A Cole Porter Companion

Edited by
DON M. RANDEL,
MATTHEW SHAFTEL, and
SUSAN FORSCHER WEISS

UNIVERSITY OF ILLINOIS PRESS
Urbana, Chicago, and Springfield

Publication of this book was supported by grants from the H. Earle Johnson Fund of the Society for American Music and from the Donna Cardamone Jackson Endowment of the American Musicological Society, funded in part by the National Endowment for the Humanities and the Andrew W. Mellon Foundation.

Manufactured in the United States of America
1 2 3 4 5 C P 5 4 3 2 1
∞ This book is printed on acid-free paper.

Library of Congress Cataloging-in-Publication Data
Names: Randel, Don Michael, editor. | Shaftel, Matthew R., editor. | Weiss, Susan Forscher, editor.
Title: A Cole Porter companion / edited by Don M. Randel, Matthew Shaftel, and Susan Forscher Weiss.
Description: Urbana : University of Illinois Press, 2016. | Series: Music in American life | Includes bibliographical references and index.
Identifiers: LCCN 2016003068 | ISBN 9780252040092 (hardcover : alk. paper) | ISBN 9780252081583 (pbk. : alk. paper)
Subjects: LCSH: Porter, Cole, 1891–1964—Criticism and interpretation.
Classification: LCC ML410.P7844 C65 2016 | DDC 782.1/4092—dc23
LC record available at http://lccn.loc.gov/2016003068

Ebook ISBN 9780252098307

A Cole Porter Companion

MUSIC IN AMERICAN LIFE

A list of books in the series appears at the end of this book.

This book is dedicated to the late Allen Forte, Faculty Emeritus at Yale University. His life and work are a profound inspiration to us all. This book would not have been possible without his conviction that the American Songbook presented profound opportunities for music scholarship. As a mentor and friend, musician and teacher, Allen was without equal.

> He brought to the traditional and somewhat standardized tasks of song-smithing a great verbal ingenuity, a brave flexibility and resourcefulness (how many of these lengthy lyrics were discarded by showtime!), a cosmopolitan's wide expertise in many mundane matters, including foreign lands and tongues, and a spirit that always kept something of collegiate innocence about it.
>
> —John Updike

Contents

Foreword

WILLIAM BOLCOM

The composer Darius Milhaud, who had known Cole Porter in his 1920s Paris days, spoke of a flower always found in his lapel. Milhaud also noted with amusement that many Paris buildings had (do they still?) an enamel blue-and-white placard affixed to the front—"Les Colporteurs ne sont pas Admis"—which meant that the scruffy, bag-toting journeymen you'd sometimes see on the street (even in the 1950s when I was young) were not admitted inside the kind of establishments Porter would have never had trouble entering.

Many years ago, driving to Indianapolis, Joan Morris and I stopped to take a look at Peru, Indiana, where the gently raised Porter hailed from. Hardly a remarkable town from what we saw—you'd be hard put to find evidence that he'd ever lived there unless you happened to be downtown when the Miami County museum, which housed a Porter collection, was open (which it wasn't that day). Even Porter's childhood home wasn't a shrine then; asking around among the townspeople about him was remarkably unfruitful. I'm told it's somewhat changed now—the Porter house is now a mini-museum with a bed and breakfast—but there isn't a Porter Boulevard I know of there to commemorate its most famous citizen.

All this makes one wonder where Porter picked up that insouciant sophistication of his. (Where indeed, for that matter, did the Astaires pick up theirs, growing up in the Nebraska that also spawned that suave country boy Johnny Carson?) Maybe it's a sense from early life of one's being somehow different from the neighbors—one's needing the roar and pace and elegance of great cities, the availability of the best of the best anytime you want—that makes so many of us escape small-town life for the capitals of the world.

It's amazing how much college had to do with many of the creators of our "classic popular song"—Rodgers and Hart doing their early show at Columbia, Ira Gershwin proudly going to CCNY—but Porter at Yale even wrote fight songs for the school among his early attempts at musical theater (though it's hard to imagine him as a jock-type sports fan). Later studies in Paris at the Schola Cantorum exposed him to a more involved harmonic language than other members of the Big Five of Broadway's golden age, a very different sophistication from Jerome Kern's Central European chordal vocabulary nearly everybody else emulated. Part of the Frenchiness Porter shares with (surprise!) Virgil Thomson is a certain spareness of musical texture. Sumptuousness is not his game—listen to recordings of Porter playing as he sings with his own metronomic *dépouillé* piano behind him, and you'll see what I mean.

Porter was just more urbane than anyone else in American musical theater history as far as I'm concerned. A man who didn't need to worry about money, he could have just lived the high life had he chosen to, but instead he worked extremely hard and meticulously on his songs. He was reportedly a slow and careful craftsman, and viewing his sheet-music manuscripts, as I did at the Secaucus warehouse (where the Harms music publishers' handwritten fair copies were stored), shows a painstaking script, the notes almost engraved into the paper—a striking contrast to the offhand fluency of Gershwin's or Vincent Youmans's handwriting. In one sheet-music engraver's copy, I saw Dr. Albert Sirmay (né Szirmai) of Harms, who made no secret of his contempt for the great American songwriters' musical unletteredness, impatiently taking over (in "Where Are the Men") from Porter's struggles in his fluent conservatory hand. Dr. Sirmay delighted in prettying up the piano parts of Harms catalog composers with added Mittel-Europa contrapuntal filigree. Gershwin must have successfully shouted the doctor down often to preserve his originals, but there is no evidence of Porter trying very hard to, and the result is that a collaborative pianist often needs to Zip-Strip away Sirmay's musical gingerbread to get to the real Porter.

What a confraternity of songwriters the 1920s produced! There exist group photographs of famous songwriters, almost as if at college reunions. As a young man, Porter complained of his not being Jewish enough to sound like Broadway; I'm not alone in suspecting that his attraction to minor-mode sultriness in some songs is a wistful attempt toward that sensibility. The most proficient creators of both lyric and music in song, he and Irving Berlin admired each other enormously. Berlin wrote a salacious party-piece parody of "You're the Top"—even dirtier than Porter's own racy double entendres—but I think the surpassing tribute to Porter from Berlin is "Let's Face the Music and Dance," with its woozy seesawing between major and minor modes, Berlin's inspiration being the very Porter songs that attempted Jewishness.

Porter's early 1923 ballet *Within the Quota*, for the Ballets suédois's Paris season and the following US tour—when else in the history did an American student composer get to have such exposure, and in Paris yet?—was his try for the avant-garde. Polytonality *à la* Milhaud was the rage, but Porter only really used whole-tone scales in his "polytonal" passages, albeit written with simultaneous key signatures in different voices, which all could have been written using one signature or none at all. I dispensed with them when I arranged the ballet for the Yale Band and the American Ballet Theater in 1970.

Porter wrote the ballet in piano score—sometimes conceived for five pianos! The orchestration used in the Ballets suédois performance was by Charles Koechlin, a quirkily fascinating character in twentieth-century French music—his compositions include the gamelan-influenced *Bandar-Log* and an orchestral suite extolling the beauties of film stars like Jane Russell and Marilyn Monroe—but the Dance Museum of Stockholm refused to let me see it or let the American Ballet Theater use it for their performance in New York in 1970, despite entreaties from the Bibliothèque nationale in Paris and Koechlin's son Yves. Time was getting short before the performance, so I holed up in a hotel on the Place de la République and sent sections of my orchestration Air Express to the copyist Lilette Hindin in New York before flying back. The job was done just in time for the afternoon rehearsal with orchestra, and *Within the Quota* went on that evening. Years later John McGlinn was able to get hold of the Koechlin orchestration and recorded it.

Already the musical language is unmistakably Porter, that *désinvolture*, or offhand manner, that choosiness, that economy. His French training gave a sophisticated gloss to the work that would show in most of his later Broadway music, separating him from the Central European flavor of so much of Broadway's golden age. Some compare Porter to Noël Coward (who also wrote a hilariously sexy parody of Porter's "Let's Do It"), but Porter could write down his own music (unlike Coward or Berlin). Unlike Kern's or Harry Warren's few examples, there is no Porter catalog of non-musical-theater works, except of course *Within the Quota*. His is a sensibility without counterpart anywhere else in the world of music.

Editors' Preface

DON M. RANDEL, MATTHEW SHAFTEL,
AND SUSAN FORSCHER WEISS

There is no denying the critical role that Cole Porter (1891–1964) has played in American music. He composed scores for dozens of Broadway musicals and films, and his songs have been included in countless other projects over the past century. Having started his musical training with his mother at an early age, Porter eventually attended Yale University (1909–13), where he wrote the lyrics and music for at least three hundred songs. Although his wealthy grandfather, James Omar Cole, pressured him into studying law at Harvard in 1913, he briefly transferred to the School of Music until opportunities on Broadway took him to New York.

Dejected by the poor reception of his first Broadway show, *See America First* (which closed after only fifteen performances), Porter devoted himself to more "serious" musical studies with composers such as Pietro Yon in New York and, most likely, Vincent d'Indy in Paris.[1] He married the rich socialite Linda Lee Thomas, and although Porter had a number of male lovers, he and his wife remained close partners until her death in 1954. The couple led a lavish lifestyle in Paris, the Riviera, and Venice throughout the 1920s, but eventually the bright lights of Broadway brought them back to New York, where several hits from Porter's fourth Broadway production, *Paris*, moved him from the exclusively social spotlight to a musical one.

Porter's eighth Broadway production ran for 420 performances and was the biggest hit of the 1930s: *Anything Goes* (1934), starring Ethel Merman. It was during this period that Porter made inroads into Hollywood, contributing to five films. Individual songs such as "I Get a Kick Out of You," "Begin the Beguine," "In the Still of the Night," "Just One of Those Things," "You're the Top," and "It's De-Lovely" were familiar to all Americans, being readily available through the sheet-music market and recordings by popular performers. Although a tragic horseback riding accident in 1937 crushed his legs, he continued to have success with his musicals, with his biggest hit, *Kiss Me, Kate* (1948), running for over a thousand performances. Even after his death from kidney failure in 1964, his musicals continued to be revised and rewritten, with revivals of *Kiss Me, Kate* (1999, 881 performances) and *Anything Goes* (1987, 784 performances) demonstrating the longevity of Porter's creative work.

His continued importance today is evidenced by the twelve published biographies (including several reprints), four DVDs related to Porter's life (including two commercial movies), over a hundred CDs devoted exclusively to his songs, a number of recent revivals on Broadway, and performances of his songs by contemporary musicians from Bono to Alanis Morissette. Porter's songs and his lyrics are timeless, speaking to audiences today as they have to so many since his first Broadway production in 1916.

That Porter occupies such an unusually prominent place in our musical history must be due in part to the breadth of the audience to which his work has appealed and continues to appeal fifty years after his death. His unique ability to balance catchy melodies, biting cynicism, clever rhymes, macaronic verse, and passionate feelings is evident in his many enduring songs. Most members of that audience would agree that although the majority of Porter's oeuvre would have to be characterized as popular music, the sophistication of his music and his poetry, as well as his unique ability to link the two, distinguishes his work from that of his contemporaries. Indeed, Porter does not fit the mold of such Broadway teams as Rodgers and Hammerstein, whose work began a trend toward the organically and comprehensively structured musical. Instead, Porter was one of the last well-known composers of the musical revue, where large-scale musical and dramatic connections are often quite tenuous. That said, the individual songs often invite a better comparison with the tradition of the Romantic lied, wherein lyric, melody, and even harmony form a symbiotic bond worthy of intense analysis and scrutiny.[2]

Such a figure would seem to be a clear candidate for serious scholarly attention. And yet, until now, the overwhelming interest has been in his biography, especially in his personal life as a figure in the New York and Paris upper crust and as a homosexual. While his homosexuality was largely suppressed in early writings on Porter (a tradition that started with the 1946 biopic *Night and*

Day), much of the recent biographical work focuses on the juicier aspects of his life and career. The works themselves—both his music and his poetry—have received significantly less attention from scholars. One of our authors (Siebert) completed a dissertation on Cole Porter in 1975, but this is the extraordinary exception that points to the surprising dearth of Porter scholarship.

The present volume aims to serve as a musicological introduction to Porter and his music, providing a map of the scholarly terrain and some tools to aid in its exploration. Our contributors—music theorists, musicologists, performers, composers, and archivists—have applied a diverse range of approaches and provide a multifaceted, multivoiced perspective on Porter and his works. The book is crafted in a way that allows readers, scholars, students, and those with a love of musical theater to wade in and out of essays, focusing as they desire on particular areas of scholarly interest: social history, analysis and criticism, or bibliographic and other evidentiary materials. The volume as a whole touches upon each of Porter's identities: Porter the poet, Porter the composer, Porter the performer, and Porter the darling of the gentry. It is divided into three broad sections framed by William Bolcom's foreword and by ideas and materials for further study. The result is a wide-ranging collection of highly distinct scholarly approaches to the composer's life and work.

As with any musicological endeavor, this book necessarily prioritizes a depth of scholarship in certain areas while leaving other areas for future studies that draw on the approaches found in the present volume. A single volume on Beethoven's nine symphonies, for instance, could never provide an in-depth picture of all thirty-seven movements but would be better served by sophisticated and quality discussions of, say, symphonies one, three, and nine. In a similar vein, the present volume creates a trajectory by focusing on in-depth explorations drawn from key musicals and films across Porter's career: *Within the Quota*, *The New Yorkers*, *You Never Know*, *Broadway Melody*, *The Seven Lively Arts*, *Anything Goes*, and *Kiss Me, Kate*. The manuscript also takes a close look at the individual gems that we know Porter's songs to be, from "Love for Sale," to "You're the Top," to "Ev'ry Time We Say Goodbye." Finally, our text provides models for every scholarly approach currently available, from archival/biographical study, to gender/reception critique, to music analysis, to issues of performance and urtext.

As stated previously, the existing Porter research is concentrated in the biographical realm. However, any biographical volume or essay prior to William McBrien's refreshingly candid 1998 biography—the most recent published volume devoted to the composer—might best be understood as a collection of entertaining anecdotes, some of which ring true, and some of which are probably fiction (often perpetrated by the composer himself). Many of the essays included here pursue aspects of Porter's biography, but, quite unlike McBrien's volume, they do so with a view to understanding his formation as a composer and poet, as well as his place in the intellectual and artistic culture of his time. The biographical work here aims to fill some of the gaps while opening doors to future biographical explorations.

Other essays in the present volume consider Porter's compositions from a variety of critical and music-analytical perspectives. The focus in these essays is on particular songs, reflecting the individualized manner in which the songs were written, published, performed, sold, and marketed. Essays by Eisen, O'Leary, Hepokoski, Shaftel, and Siebert do place groups of songs within the larger context of a single show or work, making a case for understanding connections between the songs across a longer dramatic trajectory. Randel and Walden, on the other hand, offer a different music-focused perspective, comparing songs across Porter's oeuvre or offering a highly detailed discussion of four of his most familiar songs.

A number of fundamental questions recur in the essays of this volume, and they suggest topics that will continue to require study. These topics derive in large measure from the nature of popular song and the degree to which this confounds the strategies of traditional musicological/musicotheoretical pursuits. At the fulcrum lies a series of critical questions: What defines a popular song, and in what ways is this different from the concept of a work in Western art music? If we claim to study a song by Cole Porter and bring to bear sophisticated music-analytical approaches, what precisely are we studying, and what is its relation to Cole Porter? Indeed, what would it mean to attempt a critical edition of the works of Cole Porter?

These questions derive in turn from the nature of the compositional process in this repertory. Musicologists have often studied the compositional process of a particular composer in the creation of a particular work. But in the repertory of Broadway and film songs of the 1920s to the 1950s, the role of the "composer" is not always easily defined, for several different people may have contributed to shaping what is ultimately heard by the listener or seen on a page of sheet music. Certainly, the piano-vocal scores that were prepared for the mass market present a (mostly) fixed musical source and, at least until radio and then television became ubiquitous, were the principal means of the dissemination of popular song and a primary source of income for the songwriters. However, beyond the sheet music lay the work of arrangers like Robert Russell Bennett, who prepared the works for performance in Broadway shows or in film. For theater audiences, the first encounter with these songs was in the form of such arrangements, which by their very nature differed significantly from the piano-vocal sheet music, even in matters of harmony and rhythm.

Chapters by Kapilow, Hepokoski, and Shaftel offer a somewhat cautionary tale in this regard, demonstrating how ontologically unstable the notion of a "single" Porter song can be, which challenges any simple attempt to "analyze" any song as though it were a stable object. Indeed, as discussed by Hepokoski and additionally seen in chapters by Morris, O'Leary, Walden, and Eisen, the very essence of a Porter song mutates as it proceeds through differing cultural and economic circumstances—they are images, in a sense, that themselves interact with and reflect a rapidly changing American musical culture. In some ways, these chapters just begin to unveil the dazzling complexity of what it means to regard such a work within twentieth-century culture.

And yet, there are compelling and practical reasons to focus on Porter's sheet music, which can be seen in chapters by Buchler, Randel, and Shaftel. Porter himself regularly performed his own songs at the piano and worked from the piano when composing. His few extant drafts typically consist of full treble and a good deal of the bass, sometimes with basic chord symbols. Finally, an original rehearsal score for the 1934 show *Anything Goes* survives in piano-vocal format and closely resembles the sheet music that was published after the show's premiere. Nonetheless, there are still many questions about the authorship of the sheet music, which was prepared for publication by Albert Sirmay, who was the publisher's arranger.

Following extensive study in the Porter archives at Yale, Allen Forte, in his seminal article on Porter that was published in the *Musical Quarterly* in 1993, concluded that "the definitive [musical] text is the piano-vocal score that was prepared for the sheet music market" and that "this is the form in which Porter submitted his music to the copyist, who in turn, prepared clean (fair) copy (the *Stichvorlag*) for the engraver."[3] Several of our contributors challenge Allen Forte's assessment and even argue the roles played by Sirmay and others, such as orchestrators Robert Russell Bennett and Hans Spialek, in the formation of Porter's works. Some themes—for example, his working relationship with Sirmay—recur among several of the essays because of their fundamental importance for the study of Porter's work. In the spirit of scholarly debate, particularly as it manifests itself in the exploration of new fields of study, we have deliberately preserved the partial disagreement on the Porter-Sirmay relationship that is found among several of the essays.[4]

Performers, too, have affected our impressions of Porter's music, for it is in the nature and tradition of this kind of popular music that a song can be recast in a wide variety of styles and still retain its identity. Frank Sinatra's famous interpretations differ radically from those of Porter himself (who was present at some of Sinatra's performances) or of Ella Fitzgerald, whose beautifully ornamented renditions evoke a very different vocal tradition from the great Ethel Merman, for whom Porter wrote many of his songs. Recent versions of Porter's songs by such popular artists as the Irish band U2 and Annie Lennox have again shown the stylistic flexibility and impressive longevity of his music while providing new opportunities for interpretation and analysis.[5]

The multiplicity of authorial "hands" at work in these songs complicates many of the philological instincts of traditional musicology. The nature of the surviving documents in the repertory of songs like those of Porter often does not help in establishing an "authentic" text for a song; nor does it establish the precise role of the composer in any given text. Considerations bearing on the nature of any given text would include the intended audience for that text, whether it be the amateur pianist (as would be the case for the sheet music) or the pit orchestra for a Broadway show. This complex of issues is addressed directly in the essays of Hepokoski and Horowitz and arises in other essays as well. Davis's chapter adds yet another layer to the intricate fabric of authorship in this repertory, comparing transcriptions from Cole Porter's own performances with the published sheet music.

Several authors raise questions about the relationship between text and music in Porter's songs. In the study of Western art music, it is usually assumed that the words preceded the music and were indeed the "mistress" of the music, as ancient theorists insisted. A composer in the earlier tradition makes a "setting" of a preexistent text, typically written by someone else whose identity may or may not be known. In the repertory of popular song in Porter's period, however, the music is often known to have preceded the writing of the text. As Deems Taylor states in his fine book on Rodgers and Hammerstein, "With Lorenz Hart, Rodgers followed the traditional Broadway practice of writing the music first and then handing the tune to the lyrist to find words to go with it."[6]

Porter's practice lies somewhere between these two alternatives. It is often difficult if not impossible to establish a chronological relationship between the writing of the text and the writing of the music. In many cases, it is tempting to conclude that music and text were conceived essentially together and that there was considerable back-and-forth in the working out of the finished song. Porter was committed to creating the most perfect union of words and music, whatever his working method. These topics are taken up in the essays by Kapilow and Randel, but almost all of our contributors address issues pertaining to Porter's distinctive lyrics.

Another fundamental question concerns the nature of Porter's musical formation, an issue that was alluded to earlier in reference to his unusual engagement with sheet music preparation. With whom did Porter study, what was the nature of those studies, and what did they contribute to his creative process? What was his relationship to contemporaneous songwriters, and how did this affect his own work? What was his relationship to performers for whom he created works, and what did this contribute to the character of these works? How did his early and continuing relationships with prominent figures in the arts and with high society inform his work? Porter's unusual involvement in the sheet music creation (particularly in relation to contemporaries like Irving Berlin) may stem from his impressive music education, which included studies at the Schola Cantorum in Paris, likely with well-known French composer Vincent d'Indy. Among Porter's fully scored works is the ballet *Within the Quota* (1923), reorchestrated in 1970 by William Bolcom, who writes about it in the foreword to this volume. Simon Morrison takes another look at it based on the more recent discovery of Porter's original score. The essays by Kimball (who discusses Porter's first songs and shows produced as a student at Yale), Horowitz, Weiss, Van den Brande, Davis, and O'Leary address various aspects of the above questions. Related topics are the place of Porter's work in the history of the genres of popular song and musical comedy, as well as the reception history of his work, about which Shaftel, O'Leary, and Siebert write.

Porter married Linda Lee Thomas in 1919 in romantic postwar Paris, but his relationship with Thomas was a complicated one. Although they were quite close until her death in 1954 (despite one short period in which they were separated), Porter also maintained a number of intimate relationships with men to whom he was also quite close. Although they spent much time apart, Linda became his muse, and through her connections with artists and intellectuals, she gained him access to the world of café society on both sides of the Atlantic. Aside from Linda and his mother, Kate, Porter fell under the influence of some other important women. Morris examines the influence of these women on Porter's lyrics, women such as Elizabeth Marbury, the producer of his first Broadway show, *See America First*, and her lover, the decorator Elsie de Wolfe (Lady Mendl). Porter's homosexuality and the effect it may have had on some of his artistic choices is also foregrounded in the essay by Hepokoski.

How can we imagine the course of future Porter studies, and what would be required to advance them? The first step is to take Porter seriously and overcome the image of him that continues to flourish in popular culture. It is not the classic image of a Tin Pan Alley composer of the mid-twentieth century. It is rather one derived from his busy and international social life as evoked by his posh residences in Paris and Venice, frolicking on the Lido with college buddies, entertaining in a lavish two-floor suite at the Waldorf Towers in New York, hanging out with the Hollywood set in California, or cocooning himself and Linda at their beloved estate Buxton Hill in Williamstown, Massachusetts, a large portion of which was left to one of Porter's favorite and loyal companions, Ray Kelly. Porter's life, however, centered on his music; he was not the playboy sometimes depicted in books and film. Early on, he adopted a regular routine of composing daily and for long hours, gradually developing the sophisticated harmonic, melodic, and rhythmic features that characterize his music. This process is partially documented in the notebooks and sketches he left to the Library of Congress and to Yale University.[7]

By its nature, Cole Porter's music calls for a wide variety of approaches, as is evident in this volume. This could include study of the formation of genre in an essentially commercial environment and the economics underlying or shaping that environment. In this light, the present volume's essays on songs from five of Porter's larger works, two of the biggest hits (*Anything Goes* [Hepokoski] and *Kiss Me, Kate* [Siebert]), two of his flops (*The Seven Lively Arts* [O'Leary] and *You Never Know* [Eisen]), and a movie (*Broadway Melody of 1940* [Shaftel]) only scratch the surface. With over thirty-five full-length musicals and films, there are many opportunities for future scholarship in this area. There is also plenty of room for basic source work. A Köchel-like catalog for Porter would be immensely valuable for every kind of scholarship, and Kimball's and Siebert's earlier work provides secure starting points. Of course, it would not answer every question that scholars would like to ask, but it would provide a firm basis for further Porter study, ultimately inspiring deeper insight into the life and work of one of America's most significant composer-poets.

A Note about the Cole Porter Literature

A complete guide to the relevant literature can be found in Gregory Decker's chapter, "Secondary Materials and the Study of Cole Porter." However, the number of sources devoted exclusively to Porter is very few, and so we will briefly touch upon them here. There are twelve published biographies of Cole Porter, several of which have been reprinted recently (not to mention two feature-length films and a number of biographical documentaries): Hubler (1965), Ewen (1965), Eells (1967), Salsini (1972), Schwartz (1977), Johnson (1984), Grafton (1987), Kimball and Sudhalter (1992), Citron (1993), Morella and Mazzei (1995), and McBrien (1998). While this demonstrates the great interest that musicians and music lovers have in Porter's work (and the great potential for sales of a book on Cole Porter), few of these books take a scholarly approach to his work, and not a single one of these books has any substantial discussion of the composer's music. The most recent of the above-cited works, William McBrien's *Cole Porter: A Biography* (New York: Alfred A. Knopf, 1998, reprinted in 2000), is a lengthy biographical study of Porter's life that is chock full of information but includes no scholarly engagement with Porter's music, formation, lyrics, or manuscripts. The exceptions are largely drawn from Allen Forte's intermittent studies of Porter's music over many years (two books and an article), as well as Matthew Shaftel's 1999 article.

This volume would, however, sit nicely alongside several musically sensitive books on other Broadway composers. Tim Carter's book *Oklahoma! The Making of an American Musical* (Yale University Press, 2007), Stephen Banfield's *Sondheim's Broadway Musicals* (University of Michigan Press, 1993), the same author's *Jerome Kern* (Yale University Press, 2006), and Jeffrey Magee's work on Irving Berlin all include notable examples of detailed musical considerations of songs from Broadway or Hollywood musicals.

Acknowledgments

We appreciate the assistance of Kendall L. Crilly, Music Librarian, and Richard Boursy, Archivist, at the Irving S. Gilmore Music Library at Yale University; the late Richard Warren, Jr., Former Curator, Historical Sound & American Musical Theatre Music Library at Yale University; Suzanne E. Lovejoy, Acting Music Librarian and Public Services Music Librarian, and Catherine Mansi, Assistant Music Librarian, at the Koerner Center at Yale University; and Nicholas Renouf. We also wish to thank the staff at the Music Division of the Library of Congress: Senior Music Specialist Mark Eden Horowitz, Theater Specialist Walter Zvonchenko, and Reference Specialist Susan Clermont. We are extremely grateful to Roberta Staats, James Grupenhoff, and Michael Worden for help with permissions. Finally, thanks to Joshua Mills and Samuel Burt for their work preparing and editing examples.

Notes

1. See Weiss in the present volume for a discussion of Porter's musical studies.

2. For more on the lied tradition and the parallel to Porter's work, see Don Randel, "Congruence between Poetry and Music in Schumann's *Dichterliebe*," *19th-Century Music* 38, no. 1 (Summer 2014): 30–52.

3. Allen Forte, "Secrets of Melody: Line and Design in the Songs of Cole Porter," *Musical Quarterly* 77, no. 4 (Winter 1993): 610. Forte adds a note: "Regarding this procedure and Porter's compositional process in general there is some very dubious anecdotal material recorded in published biographies of Porter, material that is unsupported by documentary evidence."

4. An article by Dominic McHugh, "'I'll Never Know Exactly Who Did What': Broadway Composers as Musical Collaborators," *Journal of the American Musicological Society* 68, no. 3 (Fall 2015), appeared after we received our proofs. McHugh discusses Porter's relationship with his collaborators and gives thanks to Hannah Robbins "for assisting my investigation of Sirmay's role in Porter's career." Robbins's unpublished paper, "Dear Doctor: Sources for the Collaboration between Cole Porter and Albert Sirmay," was unavailable, but the editors wished to acknowledge her contribution for the sake of future research into Porter and Sirmay.

5. Lennox's performance of Porter's "Ev'ry Time We Say Goodbye" was part of the album *Red, Hot + Blue: Cole Porter Tribute*, released in 1990 as a benefit for AIDS.

6. Deems Taylor, *Some Enchanted Evenings: The Story of Rodgers and Hammerstein* (New York: Harper & Brothers, 1953), 219–20.

7. Many thanks to both institutions for their critical help with the present volume.

PART 1

"What a Joy to Be Young"

From Peru to Paris via Yale and Other Academies

1

Cole Porter at Yale

ROBERT KIMBALL

In the September twilight in the fall of 1909, young men with golf bags, suitcases, hatboxes, and mandolin cases hurried from the New Haven train station to find lodging in the rooming houses that lined the York Street trolley tracks. Then upperclassmen hustled them to the intersection of College and Chapel Streets, where, linking arms, they lined up in a huge procession that was forming outside Osborn Hall. The Second Regiment Band struck up "Down the Field" and led a whirling, winding, snake-dancing torchlight parade through the city streets to the Old Campus. Chanting the Greek cheer Brek-ek-ek-coax-coax and stepping in time to "Boola" and other Yale marching songs, members of the class of 1913 arrived on campus.

The students formed a spacious semicircle in the shadow of the moon-drenched towers and witnessed the freshman-sophomore wrestling bouts. Then they were shepherded back to York Street, where they mixed it up with the sophomores in a sweating, chaotic "rush." After some mild hazing and various choruses of "Wake, Freshmen, Wake," the festivities were over, and lights went out all along York Street. Once again the strange amalgam of ritual, pageantry, and song that graced Yale before World War I had done its work, and several hundred individuals had been welded together for the first time as a class.

Cole Porter, Yale '13, settled in Garland's lodging house at 242 York Street, now the site of Davenport College, where he installed an upright piano in his single room (Porter roomed alone through most of his Yale career so that he could compose and play far into the night without disturbing a roommate) and promptly established a reputation as a fine entertainer. His classmates included W. Averell Harriman and future Yale grandees Arnold Whitridge, Sidney Lovett, and Ralph Gabriel. Porter majored in English, minored in music, studied French, and even received credit for singing in the university choir.

Porter's English courses at Yale College included English Poets of the Nineteenth Century (Wordsworth, Coleridge, Byron, Shelley, Keats, et al.), Tennyson and Browning, and Shakespeare. Porter thought Tennyson's "The Princess" had an "excellent libretto for comic opera." There is no evidence that reading Shakespeare's *The Taming of the Shrew* had any influence on Porter's future masterpiece *Kiss Me, Kate*.

The years 1909–13 were good years for anyone interested in pursuing music at Yale. When freshmen arrived on campus, they were greeted with a barrage of ads: "Pianos for rent"; "Learn to waltz, two-step, and Boston"; "Instruction in banjo, mandolin, and guitar"; "Let us build up your voice for the Glee Club trials." The Whiffenpoofs came into existence early in 1909 (Porter was a member during his senior year), and Yale's leading music professor, Horatio Parker, had his prize-winning opera *Mona* performed at the Metropolitan Opera.

Gustav Mahler brought the New York Philharmonic to Woolsey Hall for a concert of Bach, Berlioz, and Richard Strauss. Outstanding vocalists such as Geraldine Farrar, Alma Gluck, Marcella Sembrich, Louise Tetrazzini, and John McCormack attracted droves of admirers (including Porter) to their recitals. Porter's classmate Swede Reilly told me that "Cole, knowing how much I admired McCormack, took me to hear his New Haven recital."

Rather early in Porter's freshman year, an editorial in the *Yale Daily News* called for original musical compositions by the undergraduates. That summons may have encouraged Porter to submit his number "Bingo Eli Yale" in the 1910 football song competition. He had begun composing songs in earnest at his prep school, Worcester Academy, in Massachusetts. Two of his songs, "When the Summer Moon Comes 'Long" and "Bridget McGuire," survive from his freshman year at Yale.

"Bingo" was formally introduced by Eddie Wittstein and his orchestra at the Yale dining hall dinner concert on 29 October 1910. (Wittstein was a famous musical figure in New Haven for several decades.) The words to "Bingo" were printed in the *Yale Daily News*, and the song itself was successfully tried out at several football rallies.

Music at meals was a regular feature of Yale life; twice and sometimes four or five times a week, Wittstein, ensconced with his orchestra in a balcony overlooking the University Commons dining hall, performed a concert of staples from the symphonic and operatic repertoire—gems from light opera, waltzes, marches, two-steps, hits from the current musical comedies, and even an occasional ragtime piece. The concerts were always well received, and Wittstein recalled that sometimes the students kept time to the music by beating on the glasses and crockery. "Glow-Worm" was certain to evoke student participation, while a performance of the "Anvil Chorus" scattered glass and broken dishes all over the floor and nearly put an end to the concerts.

Wittstein, who conducted other Porter premieres at Yale, including his first musical comedy, *Cora*, in 1911, remembered Porter as "quiet, suave, intelligent, a real gentleman. He was a good pianist, and although not an especially talented singer he was excellent at putting over his own lyrics. I always liked him and played a lot of his football songs at the dining halls and the Yale Proms. I remember going up to his room where he told me he was influenced by the music of Richard Strauss. He was studying *Der Rosenkavalier* before it was performed in America."

In his junior year Porter's stepped-up output of football songs included the seemingly indestructible "Bull Dog." "I was standing outside Harvard Stadium on the day of the Harvard-Yale game," recalled Porter's classmate Albert B. "Baldy" Crawford. "The crowds were gathering. Inside the stadium the band was playing 'Bull Dog.' Cole came running up to me, shouting, 'Baldy, Baldy, they're playing my song, but I don't have my ticket and I can't get into the stadium.'"

As chairman of the football committee in his senior year (and, coincidentally, a cheerleader), Porter was arbiter of all Yale College football songs. In the *Yale Daily News* of 1 October 1912, Porter inserted the following notice: "Anyone who has any football songs which he would like to present to the committee will please leave them at 31 Vanderbilt before Wednesday, October 9." (Porter's room in Vanderbilt was the most expensive on campus.) Among the aspirants were Alonzo Elliott, Porter's classmate who later wrote the music for the poignant "There's a Long, Long Trail A-Winding" (Stoddart King, Yale '14, wrote the lyrics), and Douglas Moore '15, later the distinguished composer of *The Ballad of Baby Doe*, whose "Goodnight Poor Harvard" achieved wide popularity the year after Porter's graduation.

While his football songs have secured a seemingly permanent place in Yale lore, Porter's most memorable personal triumphs occurred through his association with the Yale Glee Club. In his senior year he was president of the Glee Club and the Banjo and Mandolin Clubs Association; he was also the Glee Club's principal soloist.

In those days, after exhaustive rehearsals in the fall, the university musical clubs embarked on an extensive Christmas tour, alternating years between the American South and West. These tours (the Yale Dramatic Association enjoyed similar excursions) were really elaborate social events; the members were transported from city to city in private railroad cars to appear at a mélange of formal dances, multicourse dinners, luncheons, teas, gala receptions, coming-out parties, and other holiday fetes. The concerts, duly sponsored by the Yale Clubs of the various cities, were almost an anticlimax for the exhausted young men.

It was late in the second half of these concerts that Cole Porter would solo in a number of his own creation—"Perfectly Terrible," "The Motor Car," or "A Football King." Then the piano would be pushed out to the center of the stage, and Porter would launch into a series of what he called "pianologues." Essentially, they were a mixture of song and recitative with piano accompaniment.

There are very few accounts of the exact nature and content of his act, but it might have opened with a number like "No Show This Evening" or "Music with Meals" followed by a song in French or perhaps "It Pays to Advertise," which began with the line, "I'd walk a mile for that schoolgirl complexion." Then he would surely have played his comic-treatment burlesque on the waltz from *The Merry Widow*, first in a straight piano rendition, then successively as a church hymn, as a band arrangement, and finally as it might be played on the hurdy-gurdy.

Perhaps his most renowned original composition aside from "Bull Dog" was the many-versioned "Antoinette Birby," also known as "Sweet Alice Kirby" and "Annabelle Birby" before it evolved into the form in which it is now printed in *Songs of Yale*. The humor and pathos of the musical saga of the poor girl from the country who comes to New Haven to work as a waitress at the Taft Hotel, only to be corrupted by an evil Yale man, made the piece a general favorite. Invariably the final number, Porter's own favorite, was his burlesque of Marie Dressler's treatment of the ballad "Heaven Will Protect the Working Girl."

As enthusiastic audiences brought him back again and again, he often held the stage for over thirty minutes before the Glee Club returned to conclude the concert. Porter's singing pianologue act, with its assortment of original compositions, deft burlesque, humorous patter, and topical allusions, was splendidly rendered with the superb phrasing and wonderful diction that he later demanded from the leading performers of the musical stage. It had all the ingredients of a first-class vaudeville act and was the delight of all who heard and saw it.

Yet in looking back at Porter's Yale years, the musical comedy scores he wrote for his fraternity, Delta Kappa Epsilon, and for the annual smokers of the Yale Dramat were the most significant aspect of his Yale experience for his subsequent career in the musical theater. With his five show scores—*Cora* (1911), *And the Villain Still Pursued Her* (1912), *The Pot of Gold* (1912), *The Kaleidoscope* (1913), and *Paranoia*, which he wrote for his alma mater while a student at the Harvard School of Music in 1914—Porter transformed musical comedy at Yale from what had been an occasional divertissement into a tradition that for many years held an honored place in the university's cultural life. He developed a proficiency in writing for the stage that prepared him ably for what would turn out to be a forty-year career as a composer-lyricist for Broadway and Hollywood.

Each of Porter's shows had its memorable moments, but his own favorite and the only college score he preserved until his death was *The Pot of Gold*. The book was written by Almet F. Jenks Jr., Yale '14, and the show was presented as the DKE initiation play on 26 November 1912. The story had something to do with efforts to reverse the declining fortunes of a rundown hotel and featured the inevitable hero and heroine, a group of plotting nihilists, scandal, mistaken identity, bellboys and lady guests, a chorus girl, a Southern general, an English barrister, and a generous assortment of complications and tearful reunions. All parts, including the female roles, were performed by members of DKE, who spared no expense in outfitting themselves in the finest wigs, shoes, and costumes.

On the appointed evening—after a dinner consisting of tomato soup, asparagus salad, roast turkey, ice cream, fancy cakes, and coffee, topped off with Champagne, cigars, and speeches by DKE members welcoming the neophytes—the house lights were dimmed, and the conductor, Mr. Fichtl of the New Haven Symphony, began the overture. Porter described the overture in a letter to Jenks as follows:

> It begins with the motif—Chlodoswine's yearning for Larry; then follows the waltz representing her pangs on finding him false, ending in the motif of supreme happiness, which appears again at the end of the play. Following this comes Larry's love song, then a thing in 5/4 time introducing the foreign influence on the hotel, modulating into a death march representing the monotony and decadence of the place. This is connected with the opening chorus by a movement that grows more excited as it progresses. The opening chorus is the Rainbow Song which would be sung by the guests who depart at the end of it.

In the overture and some of the extended musical sections of *The Pot of Gold*, Porter sought to "combine the splendor of Wagner and the decadence of Strauss." The courses he had taken at Yale in harmony and music history with

Professor David Stanley Smith had widened his musical knowledge; through Smith he met Professor William Haesche, who orchestrated *The Pot of Gold* for an unusually large ensemble of violins, cellos, bass, flutes, clarinets, cornets, trombone, and drums.

If the music of *The Pot of Gold* showed the influence of German Romanticism, Porter's lyrics demonstrated the literary impact of Browning and Tennyson, whom he had studied with Professor William Lyon Phelps, and a wide familiarity with artistic expression of the day. Anna Pavlova and Mikhail Mordkin of the Imperial Russian Ballet, who made such an impression on Porter during their appearances in New Haven, inspired "When I Used to Lead the Ballet," which was the hit song of *The Pot of Gold* and later a feature in his first Broadway show, *See America First*. Another standout number was "My Salvation Army Queen." With its musical burlesque of "Onward Christian Soldiers," the song was a reference to Edna May, the Salvation Army heroine of the Broadway show *The Belle of New York* who had won fame by singing "Men never proceed to follow the light, but they always follow me."

"She Was a Fair Young Mermaid" was a nod to Annette Kellerman of exhibition diving and swimming fame, who shocked the nation by appearing in her vaudeville act in a one-piece bathing suit. Musical comedy star Elsie Janis and her redoubtable Ma, perhaps the most famous of stage mothers and a formidable barrier to her daughter's love life, were the likely source of the sentimental burlesque "It's Awfully Hard When Mother's Not Along." And the Broadway kid himself, George M. Cohan, promoted Porter's unabashed tribute "Longing for Dear Old Broadway."

While *The Pot of Gold* owed something to the influence of others, there were already signs of the suave, audacious lyrics and sophisticated music that signal the unique Porter touch. The original turns of phrase and unexpected rhymes that are the hallmark of his later distinction were displayed in lines like "She was so seraphic that she blocked the traffic when she beat the tambourine"; "She's a most decided blonde—she just decided lately"; "For if you'd not neglect your figure's architecture, you've got to exercise."

Porter's skill as a musical comedy writer was recognized by almost everyone who saw his Yale shows. No less an authority than Professor William Lyon Phelps congratulated the Dramat after a performance of *The Kaleidoscope* for "having one man who is a real genius who writes words and music of such exceptional high order."

The triumphs of Porter's Yale years were followed by an almost uninterrupted series of professional disappointments, beginning with the failure of his first Broadway offering, *See America First*, a curious attempt to Americanize Gilbert and Sullivan that ran for two weeks in early 1916.

Porter was prepared to abandon songwriting for the theater altogether when, at the urging of his good friend Monty Woolley, director of the Yale Dramat, he reluctantly agreed to submit three songs for *Out o' Luck*, a comedy-melodrama concerning American doughboys during World War I. The show's success on the Dramat's Christmas tours of 1925 and 1926 helped Porter overcome the creative doldrums that had plagued him in the years after he graduated from Yale.

Henry C. Potter, Yale '26, who played the lead in *Out o' Luck*, recalls Porter's mood at that time:

> I remember well, one evening "after hours" when those of us in the Dramat sat around with Cole, singing and doing little skits, imitations of Jolson and so on. I did an imitation of some currently popular vaudeville "sob-ballad" singer. When I finished, Cole laughed heartily; then his face grew somber and he said, "But do you know? I wish to God I could write songs like that."
>
> Thank God he didn't. But not too many years after that evening along came "Night and Day" and all the glorious rest. And we Yale '25 and '26ers have always thought that perhaps we had helped him a little.

They had. Yet Porter's relationship with Yale deteriorated for a number of years. When his close friend Monty Woolley was dismissed from the Yale faculty in the late 1920s, Porter was so upset he stopped sending contributions to Yale. It took more than twenty years before there was a reconciliation. Another upsetting factor was the Yale Corporation's refusal to offer him an honorary degree despite the advocacy of Dean Acheson and other distinguished Yale graduates.

Happily, a few of Porter's Yale professors helped in an eventual rapprochement, with friendly letters often recalling the lyrics to songs he had written as an undergraduate. When Yale, thanks to Robert L. Barlow '33, established its Collection of the Literature of the American Musical Theater in 1953 (the collection's student assistants have included Dick Cavett, David Shire, and Sam Waterston), Porter served on the collection's advisory committee and sent Yale copies of many vocal scores by Victor Herbert.

While the 1950s brought Porter continued success on Broadway and in Hollywood, it was also a time of personal misfortune. Cole's mother, the great Kate, died in the summer of 1952; his wife, Linda, succumbed to emphysema in 1954; and his closest friend, Howard Sturges, passed away in 1955. In the spring of 1958 Cole's right leg, which had been crushed in a terrible horseback-riding accident in 1937, was amputated. He lost the will to write after the amputation and died in Santa Monica, California, on 15 October 1964.

There were many tributes offered at his death, but none was more eloquent than the citation that accompanied his long-overdue honorary degree from Yale University, presented at his apartment in the Waldorf-Astoria on 9 June 1960:

> Cole Porter: As an undergraduate you first won acclaim for writing the words and music of two of Yale's perennial football songs. Since then you have achieved a reputation as a towering figure in the American musical theater. Master of the deft phrase, the delectable rhyme, the distinctive melody, you are, in your own words and in your own field, the top. . . . Your graceful, impudent, inimitable songs will be played and sung as long as footlights burn and curtains go up.

Notes

In the spring of 1966, Yale University invited me to organize and prepare an inventory of the music manuscripts and papers that composer-lyricist Cole Porter had bequeathed to his alma mater. While at work on the Porter archive, I was asked by John F. Wharton, trustee of the Cole Porter Musical and Literary Property Trusts and Porter's longtime attorney, to become the artistic advisor to the Porter Trusts, a position I have held ever since.

During the years that followed I began a project that became the book *Cole* (Holt, Rinehart and Winston, 1971), a collaboration with longtime *New Yorker* writer Brendan Gill and designer Bea Feitler. Other Porter books I have edited include *The Complete Lyrics of Cole Porter* (Alfred A. Knopf, 1983) and *Cole Porter: Selected Lyrics* (The Library of America's American Poets Project, 2006).

At the Yale reunions in 1968 I spoke at a dinner with some of Porter's 1913 Yale classmates, who made me an honorary member of their class. Soon after, I wrote an article for the *Yale Alumni Magazine* titled "The Cole Porter Years." It appeared in the magazine in March 1969 and forms the basis of this essay. Much of my original research was done with the help of members of the Yale Class of 1913.

In addition, I acknowledge with gratitude the generous assistance of Robert L. Barlow, Yale '33, founder and first curator of the Yale University Collection of the Literature of the American Musical Theater; Porter's Yale College classmates George B. Cortelyou Jr., Sidney Lovett, and Arnold Whitridge; Henry C. Potter '26; Basil Duke Henning '32; New Haven orchestra leader Edward Wittstein; Yale University archivist Judith Schiff; Goddard Lieberson, longtime president of Columbia Records and founding advisor to the Yale American Musical Theater Collection; and Peter L. Felcher, trustee, and Roberta Staats, executive director, of the Cole Porter Musical and Literary Property Trusts.

2

When the Little Bluebird Starts to Sing

Porter's Musical Formation

SUSAN FORSCHER WEISS

That Cole Porter loved birds is evident from the references throughout his lyrics to members of the avian species.[1] His first known composition, which he wrote in 1901 at the age of ten and dedicated to his mother, was a programmatic work for piano entitled "The Song of the Birds." This and other early works reveal his exposure to classical music and his affinity for opera, German lieder, English and European operettas, ballet, and popular idioms. They also reveal his devotion to linking words with music and foreshadow the creativity of his mature style.

Porter's manuscripts contain multiple versions of his lyrics, hundreds of pages and snippets of paper in his own hand or produced on his typewriter. He was said to sit at the keyboard sketching into the wee hours of the morning. Many of these early manuscripts contain musical notation that seems labored; half-finished "scores" with annotations in the margins included a variety of doodles and whimsical drawings. Serious analyses of Porter's lyrics point out their assonances, internal rhymes, double entendres, puns, alliterations, and onomatopoeic utterances, and the adjectives applied to them include "smart," "sophisticated," "polished," "clever," and "witty." Porter not only kept dictionaries and thesauri at his side while composing but also conducted research to be sure that his lyrics were as polished and accurate as possible. Perhaps his fastidiousness stemmed from earlier bloopers. In 1919 he was embarrassed to find that he had mentioned both fall and spring flowers blooming simultaneously in his first hit, "An Old-Fashioned Garden."[2] "The Porter lyrics, composed at the same time as his music and indissolubly wedded to it, bar by bar, syllable by syllable, were a product of intense intellectual concentration; the seemingly effortless rhymes came not from Heaven, but from a rhyming dictionary."[3]

Peru and Worcester

Cole Porter was born in 1891 in Peru, Indiana, the only child of Kate (née Cole), the daughter of one of the wealthiest families in town, and Sam Porter, a druggist. Kate, trained in music and dance, exposed Cole to music and the arts, while Sam, an amateur musician, also imbued his son with a passion for literature, especially for the works of Robert and Elizabeth Browning.[4] At age six Cole was playing piano and violin, practicing about two hours a day. He attended the East Main Street Grade School, where he is pictured in 1899 in music class as a tiny eight-year-old among nine older female classmates.[5] He also sang in the choir of St. John's Lutheran Church in Peru and took lessons at the Marion Conservatory of Music in nearby Grant County. The school was founded in 1899 by the Nussbaum brothers, Percy, a violinist, and Hamilton, a composer who had studied piano in Berlin with Theodor Leschetitzky.[6] It was during those trips that Porter discovered "spicy" books among the shops in Marion. Later in life he noted that those novels played a role in the lyrics for such songs as "Love for Sale" and "Always True to You in My Fashion."[7]

Apparently, young Porter preferred the sound of the piano to the violin, an instrument he described as "screechy," and Kate encouraged him by playing piano duets, particularly burlesques of popular songs.[8] She also took him to Chicago for theater and opera performances. At the Auditorium Theater he heard his first performance of Wagner's *Lohengrin*.[9]

Porter's earliest surviving work, "The Song of the Birds," provides evidence of his interest in musical imagery (ex. 1).[10] Porter divided the 114-measure piano piece into six sections, each with a descriptive title. Written in F major, it is filled with ideas that stem from his exposure to classical music, in particular the nineteenth-century piano miniatures, and is sprinkled with elements from popular turn-of-the-century works such as waltzes by Franz Lehár. In a section marked "The Young Ones Learning to Sing," Cole attempted to imitate a bird's song with a chirping treble motive accompanied by open fifths that

EXAMPLE 1. Cole Porter, excerpt from "The Song of the Birds," 1901, manuscript in the collection of the Cole Porter Trust. Used by permission of the Trustees.

morph into an Alberti-like accompaniment written in the treble clef. These twenty or so measures cadence on the tonic and are followed by a shorter chromatic section of only sixteen measures with the title "One Bird Falls from the Nest," marked *pianissimo* and *lento*. Porter's clear but awkwardly written notation reveals shifting clef signs in order to effect the crossing of hands. In the next twelve measures, "The Cuckoo Tells the Mother Where the Bird Is," a modulation to C minor precedes a return to the tonic as "The Bird Is Found." This $\frac{6}{8}$ waltz-like section precedes "They Fly Away," with its upward sweeps of a three-note motive followed by a descending arpeggiated figure that makes fairly wide use of the keyboard. This closing and longest section of twenty-seven measures combines the birdlike motives with an oompah accompaniment interrupted by a short hymn-like passage at measure 103 that leads to the coda, a perpetual motion of descending and ascending sixteenths depicting the birds flying off. The piece is a bellwether of sorts, revealing Porter's attraction to dance rhythms and to birdsong, recurrent features in his later works.[11] Remarkable for a ten-year-old are the key and meter changes, to say nothing of his attempts at creating a program. Nonetheless, Porter self-deprecatingly referred to it in later years as "an obnoxious item."[12]

In 1902 Kate Porter paid S. Brainard's Sons, Cleveland's leading nineteenth-century music-publishing house, one hundred dollars to print one hundred copies of her son's "Bobolink Waltz." Porter referred to this as his "second composition, a burbling item that I wrote at the age of ten."[13] The waltz, again in F major, begins with a thirty-two-bar A section consisting of an eight-bar antecedent melody in the tonic built around a rising C major scale, followed by a short consequent phrase that moves to the dominant before returning to a repeat of the antecedent and a variation of the consequent resolving on the tonic. The craftsmanship of this ninety-six-measure waltz, while perhaps not that of the young Mozart, is extraordinary for a ten-year-old.[14]

In 1905 Porter's parents sent him to Worcester Academy in Massachusetts. The headmaster, Daniel Webster Abercrombie, took Cole under his wing and taught him, among other things, the importance of the relationship between words and music. Letters between Kate and Abercrombie demonstrate her involvement and the principal's attachment to his student. Abercrombie, a man of letters, recognized Cole's "ingenious and delightful spirit," as well as his physical frailty, evidenced by frequent trips to the school infirmary as a result of either injury or illness. Abercrombie assured Kate that Worcester would prepare Cole for an Ivy League education. He wanted the boy to understand that sound and sense must merge in his compositions.[15] Abercrombie arranged for Cole to have an instrument in his room. It was then that Porter began setting his own words to music, but regrettably only titles survive.

Even though her son made the honor roll in his freshman year, "Dr. A" wrote to Mrs. Porter complaining that the boy did too much socializing. He commented on Cole's friendships, some of which he felt were not in the boy's best interest, and on his occasional lapses in judgment. To keep Cole further from sources of distraction, especially the infirmary, Abercrombie decided to move him to a new room.

The letters reveal that Abercrombie had respect and admiration for Porter's mother and for her efforts to educate her son and build his character. When Cole failed the classics portion of the entrance exam at Yale, Abercrombie arranged for him to be tutored in Latin and Greek, sending him to Worcester Academy faculty member Alfred Dame's summer school in Campion, New Hampshire. In the fall of his senior year Cole entered Abercrombie's Greek class.[16] Also revealing is Abercrombie's uncommon attachment for Cole:

> I am already beginning to feel deeply about Cole's graduation. I shall miss him more than he can ever realize. He has been a pleasure and a piece of sunshine to me all through his course, and I love him as if he were my own son. I know that is almost as pleasant for you to hear as it is for me to be able to write it, and to know that he feels and appreciates my coming into his life in helpful ways is the cause of great gratitude to me. I am trying to strengthen Cole in all possible ways. I want him to graduate with very high honors from this school and enter college ready in his technical training and in his spirit to be a strong man. You have a dear boy who will bring satisfaction increasingly as the years go by.[17]

Abercrombie also wrote expressing his belief that Yale was the wrong place for Cole: "I want him to go to college much more mature than he has been but I regret more than I can tell you that he is going to Yale because Yale hasn't what he needs, and has what he doesn't. Its ideals are of a very boisterous athletic life."[18]

In his senior year, Porter played the piano during study halls, and perhaps as a way of rebelling against both his mother and Abercrombie, he spent most of his time acting in school plays and entering speaking contests. His grades suffered. Still, Abercrombie nominated him for valedictorian of his class, and many members of his family, with the exception of his father, came from Peru for the commencement in 1909. Most disappointing to Abercrombie was the silence following Cole's graduation. His regret is palpable in a letter he wrote on 22 February 1916 to an alumnus, Meylert B. Mullin, who sent Abercrombie a review of Porter's first Broadway show, *See America First*.

> My dear Meylert:
>
> I thank you very much for your kind note which reached me this morning, with its enclosure of the item about Cole Porter. What a genius he has for such work. I haven't laid eyes on Cole since he graduated. . . . His alienation from the school is very sad to me, and without explanation. I don't understand it. It is one of those little tragedies of my life for which I find no explanation and which always bring me real sorrow. . . .
>
> Very sincerely,
> DIWA[19]

Apparently, Porter had no further communication with Abercrombie. In 1965, a year following Porter's death, Richard Hubler published *The Cole Porter Story*, a collection of reminiscences by the composer. Porter credits "a sympathetic Greek teacher" with his success in graduating as valedictorian of his class in 1909; that same teacher also "opened the door to Homer and the New Testament in that language." After working with this teacher (almost certainly Abercrombie), Porter said he was "never satisfied to write music and allow someone else to do the lyrics—I have realized that each must be wedded inseparably to the other."

> I graduated from Worcester in 1909 as valedictorian of my class—largely because I had a sympathetic Greek teacher who suddenly opened the door to Homer and the New Testament in that language. For the first time I saw the music inherent in the words. Since then I have never been satisfied to write music and allow someone else to do the lyrics—I realized that each must be wedded to the other.[20]

Following Cole's graduation from Worcester, his grandfather J. O. Cole sent him on a summer vacation to France, Switzerland, and Germany that not only whetted Porter's appetite for travel but also "planted a love for Europe that I never lost."[21] His time there may have provided him with material that set him apart from the majority of other American-born composers of Broadway songs.[22]

College, Grad School, Paris, and New York

While at Yale, Porter majored in English and minored in music, taking courses in history, instrumentation, harmony, and what is today referred to in music curricula as applied music, most likely piano lessons. During those four years he wrote hundreds of songs and six full-scale productions.[23] He joined the fraternity Delta Kappa Epsilon, where he met Gerald Murphy, Monty Woolley, and others who would later become collaborators and intimate friends. In 1911 he wrote his first musical comedy, *Cora*, for Delta Kappa Epsilon. A year later, he collaborated with Almet Jenks (Yale '14) on the Gilbert and Sullivan parody *The Pot of Gold*, which was performed both at the fraternity house and at the Hotel Taft in New Haven.[24] Another early work, *The Kaleidoscope,* also had two performances, the first at the Taft and the second at the Yale Club of New York on 7 May 1913, weeks before Cole's graduation. A song from this show, "As I Love You," became the first of Cole's tunes to be included in a Broadway show (22 July 1915, retitled "Esmeralda" in the Hungarian-born Sigmund Romberg's revue *Hands Up*).

During his college years Porter played piano with James Reese Europe, Eubie Blake, and other black musicians when their Society Orchestra performed at fraternity house parties.[25] Noble Sissle, another black lyricist, singer, and playwright, came from Indianapolis to join Eubie Blake in Baltimore in 1915. Sissle and Blake collaborated on the 1921 musical *Shuffle Along,* arguably the first hit musical on Broadway written by and about African Americans. Cole idolized Sissle and later helped his all-black band get a slot at a famous dance hall in Paris.[26]

Porter also loved to reference dancing, in particular ballet.[27] The Whiffenpoofs performed "When I Used to Lead the Ballet," written for the Yale-Brown football game in 1912, with Cole dressed as "Pavlova." Porter's refrain rhymes "Pavlova" with "are over" and her principal in the Bolshoi, Mikhail "Mordkin," her "beautiful ballet boy," with her "lordkin."

> When I used to lead the ballet,
> When I used to lead the ballet,
> In costume so scanty
> The world dilettante
> Pronounced me a perfect joy.
> Those wonderful days are over
> When I danced with the fair Pavlova.
> For I was her lordkin,
> Her lambkin, her Mordkin,
> Her beautiful ballet boy.

The verse includes a reference to an ad for the beverages made by White Rock, whose labels depicted a diaphanously clad, fairy-like woman who gazes into a pond. The line "in costume so scanty" could not have been lost on the college men. At this time most college campus shows featured men in drag playing the female roles. The song was later included in *See America First*, produced in 1916 by Elisabeth Marbury. She was responsible for many successful Princess Theatre productions, more modest shows that represented a departure from the gaudy extravaganzas of Broadway in the early 1900s. Marbury was the lover of Elsie de Wolfe, a woman who became very important to Porter during his Parisian years and who figured in a number of Porter songs.[28]

Following his graduation from Yale in 1913, Porter took another summer trip to Europe, where the seed that had been planted in 1909 began to germinate. African American dance bands had become popular in Europe, and classical composers began to incorporate jazz and ragtime idioms into their compositions. While Cole was visiting Paris, his fraternity brother Gerald Murphy introduced him to Zelda and F. Scott Fitzgerald, Ernest Hemingway, John Dos Passos, Samuel Beckett, Archibald MacLeish, John O'Hara, James Joyce, Dorothy Parker, and Robert Benchley.[29] Stravinsky said that the first Americans he met in Paris were Gerald and Sara Murphy.[30]

In the fall of 1913 Porter entered Harvard Law School, but after an unhappy year, and with the encouragement of the law school dean, he transferred to the Faculty of Arts and Sciences, where he entered the graduate program in music. His transcript reveals that he took some classes, but it is not clear that he completed any of them.[31] In Cambridge, Porter partnered with his Yale roommate and president of the Yale Dramatic Society, T. Lawrason Riggs (a graduate student in English literature at Harvard), to produce the first of two collaborations, *Paranoia* (1914), not for Harvard but for the Yale Dramatic Association.[32] The show, subtitled *Chester of the Yale Dramatic Association* (originally called *Belle of the Balkans*) contained a parody of Debussy's *Afternoon of a Faun* and songs that are harbingers of Porter's ability to weave his personal experiences into the lyrics.[33]

Cole spent 1915 in New York. That same year he again partnered with Riggs on *See America First*, a musical based loosely on Gilbert and Sullivan. It had its first performance in February 1916 in Schenectady. Several of its numbers were reworked from his college songs.[34] On 28 March 1916, after playing in other cities, the Porter-Riggs show opened on Broadway, where it played for only fifteen performances.[35]

Among the songs are some obvious parodies of Gilbert and Sullivan, such as the echoed strains of "I Am the Captain of the Pinafore" from *HMS Pinafore* and "A Modern Major General" from *The Pirates of Penzance* in "The Lady I've Vowed to Wed" and "Announcement Ensemble" ("Engagement Ensemble").

> His nearest what? His nearest what?
> His nearest female relative!
> His nearest what? His nearest what?
> His nearest female relative![36]

The Benefits of Networking: Linda, Darius, Léon, Alice, et al.

When the United States entered the war in April 1917, Porter, perhaps despondent over the failure of *See America First*, left for Paris to work with the relief effort and serve briefly in the Foreign Legion.[37] Before leaving, he wrote to his parents that he was going to Gotham to study counterpoint with the Italian-born teacher and organist Pietro Yon.[38] In Europe during the war, operetta and Franz Lehár's beloved waltzes began to be overpowered by the sounds of Broadway and American jazz tunes.[39] Parisian clubs were alive with the imported sounds of American dance music. A review by T. R. Ybarra in the *New York Times* in December 1921, entitled "'Jazz 'er Up!': Broadway's Conquest of Europe," stated that "if an American touring music-hall Paris shuts his eyes after being shown to his seat at the *Folies Bergères* . . . he will find himself wondering . . . whether he has really left Broadway."[40] As Parisians began to shake off the horrors of war, many sought to embrace the new decade by burying the old one. This led to a backlash in some areas of the arts. In music, composers sought to cleanse French music of foreign elements. Cocteau's panegyrics to Satie claimed the composer as profoundly original while calling Wagner, Stravinsky, and even Debussy "first rate octopuses": "Enough of clouds, waves, aquariums, watersprites, and nocturnal scents; what we need is a music of the earth, every-day music. . . . The music-hall, the circus, and American negro-bands, all these things fertilize an artist just as life does."[41] Satie and Cocteau set out to create a work that would utilize the sounds and characteristics of such popular entertainment as the cabaret and the circus. Cocteau had a fascination with black musicians that reflected a wider fashionable interest in black Africa among French intellectuals.[42] Premiered by Serge Diaghilev's Ballets russes in May 1917, *Parade* became a symbol for the avant-garde of the new "everyday" music. Satie rewrote Irving Berlin's "That Mysterious Rag," a Tin Pan Alley ragtime song, and renamed it "Steamship Ragtime."[43] "More than any single event at the time, [*Parade*] set the tone for the post-war years. . . . It was a serious-humorous exploitation of popular elements in art, a turning to jazz and music hall and to all the paraphernalia of modern life, not in a spirit of realism, but with a sense of exhilaration in the absurd."[44]

Parade was not alone in creating a tapestry of idioms. Folk and burlesque elements found their way into Stravinsky's ballets, including *Petrushka* (1911) and *Renard* (1915–16), and even earlier in Claude Debussy's *Golliwog's Cakewalk* (1908). In 1918 Stravinsky included popular idioms in his *L'histoire du soldat* and *Ragtime*.[45] The combination of stringed instruments included those he had heard in bars in Geneva, including the cimbalom, popular in Hungarian traditional ensembles.[46] Using popular song within the context of serious composition set the stage for a generation of young composers anxious to seek a new direction.

In 1918, while attending a wedding at the Ritz in Paris, Porter was introduced to Linda Lee Thomas, a divorcée from a wealthy and socially prominent Virginia family. They married shortly thereafter, and she, almost a decade older, became a powerful influence until she predeceased him in 1954. One of her most important introductions was to Darius Milhaud in 1919, while the latter was working with Jean Cocteau and others on a comic ballet, *Le boeuf sur le toit*. The work was inspired by the carnival in Rio and is filled with Brazilian dance and folk tunes. It includes music for a scene in an American bar during Prohibition. The first performance took place at the Théâtre des Champs-Élysées in 1920.[47] Two years later, Jean Wiéner, a promoter of American popular dance music by Gershwin, Vincent Youmans, Fletcher Henderson, and others, opened a club named after Milhaud's ballet *Le boeuf sur le toit*.[48] Wiéner's ensemble consisted of saxophone, banjo, snare drum, and a hi-hat lent to him by Stravinsky. Milhaud attributed jazz band arrangements to Irving Berlin but also wrote of Wiéner's talent and his interest in eclectic music, from ragtime and jazz to Bach: "Jean Wiéner played syncopated music with aerial grace and sensitivity, with an especially light rhythm. We loved listening to his playing, and to that of his partner, Vance, the Negro, who was an admirable saxophonist and banjo player. Without any transition these two would pass from fashionable ragtime and foxtrots to the most celebrated works of Bach. Besides, syncopated music calls for a rhythm as inexorably regular as that of Bach himself, which has the same basis."[49] The music was a mixture of syncopated Broadway show tunes fused with French chansons and a little Parisian music hall. Ira Gershwin reported that the musicians didn't play well, and he couldn't understand how Milhaud, as well as Ravel and Poulenc, could like what they were doing.[50]

Saturday evenings at Milhaud's apartment included cocktails, performances of poetry and music, and excursions to a café for dinner.[51] Guests would also attend the circus, music hall, or cinema. Milhaud was excited about the jazz he had heard in Harlem and shared his interest with Porter, playing gramophone records for him.[52] The Porters encountered these and other artists and literati at the Milhauds' and at the home of Singer sewing machine heiress Winnaretta Singer, Princesse Edmond de Polignac.[53]

A short, undated example from the collection at the Library of Congress reveals Porter's attempt at fusing jazz and popular music (fig. 1). Although

FIGURE 1. Undated counterpoint exercise, the Cole Porter Collection, folder 2, box 1, Music Division, Library of Congress. Used by permission of the Library of Congress.

this short piece is grouped with other pieces and exercises marked by sporadic comments and directions in French, it cannot be safely assigned to his studies in Paris. Perhaps, instead, it was a product of his earlier counterpoint studies with Pietro Yon in New York.[54] Porter's notation has improved and now reveals his "left-handed" bass clefs (fig. 1a). Porter's opening chromatic line in the left hand ascends from the tonic C to the major sixth in measure 3, where it is joined in imitation by the right hand. This theme provides a palette for Porter's subsequent use of accidentals (fig. 1b), including what we now call blue notes. The rising sequences beginning in the third system are a natural outgrowth of his semitone to rising sixth motive (fig. 1c). Several places include corrections likely inserted by Porter himself at a later time (fig. 1d). These include an added E on the third beat of the fourth measure in the bass; the C in the tenor in measure 24, creating a tritone with the bass and an augmented ninth with the alto; and the change from G in the bass in measure 27, converting what would be a traditional dominant–tonic final to a plagal cadence. What appears at first to be a four-voice invention in the fantasia style of a Baroque chorale prelude is peppered with sounds that foreshadow Porter's later style. The chromatic sequences, circles of fifths, and shifting modalities are also characteristics that reappear in his 1923 ballet *Within the Quota* and in some of his most memorable songs. Consider "the change from major to minor" in "Ev'ry Time We Say Goodbye" or the Middle Eastern–sounding chromaticism in "My Heart Belongs to Daddy," a song Oscar Levant described as "one of the most Yiddish tunes ever written."[55]

Porter sailed home in 1919 to discuss finances with his grandfather. On the ship he met the theatrical producer Raymond Hitchcock, who heard Porter perform "An Old-Fashioned Garden." The song eventually made its way into the 1919 revue *Hitchy-Koo*.[56] Other songs for that show included "When Black Sallie Sings Pagliacci," referencing black performers, in particular Josephine Baker, a singer who dazzled Paris and New York in the 1920s.[57] Another song for the show, "When I Had a Uniform On," was perhaps a reference to Porter's real or fantasized experience in the Foreign Legion. In "My Cozy Little Corner in the Ritz," Porter relies on ragtime and a kind of cakewalk with an extended piano postlude, references to the sounds he heard in Parisian bars.[58]

"Since Ma Got the Craze Espagnole" included the lyric "To show to what limits our nerves have been taxed / Why she just had the bathroom done over by Bakst." Porter's relationship with Léon Bakst had begun as early as 1914, during Porter's first European trip. It was then that the Russian avant-garde designer of theatrical scenes and costumes met the Baltimore socialite Alice

Warder Garrett, possibly the "she" who "just had the bathroom done over by Bakst."[59] In 1922, after Bakst severed his relationship with the Ballets russes, he came to Baltimore to design a theater for the Garretts' home, Evergreen House.[60] John Work Garrett (1872–1942), a diplomat and heir to the B&O Railroad fortune, had married Alice in 1908. From 1914 until 1917 he served as the assistant to the ambassador to France and for the next two years served as minister to the Netherlands and Luxembourg. Alice Garrett cultivated artists, writers, and musicians, creating a salon not unlike those of Elisabeth Marbury and Elsie de Wolfe on Sutton Place in New York and Winnaretta Singer on the rue Henri Martin in Paris. "For she's taken a fancy for anything Spanish" may be a Porter reference to Alice Garrett.[61] She had herself painted in Spanish garb by the portrait painter Ignacio Zuloaga (1870–1945), one full-length portrait in 1915 that hangs above the Steinway that Cole was said to have played and a second portrait in 1934.[62] The real friendship, bordering on infatuation, was between Alice and Linda Porter. A portrait of Linda drawn by Bakst hangs on the wall leading to the second floor at Evergreen House, and there is a photograph of her in an elegant hat and coat (figs. 2 and 3).

FIGURE 2. Linda Lee Porter, 1915, Léon Bakst (1866–1924). Graphite on paper, Collection of the Evergreen House Foundation, Evergreen Museum & Library. Used by permission of Johns Hopkins University.

FIGURE 3. Linda Lee Porter, ca. 1917, photographer unknown. Collection of the Evergreen House Foundation, Evergreen Museum & Library. Used by permission of Johns Hopkins University.

A telegram dated July 1922 from Linda to Alice asks if the Garretts could rent their Paris apartment to Cole for six weeks so that he could write a revue. With the death of his grandfather in 1923, Porter's financial situation suddenly improved, allowing him to rent a palazzo on the Grand Canal in Venice. It was there in 1923 that he collaborated with Gerald Murphy on his ballet *Within the Quota*.[63] On 5 June 1923 Milhaud arranged for Porter to meet Charles Koechlin, a composer and teacher at the Schola Cantorum in Paris in the 1930s who gave him an intensive course of eight lessons in eleven days at the Ritz hotel.[64] A concert on 25 October 1923 at the Théâtre des Champs-Élysées included two of Koechlin's chorales for small orchestra (op. 76, no. 2) performed along with pieces by members of Satie's École d'Arcueil, a group of four young composers founded that year, including Henri Cliquet-Pleyel (1894–1963), Roger Désormière (1898–1963), Henri Sauguet (1901–89), and Maxime Jacob (1906–78). Satie hoped that this "school" would be the successor to Les Six. This gala, involving Rolf de Maré's Ballets suédois, also included Milhaud's ballet *La création du monde* (with cubist sets by Fernand Henri Léger) and the premiere of Porter's *Within the Quota,* the first ballet with an American theme set to music by an American composer. Koechlin had orchestrated it that September.[65] The layering and stratification in Porter's ballet are, not surprisingly, similar to those employed by Milhaud in his *La création du monde*.[66] Along with techniques approaching collage, Porter, as he did with the short counterpoint exercise discussed earlier, played with polytonality, shades of Stravinsky's *Petrushka* in the opening, a juxtaposition of twelve-bar blues and stride motives in "Cowboy," parodies on pop tunes in "The Sweetheart of the World," and in the finale, a quodlibet not unlike that found in Milhaud's *Le boeuf*. Scattered here and there are echoes of Satie's *Gymnopédies* and Stravinsky's *Les noces*, as well as allusions to silent movie piano accompaniments, Swedish waltzes, and fox-trots.[67]

The Porter ballet was considered a success in Paris and in New York, where it was presented sixty times during a two-month tour. It is not known whether Porter knew Gershwin's jazz "opera" *Blue Monday*, orchestrated by Will Vodery for *George White's The Scandals of 1922*.[68] That work shares the same bluesy rhetoric as *Rhapsody in Blue*, with syncopated figures, call-and-response patterns, and other features of early jazz.[69] Had Porter had the advantage of an orchestrator like Vodery, *Within the Quota* might have had greater success.[70] He was to have written a second ballet with Bakst's scenery and costumes, but the designer died in 1924.[71] Porter anticipated certain idioms that were to cause a stir when, months later, they found expression in Gershwin's *Rhapsody in Blue*.[72] It was likely that Gershwin's immediate success led Porter to withdraw from writing other serious instrumental works.[73] In the following year, after the failure of *Greenwich Village Follies of 1924* and the success of Gershwin's *Rhapsody in Blue,* Porter took a break from composing for the public, limiting his activities to writing and performing his songs for friends and acquaintances.

In 1923 Albert Sirmay (Szirmai, 1880–1967) arrived from Budapest, becoming the chief editor of Chappell and Company in New York, where he worked with Berlin, Jerome Kern, Gershwin, Porter, and others, translating their music into standard piano-vocal scores.[74] There is some disagreement as to Sirmay's role in notating Porter's compositions.[75] Their correspondence reveals that Sirmay was a close friend, editor, "musical secretary," and consultant.[76] He also lent Porter moral support on occasions when Porter felt his work to be inadequate.[77]

In 1928 Irving Berlin's brother-in-law Ray Goetz, a friend Porter met on the beach at the Lido, commissioned a show for his wife, the actress Irène Bordoni. That show, *Paris,* opened in New York in 1928 and ran for 195 performances, the longest run for any Porter show up until that time and one that he himself said "was an instant smash." He reported to Richard Hubler that "I was a musical comedy writer in demand—and I was never again really in the doldrums after 1928." The first of his famous list songs, "Let's Do It—Let's Fall in Love," drew rave reviews.[78] At around the same time, Porter composed music and lyrics for several other shows with international themes, including *La Revue des Ambassadeurs*, *Wake Up and Dream, Paris,* and *Fifty Million Frenchmen*.[79] "What Is This Thing Called Love?" from *Wake Up and Dream*, with an opening on a half-diminished dominant chord, shifts between major and minor keys, and unusual harmonic progressions, became a familiar jazz standard. Porter himself said the piece was inspired by a Moroccan dance.[80]

In sum, Porter's compositions can be described as an amalgam of styles, combining his early classical training and exposure to opera, ballet, ragtime, popular music, and jazz. He had an innate gift for mimicking the sounds around him, breezily absorbing the idioms and nuances of the speech and melodies he heard. His social skills provided a network of influential friends and artists who provided him with ideas and feedback. Porter is quoted as saying in those years:

> I'm becoming less and less interested in tricky rhymes. I think I used to go overboard on them. In Yale, I was rhyme-crazy. That was due to the fact that I was Gilbert and Sullivan crazy. They had a big influence on my life. My songs

> are easier than they used to be, musically and lyrically. I've never been able to get complete simplicity the way Berlin does. Sometimes, I'll take twenty-five minutes to write a song, sometimes two days. I can tell a bad line by watching audiences. The minute they look at a program, I know the line's got to be thrown out.[81]

By the late 1920s Porter had given up on the idea of becoming a serious classical composer and instead concentrated on writing sophisticated, witty lyrics, molding them to his signature musical style just for listeners who wanted to enter his world and share his encounters with elegance and artistry.

Notes

1. Among a few of Porter's lyrics with bird references: "Be Like the Bluebird," "The Sophomore," "The Kling Kling Bird on the Divi-Divi Tree," "Glide, Glider, Glide," "Let's Do It," "Sing Sing." A common thread is the insouciance of birds. "Greetings, Gentlemen" from *See America First* includes "The birds are singing merrily / Merely because they persist in ignoring life's tragedy."

2. William McBrien, *Cole Porter: A Biography* (New York: Vintage Books, 1998), 72; Richard Hubler, *The Cole Porter Story, as Told to Richard G. Hubler* (Cleveland: World Publishing Company, 1965), 17, 67; George Eells, *The Life That Late He Led: A Biography of Cole Porter* (New York: G. P. Putnam's Sons, 1967), 152.

3. Brendan Gill, "Wouldn't It Be Fun?," *New Yorker*, 18 September 1971, 48–66, 53.

4. McBrien, *Cole Porter*, 10.

5. "You're the Top: Cole Porter in the 1930s," Cole Porter Centennial Collection, Indiana History Society, Miami County, Indiana, and Koch International Classics, 1992.

6. *Grant County and Who's Who [1831–1909]* (Marion, IN: Special Company, 1909). See also the 1910 census.

7. Eells, *The Life That Late He Led*, 17.

8. Ibid., 16.

9. Hubler, *The Cole Porter Story*, 11.

10. "The Song of the Birds," manuscript is in the collection of Cole Porter Trust: Roberta Staats, Executive Director of the Cole Porter Trust, Paul, Weiss, Rifkind, Wharton & Garrison LLP, 1285 Avenue of the Americas, New York, NY 10019-064. Used by permission of the Trustee.

11. The bird motives may anticipate the inimitable "twee" renderings in songs such as "Be Like the Bluebird" from *Anything Goes*. The oompah anticipates Porter's love of circus parades and the influence of his father, who played the steam calliope.

12. Hubler, *The Cole Porter Story*, 10.

13. McBrien, *Cole Porter*, 12.

14. Franz Schubert's first composition for piano, a duet, was written when he was three years older than Porter. Recordings of Porter singing reveal that he had a high voice. F major may have been a comfortable key for him.

15. Letters of D. W. Abercrombie, Principal of Worcester Academy, to Kate Cole. The letters between Kate Cole and Abercrombie are preserved in twelve books at Worcester

Academy. Another four books are at the American Antiquarian Society in the Worcester Academy Records, 1832–1983, Worcester, Massachusetts. I am grateful to Wilfried Van den Brande and Roberta Staats for sharing these documents and to Frank Callahan at Worcester Academy for permission to use some of them here. Many letters were published in the *Worcester Review*.

16. Although he attributed the failure to lack of preparation, Abercrombie also believed that Cole bluffed his way through the test. My gratitude to Frank Callahan at Worcester Academy for providing me with this information about Cole attending Dame's summer school.

17. D. W. Abercrombie, Principal of Worcester Academy, to Kate Cole, 9 January 1909, Worcester Academy Records, 1832–1983.

18. D. W. Abercrombie, Principal of Worcester Academy, to Kate Cole, 26 September 1908, Worcester Academy Records, 1832–1983.

19. D. W. Abercrombie, Principal of Worcester Academy, to Kate Cole, 22 February 1916, Worcester Academy Records, 1832–1983.

20. Hubler, *The Cole Porter Story*, 11.

21. Ibid.

22. Most but not all of these composers were white males of European descent. There were some women who made their mark on Tin Pan Alley, such as Ann Ronell, the subject of a biography by Tighe Zimmers, *Tin Pan Alley Girl: A Biography of Ann Ronell* (Jefferson, NC: McFarland, 2009). The African American contribution is the subject of recent research by Paula Rogo and Eden E. Woldearegay, *In the Shadows of Broadway*, http://www.shadowsofbroadway.com/about/, accessed 14 December 2013.

23. See Kimball's chapter in this volume on Porter at Yale. For nearly a century, Porter was mistakenly credited with the authorship of the song "Boola." Recent research has established that it was actually Allan Hirsh (Yale '01) who adapted it from "La Hoola Boola" by the Broadway team of Bob Cole and Billy Johnson in 1898. The meaning of "Boola-Boola," however, remains one of the great mysteries of Yale College life. Porter's "Bridget" was actually his first published song that included lyrics (Detroit: Jerome H. Remick, 1910).

24. Porter claimed he was "Gilbert and Sullivan crazy" in his youth (Eells, *The Life That Late He Led*, 278). See the reference to Porter's love for Gilbert and Sullivan in Walden, this volume, note 5. The affection for Gilbert and Sullivan was felt on both sides of the Atlantic. Porter's British alter ego, Noël Coward, claimed that the lyrics and melodies "were hummed and strummed into my consciousness at an early age. My father sang them, my mother played them . . . my aunts and uncles, who were legion, sang them singly and in unison at the slightest provocation" (Graham Payn, *My Life with Noël Coward* [New York: Hal Leonard, 1994], 308).

25. Reid Badger, *A Life in Ragtime: A Biography of James Reese Europe* (New York: Oxford, 1995), 288n40.

26. Al Rose, *Eubie Blake* (New York: Schirmer, 1979), 96–97.

27. Charles Schwartz, *Cole Porter: A Biography* (New York: Da Capo Press, 1977), 85.

28. See Van den Brande and Morris, this volume. These women, Marbury and de Wolfe (later Lady Mendl), took Porter under their wings. Their apartment on Sutton Place in New York City became what might be called an "Amazonian enclave."

29. Murphy was the supposed inspiration for Dick Diver (see Van den Brande, this volume). Among others Murphy knew were the artists Fernand Léger, Constantin Brancusi, Man Ray, Joan Miró, and Pablo Picasso and the dancers George Balanchine and Isadora Duncan. The list goes on and on.

30. Amanda Vaill, *Everybody Was So Young: Gerald and Sara Murphy: A Lost Generation Love Story* (Boston: Houghton Mifflin, 1998).

31. Correspondence with the Reference Staff, 30 November 2012, Harvard University Archives, Pusey Library, Harvard Yard, Cambridge, MA, 02138, http://library.harvard.edu/university-archives/.

32. Riggs's relatives included Lawrason Riggs, a philanthropist and lawyer who served as a member of the inaugural board of trustees of the Peabody Institute in Baltimore for forty-three years. His portrait hangs in the Arthur Friedheim Music Library at the Peabody Conservatory. The music for *Paranoia* has not survived.

33. See Van den Brande's discussion in this volume of "I've a Shooting Box in Scotland," another song to reappear in Porter's first show, *See America First*.

34. That type of practice dates to the self-borrowings of Handel and other composers with a shortage of time and fast-approaching deadlines.

35. Much of the original piano vocal score survives at the Library of Congress (boxes 1 and 2 of the Porter Collection). Autographs survive for some of the parts. Although there is no orchestral score, Porter indicated slurs, bowings, and other indications for instruments.

36. And many of Porter's works are parodied today. Stephen Holden, writing in the *New York Times* on Friday, 17 May 2013, "Recalling the Life of the Party," reviewed a concert where James Naughton in a tribute to Bobby Short performed "You're the Pits," with lyrics by Robert Grode, a parody of Porter's "You're the Top."

37. Porter's picture appears in the French Foreign Legion museum. Not much is known about his time there, but stories survive of his having carried on his back a small portable piano. Morris, citing McBrien, feels that Porter made up his affiliation with the Legion.

38. Stephen Citron, *Noel and Cole: The Sophisticates* (London: Sinclair Stephenson, 1992), 39.

39. Gunther Schuller, *Early Jazz: Its Roots and Musical Development* (New York: Oxford University Press, 1968), 66. See also Glenn Watkins, *Pyramids at the Louvre: Music, Culture, and Collage from Stravinsky to the Postmodernists* (Cambridge, MA: Belknap Press of Harvard University Press, 1994), 488.

40. T. R. Ybarra, "'Jazz 'er Up!': Broadway's Conquest of Europe," *New York Times Book Review*, 18 December 1921, 3, 17.

41. Jean Cocteau, *Cock and Harlequin: Notes Concerning Music*, trans. Rollo H. Myers (London: Egoist Press, 1921), 20. There are some striking parallels between the training of Satie and Porter. In 1905, at age thirty-nine, Satie enrolled at the Schola (twenty-one years after being told by teachers at the Conservatoire that he had no talent) to study counterpoint while continuing to earn an income writing for cabaret.

42. See Watkins, *Pyramids*, 63. For more on the influence of African musicians in Paris, see Van den Brande, this volume.

43. Nancy Perloff, *Art and the Everyday: Popular Entertainment and the Circle of Erik Satie* (Oxford: Clarendon Press, 1993), 132. Apparently, American students brought syncopated music to the Continent as early as the 1880s. Brahms was said to have heard an American girl play cakewalk on her banjo.

44. Roger Shattuck, *The Banquet Years: The Origins of the Avant Garde in France, 1885 to World War I* (New York: Random House, 1968), 154. One moment in the ballet that caused controversy was a music-hall number titled "Little American Girl."

45. The latter was first written for eleven instruments, but, hoping to sell more copies, Stravinsky later provided a piano reduction (Stravinsky to Edwin Evans, 7 May 1918, personal collection). See also Barbara Heyman, "Stravinsky and Ragtime," *Musical Quarterly* 68, no. 4 (1982): 543–62; and McBrien, *Cole Porter*, 52.

46. Darius Milhaud and fellow members of Les Six (as they were dubbed by Henry Collet in 1920), the young composers Francis Poulenc, Georges Auric, Germaine Tailleferre, Arthur Honegger, and Louis Durey, adopted Satie as their paterfamilias. One of Les Six, Germaine Tailleferre, signed the guest register at the Baltimore home of Alice Warder Garrett in 1925 with a quote from her piano concerto. Also in 1925 at a soirée there, Tailleferre and Gershwin played a two-piano transcription of *Rhapsody in Blue*.

47. Rachel Franklin, "American Jazz in the Works of Jean Wiéner, Maurice Ravel, and Darius Milhaud" (DMA document, Peabody Conservatory, 1995).

48. The club replaced Bar Gaya, a popular spot for artists, writers, and musicians that had become too small. Wiéner, Milhaud, and Charles Koechlin all studied with André Gédalge at the Paris Conservatory (and had known each other since childhood).

49. Darius Milhaud, *Études* (Paris: Éditions Claude Aveline, 1927), 52; Milhaud, *Notes without Music* (New York: Da Capo Press, 1970), 120.

50. David Baskerville, *Jazz Influence on Art Music to Mid-Century* (Berkeley: University of California Press, 1975), 121.

51. McBrien, *Cole Porter*, 89. It was Linda who introduced Cole to Stravinsky and convinced Cole to enroll at the Schola Cantorum in Paris. Cole entered the Schola in 1920 for two years. D'Indy's biographer Andrew Thomson stated that Cole was among those Americans who came after the war: "Feeling the need of some solid grounding in composition, the future writer of the famous American musical *Kiss Me Kate* enrolled in d'Indy's class at the Schola. But before long he dropped out, finding the regime too academic for his particular kind of talent, which needed to blossom spontaneously. Yet, he did not repudiate his brief time there, as it proved to be a useful badge of respectability back in the States" (*Vincent d'Indy and His World* [Oxford: Clarendon Press, 1996], 198, quoting from Vincent d'Indy, *Lettres à Auguste Sérieyx etc.* [Lausanne: Éditions du Cervin, 1961], 25–27).

52. Milhaud was part of a network of artists, including Erik Satie, Robert Delaunay, Marc Chagall, and Blaise Cendrars. Cole met Cendrars, a collaborator of Darius Milhaud who wrote the book for his ballet *La création du monde*, while at a party following the premiere of Stravinsky's *Les noces*. Cendrars was the nom de plume (*cendres*, "ashes," and *ars*, "arts") of Frédéric Louis Sauser (1887–1961). Cendrars's poem to Erik Satie, "The Musickissme," contains the kind of inner rhyme scheme that permeates the sophisti-

cated lyrics that came to be associated with Porter songs. Cendrars studied medicine, philosophy, literature, and musicology at university in his native Switzerland.

53. See Van den Brande, this volume.

54. See holograph scores and sketches in pencil, box 1, folder 2 (musical exercises and student work), Cole Porter Collection, Performing Arts Division, Library of Congress, Washington, DC: approximately twenty leaves, including exercises in writing fugues, voice leading, and orchestration along with what appear to be notes taken from lectures. The contents of this folder was mixed in with all of the preceding manuscript materials. Because many of Porter's notes are in French, this is probably circa 1920, while he was studying at the Schola Cantorum in Paris. Many of these exercises, all in Porter's hand with his characteristic "left-handed" bass clef, contain some annotations in another hand, as well as the familiar Porter doodles of women with hats (see Horowitz, this volume).

55. Oscar Levant, *The Unimportance of Being Oscar* (1968; repr., New York: Pocket Books, 1989), 32.

56. Porter claimed it was one of the biggest hits of his career and thought it had sold two million copies, a bit of an exaggeration (the figure was closer to one hundred thousand). Cole's own copy of the published piano-vocal score of "An Old-Fashioned Garden" is in box 2.22 in the Porter Collection at the Library of Congress with a Waldorf Towers address label and a handwritten note, "to be returned to" Cole Porter.

57. It was during this time that George Gershwin wrote a thirty-minute opera with a melodramatic plot by B. G. DeSylva, essentially a gloss on Leoncavallo's *Pagliacci*. *Blue Monday*, written for *George White's Scandals of 1922*, was performed by white singers in blackface and took place in a bar in Harlem. The short work combined aspects of verismo opera, ragtime, band music, and jazz and anticipated *Rhapsody in Blue* (1924), his *Preludes* of 1926, and his full-length opera *Porgy and Bess* (1935). John Andrew Johnson, "Gershwin's Blue Monday (1922) and the Promise of Success," in *The Gershwin Style: New Looks at the Music of George Gershwin*, ed. Wayne Schneider (New York: Oxford University Press, 1999), 112.

58. On the implications of this song and the gay sections of the bar, see Van den Brande, this volume.

59. Along with the photo and drawing of Linda Porter in the Garretts' home, there is a photo of Bakst. Among Alice Garrett's papers, now housed in the Special Collections at the Milton S. Eisenhower Library at Johns Hopkins University, are a few letters and telegrams from Linda.

60. In the early 1920s the Garretts inherited the family mansion on Charles Street in north Baltimore, where they hosted many celebrities, including "a drunken H. L. Mencken, introducing the rhumba" in the Bakst theater. From 1920 until 1929 Garrett dabbled in Republican politics, running unsuccessfully for the Senate in Maryland in 1922. Johns Hopkins University now owns the home and its library (which is a part of the Sheridan Libraries). Numerous cultural events make use of the home and the Bakst theater.

61. Alice was involved in the arts from a young age, studying voice and developing a love of theater, the visual arts, and architecture. She published pamphlets on diverse subjects, most dealing with the arts, one of them entitled "The Development of Music

in America." Letters, as well as her published papers on the arts, survive in the archives at Johns Hopkins University.

62. The first of these may have been the inspiration for "Since Ma Got the Craze Espagnole." Zuloaga also was commissioned to do a seated portrait of Alice's husband, John Work Garrett, after he became ambassador to Rome (1929–33); a Spanish landscape; a painting based on the opera *Goyescas*, written by Enrique Granados in 1915; and a landscape of Calatayud in Aragon. Porter was thought to have entertained guests on the Garretts' Steinway at least once, but, oddly, neither his nor Linda's name appears among the many signatures in the Garretts' guest books, nor do the signatures of other personal friends of Alice's such as Zuloaga and her decorator Billy Baldwin. Throughout the 1920s and 1930s the Garrett guest books reveal signatures and doodles or musical quotations by Léon Bakst, Edith Wharton, Ezra Pound, Frank Lloyd Wright, Marcel Proust, Andrew W. Mellon, George Gershwin, Olga Samaroff Stokowski, Willem Mengelberg, Bruno Walter, Princesse Edmond de Polignac (Winnaretta Singer), the Damrosches, Arturo Toscanini, Ernest Schelling (composer, pianist, and the first conductor of the Young Persons Concerts of the New York Philharmonic in 1924), Béla Bartók, the Crowninshields, and Walter Lippmann, among others.

63. Robert Kimball, *The Complete Lyrics Of Cole Porter* (New York: Knopf, 1983; repr., New York: Da Capo Press, 1992), xxviii. Van den Brande explores Italian influences in the next chapter in this volume. Porter must have longed for the Lido. In the late 1930s, following his riding accident, he rented a home in Lido Beach, New York, perhaps to bring back memories of his beloved Venice and the intimate friendships he cultivated while there.

64. Robert Orledge, "Cole Porter's Ballet 'Within the Quota,'" *Yale University Library Gazette* 50, no. 1 (July 1975): 19–29. The lessons were held at the Ritz Hotel. Koechlin complained to Henri Sauguet in a letter dated 19 September 1923 that while he was busy with the score, "it was a difficult task, because a more substantial orchestra was needed" ("Cher ami . . . A ce moment, j'orchestre un ballet de l'Americain Cole Porter, c'est un travail difficile car il y faudrait un orchestre plus nourri; mais enfin j'espère que ça sonnera tout de même") ("Charles Koechlin, 1867–1950: Correspondence," *La revue musicale* [1982]: 64). Koechlin gave Cole five further lessons between 23 January and 5 February 1924. Other Koechlin students included Germaine Tailleferre (1916–23); Roger Desormière (1916–23, 1926–27); Francis Poulenc (1921–23, 1925); and Alexander Steinert, who graduated from Harvard with a degree in music in 1923, studying with Charles Martin Loeffler, also a teacher of Milhaud. Steinert, heir to the Steinway Piano fortune whose father brought Nathan Milstein, Gregor Piatagorski, and Vladimir Horowitz to the United States, also studied with d'Indy at the Schola in 1922. He had a long career in music as a conductor, and he wrote music for film, eventually succeeding Albert Sirmay as Porter's amanuensis in the early 1950s, when the two former Schola students began meeting to play two pianos.

65. In it, a Swedish immigrant—Jean Börlin, also the principal dancer in Milhaud's ballet—meets a variety of American "types": an heiress, a colored gentleman, a jazz baby, and so on. Borlin was also the principal dancer in the Francis Picabia–Erik Satie collaboration *Relâche* (also for the Ballets suédois in 1924) and was later involved in *The Seven Lively Arts* (1944). See Morrison, this volume.

66. Matthew David Luttrell, "An American Songwriter in Paris: Cole Porter's Ballet *Within the Quota* with Comparison to Darius Milhaud's *La Création du monde,*" DMA doc., Arizona State University, 2010, 5–7.

67. The thematic material relies on three basic themes subdivided into smaller motives occasionally presented in ostinato form. Porter includes half-diminished seventh chords and favors tonal ambiguities throughout the work. Poulenc told Koechlin in a letter that he loved the orchestration. Milhaud said, "I found the score redolent of the pure spirit of Manhattan, with wistful blues alternating with throbbing ragtime rhythms. This odd partnership between the technician of counterpoint and fugue and the brilliant future 'King of Broadway' was an outstanding success" (Robert Orledge, *Charles Koechlin [1867–1950]: His Life and Works* [Chur, Switzerland: Harwood, 1989], 28).

68. Also called "Opera a la Afro American."

69. Gershwin later had lessons in harmony, composition, and orchestration from Henry Cowell, Wallingford Riegger, and Arnold Schoenberg. Although neither Gershwin nor Porter orchestrated his works, Gershwin, who relied on Ferde Grofé for *Rhapsody in Blue*, went on to orchestrate his Concerto in F (commissioned by Walter Damrosch in 1925).

70. However, the jazz element in *Within the Quota* lies more in the music than in the orchestration. Jazz apparently did not appeal to Koechlin's tastes. The manuscript in the Bibliothèque nationale (F-Pn MS 15472) reveals that Koechlin added an alto saxophone as an afterthought, and the opening theme of the "Jazz Baby" is given to the English horn doubled at the octave on the piccolo. After four bars this opening theme passes on to two bassoons in their highest register. Overall, Koechlin's end product is distinctly French rather than American, infused with Parisian colors. Koechlin complained, "It was a difficult task, because a more substantial orchestra was needed." Simon Morrison, elsewhere in this volume, reveals that Porter's original score was filled with these elements, which are all but neglected in Koechlin's orchestration.

71. See Bolcom and Morrison, this volume.

72. Paul Whiteman commissioned the piece in 1924. See Allen Forte, "Secrets of Melody: Line and Design in the Songs of Cole Porter," *Musical Quarterly* 77, no. 4 (1993): 625, on Cole's jazz harmonies, as well as Bolcom, Kimball, and Morrison, this volume.

73. Robert Kimball and Richard M. Sudhalter, *You're the Top: Cole Porter in the 1930's* (Indianapolis: Indiana Historical Society, 1992), 2.

74. His own operettas were pastiches of Viennese waltzes and Hungarian czardas mixed with Wagner and Gilbert and Sullivan. It comes as no surprise that Sirmay was editing popular editions of piano versions of arias from grand opera, American folk songs, and Gilbert and Sullivan. In a review of a performance of Gilbert and Sullivan in the *New Yorker* ("Musical Events," 22 November 1941), Robert Simon wrote of a new edition of the operettas by Deems Taylor: "The songs have new piano arrangements by Dr. Albert Sirmay, who has adjusted matters for the convenience of those of us who aren't exactly virtuosi. The helpful 'Doc' Sirmay also has transposed certain airs into keys, which bring the music within the vocal ranges of unterrified amateurs."

75. Michael Feinstein believes that Sirmay would help notate the piano score during production and would later simplify the songs (Michael Feinstein and Jan Jackman, *The Gershwins and Me* [New York: Simon and Schuster, 2011], 14). I agree with Allen Forte that Sirmay changed little of Porter's music.

76. Albert Sirmay, Emerich Kalman, and Victor Jacobi were, with Franz Lehár, leading composers of the Silver Age of Viennese operetta. Kalman was said to be Hitler's favorite operetta composer. It is regrettable that so little is known about Sirmay. Efforts to discover more ended in blind alleys; his influence on generations of Broadway composers calls for more research.

77. The 1928 Broadway show *Rosalie* originally had seven songs by Gershwin and eight by Romberg, but it was Porter's music that was used for the 1937 film. He wrote "Rosalie," the title song; more than five hundred thousand copies of the sheet music were sold. Sirmay wrote that Cole was wrong about his final version, claiming it wasn't very good; it was the best, and it was the one Louis B. Mayer liked. Mayer wanted a honky-tonk number rather than something for Nelson Eddy.

78. Hubler, *The Cole Porter Story*, 22.

79. See Van den Brande, this volume, on the significance of the Café Les Ambassadeurs. One can speculate that *La Revue des Ambassadeurs* may also have been a tribute to the Garretts, who, as ambassadors, spent time in Switzerland ("Alpine Rose," "Hans"), but also to Cole's own Francophilia ("Lost Liberty Blues" and "Military Maids") and love for the exotic ("In a Moorish Garden" and "Almiro"). George Gershwin was the accompanist at the premiere in 1928. Porter's affection for dance, blues, and jazz is heard in a number of songs, including "You and Me" and "Blue Hours." His lyrics contain the customary references to birds: bluebirds singing the blues and a serenade sung in Marrakech by "a swallow who was winging through the garden." Happily, the orchestral arrangements by Fred Waring, thought to have been lost, were recently discovered in the Waring Archive in University Park, Pennsylvania. Much of the printed piano-vocal music survives. See James Barron, "Cole Porter's Lost Show Unearthed," *New York Times*, 23 June 2014, C1, C6.

80. Van den Brande, this volume, suggests that the song might relate to Porter's despair over the end of his affair with Boris Kochno.

81. Gilbert Millstein, "Words anent Music by Cole Porter," *New York Times*, 20 February 1955.

3
Cole Porter, European

WILFRIED VAN DEN BRANDE

I vividly remember my first encounter in Manhattan with Robert Kimball, aptly described by Porter biographer William McBrien as "the dean of Porter studies."[1] We had lunch at Sardi's, and Robert asked me what specific book or article, in my opinion, came closest to capturing Porter's spirit. To our joy, we discovered that, for both of us, Moss Hart's foreword to the *Cole Porter Songbook* won the prize: it is a vivacious, sympathetic, firsthand account by someone who traveled and worked with Porter—someone who knew him well.[2] The story is famous: in 1933 the young Moss Hart, carrying with him a letter of introduction from Irving Berlin, encounters Cole Porter at the Ritz bar in Paris and hands him a present from a friend:

> George Hale asked me to bring this to you. . . . Two long, thin slabs of gold with the initials "C.P." engraved on them lay somewhat nakedly on the white satin. "What are they?" "Garters," he replied. I watched, astonished, as he lifted each of his trousers legs, revealing a gold garter on the sock above each leg, removed the old ones from each and put the new ones on, and in further astonishment I heard him call, "hey, Jimmy!" to the barman and toss the old gold garters across the bar. [A first encounter that contains] some of the gaiety, the impishness, the audacity and the wonderful insouciance of some of his songs. . . . Words and music that had an abandon, a stunning freshness, a dash and a lyrical agility that were completely new to our ears.[3]

Hart's depiction of Porter as a jet-set man, a character stepping right out of *The Great Gatsby*, is utterly convincing—the world of the affluent was his natural environment. Starting from this image, I will attempt to paint a portrait of Cole Porter's life in Europe between the late 1910s and early 1930s. The persons and places he encountered there left their mark on a multitude of his songs, and, through Porter's unique perspective, perhaps we can view this special period of history in fresh and vibrant colors.[4]

Cole Porter, European: Linda

Whereas the role of Porter's wife, Linda, is too often dismissed with a benign smile because of Cole's homosexuality, Moss Hart rightly focuses on the enormous importance of Linda in his life: "She was a woman of immense delicacy with an enchanting turn of mind, a legendary beauty herself, [who] lent something of her own radiance and splendor to their life together."[5] As a rich divorcée originating from a Kentucky family, Linda Lee Thomas encountered Cole at the marriage of socialites Ethel Harriman and Henry Russell in Paris. She was intrigued by the smart, sophisticated gentleman who so wonderfully entertained at the piano, drawing people in with his witty, double entendre–laden songs. As the resulting friendship turned into love, Linda became his "finishing school"—almost eight years his elder, she'd become a second mother figure, as influential as the "great Kate" herself.[6] Her friend Bernard Berenson, an art connoisseur and historian, remembered her as "a great beauty with great brains."[7] Sophisticated and socially well connected, she "collected first-rate antiques and art objects, particularly old Chinese arts, . . . mingled with ease among nobility and royalty; and she cultivated and counted as friends many of the most distinguished minds of the times, among them G. B. Shaw, John Galsworthy, Winston Churchill."[8] Her sensibilities matched well with Cole's and played a role in his music as well. "Linda was devoted to old-fashioned customs but not to old-fashioned people. She saw [Porter] correctly as redeeming the, at times, crass business of Broadway with what those of Linda's background valued more than anything else: style." "She was the air that made Cole's sails move," and "unless she was sold on a song, Porter kept working at it."[9]

Cole and Linda kept a stylish home in Paris: "The Porters set up housekeeping at Linda's house at 13, rue Monsieur, in the fashionable Quartier des Invalides. Thanks to Linda's great taste, the interior was an Art Deco symphony: zebra rugs on highly polished marble floors, red lacquered chairs with cushions covered in white kidskin, settees covered in suede, platinum-colored wallpaper, and a huge basement room entirely lined with mirrors and used solely for dancing and parties."[10] Linda was well connected in Paris, and her circle of friends featured prominent names. In an autobiographical interview with Richard Hubler, Porter tells of a visit to the Duke of Alba in Seville, where the Prince of Wales, "a terribly shy, amazingly blond young man who was in love—at the time—solely with American music. . . . [H]earing some of the most remarkable flamenco tunes, [he] drew me out onto the balcony. 'Cole,' he whispered, 'what wouldn't I give for just five minutes of good old American ragtime!'"[11] Schuyler Parsons, perhaps Linda and Cole's matchmaker without realizing it, also introduced Porter to Charles Lindbergh, who flew his *Spirit of St. Louis* across the Atlantic. Porter, giving in to his natural curiosity, was at Le Bourget when Lindbergh landed, and he was also present at the exclusive dinner Parsons organized; the occasion may have inspired Porter to write one of his early double entendre songs: "Pilot Me."

Elsie de Wolfe

In *Hitchy-Koo of 1919*, Cole frequently references the high-society life he's living. One fascinating song concerns his friend Elsie de Wolfe, "the leading decorator of the nation." A marvelous woman with tremendous taste and a great sense of humor, "she was one of the most flamboyant and influential women of the late-nineteenth and twentieth centuries, [whose] parties were *de rigueur*. Her skills as an interior decorator revolutionized twentieth-century design, her advice on art and decoration helped build the collections of Fricks, Vanderbilts and Morgans. She nursed on the front lines during World War I [and] marched down Fifth Avenue for women's rights."[12] Porter had met her years before, when she was still an actress and partner of Elisabeth Marbury, the producer who gave him his first chance on Broadway with *See America First*.[13] This utter flop seems not to have destroyed the relationship between the two friends. Elsie, along with Elisabeth Marbury and Anne Morgan—the three graces—owned one of *the* meeting points among the Paris jet set: the Villa Trianon in Versailles, where even the illustrious Comte Robert de Montesquiou ("Charlus" in Proust's *À la recherche*) would enliven the parties with his mordant wit. Here, Elsie was hostess to a "standard mixture of diplomats, entertainers, wealthy Americans, cosmopolitan Europeans and young beauties of both sexes."[14] In her surprise marriage (at a relatively advanced age) to Sir Charles Mendl, she followed Cole's example of a *mariage blanc*.[15]

"That Black and White Baby of Mine," which Porter wrote for *Hitchy-Koo of 1919*, reflects Elsie de Wolfe's decorating taste when the heroine of the song has her whole life redesigned in a strict black-and-white color scheme. When

Elsie moved on to her "beige" period, her comment upon arriving at the top of the climb to the Acropolis became legendary: "My colour!"[16]

At the Villa Trianon, Bernard Berenson, who advised the world on Italian Renaissance paintings, was a treasured guest. BB, as they called him, maintained a lifelong correspondence with Linda (and Cole now and then) and was very well acquainted with the art dealer *par excellence*, Sir Joseph Duveen. Joe Duveen makes an appearance in such Cole Porter songs as "The Blue Boy Blues" and one of Porter's most wonderful gems, "Looking at You":

> I've gone afar,
> Collecting objets d'art,
> I know the whole game by heart.
> Why, Joe Duveen
> Will tell you what I mean,
> 'Twas I who gave him his start.
> But since I looked, dear,
> In your direction,
> I've quite forgotten my art collection.
> To be exact,
> You simply prove the fact,
> That nature's greater than art.

In this verse, we see what Hart means when he asserts that Cole Porter lifted the popular song to an entirely new level "with a velocity of a meteor streaking across the sky."[17] Indeed, as Alan Jay Lerner contends, "he seemed to spring from nowhere, like Jupiter from Minerva's head [*sic*]—all made."[18]

Elsa Maxwell

When it came to organizing parties, Porter's partner in crime was his friend Elsa Maxwell. Through Porter's friendship with Elsie de Wolfe, Maxwell, who started out as a modest pianist/accompanist and who could not exactly be described as a beauty queen, found herself among the European/expatriate elite. Elsa soon discovered that she could "[earn] her income by no profession known to the dictionary: promoting and hustling in the world of the rich and famous performing favors of a delicate social nature with the unspoken understanding that she would be tipped with a jeweled trinket suitable for resale."[19] As Charles Schwartz describes, "Her masterminding of society charity affairs for the benefit of the allies during World War I had put her on the map as an 'upper-echelon social director.'"[20]

Elsa's frauds are legendary—her mother must have died twenty-five times, for Elsa was always asking her friends for a little help with the funeral costs—but her ideas were grand. "Everyone liked her, because she was too unattractive to threaten and had a keen sense of fun."[21] In a notorious hoax, Elsa and Cole invented a phony social-climbing couple from Tulsa, Oklahoma, and then filled the pages of the international edition of the *New York Herald Tribune* with fictitious stories and letters by and about the Fitches. "Mister and Missus Fitch" even had a papal audience before Porter, probably having grown tired of the story, had them die in a tragic car crash.

Schwartz credits Elsa Maxwell for "spreading the word about Cole in the early days, with the result that he became a kind of cause célèbre among the elite considerably before the masses knew about him."[22] In their musical *Jubilee,* Moss Hart and Cole Porter based a character on Elsa, "as close to the original as skin"—"My Most Intimate Friend" portrays Elsa from head to toe.[23] As a surprise birthday present, Porter wrote Elsa a song in the late 1920s, "I'm Dining with Elsa" (and her ninety-nine most intimate friends), for which the music remains lost.[24] In his exquisite biography, Sam Staggs writes about Elsa's important role in luring Cole Porter to the Waldorf Towers: "Elsa's rent was free, at least for a long time. . . . She moved in the year the hotel opened because, she said, 'Lucius Boomer, the president, made the offer thinking my presence might bring other more-desirable guests. Boomer was right; the Towers filled up with friends.' Among them the Shah of Iran, the Duke and Duchess of Windsor, Marilyn Monroe and . . . Cole Porter."[25] In her autobiography, Elsa recounts visiting Cole in the hospital after the riding accident that crippled both of his legs and was thereafter responsible for a life full of pain. The ordeal would have been bad enough for anyone, but it was doubly harrowing for a *bon vivant* with Cole's ebullience and zest for life. But even from his hospital bed, Cole led the parade: "Now I know fifty million Frenchmen can't be wrong," he said. "They eat horses instead of riding them."[26]

A Jet-Set Environment

Porter was an indefatigable sightseer, a tourist *avant la lettre*. He traveled the world and the seven seas, his insatiable curiosity leading him to exotic countries, resulting in exoticist (if not absolutely authentic) musical borrowings. As an amateur Egyptologist, Linda was a friend to Lord Carnarvon and Howard Carter, the latter even guiding the Porters when they took a two-month trip down the Nile in a luxurious riverboat. This trip may have inspired Cole in later writing "Ruins," in which he pokes fun at people who are seemingly out of touch with the remains of history. "Why Don't We Try Staying Home" is a variation on the same theme.

I agree with Ethan Mordden that Porter is at his most characteristic in the largely forgotten classic "The Kling Kling Bird," with its unusual structure, its powerful rhythmic synergies, and its playfully bawdy lyrics recounting a young lad's travels to exotic lands.[27] Porter also betrays his wanderlust in his first song to have a commercial recording—and perhaps his earliest masterpiece—"I've a Shooting Box in Scotland," written for *Paranoia* (1914) and later to be included in Cole's first Broadway show, *See America First* (1916). Its third verse lists residences all over the globe, depicting what Porter's life would be about:

> Having lots of idle leisure
> I pursue a life of pleasure
> Like a rolling stone in constant agitation.
> For tho' stay-at-homes may cavil,
> I admit I'd rather travel
> Than collect a crop of mossy vegetation.

Apart from Paris, there was one city that won his heart: Venice. As a child, Porter had fallen in love with "the polychrome curtain that hung at the Emeric Theater on West Fifth Street. . . . This marvel depicted the Grand Canal in Venice in all its exciting detail, and by the time Cole was ten years old, he had resolved that one day he would occupy one of those Venetian Palazzos."[28] When Porter's grandfather J. O. Cole died, Kate decided to split the inherited fortune with her son, allowing Cole to fulfill his dream: for five consecutive years, Cole and Linda spent their summers in La Serenissima, the first at the Palazzo Barbaro, the second at the Palazzo Papadopoli, and then three years at the Ca' Rezzonico (where one of Porter's idols, Robert Browning, had died). In Venice, as elsewhere, Porter found himself at the center of high society. In her memoirs, Diana Vreeland, fashionista and editor of *Vogue* magazine for many years, describes how much she appreciated her friend Cole's presence in Venice: "At six in the morning [he would] go out with his gondolier and change positions with him. . . . Cole would stand in the back, with the big oar, and wearing a little navy pullover . . . he would feel the rhythm of the gondola. Everything with him was rhythm. That's why he's so contagious. . . . He looked so appetizing, such a gentleman, a *mondaine* chap, he was what you'd call a big-time gent. He had the *patina* of the world."[29] Not everybody was equally delighted, however. The founder and impresario of the Ballets russes, Sergei Diaghilev, very much opposed to the jazz invasion of Europe, wrote to his assistant Boris Kochno in 1926: "The whole of Venice is up in arms against Cole Porter because of his jazz and his Negroes. . . . They are teaching the 'Charleston' on the Lido Beach! It's dreadful! The gondoliers are threatening to massacre all the elderly American women here. The very fact of their [Linda and Cole Porter's] renting the Palazzo Rezzonico is considered characteristic of *nouveaux riches*." Porter had been friendly to the Ballets russes, though, always ready to help the company in its ever-dire financial straits. In the summer of 1924, Cole and Linda hosted an evening of ballet by Diaghilev and Kochno at the Palazzo Papadopoli: two male duets from *Les matelots* (Georges Auric) and a selection of Francis Poulenc's *Les biches* with Kochno humming the music of *Les matelots* to Porter, who was accompanying, as there were no scores to be found.

Complicating the relationship was that Cole had fallen madly in love with the young and beautiful Boris Kochno. One of the most interesting passages in McBrien's biography deals with Cole's correspondence to Kochno, highlighting his euphoria at the beginning of their relationship and his despair soon after. His letters are very close to the spirit of "What Is This Thing Called Love?" As Stephen Citron notes, "This was the only time in his life, Cole fell desperately in love."[30]

Cole Porter, European Songwriter

Many of Porter's songs display a keen sense for Europe's history and historical figures: George Sand and Chopin make regular appearances, as do Catherine of Russia (*Anything Goes*, 1934), Isabella of Spain, and Abelard and Heloise.[31] He even dedicates half a show to another historical figure, Madame du Barry: *Du Barry Was a Lady* (1939) contains one of Cole's most hilarious songs, "Give Him the Oo-la-la," the music of which cleverly quotes "La Marseillaise" at the lines: "If Napoleon at Waterloo-la-la had an army of debutantes / To give the British the well-known oo-la-la, / He'd have changed the hist'ry of France."

Cole's songs reference not only Europe's history but also its art and mythology. *Kiss Me, Kate* (1948) shows Porter's European spirit not only because it is based on Shakespeare's *The Taming of the Shrew* but also because it pays homage to Italian dance forms (the tarantella "Where Is the Life That Late I Led") and Mozart's "catalog aria," sung by Leporello in *Don Giovanni*. *Out of This World* (1950) gives us Jupiter, Mercury, and the brilliant song "They Couldn't Compare to You":

> So, at once, I started cruising,
> Found the Muses so amusing,
> That I even got a kick outa Terpsichore. . . .

After that I staged an orgy
For some friends of Lucretia Borgie . . .
After having had a party with Phoenicia's goddess Astarte.
Well I raised a bit of hell with Penelope. . . .
There was Galatea and mean Medea
And Sappho one of the best.
There was Nefertiti
A perfect sweetie
And gay Mae West.

(Admittedly, Mae West is not a traditional figure in classical Mediterranean mythology.)

No one captured the essence of "la Ville Lumière" as did Cole. Cole lived Paris from the inside, mocking superficial tourism in *Fifty Million Frenchmen* (1929):

You come to Paris, you come to play.
You have a wonderful time, you go away.
And, from then on, you talk of Paris knowingly;
You may know Paris, you don't know Paree.

Growing older, Cole Porter retired to an imaginary Paris, to the Paris of Toulouse-Lautrec, and even composed his *Can-Can* (1953) in that vein. "C'est Magnifique" and "Montmartre" are two fabulous tributes to the joy of a utopian Paris, and in *Silk Stockings* he has an American impresario convince a Russian commissar that "Paris Loves Lovers." Citron writes that Cole's "shifting from the major to minor mode more closely resembles the ambivalent French chansons popular around Pigalle than true Yiddish music" often associated with Broadway.[32] The 1928 songs "Blue Hours" and "Fish" evoke the spirit of Montmartre and allude to the rue Pigalle, respectively. His "I Love Paris" became the anthem of the City of Light, no mean feat for a nonnative son in a country as famously chauvinistic as France. In the undeservedly underrated movie *Les Girls,* the great Gene Kelly finds himself in Paris and sings:

Les Girls, Les Girls,
Ah, comme je les aim-e. . . .
J' les trouve supreme-es
De la plant-e des pieds
À la racine des ch'veux
J'ador-e, mais oui
Les Girls.

Cole Porter, Musician: The Classical Music Scene

Cole Porter was at the center of the musical/artistic scene in 1920s Paris, and perhaps no vignette captures it better than this: in 1923 "les Colporteurs" (as they were called in "le tout Paris," playing off the French term for door-to-door salespeople) were present at the after-party for Stravinsky's *Les noces*—a champagne dinner on a boat in the Seine. The guest list reads like an artistic who's who in Paris: Stravinsky, Picasso, the Princesse de Polignac, Misia Sert, Jean Cocteau, Darius Milhaud, Sergei Diaghilev, Serge Lifar, Ernest Ansermet, Gilbert Seldes, Blaise Cendrars. . . . "Picasso rearranged the toy decorations into a giant assemblage, Marcelle Meyer played Scarlatti on the piano, Goncharova read the guests' palms . . . and Jean Cocteau scurried around the deck with a lantern, sticking his head through the portholes to proclaim, 'On coule' (we're sinking)."[33]

The after-party was organized by Gerald and Sara Murphy (the models for Nicole and Dick Diver in their friend Scott Fitzgerald's *Tender Is the Night*). Porter had met Gerald at Yale, where Gerald introduced the somewhat odd fellow from Peru, Indiana ("wearing checkered suits and a silk tie"), to Murphy's influential friends, thus allowing Porter to gradually develop into Yale's court composer. The charming couple was treasured by many artists: Gerald had become very active in the Paris painting scene and helped Natalia Goncharova in repairing damaged scenery for Diaghilev's Ballets russes, and Sara was a source of infatuation for Picasso, Fitzgerald, and Hemingway. Gerald eventually gave up a promising painting career to take charge of the family business—Mark Cross fine leather retailers on Fifth Avenue—from his father, Patrick Murphy. Not surprisingly, Porter mentions Mark Cross in one of his charming list songs, "I Introduced."[34]

In Paris, as a regular guest at the Princesse de Polignac's salons, Porter met the *fine fleur* of the Parisian music scene, including the young Arthur Rubinstein, "who played his best when he primed on my best champagne."[35] (In his biography, Rubinstein complains that the affluent Winnie de Polignac was very stingy.) Francis Poulenc was yet another acquaintance from the Princesse de Polignac's circle; he dedicated a *mélodie* to Linda Porter: "Carte-Postale," the second of his Guillaume Apollinaire cycle.

While in Venice, Diaghilev wasn't the only one to complain about Porter's festive activities: as a reaction to the launching of the Galleggiante, Porter's party barge that enjoyed only one journey, author Didymus Belcampus (better known in English circles as Sir Thomas Beecham) privately published a delightful pamphlet, *The Tragical History of Young King Cole*:

> Young King Cole
> Was a jolly youthful soul
> And a jazz-band king was he.
> He launched a dainty barge
> On the fashionable marge
> Of the Adriatic Sea. . . .
> Young King Cole—I confess I find it droll
> Composed when his hours were free;
> And graciously he'd strum
> On the soft melodious drum,
> His dusky-toned harmony. . . .
> Young King Cole—Sacred fury in his soul—Now blared all day at the sea
> Each morn he'd syncopate
> Every night he'd ululate
> To a grateful Italy.[36]

Surely Cole Porter was thrilled to be the object of gentle slander by such a giant of classical music. His riposte was of an equally high profile: in "Operatic Pills" (*Wake Up and Dream,* 1929) Porter has Sir Thomas complain,

> I've begged all of England's classes
> To invest in op'ra glasses
> But in spite of my insistence, they refuse.
> 'T would be infinitely prop'rer
> If they went to hear the op'ra
> 'Stead of going to these barbarous revues.

Being the son of Sir Joseph Beecham, who was equally the father of the world-famous pills, Sir Thomas proposes a remedy:

> If you take one pill
> You'll hear the Barber of Seville
> If you take two pills
> You'll hear Louise
> If you take one more,
> The Song of the Toréador
> Will come thund'ring over the breeze.[37]

Both the pamphlet and the song lyrics have a light-hearted tone that attests to a possible mutual admiration.

Porter's Musical Ambitions

Winnaretta Singer, Princesse Edmond de Polignac, was an important patroness in Parisian music circles and supported a great many composers, including Igor Stravinsky. At one point, she "contrived to secure additional revenue for him by suggesting that he teach composition—to Cole Porter."[38] Linda also hoped that Porter "would devote his talent to 'serious' music. The preceding summer she had invited Stravinsky down to Antibes to teach her husband harmony and composition; after a consultation with the Murphys, Stravinsky had declined."[39]

The exact story of the Stravinsky-Porter relationship seems to have been a bit more involved, though. Porter asked composer Paul Thévanez, Jean Cocteau's lover, to arrange an introduction. Thévanez, perhaps reading a bit much into the situation, wrote to Stravinsky: "He will pay you whatever you want. He's a very nice young man, intelligent and gifted, and a multi-millionaire."[40] In a letter to the princess, Stravinsky explains his side of the story:

> I would also like to tell you that mister Cole Porter has abruptly renounced to take lessons with me. When I saw him last, I had a contract that was drawn up and signed by him, accompanied by a letter. He asked me to let him know by lawyer if (and I underline) there *was anything in the contract that might not be to my liking.* So I did, and offered him a counterproposal, that only included a few precisions to his contract, that had only guaranteed me half of the announced sum. After which his lawyer announced to me the somehow unexpected news of Porter's refusal. Unexpected, because it was Porter himself who urged me to make the changes. I do not hide to you the fact that I feel hurt by his behavior and I regret that he troubled you for nothing.[41]

Boris Kochno corroborates the evidence: "With the Princess Edmond de Polignac acting as go-between, Porter had asked Stravinsky to give him lessons in orchestration. Nothing came of it because Stravinsky demanded such an exorbitant fee."[42]

At Princesse Winnie's Paris domicile or at her Venetian Palazzo Contarini, Porter came across Darius Milhaud several times. Although most biographies credit Gerald Murphy—who wrote the scenario and created the sets for the ballet *Within the Quota*—for asking Porter to write the music, it was actually Milhaud who thought of Porter when Rolf de Maré of the Ballets suédois asked him to recommend an American composer for a project.[43] Milhaud also introduced Porter to the ballet's future orchestrator, Charles Koechlin. On 5 June 1923 Koechlin met Cole at the Porter residence, 13, rue Monsieur, at a dinner specially arranged by Milhaud. Koechlin accepted the orchestration assignment, and, what is more, "he gave Cole an intensive course of eight lessons at the Ritz over the next eleven days, though overcharging his normal price."[44] A few months later, there were to be five more lessons.

This information, though published by Robert Orledge in the *Yale University Library Gazette*, was never taken up in any Porter biography, but it sheds important light on Cole Porter's musical ambitions and dedication. Indeed, there may be more to Porter's serious musical studies than some biographers imply. For example, one biographer of note told me that Cole "was always skipping classes, going to the Café de Flore instead."[45] Charles Schwartz is even harsher: "Probably the most substantial benefit that Cole derived from the Schola [Cantorum] was not so much a musical as a public relations one. Over and over in later years he would speak pridefully, for press purposes, of his studies at the Schola and his work with Vincent d'Indy, each of which were minimal at best."[46]

In Porter's defense, Margaret Case Harriman states in her profile of the composer that he gave up his studies at the Schola "when he found the influence of the French classical school was interfering with his own sense of rhythm."[47] George Eells sheds more light on why Porter didn't complete his studies at the Schola: "While Cole accepted the discipline of classicism, he could not subscribe to d'Indy's rejection of modern experimentation. As a creative individual, Cole was unable to ignore the new rhythms he had detected in contemporary, especially American, life. He became restive, worrying that he was stifling his imaginative impulses. By limiting himself to the rigid forms of the past, he felt that he would be rejecting everything fresh in his work."[48]

The Influence of Opera

Cole's love for and infatuation with opera date back to his childhood, when his mother took him on excursions to Chicago.[49] The conductor Eddie Wittstein recounts going to Porter's room at Yale and finding him "studying *Der Rosenkavalier* before it was performed in America."[50] Of his travels in Italy, Porter mentions: "We attended opera not only in Milan but in every small Italian town—where the artists were often better than those at the highly touted La Scala."[51] According to Robert Kimball, the Porters would attend opera performances with the score on their laps and a flashlight in hand. One might assume that Porter's use of a large tessitura for his songs was triggered by his frequent opera visits: "From the start, Porter's songs called for trained, theatrical singers like Ethel Merman, who could put over his tongue-twisting lyrics and make challenging melodies appear effortless. Broadway composers usually kept their melodies within an octave or so; Porter's often extend that range an additional half octave, demanding an almost operatic technique. A typical Porter move . . . is to start a song in a low register and then push the line ever upward until it has an almost Wagnerian intensity."[52] This fusion of a classical operatic feel for the voice with a topical modernist touch appears in many of Porter's songs, such as "Bring Me Back My Butterfly," where Porter glides with an engaging ease between cabaret and Puccini's own *Madama Butterfly*.

Leo Smit, whose career as composer, pianist, conductor, and educator spanned seven musical decades in the United States, discusses Cole's classical background and inspirations in the liner notes to his classically inspired recording with Jan de Gaetani.[53] According to Smit, "Porter was consciously aware of the serious problems of musical craft and . . . was able to conceal the many beautiful solutions from unsuspecting ears while easily charming them." Smit sees clear influences "ranging from the classical past to his contemporaries of the 1920s: from Tchaikovsky Porter adapted an expressive and declamatory style ('Easy to Love'), whereas 'What Is This Thing Called Love?' was created through the miraculous travaille of . . . Beethoven, Schubert and Brahms."[54] Smit was preceded by Cole's editor Alfred "Doc" Sirmay in linking him to Schubert: "I myself have a personal affair with your song 'Ev'ry Time.' It chokes me whenever I hear it, it moves me to tears. This song is one of the greatest songs you ever wrote. . . . It is no less a gem than any immortal song of a Schubert or Schumann."[55]

Bricktop

Paris was not only a haven for white expatriates and highbrow classical musicians, it was also a magnet for African American performers, who enjoyed a freedom and appreciation they could never have dreamt of in the United States. (Besides, there was no prohibition in the City of Light, and the cost of living was quite low.) One of the main places of attraction was Chez Bricktop, a famous club at 66, rue Pigalle. As the doyenne of Paris's café society, Ada Smith (called "Bricktop" after her flaming red hair) drew many celebrated figures to her club, including Cole Porter, the Duke and Duchess of Windsor, the Aga Khan, and F. Scott Fitzgerald—as Fitzgerald once quipped, "My greatest claim to fame is that I discovered Bricktop before Cole Porter did."

Bricktop's description of the atmosphere in her club is quite informative:

> It was a wonderful time. My small place was filled every night with Cole Porter and his friends, or Cole Porter's friends, or friends of Cole Porter's friends. . . . You didn't have to pretend in my place, you could just be yourself. . . . Noel Coward would hit the door, and then he'd hit the piano. He'd say, "How 'm I doin'? How 'm I doin', Bricky?" He was always trying to make somebody. Cole would try out his new tunes, too, but never when there were a lot of people around.[56]

If there were one song that might epitomize Bricktop, it would be "I'm in Love Again." The song evokes a highly intoxicated character with a devil-may-care attitude toward the consequences of one's actions. This was the song Bricktop was singing the first time she saw Porter, who did not walk out, which is "what he usually quietly does, if he doesn't approve of the singer."[57]

Cole Porter met Bricktop at the first Paris club where she entertained, Le Grand Duc. As she recounts:

> One morning in the late fall or early winter of 1925 a slight, immaculately dressed man came in, and ordered a plate of corned-beef hash with a poached egg on top (we served them courtesy of the house) and a bottle of wine. By morning, I mean between three a.m. and six a.m. I got up to sing and could sense that the man was watching and listening with more than ordinary interest. . . . When he got up to leave . . . drummer Buddy Gilmore came through the door. He grabbed the stranger and started hugging him. "Who was that?" I asked. "That was Cole Porter." "Oh, my God!" I said. "I've just been singing one of his songs." . . . Cole came back the very next night. Pretty soon he sent for me. What he wanted to know was, could I dance? I couldn't believe it when he asked, "Can you dance the Charleston?"[58]

When Porter introduced Bricktop (and the Charleston) to Elsa Maxwell, "she clapped and shrieked. . . . Me and the Charleston were something new for her to play with. I was in."[59]

Bricktop considered Cole and Linda Porter to be "real friends," and her testimony about Cole's personality is one of the most striking and insightful ever: "A lot of people thought that Cole was a strange man—cold, indifferent, rude. But I didn't know that Cole Porter. He was shy, and shy people have problems—especially if they're prominent. He wasn't very good at dealing with hurly-burly newspapermen. . . . He couldn't stand plain snobs or social climbers, and, he'd go out of his way not to be rude. . . . [O]ne of the best friends I've ever had."[60]

Hutch

Having witnessed a Ku Klux Klan raid when performing in Florida, Grenada-born pianist Leslie Hutchinson decided to try his luck in Paris. It was only a matter of time before Hutch would bump into Cole, which, through Bricktop, he inevitably did. They shared expensive tastes, and at the impressionable age of twenty-five, Hutch began to copy Porter in his ways, even down to wearing a carnation in his lapel. For his part, "Cole was willing to teach his protégé, socially, intellectually, musically and Hutch was keen to learn. . . . Cole had about him a subversive irony which he used to oust pomposity in favor of style. This swiftly became a key component of Hutch's way of presenting himself."[61]

Cole, who had a well-known *faiblesse* for black men, appreciated Hutch's rare combination of attributes—musical abilities, good looks, quick wits, great skills in acting and timing. The two men would sit for hours at Cole's house, trying out new numbers on a white double piano. Hutch, who possessed a husky baritone voice in addition to his impressive pianism, quickly became one of Cole's favorite exponents of his songs, with Cole showing him exactly how he wanted them performed. (And according to Cole's friend Monty Woolley, "Cole loved to recount to male friends that Hutch's talents went far beyond the keyboard.")[62] Linda and Cole hired Hutch and his band to play at their parties in Paris and Venice, and with Hutchinson's Royal Six he played on Cole's famous "floating nightclub," the Galleggiante. As Hutch reports: "I was lucky being in Paris at the time when Cole Porter was starting to write his really big hits. Cole took me under his wing, taught me how to sing his songs, introduced me to the right people and I was later introduced to London society through him. He was the greatest man in music ever known. He's an education."[63]

Hutch fervently wanted to be treated on a par with the other guests, not just to be tolerated as an exotic black performer, and through Cole, he felt he was moving up in society. As he saw it, not having to sing for his supper meant that he was being accepted as he was. But as Charlotte Breese observes, this acceptance may have been quite shallow: "The expatriate Americans were being daring in crossing the colour line, but they were far from home, in a city where blacks happened to be fashionable. They were only toying with the exotic." In Hutch's case, his welcome might have lasted longer had he not overplayed his hand with Lady Edwina Mountbatten. Their relationship lasted a very long time—even beyond the trial in which Lady Mountbatten had to deny her "inappropriate" relationship with a black man—and when she got Hutch to come to London, he became a superstar. According to Monty Woolley,

> Hutch would sit up at his highly polished concert grand Steinway with the lid up, dressed in white tie and tails, a large white handkerchief up his sleeve. It would be drawn out in a carefully calculated gesture, Hutch using it to mop his sweat-beaded forehead after each number. Titled society women seeing this gesture went into near-hysteria. Aside from his considerable skill at the piano, Hutch was recognized throughout Europe as a legendary stud, and his liaisons with a succession of celebrities, from Cole Porter to Edwina Mountbatten to Merle Oberon, made him as much in demand for his sexual prowess as for his music.[64]

In the end, however, Hutch became a bit too careless about hiding the extra-musical reasons for his success among the jet set and became persona non grata. His exploits, however, were immortalized in the Porter song written especially for him: "I'm a Gigolo."[65]

Cole Porter, Hedonist and Humanist: On the Fringes of Society

It is no secret that Cole Porter, in a world that was still very much influenced by class distinction, was part of a social stratum that could command the world on a whim with a single gesture, and the world would oblige. He followed the motto: "Class is what you display, sex is what you hide."[66] It was hidden, but still very present. Always the debonair sophisticate, Cole Porter lived a life that would have been perceived as extremely provocative had it not been tempered by power, means, and, most of all, style—all of which allowed him to cover his traces. The cover-up would last until Monty Woolley, perhaps in need of some extra cash or just in need of all the attention he could still get, revealed the smutty details of Porter's "darker" side.

If there was one friend who may have severely damaged Porter's reputation, it was definitely Monty Woolley. A fellow Yale alumnus, Woolley directed three important Porter shows (*Fifty Million Frenchmen*, *The New Yorkers*, and *Jubilee*) and as an actor had become famous for his role of Sheridan Whiteside in *The Man Who Came to Dinner*. Monty was Cole's sparring partner in cruises around New York City's waterfront bars and bordellos. Whereas Porter, though assertively gay, would never discuss the issue in public, Monty was not one to stay tongue-tied. "He never tired of recalling the many years of friendship," author David Grafton recalls. "I was fortunate enough to have been brought into that magic circle created by the witty and often caustic tongue of Monty Woolley, and during one of our late afternoon conversations in the bar of New York's Hotel Astor, he gave a detailed insight into the hasty departure of the Porters from Venice."[67] Schwartz provides the colorful details: "Cole was forced to leave at the invitation of the police when, in the summer of 1927, they raided the Palazzo Rezzonico and found a party in full swing in which a slew of handsome Italian boys dressed in Linda's fancy clothes (she was away at the time) were cavorting for Cole and several of his friends. To the dismay of the police chief who conducted the raid, his own son was among the boys in drag at the party."[68]

Grafton is quoted by McBrien when he discusses this other side of Cole Porter: "According to Woolley, both he and Cole took most of their sexual pleasures in Harlem. . . . Woolley with the intensity he gave to the first reading of a play he was about to direct, extolled the physical virtues of the young black studs who inhabited the many houses of male prostitution that dotted the Harlem landscape."[69] More bluntly, Charlotte Breese states that "Hutch pimped for Cole and his friends. He took them to the lowlife nightclubs of Montmartre, and organized sleazy parties for them."[70] With a spoonful of sugar, McBrien tries to soften the fact that Porter paid for sex: "There is no evidence that he treated these men cruelly or felt in any fashion superior to them."[71]

Empathy and Censorship

The two most detailed biographies of Porter dwell on this dark side and paint a portrait of a cold man made untouchable by his wealth. In these biographies, there is little room for Cole's generosity, his (for the era) shockingly open attitude toward African Americans, and his genuine respect for talent. In particular, two important facts seem to be ignored completely: Cole Porter shared a strong empathy with the outcasts of society, and his life was one of opposition to any kind of censorship.

Porter's habitat of Paris was a city of tolerance where the gay and lesbian scene could thrive. This *laissez-faire, laissez-passer* attitude appealed not only to Porter: there were Gertrude Stein and Alice B. Toklas; there was the world of Diaghilev's Ballets russes; and on the Rive Gauche, Natalie Barney created her "Sapphic Temple." Paris was a city of the free, and I fully concur with Robert Kimball's assertion that we should remember Cole as an apostle of freedom, fighting against any form of censorship. Cole brazenly poked fun at the *arrivistes* of society and even dared to mock the powerful "old money families" who sat comfortably at the top of the social pyramid.[72] With "The Lost Liberty Blues," written for *La Revue des Ambassadeurs* in 1928, Porter offers a sardonic critique of his homeland through the voice of America's Statue of Liberty—compared to the Paris in which he lived, the ideals embodied by this "innocent public monument" were censored and restricted in the land of the free. Says Miss Liberty:

> Once, my country, France,
> Had a Yank romance,
> So she gave me to Uncle Sam.
> But he's changed me so
> That I hardly know
> What I'm meant for or who I am.
> He's made a mess
> Of my chance for success,
> And I'm not worth a damn.

Another example of Porter's social/political conscience is his pointed "Love for Sale" from *The New Yorkers* (1930). The song was banned from American radio for years, much to Porter's dismay: "I can't understand it. You can write a novel about a harlot, paint a picture of a harlot, but you can't write a song about a harlot."[73] The song is no less breathtaking a work of art than any of the major Schubert lieder, and though it bears similarities to "Der Wegweiser" and "Das Wirtshaus," it "is immensely original, it has no cliché in it whatsoever."[74] With its haunting melody, Porter brings us uncomfortably close to a girl singing of her sad fate as she advertises her services. His enormous empathy for the character was too much for American society to handle: when *The New Yorkers* opened in 1930, "Love for Sale" was originally sung by the (white) Kathryn Crawford, but in response to immediate criticism, the song was quickly given instead to Elisabeth Welch, who was black.

Difference and Art

To define Porter's art, Ethan Mordden suggests a focus on its "difference":

> Living in absolute liberty enabled Porter to exploit his talent even as he worried how far beyond popular he dared go. . . . The subject matter of Porter's shows redoubles his wicked side, treating socially and sometimes legally marginal characters. The folks represented by Ethel Merman, Jimmy Durante, William Gaxton, Victor Moore, and Bert Lahr in various Porter titles could be read as a

> rejection of "correct" citizenship: as a preference for the subculture of the Different. . . . Porter's music, too, is Different: the sensation of his tunes hungrily gliding over the steady $\frac{4}{4}$ beat under them suggests a "special" existence floating above conformist. No other lyricist of his day sounded as worldly as Porter, as naughty, as vivacious. . . . Porter's truest true love isn't true at all but achingly hot and unencumbered by bourgeois cautions, and his double meanings can be so subtle they lurk rather than leap at one.[75]

This "difference" resulted from the multiple perspectives that shaped Porter in Europe, a place where his substantial mind, means, and determination could take him to different strata of society or different places and atmospheres on a momentary whim.

Mordden states, "To a man like Porter, art was stylized autobiography."[76] This calls to mind the philosophy of the late Michel Foucault, who, in a final ethical turn at the end of his life, urged people to make works of art out of their lives. This suggests the dynamic concept of the *souci de soi* (care of the self), referring back to the antiquity Cole Porter loved so much. He was a true *carpe diem* hedonist who nevertheless had a stoic attitude toward composition. Although he was never driven by financial needs, he still worked several hours a day on his songs.

Brendan Gill writes: "All of his life he will be accused of being a snob and all his life he will deny the charge, but his snobbery, real or imaginary, is beside the point, which is that at every turn, he furnished the world with far more joy than he got back. In the unspoken bargain between genius and the rest of us, it is the rest of us who come home with full hands and, in this instance, dancing feet."[77] The accusations regarding Cole being cold, rude, or perverted can be answered in just the same way.

Cole Porter is the product of a special time, and both his life and his art are extraordinary prisms through which to view the history of the twentieth century. He stood at the center of the Roaring Twenties in Paris and of the 1930s and 1940s in New York and Hollywood, a product of the upper class, the personification of the notion of "style" and of a philosophy that strives for a quality interpretation of life with an emphasis on creating beauty and well-being. But at the same time, he served as a subversive figure within his social order, openly displaying his considerable empathy for the outcasts of society, for his fellow men both black and white, and for persons whose sexuality differed from societal norms. His songs, some of the most outstanding of the twentieth century, songs that explore and express the *condition humaine* in the best tradition of the nineteenth-century European lied, allowed him to transcend life's struggles and hardships. Perhaps through them, both the performer and the audience, coming home with full hands and dancing feet, might do so as well.

Notes

1. William McBrien, *Cole Porter: A Biography* (New York: Alfred A. Knopf, 1998), x.

2. No book, though, comes closer to Porter's true spirit than Robert Kimball and Brendan Gill, *Cole* (New York: Holt, Rinehart & Winston, 1971). This splendid coffee-table book is a treasure trove, with hundreds of pictures and meticulous comments on the songs. It has served as a factual reservoir for later biographies. Next to Kimball and Gill's *Cole*, essays by Ethan Mordden and Brendan Gill, which were written for the *New Yorker*, are close rivals to Moss Hart's text.

3. Moss Hart, *Act One: An Autobiography* (New York: Random House, 1959), 2. For a description of the Ritz bar, see Stephen Citron, *Noel and Cole: The Sophisticates* (New York: Oxford University Press, 1993; repr., with new introduction, Milwaukee: Hal Leonard, 2005), 54: "At that time the Ritz had two bars, a men's bar on the left (a frequent gathering place for homosexuals) where, as Beverley Nichols noted, 'Cole Porter, looking like a startled leprechaun, could sip a Pernod and cast his dark, syrupy little eyes to the white and gold ceiling, and think out his devastating little rhymes' and a mixed bar on the right. Once the Cole-Linda liaison was a *fait accompli*, the couple switched from the left to the right-hand one."

4. For a chronological performance of more than 320 Cole Porter songs, see www.coleporteranthology.com.

5. Hart, *Act One,* 3.

6. Robert Kimball, *The Complete Lyrics of Cole Porter* (New York: Knopf, 1983; repr., New York: Da Capo Press, 1992), 123: "'Kate the Great' is an unused song written for Ethel Merman. Madeleine Smith, Porter's secretary, has said that Porter often referred to his mother as 'The Great Kate.' Other 'Kate' creations by Porter include 'Katie of the Y.M.C.A.,' 'Katie Went to Haiti' (*Du Barry Was a Lady*, 1939), and, of course, the show title *Kiss Me, Kate* (1948)."

7. Kimball and Gill, *Cole*, 250.

8. Charles Schwartz, *Cole Porter* (New York: Dial Press, 1977), 53. See also Weiss, this volume, highlighting the Alice Garrett–Linda Porter friendship.

9. First quote, Arnold Saint Subber in Allen Albert and Bobby Short, *You're the Top: The Cole Porter Story* (Winstar Home Entertainment, 1998, DVD); second quote, Robert Kimball, interview in McBrien, *Cole Porter,* 67.

10. David Grafton, *Red, Hot and Rich! An Oral History of Cole Porter* (New York: Stein & Day, 1987), 52.

11. Richard Hubler, *The Cole Porter Story, as Told to Richard G. Hubler* (Cleveland: World Publishing Company, 1965), 19. Editor's note: Linda wrote to Bernard Berenson about Jimmy Alba, as she called him. In these letters, she discussed their relative health, the birth of Alba's grandchild, his illness, and his eventual death in 1953, the year before she herself died. Archives of Biblioteca Berenson, Villa I Tatti: The Harvard University Center for Italian Renaissance Studies, courtesy of the President and Fellows of Harvard College.

12. Jane S. Smith, *Elsie de Wolfe: A Life in the High Style* (New York: Atheneum, 1982), front and back flaps.

13. See also Weiss's comments in this volume on Elisabeth Marbury.

14. Smith, *Elsie de Wolfe,* 216.

15. See Morris, this volume.

16. Elsie is also featured in the title song of *Anything Goes*: "When you hear that Lady Mendl standing up / Now turns a handspring landing up—On her toes, / Anything goes." See Morris, this volume.

17. Hart, *Act One,* 2.

18. Alan Jay Lerner in Friends of the Library, *Cole Porter: The Life That Late He Led* (Los Angeles: University of Southern California, 1967), 11.

19. Ethan Mordden, *The Guest List: How Manhattan Defined American Sophistication* (New York: St. Martin's Press, 2010). See also Morris in this volume.

20. Schwartz, *Cole Porter,* 63.

21. Mordden, *The Guest List*, 201.

22. Schwartz, *Cole Porter,* 63.

23. Mordden, *The Guest List,* 201.

24. Elsa Maxwell, *R.S.V.P.: Elsa Maxwell's Own Story* (New York: Little, Brown and Company, 1954), 127–28.

25. Sam Staggs, *Inventing Elsa Maxwell* (New York: St. Martin's Griffin, 2012), 185.

26. Maxwell, *R.S.V.P.*, 127–28.

27. Ethan Mordden, "A Critic at Large: Rock and Cole," *New Yorker*, 28 October 1991, 91–113, 99.

28. George Eells, *The Life That Late He Led: A Biography of Cole Porter* (New York: G. P. Putnam's Sons, 1967), 24.

29. Diana Vreeland, *D.V.* (New York: Alfred A. Knopf, 1984), 167.

30. Citron, *Noel and Cole,* 60.

31. "Georgia Sand" in *Nymph Errant* (1933) or "The Leader of a Big-Time Band" in *Something for the Boys* (1943). The latter song has the fabulous lines: "When, in Venice, Georgia Sand with Chopin romped / Her libido had the Lido simply swamped. / But today who would be buried in the sand? / Why, the leader of a big-time band." Isabella is another favorite of Cole's. She's also featured in the above-mentioned "Since Ma Got the Craze Espagnole" (*Hitchy-Koo of 1919*): "She rants round the home / Simply clad in a comb / Shouting, 'I'm Isabella, / Where's that Ferdinand fella?'" A wonderful hint to *los reyes católicos*.

32. Citron's comments are contrary to what Richard Rodgers asserted in his autobiography, *Musical Stages*: "it is surely one of the ironies of the musical theatre that, despite the abundance of Jewish composers, the one who has written the most enduring 'Jewish' music should be an Episcopalian millionaire who was born on a farm in Peru, Indiana." Cole had declared to him that he'd found that he had discovered the formula for success: "I'll write Jewish tunes."

33. See Weiss, this volume, on Jean Cocteau and the impetus of *Parade* for combining jazz and classical idioms. See Morris in this volume for more on "les Colporteurs." The quote is from Amanda Vail, *Everybody Was So Young: Gerald and Sarah Murphy: A Lost Generation Love Story* (London: Warner Books, 1999), 119.

34. See Weiss, this volume.

35. For more on the Parisian music scene, see Weiss, this volume. The text quote is from Hubler, *The Cole Porter Story,* 18. Another friend Porter mentions (in an interview with Hubler) is opera diva Mary Garden. It was she who introduced Cole to Antibes, where both the Porters and the Murphys decided to stay one summer. Gerald and Sara decided to come back during the following summers, creating the Villa America, whereas the ever-wandering Porter decided to move on.

36. Kimball and Gill, *Cole*, 75.

37. Kimball, *The Complete Lyrics*, 79.

38. Sylvia Kahan, *Music's Modern Muse: A Life of Winnaretta Singer, Princesse de Polignac* (Rochester, NY: University of Rochester Press, 2003), 229.

39. Calvin Tomkins, *Living Well Is the Best Revenge* (New York: Modern Library, 1998), 39.

40. Kahan, *Music's Modern Muse,* 229.

41. Igor Stravinsky to Winnaretta Singer Polignac, 18 July 1922, Fondation Singer Polignac. I am grateful to Prof. Sylvia Kahan for sharing this information with me.

42. Boris Kochno, *Diaghilev and the Ballets Russes* (New York: Harper & Row, 1970), 222.

43. Gerald had very convincingly swept audiences at the Salon des indépendants with his "cubistic studies of machinery" and especially his "extraordinary construction of skyscrapers topped with electric signs." His design for the "American" booth at an international charity benefit gave him an even greater cachet (Vail, *Everybody Was So Young,* 111). With his experience in his work for the Ballets russes and with his artistic reputation as a painter, Murphy had been the right choice for the libretto, scenery, and costumes of *Within the Quota.*

44. Robert Orledge, "Cole Porter's Ballet 'Within the Quota,'" *Yale University Library Gazette* 50, no. 1 (July 1975), 21.

45. Stephen Citron, personal letter, August 2011.

46. Schwartz, *Cole Porter,* 57.

47. Margaret Case Harriman, *Take Them Up Tenderly: A Collection of Profiles* (New York: Alfred A. Knopf, 1944), 142.

48. Eells, *The Life That Late He Led,* 55.

49. See also Weiss, this volume.

50. Robert Kimball and Richard M. Sudhalter, *You're Sensational: Cole Porter in the '20s, '40s & '50s* (Indianapolis: Indiana Historical Society, 1999), 1.

51. Hubler, *The Cole Porter Story,* 20.

52. David Schiff, "One Swell Party," *Atlantic Monthly,* July 2004, 179, http://www.theatlantic.com/past/docs/issues/2004/07/schiff.htm.

53. This recording is lauded by Ethan Mordden, *Broadway Babies: The People Who Made the American Musical* (New York: Oxford University Press, 1983), 217.

54. Leo Smit, "The Classic Cole Porter," *Saturday Review,* 25 December 1971, 2. "What Is This Thing Called Love" always catapults me back to singing Schubert's Winterreise, especially a song like "Auf dem Flusse," which shares the same alternation between despair and ecstasy.

55. McBrien, *Cole Porter,* 287.

56. Bricktop and James Haskins, *Bricktop* (New York: Atheneum, 1983), 122.

57. Ibid., 100.

58. Ibid., 100–101.

59. Ibid., 101.

60. Ibid., 112.

61. Charlotte Breese, *Hutch* (London: Bloomsbury, 1999), 39.

62. Grafton, *Red, Hot and Rich,* 61.

63. Breese, *Hutch,* 40.

64. Grafton, *Red, Hot and Rich,* 61–62.

65. Breese, *Hutch,* 39.

66. Mordden, "Rock and Cole," 93.

67. Grafton, *Red, Hot and Rich,* 61.

68. Schwartz, *Cole Porter,* 77.

69. Grafton, *Red, Hot and Rich,* 107; McBrien, *Cole Porter,* 129.

70. Breese, *Hutch,* 42.

71. McBrien, *Cole Porter,* 129.

72. Being a Yale alumnus, Porter was definitely "old school," but one thing he severely regretted was not to have been part of the "old money" league by birth. His grandfather was a self-made man who had realized his dream of striking it rich and investing his money well.

73. McBrien, *Cole Porter,* 137.

74. Wim Henderickx, personal interview, February 2013.

75. Mordden, *The Guest List*, 252.

76. Mordden, "Rock and Cole," 101.

77. Kimball and Gill, *Cole*, x.

4

Landed

Cole Porter's Ballet

SIMON MORRISON

There is no doubting the importance of Sergei Diaghilev's Ballets russes in the history of musical and choreographic modernism. But the stress placed on Diaghilev's achievement has come at the expense of another organization no less innovative in terms of its aesthetic risks and rewards. That was the Ballets suédois, which in 1923 premiered a brief ballet-pantomime to music by the untested Cole Porter.

The Ballets suédois occupied the Théâtre des Champs-Élysées in Paris during the first half of the 1920s. There was little Swedish about it, except for its founders, Rolf de Maré and Nils Dardel, and its choreographer, Jean Börlin. Most of what they staged cannot properly be labeled ballets. The music and dance of the mature productions aspire to the condition of collage; they are bric-a-bracs of competing forms, styles, and genres. The Ballets suédois ended up privileging nonballets with, at the extreme, nonscores performed to nonchoreographies in front of nondécors. The circus, vaudeville, and cinema (particularly the films of Charlie Chaplin and Mary Pickford) informed its repertoire in equal measure. Reviewers observed that the Ballets suédois seemed much less interested in staging dance and pantomime than in performing ideas, many of which concerned the darker aspects of modern life. Börlin was the first choreographer I know to set a ballet in an insane asylum (*Maison de fous*, 1920) and the first to experiment with an admixture of live and recorded sound.[1] With one of his last works, *Relâche* (1924), he willed ballet—and then himself—out of existence.

Scholarship on the organization is scant even as the record of performances runs long. The Ballets suédois appeared some 2,600 times in some 270 cities, towns, and resorts in Europe and the United States.[2] That does not necessarily justify academic study. But the fact that the troupe helped to define French modernism, informed the careers of the composers collectively known as Les Six, and provided Diaghilev with serious competition certainly does. Pertinent to Porter is the organization's commitment to negating the divide between "popular" and "serious" music.

The archive of the Ballets suédois is kept at the Dance Museum in Stockholm, but cataloging has been slow. In addition, Börlin's eclectic choreographic annotations in Swedish and French have yet to be decoded. The museum also houses the orchestral score of the Porter ballet, which was completed by Charles Koechlin under the title *Within the Quota*. Studio photographs and two pages of musical sketches are preserved in Paris at the Bibliothèque nationale, and the Victoria and Albert Museum in London and New York Public Library for the Performing Arts have programs and advertising materials.

The key source for the discussion that follows, the original three-piano (in places four-piano) score, is preserved in the Cole Porter archive at Yale University along with some clippings and a 1975 article by the musicologist Robert Orledge for Yale's *Library Gazette*.[3] The score is just under fifteen minutes if played straight through, which the orthographic vagaries make hard to do. The faint, yellowed manuscript is replete with errors (missing flats and sharps, incorrect clefs) and incomplete harmonies. It seems like the product of an enthusiastic but inexperienced composer who had cut his teeth composing for Yale College productions but was not entirely prepared for symphonic composition. Technical problems aside, the score is also, I believe, a marvel—a modest one perhaps, but much bolder in its substance than Koechlin's cleaned-up, highly Europeanized orchestration. Porter endorsed that orchestration, and the impulse behind it, which finds Koechlin seeking to abstract and estrange Porter's American idiom, to give it a kind of expat identity. Judging from the reviews, however, Koechlin's scoring did no favors for the Ballets suédois, or for Porter, who turned back to Broadway. Although the score did not survive the organization that commissioned it, *Within the Quota* became known, even in absentia, as the first "jazz" ballet.

The scenario is by American artist and writer Gerald Murphy, a friend of Porter since their days together as undergraduates at Yale.[4] They first met in

1910, when the gadabout Murphy smoothed the entry of the foppish sophomore from Indiana into Delta Kappa Epsilon, a premier fraternity, and the exclusive Glee Club.[5] Murphy's father was the owner of the Mark Cross luxury leather goods firm, with a flagship store on New York's Fifth Avenue, and Gerald grew up hobnobbing with the well-heeled Wiborg family on their six-hundred-acre estate in East Hampton.[6] (He would marry the eldest of Frank Wiborg's three daughters, Sara, in 1916.) Cole was from what was then dismissively called the Middle West, but he was no rube. His maternal grandfather, J. O. Cole, was a self-made millionaire who began building his fortune during the California gold rush as the proprietor of a general store. He came to own valuable farmland in Indiana and resource-rich lands in West Virginia as well. Cole's father was a successful druggist, with three stores in their hometown of Peru, Indiana, seventy-five miles north of Indianapolis.[7] As a sophomore at Yale, Cole distinguished himself as the composer of a football song, "Bingo Eli Yale." He spent the years after graduation trying to translate his theatrical success at college into a career on Broadway. But soon after his 1916 project, *See America First*, flopped, a chagrined Porter set out for Paris.

There he fell in with the fashionable expat crowd. He met—and married—American divorcée Linda Thomas, described by an acquaintance as "the Beauty of the Peace Conference time in Paris—a lovely, lovely creature."[8] He enjoyed her company, and she tolerated his homosexuality. In the summer of 1921 the Porters came together with the Murphys, who were traveling through Europe at the time, and the foursome joined the glitterati of Paris, with frequent sojourns to the Mediterranean and Italy. They were fixtures in the free-and-easy world of Ernest Hemingway's *A Moveable Feast* and Roger Shattuck's *The Banquet Years*. But Porter's biographer William McBrien notes that the would-be composer quietly suffered some professional anxiety. "The twenties were for Cole a time of uncertainty, self-doubt, and confusion about his musical gifts," he writes, "which he successfully disguised by assuming the role of a boulevardier."[9]

Murphy stepped in to offer Porter his first big professional opportunity. When approached by the Ballets suédois impresario Rolf de Maré to create a work to be staged alongside Darius Milhaud's neoprimitivist, jazz-inflected ballet *La création du monde*, Murphy in turn proposed that Cole Porter write the music. Milhaud personally offered the commission to Cole in the salon of their mutual friend Winnaretta Singer, the Princesse de Polignac.[10] That summer, the Porters resided in Venice at the famed Palazzo Barbaro, immortalized by Henry James in *The Wings of the Dove*. Gerald and Sara joined them at the Casa

Papadopoli on the Grand Canal for two weeks in August so that the two men could work together on the ballet.[11] Linda amused herself on the local party circuit, while Porter trolled the canals in search of the carnal pleasures of the gay "rough trade." Gerald may have not shared Porter's particular tastes, but Sara was ill at ease. She returned to their hotel in Antibes, where she continued a summer dalliance with Picasso. When the piano score was completed, Porter presented it, on de Maré's request, using the four best pianists he could find (one came from Venice, the other three from France).

Perhaps swayed by Hemingway's much later, ungenerous appraisal of his former friends, Robert Orledge is quick to dismiss Murphy, Cole, and their entire milieu, denigrating Murphy's preperformance interviews for *Within the Quota* as "reflect[ing] the superficiality and grand gestures of the social circles in which they moved."[12] Yet these circles were hardly shallow, including such profound talents as Pablo Picasso, Fernand Léger, Jean Cocteau, Igor Stravinsky, Hemingway, and F. Scott Fitzgerald. Neither Sara nor Gerald was a mere dilettante, for that matter; both had studied painting with the Silver Age artist Natalia Goncharova and made themselves known to Diaghilev, who enlisted their help in refurbishing sets and décor for the Ballets russes' spring season of 1922.[13]

With Gerald's assistance, Sara designed the costumes for *Within the Quota*, originally titled *Landing*. She modeled the character of the heiress on her own sister, Mary "Hoytie" Wiborg.[14] The rest of "the Hollywood cast of characters," as described by the Murphys' biographer Amanda Vaill, were "dressed in clothes from a semiotician's sign book: the Tom Mix–like cowboy wore furry chaps that might have been stolen from a grizzly bear and what looks like a twenty-gallon hat; the sheriff had a dinner plate–sized star for a badge; the gilt-haired Mary Pickford type was bedecked with roses."[15]

There is no real plot, just a series of encounters leading to a distinctly modern American happy ending: fame conquers all. The choreographer, Jean Börlin, took the lead role, as he did in all of his creations, playing the part of an immigrant who, upon passing through Ellis Island, meets various clichéd American types extracted from the silent screen. The as-yet-to-be hero is number thirteen within the immigration quota, so he wears that number as a tag on his ill-fitting town suit. He first encounters a fabulously bejeweled heiress, a role taken by the flouncy, pliable Klara Kjellblad. Next appears a strutting "colored gentleman" in natty attire (trim suit, pink shirt, straw hat, bow tie, tap shoes, and white socks). The part, performed in blackface by Kaj Smith, inspired the catchiest music in Porter's score. (In keeping with the vogue for black culture at the time, de Maré demonstrated a keen fascination with blackface minstrelsy throughout the 1920s, later mounting a "show of authentic Negro vaudeville" at the Théâtre des Champs-Élysées.)[16] There follows a posh "jazz baby" inspired by the mercurial femme fatale actress Pola Negri; the role was danced in a slit gown by the black-haired, pale-skinned Ebon Strandin. Lastly there is a deeply tanned, constantly squatting cowboy (Paul Eltorp). The encounters leave the immigrant confused and puzzled, especially since each figure in the parade of clichés gets accosted by a kind of figure of fate: a prohibitionist, who drinks the bottle that he confiscates; then a tax collector; a sheriff; and finally a film censor. The censor, performed for much of the run by Toïvo Niskanen, follows the appearance of a movie star in long curls, pink ribbons, and heart-shaped necklace pendant. She represents the silent film comedienne Mary Pickford. The part was played by Edith von Bonsdorff. Ultimately, Vaill argues, the scenario explores an especially American form of "patriarchal disapproval" that the European conquers only by becoming famous.[17]

Perhaps the most enduring aspect of the ballet has been its backdrop, painted by Murphy. Ripping a page from Picasso's and Braque's still recent *papiers collés*, which used pages from *Le Journal* to comment on art, life, and their intersection, Murphy reproduced the front page of an American newspaper, replete with scandalous headlines. UNKNOWN BANKER BUYS ATLANTIC reads one, DANCER RENEWS HEART-BALM CASE another. The latter, as Vaill astutely notes, echoes an actual case of a jilted showgirl who sued Cornelius Vanderbilt Whitney for a million dollars.[18] Gerald even inserted an inside joke into his drawing for the programs, one that Vaill catches and explains. "Gerald's cover collage of New York City" featured the city's landmarks, among them the Mark Cross store, the business that Gerald's family had founded and owned. "Only the most observant (and knowledgeable)" in the audience for the premiere, Vaill writes, "would have noticed that the Mark Cross store on Fifth Avenue, with the company logo painted on the side of the building," peeked through the space beneath the towering immigrant's legs.[19] With this in mind, Vaill argues that the scenario of *Within the Quota* proved a kind of wish fulfillment for Murphy: "In the end the European overcomes that disapproval"—the moralizing, conservative pushback against modernism—"because he becomes a star. Perhaps Gerald hoped for the same thing."[20] His backdrop did at least, and a host of artists followed his example, incorporating the look and language of the newspapers in their art.[21]

Porter, of course, later found fame, having altogether abandoned "serious" composition, and Murphy's reputation as an artist has risen in recent decades.

At the time, *Within the Quota* made little impression, however, on French critics. The reviews of the 25 October 1923 premiere are slight and repetitive, providing the basic details of the collaboration without interpretation. The review from *Bonsoir* reveals that even one month before the premiere, Börlin, Murphy, and Porter were still planning to call the ballet *Landed*.[22] It was the curtain-raiser to *La création du monde* when performed in Paris but part of a broader mix of pieces when taken on tour to the United States from 26 November 1923 to 1 March 1924. There it was featured alongside *Skating Rink*, *Les vierges folles* (The foolish virgins), and some Swedish folk fare. The American reviews are slightly more detailed than the French, providing both the plot and some details of the scenic blocking.

According to one audience member, the immigrant is first seen gazing at "the back drop of a flaming yellow journal, screaming its violent headlines of divorce, bootlegging, and graft." Amid the luridness is news that an "unknown banker" has purchased the Atlantic Ocean. The confusion in the immigrant's tired brain is captured by the "mixture of syncopation, strange dissonance and musical topsy-turvieness."[23]

Performed sixty-nine times, the ballet found success on its native soil. Orledge mischaracterizes the American experience of the ballet itself, quoting the predictably conservative New York critics Deems Taylor and Francis Perkins but ignoring other voices. Vaill argues instead that *Within the Quota* "received the equivalent of a hero's welcome" and proved "immensely popular" on the American tour.[24] Indeed, it took pride of place on the program when the ballet it was once meant to precede, *La création du monde*, was dropped on the road. The supposed failure of the piece becomes a necessary construct in Charles Schwartz's 1979 biography of Cole Porter by way of explanation for Porter's turn back to Broadway. Schwartz is determined to see the ballet as "an important turning point in Cole's personal life" as well, imagining a breakdown between the Murphys and Porters along aesthetic lines, with Sara and Gerald mingling with artists and intellectuals in Paris, while the Porters "were drawn ever more to social and theatrical pursuits."[25] Yet such supposed divides—between the serious and the theatrical, art and entertainment, intellectual and social—are what American transatlantic modernism, the modernism of the Ballets suédois, meant to ruin.

That the sound of *Within the Quota* "is distinctly French and restrained," an inflection Orledge credits to Koechlin, is thus no failure but a telling strength. And there is not much traction in portraying Porter as compositionally hapless; he had, after all, studied counterpoint and orchestration at the Schola

Cantorum in 1920.[26] Instead, the aesthetic mixture of French and American, Koechlin and Porter, Murphy and de Maré reflects the depths of the ballet's cultural origins, not the surface of its surroundings. The Americanness of the score owes precisely to its expatriate identity. Murphy's explanation of the concept behind *Within the Quota*, one that irks Orledge, turns out to be both apt and revealing. "It is nothing but a translation on to the stage of the way America looks to me from over here," Murphy explained in an interview for the European edition of the *New York Herald*. "Paris is bound to make a man either more or less American." Porter echoed such sentiments, adding that "it's easier to write jazz over here than in New York . . . because you are too much under the influence of the popular song in America, and jazz is better than that."[27] And as Murphy reminisced to his friend and biographer Calvin Tomkins about the entire "jazz age" in Paris, "even though it happened in France, it was all somehow an American experience."[28]

It was also a very modern experience, a true transatlantic journey in form and content. The magic in Porter's score resides in its ingenious combination of the aesthetic highbrow and lowbrow. An American vernacular is heard in the simple diatonic tunes that grace each of the movements and the syncopations beneath them. The highbrow resides in the juxtaposition of Stravinskian polychords and polymeters in the tableaux accompanying the contemporary American characters (the heiress, the colored gentleman, the jazz baby, and the cowboy) versus the Schoenbergian atonality in the intervening "reformer" episodes. These latter constitute forces of musical as well as social repression, the structuring discourses that define the real, the imposed quotas. The progressive characters are assigned consonant tunes, stable refrain forms, and danceable ragtime undulations. Those that push back against the modern exist in a melodically, harmonically, and rhythmically amorphous realm. The one complication in this dichotomy concerns the odd quotation of the governing motif of Handel's "Hallelujah" chorus that appears at the start of the "Heiress Reformer" movement. Orledge puzzled over the allusion, but it seems to be an in-joke of the kind that defines the décor of the ballet. For a composer like Porter, the "Protestant" Handel's four-part, four-square chorale textures (those that Porter himself was steeped in as a student of the Schola Cantorum) would have been no less oppressive than Schoenberg's free atonality; after all, Schoenberg had declared himself heir to the Baroque masters.

Here is the essence of Porter's exposure to European academic composition. Back in New York he was a creature of the music hall, a song-and-dance man. The teachers of the conservatoires and European lords of the Western canon are figured in *Within the Quota* as his reformers, sheriffs, and censors. Thus the lowbrow characters doing the entertaining in the ballet are privileged over the unentertaining figures reining them in. Porter's presumed dilemma—that of a popular composer moving in elite musical circles—is built into the music.

The opening establishes the basic elements of the entire score: a two-measure hypermeter that places emphasis on the third beat of the even-numbered measures; and an emphasis on the intervals of the octave, the minor seventh, and its major second inversion.[29] Starting with the heiress movement, the minor seventh chord serves as the harmonic ground, but Porter also emphasizes, as he does in such songs as "Night and Day," trichords consisting of pairs of semitones and, alternately, pairs of whole tones.[30] For example, G and A are paired in cadential opposition to C and D; the grace notes are flats. "The Sweetheart of the World" theme falls comfortably within the range of a fifth, including all of the pitches listed here plus B♭.

For the colored gentleman, Porter creates a texture littered with wrong notes on the off-beats and *Petrushka*-like tritone-partitioned chords for the breaks. The goofiness of the ragtime is enhanced by passages of hemiola. For the cowboy, he relies on a Stravinskian overlay of meters. The third piano part represents the ambling of a horse; the second piano depicts the cowboy's bobbing up and down in the saddle. In the first piano part, the repeated melodic figure outlining an E–B♭ diminished fifth evokes, at least in my imagination, the twirling of a lasso. The jazz baby sounds fittingly lascivious: a tune slinks by semitone and augmented second in mixed rhythmic values. The various reformer episodes have motivic points of connection with those assigned to the cinematic caricatures but are subject to grotesque distortion. They recur intact but find themselves in the wrong key, on the sharp side of the circle of fifths as opposed to the flat side.

The dramatic and musical conflict between progress and reform, modern and antimodern, extends to suggest a kind of ambivalence about the age of mechanical reproduction. *Within the Quota* wrestles with the worlds of musical theater and the cinema. Similar fantasies and anxieties about different media are played out elsewhere in the Ballets suédois repertoire: live orchestral music comes out of gramophones; cameras malfunction (regurgitating the subjects they have swallowed); toys run amok. *Relâche* is famous for its cinematic entr'acte, but the film (shot by René Clair to music by Erik Satie) is experimental, densely avant-garde in its privileging of the texture of the moment over chronological time. *Within the Quota* represents a unique—and melancholic—surrendering to time and technology. As Vaill points out, the avant-garde predecessor to *Within the Quota*, Cocteau's and Satie's *Parade*, was a Ballets russes production "about how the advertising image, the sideshow, comes to be more important than the real attraction inside the circus tent." *Within the Quota*, in contrast, "was about how the image *becomes* the real attraction."[31]

The ending of the score bears witness to this cinematic dissolve. Titled "The Sweetheart of the World," the rhapsodic tune that rises from its twinkling accompaniment almost begs for a crooner to perform its unwritten lyrics in a smoky cavern somewhere. For the cinematic apotheosis, Porter relies on a clever acoustic trick. The tune is sextupled in rapid triplets two octaves above, generating a shimmering effect. This is the musical equivalent of the now-standard Hollywood practice of blurring a love scene with a pulled-back, expanding shot, syrupy strings, the sound of the sea, and so on. In Porter's score, chromatic scales ascend at the last ever higher.

Porter's sweetheart music is an emblem of the kinds of characters that Mary Pickford tended to portray and of the plight of the immigrant as captured on film in the 1920s. Börlin himself merges here with Pickford, a comedienne forever associated with the part of the "tragic little orphan, lost in the cruel world, at the constant mercy of Fate"—but when times get tough, plucky and strong-willed enough to "storm off and do something about it."[32] From the reviews, it seems that Börlin performed, in many of his productions, on the edge of mawkishness, repeating himself when inspiration failed, indulging in clichéd gesture and privileging the kind of athleticism that ballet historians derided as the balletic equivalent of steeplechasing. The Pickford character and Börlin's immigrant perform a miniature pas de deux, ballet's corseted emblem of romantic ecstasy, as the cameras click and the lightbulbs flash, and as the upper strings (the right-hand part in the third piano) rise heavenward in chromatic runs. The show ends with the protagonist not lost in the New World but lost in the stars. The rest of the characters dip and spin as the curtain descends. The ballet concludes somewhere between the real and the fantastic, no longer within the quota of either. This blurring of divisions between media, between perceptual registers, is the essence of the modernist aesthetic and what gives the slight works of the Ballets suédois such conceptual heft.

In real life, too, Börlin strove for the heavens. But there was no happy ending for him. Following the dissolution of the Ballets suédois in 1925, after de Maré discovered that the company manager had swindled him, Börlin came to the United States seeking a new start, a new career, but he died a victim of drugs and alcohol and the attendant heart and liver disease just five years later, at age thirty-seven. He had effectively worked himself to death in the service of the company that de Maré, his lover and mentor, had bankrolled.[33]

To look for the steps and gestures Börlin created for *Within the Quota* is to confront an abyss. Nothing remains, not even in Börlin's notebooks. But that bald fact did not hamper Millicent Hodson and her husband, Kenneth Archer. Specialists in the dubious art of ballet reconstruction, they relied on the extant costume drawings and studio photographs to "reconstruct" *Within the Quota* for the Royal Swedish Ballet in June 1998.[34] Since none of the original stage action survives in any form, the reconstruction relied on guesswork. Hodson and Archer watched silent films and looked at fashion magazines from the period, assuming they had fueled Börlin's imagination, then came up with steps and gestures based on how the characters in those films conducted themselves. The photographs of the time were black and white, but of course that does not mean Börlin's production lacked color. Yet Hodson and Archer made it seem that way. They also decided that the heiress was meant to look like Gloria Swanson, even though there is no evidence to support that contention. Moreover, the jazz baby does the shimmy not like Pola Negri but instead like the famous flapper Clara Bow. Hodson and Archer also decided that it would look good to add another character to the cast: a filmmaker. The new-old *Within the Quota* was meant to delight and as such lacked the cynicism built into the original. No one was fooled into thinking that the choreography was authentic, however, and even as a mockup it had its problems. It looked like a flipbook; it was anachronistic in its sourcing. As Judith MacKrell put it in the *Guardian*, "The choreography with which Hodson reconstructs these characters relies too heavily on predictable, stereotypical moves. As a result, it looks as though it could have been made at any time between then and now."[35]

The history of *Within the Quota* since 1923 has not been impressive, which is not solely the fault of Hodson and Archer's methodologically problematic reconstruction. In 1970 the American Ballet Theater (ABT) performed a kind of homage to *Within the Quota* titled *Times Past*. The *New York Times* preview article, by Anna Kisselgoff, is incredibly off the mark in its assertion that *Times Past* was a revival of *Within the Quota* based on inspired research by Robert Kimball, longtime curator of Yale's Musical Theater Collection.[36] In truth, the "musical detective story" ended in failure, with the Stockholm Dance Museum mysteriously refusing to provide Kimball with a copy of the Koechlin orchestration, which had been in its collection since 1968.[37] The refusal obliged ABT to rely on a two-piano arrangement by William Bolcolm. Orledge describes the orchestration of that two-piano version—the orchestration also used by Hodson and Archer in their reconstruction—as sounding in places like "Henry Mancini," meaning that it strove, in its brass and percussion writing, for a banally pleasing *Pink Panther* sound. Orledge prefers Mancini to the Debussy-derived Frenchness of the Koechlin orchestration, whose single reference to jazz convention, a modestly deployed alto saxophone, seemed an "afterthought," entered into the score in haste in a different-colored ink.[38]

So Porter's jazz ballet, one of the first ballets on an American topic by an American composer, has never actually been orchestrated in Porter's own idiom, which was more a part of New York's Tin Pan Alley than Paris's Ballets suédois and Ballets russes. But to achieve that idiom would entail creating a new version of *Within the Quota*, one that reimagines a vernacular that never existed in the first place—at least not at that time. Recall that Porter himself had not yet found his way on Broadway in 1923. Perhaps, however, the fiction of such an endeavor could be in keeping with the truth of the original musical and cultural context. Once the immigrant lands in the United States and finds the forces aligned against him, he dissolves into the Hollywood illusion that the real America might have denied him. The surreal is preferable to the real in the plot. Might it not be for the music as well?

Notes

I am grateful to Laura Ong and Lisa Snyder for their assistance researching this article.

1. I have in mind here *Les mariés de la tour Eiffel* (The newlyweds on the Eiffel Tower, 1921). The characters include two gramophones, into which unseen actors speak semicoherent lines. Their words are thus live and recorded at the same time. This condition also pertains to the background music, composed by Georges Auric, Darius Milhaud, Francis Poulenc, Germaine Tailleferre, and Arthur Honegger—five members of the group of Parisian iconoclasts known as Les Six. Though we hear a live orchestra, their music tries very hard to sound as if it were emanating from wax cylinders and piano rolls.

2. For the specifics, see Mathias Auclair, Frank Claustrat, and Inès Piovesan, *Les Ballets suédois: Une compagnie d'avant-garde (1920–1925)* (Montreuil: Gourcuff Gradenigo, 2014).

3. Robert Orledge, "Cole Porter's Ballet 'Within the Quota,'" *Yale University Library Gazette* 50, no. 1 (1975): 19–29. Porter's manuscript is found in folders 65–66, box 8, MSS 82, Cole Porter Collection, Irving S. Gilmore Music Library, Yale University.

4. The finest biography of Gerald and Sara Murphy is the most recent: Amanda Vaill, *Everybody Was So Young: Gerald and Sara Murphy: A Lost Generation Love Story* (Boston: Houghton Mifflin, 1998).

5. On this first meeting, see Vaill, *Everybody Was So Young*, 35–36; and William McBrien, *Cole Porter: A Biography* (New York: Alfred A. Knopf, 1998), 31–32. Biographical details in this paragraph are drawn from both sources.

6. On Frank B. Wiborg's East Hampton estate, known as The Dunes, see Wendy Goodman, "A South Fork Story," *New York Magazine*, 17 July 2006, http://nymag.com/arts/all/features/17561/, accessed 16 August 2014. The six-hundred-acre expanse would today be valued at over $1 billion.

7. McBrien, *Cole Porter*, 5–9.

8. As quoted in ibid., 73.

9. Ibid., 74.

10. Ibid., 89. See also Vaill, *Everybody Was So Young*, 122–24. Vaill notes that because "de Maré's pockets were as deep as Diaghilev's were shallow," the Ballets suédois could afford to buy talent. In the case of *Within the Quota*, he went with the relatively unknown Murphy and Porter because the priority was to find Americans to work on a project slated for the upcoming 1923–24 tour of the United States.

11. Vaill, *Everybody Was So Young*, 128.

12. Orledge, "Cole Porter's Ballet," 24.

13. Vaill, *Everybody Was So Young*, 105–7.

14. Ibid., 131.

15. Ibid.

16. On blackface performance in Paris, see especially Petrine Archer-Shaw, *Negrophilia: Avant-Garde Paris and Black Culture in the 1920s* (London: Thames and Hudson, 2000); and Jody Blake, *Le Tumulte noir: Modernist Art and Popular Entertainment in Jazz Age Paris, 1900–1930* (University Park: Pennsylvania State University Press, 2003).

17. Among the many sources on American modernism and celebrity, see in particular Aaron Jaffe, *Modernism and the Culture of Celebrity* (Cambridge: Cambridge University Press, 2005); and Jonathan Goldman, *Modernism Is the Literature of Celebrity* (Austin: University of Texas Press, 2011).

18. Vaill, *Everybody Was So Young*, 132.

19. Ibid.

20. Ibid.

21. Among them were novelist John Dos Passos and painter Stuart Davis. See, in particular, Christopher Benfey, *American Audacity: Literary Essays North and South* (Ann Arbor: University of Michigan Press, 2009), 97; Sidra Stich, *Made in the U.S.A.: An Americanization in Modern Art, the '50s & '60s* (Berkeley: University of California Press, 1987), 110–15, among many others.

22. André L. Daven, "Jean Borlin revient de Stockholm," *Bonsoir*, 19 September 1923.

23. W. H. H., "Swedish Ballet Topsy Turvy Hit" [1923], folder 66, box 8, Cole Porter Collection.

24. Vaill, *Everybody Was So Young*, 133.

25. Charles Schwartz, *Cole Porter: A Biography* (New York: Da Capo Press, 1979), 84, 86.

26. McBrien, *Cole Porter*, 74.

27. As quoted in Orledge, "Cole Porter's Ballet," 24–25.

28. Calvin Tomkins, *Living Well Is the Best Revenge* (1962; repr., New York: New American Library, 1972), 11.

29. I derive the detail about hypermeter from Matthew Shaftel, "From Inspiration to Archive: Cole Porter's 'Night and Day,'" *Journal of Music Theory* 43, no. 2 (Autumn 1999): 326.

30. Ibid., 329–31, 333, 335.

31. Vaill, *Everybody Was So Young*, 131.

32. Kevin Brownlow, "A Tribute to Mary Pickford," http://www.cobbles.com/simpp_archive/mary-pickford_brownlo.htm, accessed 16 August 2014.

33. On these points and the Ballets suédois in general, see George Dorris, "Jean Borlin as Dancer and Choreographer," *Dance Chronicle* 22, no. 2 (1999): 167–88.

34. On the purported reconstruction, see Kenneth Archer and Millicent Hodson, "Recreating the Quota," *Dance International* 29, no. 1 (Spring 1998): 21–27. Much of the research for the reconstruction is suspect, to be polite. Archer and Hodson write, nonsensically, that Smith and Börlin would have taken inspiration for the colored gentleman "from Gerald Murphy, who was a genuine expert on American folk art, particularly Black music." And as pure conjecture, they add that "just before moving the family to Paris he and Sara must have seen the New York sensation of spring 1921, Noble Sissle's and Eubie Blake's *Shuffle Along*" (ibid., 27). At the time, the Murphys lived in Cambridge, Massachusetts, where Gerald was pursuing a degree in landscape architecture at Harvard.

35. Judith MacKrell, "Jean Who?," *Guardian*, 17 June 1998.

36. Anna Kisselgoff, "Ballet by Cole Porter to Be Danced Here," *New York Times*, 5 May 1970.

37. Ibid.

38. Orledge, "Cole Porter's Ballet," 27.

PART 2

Porter the Poet and Performer

5

Lists of Louche Living

Music in Cole Porter's Social World

MITCHELL MORRIS

Asked once whether his songs would endure, Cole Porter replied, "I never gave it a thought. . . . My enjoyment was in writing them."[1] Both the question and the response might seem little more than journalistic chitchat, but the implications are worth a bit more attention. Take first the question itself—passing "the test of time" is a notion that brings with it a set of assumptions about music and value that have a long trajectory in music history. Contemporaneity is all well and good, that question seems to say, but enough about the present: Will Porter's songs, we ask, be rich enough, tenacious enough, to survive past the moment of their currency? Monumentality, on the order of the work of a Catullus or a Dante, of a Raphael or a Boucher—or, more pointedly, a Mozart or a Schumann—is proof, in our casual conversations, of high value. (T. S. Eliot's women coming and going were "talking of Michelangelo," not just a nobody.) Porter's response rather disingenuously evades the question's implications in favor of a pose of frivolity, masking fundamental disagreements with its premises.

The history of this idea of seriousness in art is a long one, of course, and a full accounting would be long and, though undoubtedly interesting, not particularly companionable; for an enormous weight of commentary and practice, from Alexandrian canon makers to Renaissance humanists and on to German Idealist philosophers (to take three important nodes) backed the notion that there was such a thing as Greatness in Art, produced by Great Artists; that this Greatness was bound up in notions of "works," objects of literary/artistic/

musical value that, in outliving the original occasions of their production, were somehow permanent; that this permanence caused works to be somehow "self-contained"; that therefore the proper way to approach them was quasi religious, treating the work as something like aesthetic Scripture. This is all pretty heavy going. But by around 1800, musicians and commentators of all sorts had begun to invest heavily in the notion.[2] (It's worth noting that such energetic goals could have a downside: to make art with an eye to eternity requires a certain disregard of the immediate social world. Romantic artists and surly teens alike, clinging to the authenticity of Artistic Vision, tend to refuse social embedding as damaging compromise. Integrity and hostility to communication can appear remarkably similar.)

The resistance to such seriousness took many forms during the nineteenth century, and one of its most important strands led to a bifurcation between the more monumentally minded and the more commercially conscious (usually placed under the rubric "light" or "popular") composers/works. Raymond Knapp has provided a rich account of the traditions and practices (mostly from the popular side) that converged in the creation of the American musical, and I would particularly stress the way his discussion includes the tensions between currency and endurance.[3] The verse of a classic Tin Pan Alley song, to take a vivid example, shows this tension particularly well in the problem of the verse, the introduction that sets the mise-en-scène for the principal topic(s) of the song's chorus. As Knapp observes, "Although the emergent type of song . . . continued usually to include clarifying and situating verses, these most often were much shorter, sometimes served as little more than introductions, and occasionally simply were not provided even for their original presentation on stage. . . . As was quickly learned within the time-restrictive environment of recording in the 1920s, the new Tin-Pan Alley song, uprooted from the stage, worked best without its verses, as a fragment of expressivity whose specific context remained somewhat fluid."[4]

Knapp, in describing the process of decontextualization that increasingly turned songs from their initial ecosystem into the freely circulating scripts we now call "standards," demonstrates one way of trading currency for endurance. But though an effective way to adjust a song into a less concrete and therefore more flexible item, there was still another problem: many a song's chorus still contained specific details of word or musical gesture that required specificity to register as important. If we aftercomers cannot recognize a dropped name or a stylistic allusion, what then? Our custom is historical excavation; we track down references and create glossaries to amplify our delectation (that is, when we do not simply ignore the problem and joyously stick with our mishearings).

But even this becomes difficult when the song in question is so variable, extant in enough multiple forms, that we must also decide, as we engage, just exactly what it *is* that we engage with.

Such as Cole Porter's songs. Start with this observation: in many of Cole Porter's renditions of songs from earlier in his career, he was happy to alter verses to suit the guests he had with him. Ethel Merman claimed that he admired her because "I never change a word. . . . I don't tamper with the melodies or the rhythm."[5] Maybe so; but Porter did not abide by the same rule. It seems clear that for him, the immediate social occasion trumped the stability of his own song's "text," its presumed intactness as a consistent work. This mutability highlights a fundamental interpretive problem. All songs, to take one instance, begin their lives as contemporaries: we hear them freshly introduced into the world, which is primarily the everyday world, and their attachments to Now are usually at least partially straightforward. At the moment of their appearance they are at their most alive, but they immediately start dying, the newness rubs off them like the down off a peach, and the surroundings that lit them up—the allusions to current topics, the concessions to current taste, the invention of novelties and ornaments, and so on—gradually fade away. Try as we may to hold on to them as a present tense, they inevitably slip into pastness, whether a particular texture of nostalgia or simple(?) old-fashionedness-on-its-way-to-antiquity. Should we try to reconstruct the past contexts in which the song was new, we may actually reembody the songs, but the quality will always be different. We can restore the original song no more easily than we can put actual flesh on a fossil or find a whole body for a footprint. But our reconstructions might still give a sense of the work the songs first meant to do.

My discussion offers several ways to think about how music appeared in Cole Porter's social world. The term "musicking," coined by musicologist Christopher Small to incorporate all musical performance acts, from composing to playing to listening to dancing, under a single rubric, is an excellent label for Porter, whose personal performances were as central to his life as his songwriting. He was a consummate musicker: his passion for music was always socially embedded to a degree that complicated any straightforward decontextualization. And in this respect, he was united with many of his friends and allies. This becomes clear from a brief account of his earlier career.

Musicking a Glamorous Life

Porter's commitment to the sociability of songwriting was already in evidence during his boyhood at the Worcester Academy, his boarding school; although a good violinist capable of playing estimably genteel parlor music, he preferred inventing jaunty songs that quite often lampooned the faculty in lyrics rife with saucy double entendres and puns.[6] The commitment deepened during Porter's college years, when his musical brilliance made the centerpiece of his quest for social triumph.

Porter's status as an outsider to eastern society and its mores was obvious from his arrival at Yale—thanks, for instance, to his midwestern tastes in dress. His friend Gerald Murphy (a Boston aesthete who was heir to the Mark Cross Company) met Porter as a sophomore and recalled him "in a checkered suit and a salmon tie, with his hair parted down the middle and slicked down, looking like a Westerner dressed up for the East."[7] (The apparent incongruity of *dandysme à l'Indiana* would be modified over the years to a transatlantic panache.) Common musical interests overrode Murphy's bemusement at Porter's clothes, however, and the two became close friends. Another close friend was the flamboyant Monty Woolley, from a rich New York family, who took to Porter and became a great mentor. Such durable friendships, together with Porter's nonstop and hugely popular musical activities, brought him vast social acclaim even while his grades shriveled into an assortment of so-sos and by-squeaks.[8] Some songs would soon find their way into the hands of publishers—and their friends.

Porter's upperclassman time at Yale was a frenzy of creativity; at the center were four musical comedies, two for his fraternity, Delta Kappa Epsilon (DKE), and two for the Dramatic Association. Together with his eccentricities of dress and manner, such constant, high-profile musicking made him one of the most unforgettable figures in the college social scene. And the connection to Yale's ongoing rounds of musical comedies and revues continued even after Porter entered Harvard Law School in 1913 to pretend to study (a sop to an irate rich grandpa).[9] Among the figures attracted to Porter's youthful talent was the imposing theatrical/literary agent and producer Elisabeth Marbury, and her interest took Porter out of law entirely. Impressed with some of the published songs, Marbury cultivated Porter, providing introductions to Sigmund Romberg and Jerome Kern and producing his first Broadway musical comedy, *See America First*, in 1916.

To understand what went wrong—because it did go wrong—a few details about New York's theatrical world before World War I are in order. First and foremost it is worth knowing that there was no clear separation between "amateur" and "professional" performance. A large number of productions featured performers who were primarily society figures or mixed trained and untrained actors freely. Some productions were more important as social events than as commercial enterprises. And New York upper-class society, though much less stable than it had been during the late nineteenth century, had not yet lost most of its authority in matters of culture making.

In conception and design, *See America First* was an outgrowth of Porter's Yale-ish style: a farrago of cheek and sensation held together by little more than the stage curtain. Marbury's predominantly social production was a failure with professional critics, and the show quickly folded.[10] Soon thereafter the United States entered World War I, and Porter sailed to France, where he volunteered for humanitarian war relief (his claim to have joined the French Foreign Legion was a spoof), socialized when possible, and continued songwriting. Among his old friends in Paris were Monty Woolley and Howard Sturgis (another of their set from Yale). After the war's end, the Parisian social world expanded dramatically, with ever more Russian émigrés mingling with British and American expatriates, plus assorted other nationalities in a rich array of artistic and social modernities.

The American presence in Paris was particularly vibrant, thanks to the enormous cultural prestige of its modernist styles—jazz, above all, seemed to embody the hyperfuturistic primitivism often deemed particularly American (Negroes! Jazz! Cars! Skyscrapers!), though it served also as a musical analogue to the strains of primitivist modernism coming in from European colonial possessions: How else could jazz come to be treated as the sonic equivalent of an African mask? It's worth remembering that in the 1920s, jazz and its popular music kin could seem as definitively Modern as the most severe products of the European avant-garde—and to many people, a more persuasive and rewarding Modern than its rivals. It is mostly the musical politics/polemics of the later avant-garde and jazz worlds that has obscured this fact. The decade is not known, after all, as the Avant-Garde Age. And to the degree that American style could be a metonym for American financial and military power (this wasn't hard to do), its authority was enhanced. Surveying the scene, art critic Wanda M. Corn has noted that "the rivalry between Paris and New York did not originate in the thirties and forties but rather in the teens and twenties when the French avant-garde, for the first time in its history, began to look enviously across the seas."[11] In any case, American culture—particularly its mass culture—was in its acutely fashionable phase in the immediate postwar period, and its exponents, whether artists or socialites, were abundant and highly visible. This was the matrix within which Porter's fundamental style was formed. And its crucial figure was Porter's wife.

Linda Lee Thomas was a wealthy American divorcée eight years Porter's senior, living in France after the Armistice; the two met at a wedding of

American friends at the Paris Ritz. Fabulously elegant and poised, with a spectacular eye for style and fashion, Thomas had a rich and exalted circle of friends—and she was smitten with Porter's talent and charm. He was equally dazzled by her beauty, taste, and worldliness. Neither of them apparently objected to a *mariage blanc*—companionship and affection were more important than consummation.[12] (And in any case, complex marriages and equivalent alliances between people of incommensurate sexual tastes were a commonplace in the High Bohemian circles that had begun to overlap a large segment of traditional Anglo/Franco elite society. I will return to this.)

The immediate obstacle to be overcome was financial—Porter's inheritance was still held by his grandfather, who was displeased with his grandson's apparent fecklessness. Hoping to wrench some funds to make the marriage possible, Porter sailed for America—and met Raymond Hitchcock, a New York producer who introduced Porter to Max Dreyfus, head of T. B. Harms, one of the most important song publishers in Tin Pan Alley. Dreyfus, who was to become Porter's major publisher, placed individual songs in shows by other composers; Hitchcock commissioned Porter for the score to his *Hitchy-Koo of 1919* (modestly successful, with one tune, the atypical "Old-Fashioned Garden," a big hit).[13] Between royalties from the song, money from his mother, and a loan from a Yale friend, Porter and Thomas were able to marry, on 18 December 1919.

For the years until Porter's inheritance finally arrived, and until his royalties began to accumulate, Linda Porter underwrote an opulent life largely centered in Paris.[14] "Les Colporteurs," as they were sometimes known, circulated among a glittering crowd of expatriate Americans, Britons, and Russians, not to mention their French hosts. Linda, who was convinced that Cole should make himself into a "serious" composer, sought opportunities for her husband, using all her connections. An attempt to interest Diaghilev in commissioning a ballet came to naught—Diaghilev loathed jazz and Americans, so Porter lost out twice. Stravinsky was unwilling to give composition lessons. George Bernard Shaw, John Galsworthy, and Arnold Bennett declined to write libretti. But Linda persisted and soon persuaded Cole to take classes at the Schola Cantorum, one of the most prestigious training grounds for serious French musicians. (Although an ambivalent student, he acquired significant if usually disavowed compositional skills.)

But Linda's greatest success came in at last getting a commission for Cole from the Ballets suédois. The pivotal figure in this process was Cole's Yale friend Gerald Murphy, who had moved to Paris with his family in 1921 and had begun to study painting briefly with Natalia Goncharova.[15] Invited to create a work for the Ballets suédois, Murphy suggested Porter as the composer—it was to be an *American* ballet—and he and Linda arranged that the invitation would be issued by Darius Milhaud when all were at a *soirée chez* the Princesse de Polignac.[16]

Unfortunately, the Ballets suédois collapsed acrimoniously in 1925, and in the brouhaha, Porter's score was believed lost. (In fact, it was misplaced, only to be rediscovered.)[17] The urgencies driving music historians have never seemed to include a place for Porter's ballet, even as they exalted Milhaud's *La création du monde* into one of the representative works of the decade. It's as if historical circumstances and practices united for years to underscore Porter's apparent willingness to distinguish between his work and "serious composition"—and his determination to stick with his sociable métier. And throughout the 1920s, despite occasional successes with a song or two, he continued to live in Europe as a social figure who, oh yes, did write an occasional song or two.

Café Society, or the Use of Gossip

In fact, the social world in which "les Colporteurs" moved was an extraordinary outgrowth of a number of social currents under way since the late nineteenth century. With the increasing improvements in transportation, particularly the fully equipped ocean liner—such as the White Star Line's RMS *Oceanic*, launched in 1870—a thoroughly transatlantic elite society became possible. (First-class accommodations, making money and status especially vivid in close quarters, also hosted increasing connections between the plush travelers who crossed the sea.) The last decades of the nineteenth century witnessed an increasing density of social connections that we can visualize as a network between London, Paris, and New York. This pattern persisted even as the established lines of caste began to break up with shifting economic patterns and the rise of the mass media. The social groups such as Mrs. Astor and the 400, who dominated New York Society in the Gilded Age, increasingly found themselves seated next to people of the theater, High Bohemians, and other sorts whose disreputability was less important than their fame (and sometimes money). Increasingly, the social worlds of the cultural capitals overlapped and merged, so that by the 1920s, to speak of Paris, London, or New York was likely to require mention of their counterparts.

The advent of World War I intensified such social changes to a degree that would probably have been inconceivable two decades earlier, and alongside the social dislocations (which should not be understood as social leveling—egalitarianism was not a priority), the most vibrant feature of the war's aftermath was the ascent of the United States as a cultural/economic power. Historian Ann Douglas summarizes: "All historical circumstances in 1918–28 decade—America's exemption from the economic consequences of the Great War, a war that devastated its European and English rivals, the congeniality of the violent and innovative mood abroad to America's longstanding cultural disposition, and its possession of new technologies and unsuspected treasures of elite and popular art of major importance to modern needs—these seemed effortlessly to conspire to assure the country's global preeminence."[18] Douglas sees the core of the change in Manhattan to be driven by the vast expansion of the African American population in the city. The phenomenal cultural vibrancy of Harlem attracted the attentions of white New Yorkers as well, especially upper-class scapegraces, artists, intellectuals, and political radicals who made up the High Bohemian world associated with Greenwich Village. Carl Van Vechten, journalist and critic, novelist, later important photographer, was central to this project as a publicist of the New Negro Movement, at every opportunity promoting Langston Hughes and Countee Cullen, Bessie Smith, and Ethel Waters to white publishers and audiences. In his private life, too, Van Vechten arranged a social life that exuberantly crossed boundaries of race, class, and sexual tastes, blended in a solvent of music, scandalous behavior, and bootleg gin. A party might also include Tallulah Bankhead, then making her name as a young actress attached to the Algonquin Round Table with a habit of outrageous statements, or George Gershwin, on the way to his greatest fame, or F. Scott and Zelda Fitzgerald, alongside the Harlem artists Van Vechten adored. Douglas's term for this insistent blending of races and classes, taken from Dorothy Parker, was "mongrel," and it acutely registers the anxieties about miscegenation (and social leveling) that sparked the moral panics that always accompanied the giddy antics of Jazz Age celebrities: traditionally illicit combinations and crossover seemed, in commercial culture and the mass media, to be everywhere.

To return to France, where the Porters await. In musical terms, what mattered most about America was jazz, and the "mongrel" social scene of the 1920s was constantly marked by its presence. One striking example concerns Ada "Bricktop" Smith, a mixed-race artist who by 1924 had moved from New York to Paris to open a cabaret, Le Grand Duc. Cole Porter, who dropped by one evening, found her singing one of his songs; he appeared the next day to ask if she could dance the Charleston, and she demonstrated. In short order, she found herself teaching the dance at his cocktail parties to the international smart set. (Jazz was for its twenties aficionados dance music above all, and the radical shift in comportment that its dances promoted was as much a part of its scandal as anything in its sound or lyrics.)

These ebullient personalities and their audacious violations of social codes might have been of only restricted interest had it not been for the huge expansion of the mass media press during the period. Publisher Condé Nast had acquired *Vogue*, a magazine aimed at American Old Society, in 1905; by the 1910s he had launched overseas editions in Britain, Spain, Italy, and France. In 1914 he transformed another magazine, *Dress*, into *Vanity Fair*. And in 1925 he launched the *New Yorker*. All three magazines were distinguished by sophisticated and strong-minded editors who tended a huge stable of brilliant writers and artists: not coincidentally, they paid careful attention to the goings-on of this new and exciting mongrel social world.[19]

The best term for this network of personalities, events, and reportage is perhaps "café society." Society journalist Lucius Beebe popularized the term as a label for the people who commonly appeared in his weekly column in the *New York Herald Tribune*; it captures the way in which "private" events increasingly took place in a semipublic that included press coverage. The increasing circulation of the Condé Nast magazines meant that access to the styles and textures of café society was increasingly available to an array of readers in places far removed from the cultural centers of the Jazz Age. And the central rhetorical mode of this commentary was gossip. The effervescence of these new urban hybrid cultures was especially hospitable to the outrageous in word and deed, and the magazines defiantly claimed allegiance to their indecorous ways. Herbert Ross, first editor of the *New Yorker*, famously claimed that his magazine was not aimed at "the old lady in Dubuque" but by implication at urban sophisticates—and the people in Dubuque who perhaps wished to be elsewhere.[20] For these audiences, gossip was especially important for the sense it could give of being on "the inside." This feeling could be all the more appealing because it was also possible for experienced readers to learn how to read between the lines, either to glean the essentials of what was *not* being said or simply to thrill at the awareness that the not-said was present and the real point of the story. Café society, always ready to accommodate eavesdroppers, was a natural home not only of the spicy anecdote but more generally of the thinly veiled reference, the double entendre, the clever pun, and the occasional rude phrase. This was a natural home for Porter, who was known at Yale for his trademark "What's the latest dirt?"[21] And gossipy reference to his friends and comrades was a staple of Porter's lyric making. To be sure, many of the lives of Porter's comrades were not very private—at least for those who had the code. For those who could hear, the news about such figures was everywhere, and of magnificently doubtful virtue.

Decoding Cole

From early in his career, Porter loved references to historical as well as contemporary figures, usually in some brash situation that flatters his audience (we recognize the reference and we get to poke fun at it too). Porter as a lyricist loved metonymic things, particularly lists. On the one hand, these lists frame a particular kind of eroticism—they most often appear in songs of romance (however ambivalent) and employ potentially endless wit, since the list could hypothetically continue to exhaustion, in the service of courtship.[22] But the list also serves to create an implied social world in which Cole's immediate audience, who certainly recognize the references, are joined by a larger and more inchoate audience through magazines, recordings, and radio, joined together by their sense of inclusion. And now we return to the difficulties of Porter's intense social embeddedness—since he depended heavily on the evanescence of the current reference, his lists can have an unusually short cultural half-life. Even when some brief excavation securely identifies a reference, it takes a great deal of time to unpack the halo of associations that are compressed around it, and that time is the death of wit.

But though the wit be diminished in explication, the richness that comes from reconstructing the social network condensed into a single reference offers a different set of rewards. By way of conclusion, let me turn to a single verse from the ever-popular standard "Anything Goes":

> When you hear that Lady Mendl standing up
> Now turns a handspring landing up—On her toes,
> Anything goes.

Lady Mendl was earlier in her life known as Elsie de Wolfe. Brought up on the margins of New York Society, she had taken to the stage as an amateur actress before being hired professionally. She was better at posing than acting and by 1903 had given up the stage to become arguably the inventor of modern interior decoration as a career. By then she had been living for over a decade, more or less openly, in a relationship with Elisabeth Marbury, who had produced *See America First*. (It is said that they were referred to behind their backs as "the Bachelors.") Just as de Wolfe was launching her new career, Marbury became involved with Anne Morgan, daughter of J. P. Morgan, the financier and a devoted philanthropist. Together, Marbury, de Wolfe, and Morgan bought and refurbished (Elsie's doing) the Villa Trianon near Versailles and spent more than a decade in an uneasy three-way partnership.[23] (Eventually, Anne Vanderbilt, a close friend of Morgan's and Marbury's, seems to have become part of the circle as well.) In the theatrical circles that impinged on New York's upper strata, such sexual styles were a commonplace. Mercedes de Acosta, brought up in New York Society, spent much of her amazing life seducing an astounding array of great actresses during this time, from Maude Adams, Eva Le Gallienne, and Isadora Duncan in New York to Greta Garbo and Marlene Dietrich in Hollywood.[24] In this light the young Tallulah Bankhead, said to have accosted strangers at the Algonquin with the line "I'm bisexual. What do you do?," seems less *outré*.

De Wolfe's dazzling success as a decorator was a mixture of social status, taste, and an unerring ability to stay *au courant*. Trading on her social connections as well as her distinct sensibility, de Wolfe rejected the heavy, dark styles of late Victorian taste in favor of much lighter, airier interiors. Chintz, wicker, rococo antiques, treillage, and any number of other decorating innovations can be credited to her.[25] It didn't hurt that she had a gift for the *bon mot*: "I believe in optimism and plenty of white paint!" Upon seeing the Parthenon for the first time: "Beige—my color!" Particularly attached to the Villa Trianon, de Wolfe spent more and more time in France, as her relationship with Marbury became attenuated—and their separation culminated in Elsie's 1926 companionable *mariage blanc* to Sir Charles Mendl, a somewhat parvenu British diplomat who was a close friend. (Their social circle found the match bemusing. Elsie's French housekeeper, when informed, exclaimed, "C'est une blague!") He was fifty-six; she admitted to fifty-eight (she lied). "Les Colporteurs" were part of the wedding party. And Elsie's life as Lady Mendl was as audacious as her earlier incarnations. Hence Cole Porter's reference to a scandalous event, in which Lady Mendl entered a fancy dress ball in Paris in the guise of a can-can girl and performed an expert backflip. Ensconced at the Villa Trianon, Lady Mendl continued as a hostess of almost unendurable power, with her parties regularly featuring music by Cole Porter or by their mutual friend Elsa Maxwell.[26] When her hair began to gray, de Wolfe had her hairdressers dye it blue; later on, she would occasionally adjust her hair to match her outfits. At the villa, she had a pet cemetery for her various dogs, with each headstone emblazoned "The One I Loved Best." And the stories go on. . . . The point, of course, is that some number of these tales would be known by nearly everyone in the room when Porter was playing for his friends—but thanks to the press, many of the tales would be known by the larger public as well. And the halo of knowledge surrounding that little mention in a Cole Porter list stood metonymically for all the anecdotes about Elsie that framed her within the social world that she inhabited and performed.

Encasing this dense tangle of reference is an infectiously rollicking tune, with its jazzy, raggy syncopations falling over into the breezy refrain. The song is actually at its most impressive, somehow, in Porter's own solo rendition, not least because of the exquisite detail in which he renders archness in multiple tones. And the presence of Porter's own recordings brings back the questions of musicking: a song for Porter, his own renditions seem to suggest, are less things in themselves than they are literally pretexts for performance.[27]

In Porter's genial mockery, we find condensed many of the historical currents I've been tracing in the service of exalting a sensibility in which the fact that the present is fleeting is the cornerstone of its charm. Change, and the pleasures of merely circulating in the lush/louche social world Porter extolled, could indeed be a rival to the stonier delights of grand permanence and Masterworks. He spoke true, surely, when he said that the "enjoyment was in writing them." And despite his songs' later bleaching—made inevitable by their commitment to the transient—they remain, in the charm of their clever sociability, "a sexy place to be invited."[28]

Notes

1. Quoted in George Eells, *The Life That Late He Led: A Biography of Cole Porter* (New York: G. P. Putnam's Sons, 1967), 305.

2. Lydia Goehr's *The Imaginary Museum of Musical Works* (New York: Oxford University Press, 1992) is the exemplary discussion of this problem in music. For an extension of these ideas to American popular song, see Mitchell Morris, "Narratives and Values," in *The Oxford Handbook of the American Musical*, ed. Raymond Knapp, Mitchell Morris, and Stacy Wolf (New York: Oxford University Press, 2011), 9–19.

3. Raymond Knapp, *The American Musical and the Formation of National Identity* (Princeton, NJ: Princeton University Press, 2005), esp. 19–99.

4. Ibid., 70–71.

5. Quoted in William McBrien, *Cole Porter: A Biography* (New York: Alfred A. Knopf, 1998), 166.

6. Ibid., 25. Sadly, none of these songs survive. See Weiss, this volume.

7. McBrien, *Cole Porter*, 31.

8. See the description in Charles Schwartz, *Cole Porter* (New York: Dial Press, 1977), 23–26. See letters from the headmaster to Porter's mother in Weiss, this volume.

9. McBrien, *Cole Porter*, 50–51; Schwartz, *Cole Porter*, 34–35.

10. Schwartz, *Cole Porter*, 41–43.

11. Wanda M. Corn, "Identity, Modernism, and the American Artist after World War I: Gerald Murphy and Américanisme," *Studies in the History of Art* 29, Symposium Papers XIII: Nationalism in the Visual Arts (1991): 151.

12. McBrien, *Cole Porter*, 70–72; Schwartz, *Cole Porter*, 50–54. See Weiss, this volume, for more on Linda and her influence.

13. McBrien, *Cole Porter*, 70–72; Schwartz, *Cole Porter*, 54–55.

14. At her death, in fact, she would leave her husband nearly two million dollars. Schwartz, *Cole Porter*, 60.

15. Despite the brevity of Murphy's career (he stopped painting after a decade, devastated by the deaths of two of his children), he was a brilliant artist who was highly regarded by the Parisian art world; with his wife, Sara, he was a major figure in the Franco/Anglo scene of 1920s France.

16. The preceding account is condensed from McBrien, *Cole Porter*, 72–91. See Bolcom, Weiss, Van den Brande, and Morrison, this volume, for more on both ballets, premiered on the same evening at the same theater.

17. See Morrison's account in this volume.

18. Ann Douglas, *Terrible Honesty: Mongrel Manhattan in the 1920s* (New York: Farrar, Straus and Giroux, 1995), 3–4.

19. Mary E. Davis has pointed out how important these magazines were to the Parisian music scene in *Classic Chic: Music, Fashion, and Modernism* (Berkeley: University of California Press, 2006).

20. Three useful discussions of the *New Yorker*, in particular, are Earl Rovit, "Modernism and Three Magazines: An Editorial Revolution," *Sewanee Review* 93, no. 3 (Fall 1985): 540–53; Don Hausdorff, "Politics and Economics: The Emergence of a 'The New Yorker' Tone," in "The New Yorker from 1925 to 1950," special issue, *Studies in American Humor*, n.s. 2, 3, no. 2 (Spring 1984): 74–82; and Thomas Grant, "Mythologizing Manhattan: The New Yorker's New York," *American Studies* 28, no. 1 (Spring 1987): 31–46.

21. Schwartz, *Cole Porter*, 30.

22. David Savran identifies a distinctly queer moment in Porter's employment of lists in a meticulous close reading. See "'You've got that thing': Cole Porter, Stephen Sondheim, and the Erotics of the List Song," *Theatre Journal* 64, no. 4 (December 2012): 533–48.

23. The complexly intertwined biographies of these women are ably recounted in Alfred Allan Lewis, *Ladies and Not-So-Gentle Women* (New York: Viking, 2000).

24. See the marvelous account in Lisa Cohen, "Fantasia on a Theme by Mercedes de Acosta," in *All We Know* (New York: Farrar, Straus and Giroux, 2012), 149–94.

25. Excellent photographs of de Wolfe's innovations can be found in Nina Campbell and Caroline Seebohm, *Elsie de Wolfe: A Decorative Life* (New York: Panache Press, 1992).

26. Elsa Maxwell, from San Francisco's High Bohemian world, would have seemed unlikely to flourish in café society; plump, short, plain, and unquestionably "mannish," her passport to this world was an almost supernatural ability to play by ear, along with a substantial amount of wit. She established herself as a party thrower for aristocrats, giving about two large parties a week for over thirty years. See Sam Staggs, *Inventing Elsa Maxwell: How an Irrepressible Nobody Conquered High Society, Hollywood, the Press, and the World* (New York: St. Martin's Press, 2012).

27. See Davis, this volume.

28. "In a way no other songs of the period did, Porter's created a world. It was a between-the-wars realm of drop-dead chic and careless name-dropping insouciance. And it was a sexy place to be invited" (Walter Clemons, *Vanity Fair*, quoted on the back cover of Robert Kimball, *The Complete Lyrics of Cole Porter* [New York: Knopf, 1983; repr., New York: Da Capo Press, 1992]).

6

Which Comes First, the Music or the Lyrics?

"You're the Top"

ROB KAPILOW

In a breezy 1955 interview with *New York Times* reporter Gilbert Millstein, after some witty introductory chitchat about Porter's dogs, Pépin le Bref (a gift of Merle Oberon) and Berthe (a companion for Pépin purchased by Porter), Porter's refusal to go to opening night parties to wait for reviews (instead, he goes to sleep and has his valet, Paul, simply nod or shake his head the next morning when Porter wakes up), and his ability to write music anywhere, even while sitting between two bores at a dinner party, Porter suddenly stops the interview and says, "When are you going to ask me which comes first, the music or the lyrics?"

In the repertoire of interview clichés, this surely tops the list, and it is almost impossible to find an interview with any of the great songwriters from Kern to Sondheim that at some point doesn't get around to the question. The answers are, of course, as varied as the composers, and many, if not most, great songwriters have done both. Richard Rodgers, for example, nearly always wrote the music before Lorenz Hart's lyrics (largely because Hart hated to work, could rarely be found when a score had to be written, and needed the stimulus of a tune to get anything done) but after Oscar Hammerstein's. Porter's stock answer to the interviewer, repeated in many other places in almost identical words, was:

> First, I think of the idea and then I fit it to a title. Then, I go to work on the melody, spotting the title at certain moments in the melody, and then I write

> the lyric—the end first—that way, it has a strong finish. It's important for a song to have a strong finish. I do the lyrics like I'd do a crossword, I try to give myself a meter which will make the lyrics as easy as possible to write without being banal. On top of the meter, I try to pick for my rhyme words of which there is a long list with the same ending.[1]

Porter's writing style has been described in various ways. In an interview with Richard Hubler, Porter stated that he worked away from the piano, writing the words and music almost simultaneously. Robert Kimball claimed that "first he created the opening and finish of a song, then proceeded from both beginning and ending toward the middle."[2]

Though it can be entertaining and enlightening to read this kind of information about the creative process, in the end it makes absolutely no difference to the final product. In a great song, whether the words or the music was written first, it is the combination that counts. Though the words might or might not be satisfying on their own, and though the music might or might not be satisfying on its own, once the two elements join to make a song, the lyrics cease to have a purely literary meaning, and the music ceases to have a purely musical meaning. Both music and words become part of a new unit—a dyad—and cannot be fully understood independently. Porter's sophisticated lyrics, with their elaborate rhymes and imaginative imagery, are spectacular in and of themselves, but, as I will try to show in great detail in this essay, it is the way they combine with the music that makes them unforgettable, and there is no more perfect example of this than one of Porter's most famous songs, "You're the Top," from perhaps his most famous show, *Anything Goes* (ex. 1).

The verse that begins "You're the Top" is not only a perfect introduction to the song but also a perfect introduction to the art of Cole Porter and in particular to his rhythmic genius. The opening lyric is classic Porter with its quintessential highbrow/lowbrow juxtapositions. It begins not with normal, everyday English, "When I try to speak poetically," but with high-toned diction, "At words poetic," immediately followed by the lowbrow, "I'm so pathetic that I always have found it best." This initiates a virtuosic, erudite, quadruple rhyme filled with "slangy," colloquial contractions—"Instead of getting 'em off my chest, to let 'em rest, unexpressed." (Best, chest, rest, unexpressed!)

Though it seems like nothing could possibly ruin these fantastic words, if I simply alter Porter's rhythm and repeat a leaden, boring, quarter-quarter-eighth-eighth-quarter rhythm in every measure, the lyric's wit, energy, and humor completely vanish (ex. 2). In comparison, Porter's wonderful syncopation in measure 5 brings the lyric "At words poetic I'm" to life, and he could

EXAMPLE 1. "You're the Top" (from *Anything Goes*), mm. 1–20. Words and music by Cole Porter. Copyright © 1934 (renewed) WB Music Corp. All Rights Reserved. Used by permission of Alfred Music.

EXAMPLE 2. "You're the Top," mm. 5–8, recomposed.

easily have copied that rhythm in the next measure for "so pathetic I." But the extra eighth note for "that" causes the two eighth notes at the end of measure 6 (followed by four more eighth notes at the beginning of measure 7) to push forward to a kind of "mini punch line" to end the thought on "always have found it best," with four chords per measure in the accompaniment for the first time helping to drive to the word "best."

One of the things that makes Porter's elaborate wordplay so effective is the masterful way he allows his audience time to process his sophisticated lyrics. He could easily have finished this first musical unit and gone straight into the second one with three emphatic quarter notes, as in example 3. But instead, Porter holds "best" for two and a half beats (m. 8) to allow the comma in the thought and the whole first clause to register while also giving the audience a moment to wonder what the rest of the sentence will be. Always have found what "best"? (with the eighth notes on "instead of" pushing strongly into the next unit).

Simply writing a clever rhyme is one thing, but having it "land" has everything to do with how it is set musically. To set the verbal rhyme of "always have found it best" and "getting 'em off my chest," Porter creates a musical rhyme, taking the rhythm of "always have found it best" (mm. 7–8) and using the same rhythm and basic melodic shape for "getting 'em off my chest" (mm. 9–10).

Rhythm can beautifully set the meaning of an individual word as well. For the line "to let 'em rest," right on the word "rest" Porter has the music "rest" for four beats—the longest vocal note in the entire song. At the same time, the harmony gives an added meaning to the word. To show the unexpressed emotion that Billy refuses to reveal, there's a lovely dissonant F resolving to E♭ in the accompaniment under "rest." (A first inversion E♭ chord would have been perfectly sufficient.)

EXAMPLE 3. "You're the Top," mm. 6–8, recomposed.

The entire phrase has been leading up to a single word, "unexpressed"—the punch line, so to speak—and no one was a greater master of the punch line than Porter. Not only does the preceding word, "rest," wittily rhyme with "unexpressed," but its long note sets up and underlines "unexpressed" as well. Once again, though it might seem like the lyric in and of itself supplies all of the wit, it is how it is set musically that actually makes it funny, as two alternate versions that are clearly not funny demonstrate. My rhythmically plodding version of three quarter notes shown in example 4a is anything but funny. The syncopated version in example 4b is slightly funnier, but it is the dissonant B♮ in Porter's version, example 4c, that gets across the irritation of the unexpressed thoughts and combines with the rhyme and syncopation to make this the perfect, witty, Porteresque punch line.

A phrase like this one immediately creates a pattern and a set of expectations for the listener. As is so typical of Porter, he begins the next phrase as if to copy the first one. An exact copy would sound like example 5a, but on "miss a bar," instead of D–A–C, Porter leaps higher, E♭–C–D, and "misses the bar," that is, gets it wrong (mm. 15–16, ex. 5b).

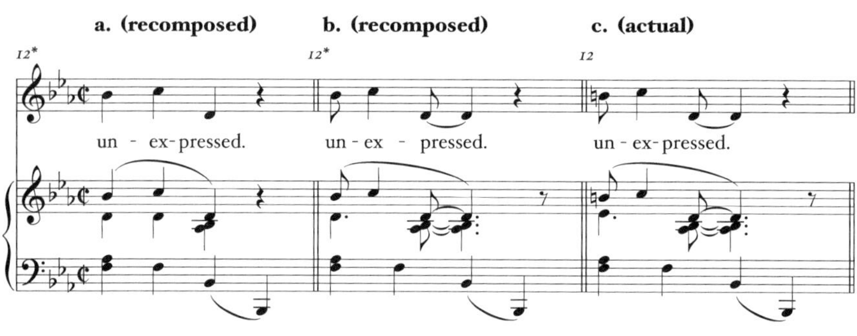

EXAMPLE 4. "You're the Top," m. 12, recomposed (a and b) and actual (c).

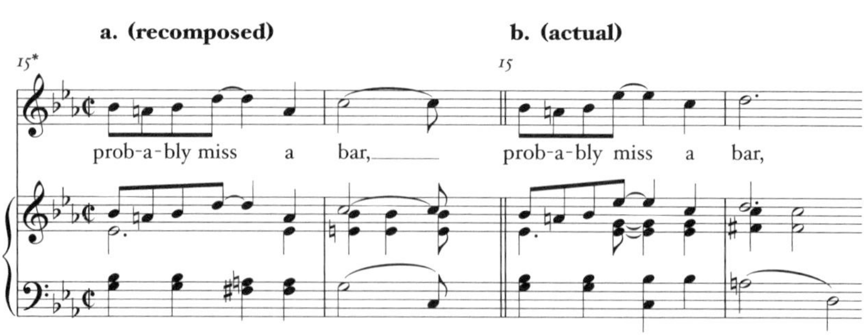

EXAMPLE 5. "You're the Top," mm. 15–16, recomposed (a) and actual (b).

"Missing the bar" moves the music dramatically out of the song's major key into minor, and once again the inextricability of music and lyrics is what makes Porter great. To end the verse, Porter gives us another typical, highbrow/lowbrow, witty, inner rhyme—"But if this *ditty* is not so *pretty*"—and to set the rhyme he uses the identical melody in both measures (mm. 17–18). He could easily have used the same harmony in both measures as well, but instead, Porter beautifully reharmonizes the melody—minor for "ditty," major for "pretty."

Finally, the introduction ends not with a straightforward, conventional, symmetrical, octave leap (B♭–B♭) on "great you are" but with a dissonant leap of a seventh instead (m. 20). In addition, though the little piano decoration of this figure seems to be a harmless connector to the chorus that follows, it will actually become crucial musical material for Porter to use later in the song.

According to a *New Yorker* writer, Margaret Harriman, "You're the Top" was composed in Paris "during a supper at Boeuf sur le Toit when Cole and Mrs. Alistair Mackintosh entertained themselves by making up a list of superlatives that rhymed. . . . Porter considered the song 'just a trick' and thought people would soon be bored by it."[3] Rather than being bored by it, people joined in, and "newspapers continued to report that the game around town in the winter of 1934–35 was writing new verses to 'You're the Top,' sometimes lewd ones."[4] Ethel Merman, for whom Cole wrote the song, said it "brought audiences to their feet because it was a new kind of love song. There had never been a song like it before. A complete original. So I wasn't surprised that at the peak of its popularity Cole received three hundred parodies a month."[5] And though we tend to think of the song primarily for its wit, it is in fact a new kind of love song.

Since so much of the greatness of any theater song depends on the opening idea of its chorus, let me build up this famous beginning from ordinary to great in four steps. Once again, the inseparability of music and lyrics, as well as Porter's superb use of rhythm, is beautifully illustrated by his setting of the song's title words, "You're the Top." My first version, example 6a, with a quarter note for each word of the lyric, is so dull and boring that it is almost the antithesis of the lyric. In this version, Reno is anything *but* the top. The version in example 6b, which syncopates just "the top," is slightly more interesting, but Porter's vocal line, example 6c, which syncopates "You're" as well, brings the lyric to life. The accompaniment, however, helps create the exuberance of this opening as much as the vocal line. All three of my versions had the piano simply leap squarely and symmetrically two octaves from B♭ to B♭. But Porter's version leaps a full step higher, to a C (ex. 7), and this exhilarating leap instantly creates the mood of the lyric before the singer has sung a syllable.

EXAMPLE 6. "You're the Top," mm. 21–22.

In terms of this essay's central premise, the piano's leap has no meaning without the lyric, and the lyric has no life without the rhythm of the vocal line and the piano accompaniment underneath. Words and music are inseparable. This one asymmetrical leap, in a sense, encapsulates the exuberant emotion of the entire song. The wonderful B♮ in Porter's chord underneath the word "You're" in measure 21 as opposed to the boring B♭ in my three versions contributes to the excitement as well. In addition, the little piano figure in measure 22 that follows the lyric sounds like a simple piano "fill," but it actually comes from the piano decoration in measure 20 at the end of the verse, followed by a witty reharmonization in measure 23 of the opening B♭–C leap of measure 21 to conclude the brief piano interlude.

Porter was a master at having his lyrics unfold at the perfect pace for the audience to follow. The one-and-a-half-measure piano interlude after "You're the top!" gives the listener time to get ready to hear the witty lyric that follows. To convey the gradual unfolding of the idea, Porter keeps the three notes of "You're the top!" as the core, making them the first three notes of "You're the Coliseum." Since in a popular song the plot must develop quickly, instead of repeating the melody, harmony, and piano "fill" of "You're the top!" when the words repeat, he does the phrase a third lower in minor and then stays in minor to set the rhyme, "You're the Louvr' Museum."[6]

The slow narrative pacing in the first eight measures of the chorus, with piano fills in between each vocal entry, allows Porter to increase the excitement in the next eight measures as the images start to come more and more quickly. Once again the core three-note figure that began the vocal line on "You're the top" (A♭–G–B♭) and was repeated a third lower (F–E♭–G) as the words repeated, kicks off the second half of the chorus still a third lower (D–C–E♭) as the first three notes of "You're a melody." The complete five-note idea is immediately sequenced higher on "from a symphony," but notice the beautiful suspensions

EXAMPLE 7. “You're the Top,” mm. 21–37.

in the accompaniment in measures 30 and 31 that give the "melody" from "Strauss' symphony" an elegant classical feel.

The punch line of the chorus, like the punch line of the verse, is again classic Porter. Building it up from ordinary to great in three steps shows Porter's effortless command of rhythm, harmony, and text setting and once again the utter inseparability of music and lyrics. Example 8a keeps Porter's pitches in the vocal line but flattens out the rhythm by eliminating all syncopations and repeats the harmony of the first measure in the second measure in the piano part. Though the highbrow lyrics are witty, "You're a Bendel bonnet [Ascot in the English version], / A Shakespeare sonnet," with my rhythm and harmony (ex. 8a) the effect is utterly banal. Example 8b improves the rhythm and the overall effect by adding syncopation, but the repetition of the melody and

EXAMPLE 8. "You're the Top," mm. 33–34, recomposed (a and b) and actual (c).

harmony in both measures makes the two images—the bonnet and the sonnet—indistinguishable. But example 8c, Porter's version, shifts from minor for the bonnet to major for the sonnet, and this reharmonization of the melody pushes the musical narrative forward, individuates the two images, and sets up the masterful punch line that ends the first half of the chorus.

The lyric of the punch line is again classic highbrow/lowbrow Porter. The two highbrow references—a Bendel bonnet and a Shakespeare sonnet—are followed by the quintessential "pop" culture reference: "You're Mickey Mouse." Though it seems like the lyric provides all the wit necessary, the punch of the punch line is completely dependent on Porter's musical setting. Rhythm and pitch combine superbly to make the line funny. My all-quarter-note version in example 9a, with a D on "Mick," falls completely flat. Keeping the quarter-note upbeat and the D but syncopating "Mickey Mouse," as in example 9b, is slightly wittier, but Porter's version, in example 9c, syncopates the upbeat as well and then, after all of those vocal Ds in measures 33 and 34, leaps to an F on "Mick"—the highest vocal note of the entire song—to punctuate emphatically the punch line. The voice has been carefully and steadily heading up to this high F since the low D that began the thought back in measure 29. Rhythm, harmony, melody, and lyrics all combine to make these eight bars one irresistible push to the punch line.

In terms of their overall form, theater songs of the twenties and thirties were usually divided up into either two or three parts. (A song like "Begin the Beguine" is a striking and wonderful exception.) Musically speaking, the standard AABA thirty-two-bar song form was a three-part form with a contrasting middle section, creating a journey fundamentally centered on "home–away–return." Equally common, however, were simpler two-part forms consisting of a single eight- or sixteen-bar idea done twice, frequently with slight changes the second time through to make a convincing ending. Because "You're the Top" is really a song about a single idea—a man and a woman taking turns complimenting each other with an endless witty array of superlatives (i.e., You're this, you're this, you're this)—contrasting music isn't the point, so when the second half of the chorus starts exactly like the first, we sit back and get ready to enjoy a new, over-the-top list of superlatives and expect the same music.

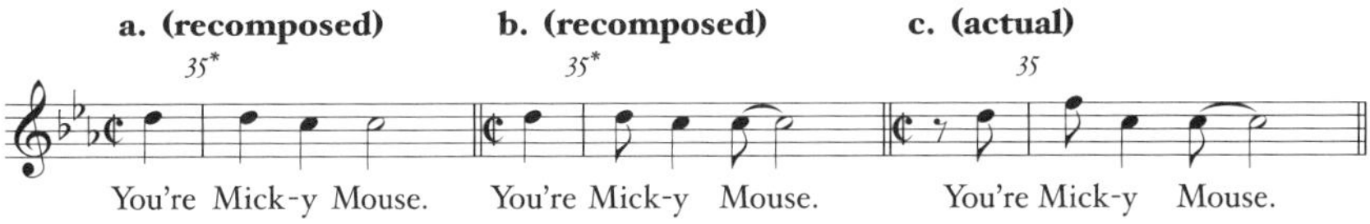

EXAMPLE 9. "You're the Top," m. 35, recomposed (a and b) and actual (c).

Porter begins to change the music harmonically in a subtle way on "of the *Mona Lisa*" (mm. 43–44) by essentially substituting E♭ dominant seventh chords for the earlier G dominant seventh chords. But the more dramatic musical changes begin precisely at the moment where the lyrics change. Up until this point, the entire chorus had been about Reno—about "*you*." "*You're* the top. *You're* the Coliseum, the Louvre Museum, a Bendel bonnet," and so on. Now the focus shifts from "*you*" to "*I*," and the imagery changes completely. Positives are replaced by negatives: "*I'm* a worthless cheque, a total wreck, a flop." Consequently, the rhythm, harmony, and vocal line are all altered, and the word "flop" that ends the clause arrives a full step higher (m. 48), with the accompaniment chord on beat 3 serving as a perfect exclamation point.

Having shifted the focus back to "I" from "you," Porter then invents a completely new, wonderfully self-deprecating, sublimely syncopated ending to finish the song: "But if Baby I'm the bottom, / You're the Top." The music perfectly encapsulates the meaning of the text here as the final "You're the top" is sung on a high E♭ at the top of the range of both the singer and the song. It literally is "the top." Though the vocal line is finished, in classic Porter fashion the wit continues till the final instrumental note, as he takes the opening piano fill of measure 22 and reharmonizes it two octaves higher in measure 51. Then, instead of simply resolving and ending dully on the beat, as in example 10a, Porter, in example 10b, delays the final E♭ resolution until the last instant—the song's final note.

Coda

Porter often quoted his teacher and the headmaster at the Worcester Academy, Dr. Abercrombie, who said, "Words and music must be so inseparably wedded to each other that they are like one," and I am not proposing anything radically new by focusing on their inseparability. Yet perhaps because of the brilliance of Porter's lyrics, there has at times been an undervaluing of his music or, more

EXAMPLE 10. "You're the Top," mm. 51–52, recomposed (a) and actual (b).

accurately, an incomplete appreciation of the way even his most dazzling lyrics are dependent on his music to create their effect. A song like "You're the Top" is justly famous for its seemingly endless outpouring of sophisticated, witty lyrics, yet as I have tried to show through the many intentionally weak, alternate versions I have composed for this essay, it is Porter's equally sophisticated harmonic, melodic, and rhythmic genius that brings these lyrics to life.

Though "You're the Top" was a highlight not only of the original 1934 Broadway production of *Anything Goes* but of every subsequent revival, the song's placement in the show continually shifted. As was common in Porter's shows, not only were songs frequently moved around within a show, but songs from other shows were frequently interpolated as well, and the 1962 revival of *Anything Goes*, for example, incorporated "Take Me Back to Manhattan" from *The New Yorkers*, "It's De-Lovely" from *Red Hot and Blue*, "Friendship" from *Du Barry Was a Lady,* and "Let's Misbehave" from *Paris*. This ability to move songs freely from scene to scene and show to show goes to the heart of an important aspect of Porter's music that is important to touch upon even in an essay focused on a close analytical reading of a single song.

In the post-*Oklahoma* world of musical theater, songs were designed to grow meaningfully out of their plots and to comment on those plots and the characters they contained. The great Porter shows of the 1920s and 1930s, however, were really song-and-dance shows, not integrated book musicals. Porter's songs grew not so much out of a show's individual plot situations but rather out of life's universal plot situations. His songs treat our most powerful emotions with sophistication, grace, and wit and transport us to a world where everyone is perfectly dressed, has impeccable manners, and speaks in perfect rhymed couplets. The often silly, frequently convoluted plots of many of Porter's shows may no longer seem topical or relevant to us today, but as long as there is love, loss, yearning, and regret—and there will always be love, loss, yearning, and regret—there will always be Porter.

Notes

1. 1955 interview with *New York Times* reporter Gilbert Millstein.

2. See Richard Hubler, *The Cole Porter Story, as Told to Richard G. Hubler* (Cleveland: World Publishing Company, 1965), 39, and Robert Kimball, ed., *Cole Porter: Selected Lyrics* (New York: The Library of America, 2006), xvi.

3. William McBrien, *Cole Porter: A Biography* (New York: Alfred A. Knopf, 1998), 169.

4. Ibid., 170.

5. Ibid., 171.

6. Notice how Porter refuses to resolve the G dominant in measure 28 to C minor so that the deceptive resolution to A♭ in measure 29 makes the subdominant sound fresh.

7

"I Hate Parading My Serenading"

The Historical Record of Porter as a Performer

ERIC DAVIS

In 1969, after evaluating, organizing, and creating an inventory for the Cole Porter Collection at Yale, Robert Kimball reported his findings in the *Yale University Library Gazette*.[1] Porter's generous bequest to his alma mater, which has significantly eased the challenges of researchers and biographers, is a treasure trove of photos, scrapbooks, memorabilia, journals, manuscripts, librettos, music and lyric notebooks, published and unpublished scores, and extensive collections of rare books and recordings. His record collection was both large and significant, containing the most comprehensive gathering of recorded interpretations of his own music to be found in one place, including many of the recordings Porter made of his own performances. Referring specifically to the commercial recordings for Victor Porter made in 1934 and 1935, Kimball wrote that "they provide valuable insights into some of the qualities which he wished emphasized in the performance of his songs."[2] Apart from their historical value as documents of the composer's playing, these records indeed give us a sense of the style Porter was familiar with when he wrote his songs and yield an abundance of information about the interpretive freedoms and constraints he preferred.

Cole Porter's ability as a performer is known to most people today through a combination of primary and secondary sources.[3] In addition to many anecdotal references in books, there are several newspaper articles, a radio transcription, eight commercial sides, and three sets of demo recordings from *Jubilee*, *Can-Can*, and *Adios, Argentina*. Together these reveal aspects of Porter's ability to interpret his own music from several perspectives, some objective, others strictly a matter of personal opinion. The sum of these parts gives the impression of an entertainer who, in his prime, was capable of conveying the full measure of wit, elegance, passion, and sophistication expressed in so many of his songs. If some firsthand accounts are less than complimentary, others offer genuine praise that is corroborated by the mature artistry reflected in the commercial recordings. After surveying published reports and eyewitness accounts of Porter's abilities, I will evaluate his performing style through close analysis of some of the records. In addition, I will compare aspects of his performances with those of some of his favorite singers in order to identify shared stylistic elements, as well as ways in which Porter's interpretations were unique. Though it will be impossible to appreciate the full measure of Porter's art (or, for that matter, to know his limitations fully) from the scant historical evidence that documented his performing, we certainly have more to work with than is the case with Irving Berlin, Jerome Kern, Vincent Youmans, and Richard Rodgers. The recordings not only make it possible to reconcile Porter's reputation as a performer with the evidence he left behind but also give us a rare opportunity to gain some insight into the interpretive qualities Porter was accustomed to and was able to bring out in the performance of his music.

Opinions may differ about Cole Porter's musical abilities, but one thing can be said with certainty about him: for the better part of his life, he was constantly at the piano playing his own songs. For him, the piano was central to work and play, both of which he took seriously and engaged in with uncommon vigor and intensity. Throughout his life, he performed with regularity for his friends and acquaintances, who were often people of great distinction in the arts and society. And yet for all of Porter's willingness to play for people in intimate settings, his public performances were infrequent and mostly took place during his college years at Yale.

His commercial recordings—all made over a three-month period between October 1934 and January 1935—represent another public activity as a musician and provide an invaluable window into his interpretive abilities at the height of his powers.[4] They display Porter as a polished, confident performer with enough technique at the piano to support his refined musical sensibility and great rhythmic energy. The success of Porter's recordings in conjunction with the triumph on Broadway of *Anything Goes* led to his only appearance as a performer on radio in late 1934. The upward trajectory of his career during the years just before his debilitating riding accident in 1937 likely would have given him greater opportunities to perform in public as time went on.

No doubt much of his diffidence about playing in public in later years can be attributed to his physical condition following the accident and the multiple surgeries he endured in order to preserve his legs. Considering all the evidence, though, it is hard to avoid the conclusion that, even before the accident, he was a modest, even shy, performer even within the friendlier confines of his home and other private locations where he demonstrated his music and entertained. The amusing irony of the confession "I hate parading my serenading" is that in fact he really did like performing, but mostly when the company was intimate (at least as intimate as an Elsa Maxwell party could be), and his gesture of feigning reluctance was appreciated in its fullest sense. Had he had the drive or the financial need to play music in public for a living, early accounts of his mastery suggest that a career as a performer was his for the taking. But Cole Porter's life in Europe among the social and artistic elite ensured that his talents were not cut out for vaudeville or Tin Pan Alley, as they were for so many aspiring songwriters in the 1920s. Instead, as he lingered in Europe, he cultivated a sophisticated style of songwriting and performance more suited to the aristocratic salons of Paris and Venice than the publishers' and producers' offices of Manhattan; and he maintained this style throughout his life, even after Broadway developed a taste for Cole Porter and his career took off.

While Porter sought musical training at Harvard and the Schola Cantorum in Paris, much of his instrumental skill as a performer of popular songs seems to have been acquired as an autodidact. He was proficient enough at reading nonetheless to play two-piano music with Dr. Albert Sirmay and Alexander Steinert, both of whom were outstanding musicians. Sirmay was a Hungarian composer of many operettas, musical comedies, and musical plays who worked for years at the Chappell music publishing house as an arranger and editor.[5] At different times he worked with Jerome Kern, George Gershwin, Richard Rodgers, and other songwriters to assist them in scoring their music for publication, as he did for Porter throughout most of his career. Longtime Porter friend Ray Kelly recalled that "at the Waldorf, Cole had two grands back to back and he and Sirmay would play like crazy—Cole Porter tunes."[6] Steinert, a conductor who was on the original production team of *Porgy and Bess*, was a musical associate and friend of Porter's who worked on several of his projects beginning in the late 1940s. The conductor had first known Cole

Porter when they studied at the Schola Cantorum, but they had since taken very different paths. Patricia Morison recalled Steinert and Porter playing classical music together at the composer's Brentwood home around the time she was auditioning for *Kiss Me, Kate*.[7] Later, when describing their two-piano sessions, Steinert confirmed that Porter's musical predilections tended toward late Baroque and Classical styles: "After that we did a considerable amount of playing. I was fascinated because Cole's taste ran true to form. He liked any music that was stylized or classical. He didn't go in for the heavy romantic music. It would be Scarlatti, it would be Haydn, a couple of things of Bach's. And he would get so excited about it."[8] Porter's skills as a duo pianist are amply in evidence on the 1935 demos he made for *Adios, Argentina*, where he performed with Victor Piemonte on most of the twelve recordings that were produced for Fox at Brunswick Studios.[9]

Some insight into the limits of Porter's musicianship comes from Benay Venuta, who recalled that Porter could not transpose his songs from *Anything Goes* down a whole tone at sight when preparing her to take over for Ethel Merman.[10] On the assumption that he had already worked out the accompaniments from lead sheets created for Merman, it seems entirely plausible that Venuta's request for a lower key left him with no other recourse than to have the rehearsal pianist, Lew Kessler, step in. Porter certainly had his own preferred keys for the songs (e.g., "You're the Top," E-flat; "Anything Goes," B-flat), and these were likely the ones that he memorized and had comfortably in his hands. Transposing, however, was simply not a skill he needed to acquire to develop his songwriting craft.

Some of the great song composers—notably Jerome Kern, George Gershwin, and Vincent Youmans—came from the ranks of rehearsal pianists and learned to transpose while working in publishing houses and for Broadway producers in their youth. Porter's wealth allowed him to live in Europe free of the need to work his way up on Broadway, as so many other aspiring songwriters had done. At the same time, the division of labor on Broadway and in Hollywood allowed songwriters to focus on their craft, which was time-consuming in itself. They were rarely required to play for the cast, as, say, Marc Blitzstein needed to when preparing *The Cradle Will Rock*, produced by the WPA in 1936. Nonetheless, Porter would sometimes make an appearance at the beginning of rehearsals to introduce his songs to the chorus. Miriam Nelson, who appeared in two Cole Porter shows in the 1940s, recalled that "he would come and demonstrate [the songs] for us so we would hear them and then the rehearsal pianist would take over."[11] One such demonstration was captured in a photo session during rehearsals for *Panama Hattie*, where we see him playing for chorus members Vera Ellen, Renee Russell, and others.[12] Given the heavy responsibility of songwriters to the success of any show, most composers were simply not expected to possess any more musical skill than was required to create a good score.

Specific accounts of Porter entertaining or demonstrating his music at the piano paint an uneven portrait. Much of the criticism seems to concentrate on his piano playing, which was never virtuosic and thus did not always impress. Jazz and stride piano styles that emerged in the wake of the ragtime era were a staple accompaniment for popular songs in the 1920s and 1930s, particularly those conceived with a strong dance rhythm. Elisabeth Welch, who played the role of an odalisque in Porter's *Nymph Errant*, was evidently comparing Porter disparagingly to the great pianists she knew from her work in black musicals during the 1920s when she said that, as a pianist, "he had a terrible left hand."[13] This comment is reminiscent of Ethel Waters's complaint about Fletcher Henderson's lack of rhythmic drive when she first met him in 1922, counseling him to study the piano rolls of James P. Johnson.[14] It is not surprising that Welch, who was accustomed to working with pianists who had a well-developed ragtime or stride bass in their technique, perceived Cole Porter's lighter approach to rhythm to be a weakness in his playing. Acknowledging the typical role of the left hand in rendering early American popular music at the piano, a journalist for *Vanity Fair* gave a perceptive illustration of Porter's pianism in a 1931 portrait, noting that "in playing the piano he uses his left hand little—though with great effect."[15]

Some of the finest songwriters were indeed brilliant pianists, and their music is often imbued with their instrumental skill. Virtuosity, however, was certainly not a prerequisite of success among composers. Noël Coward made a comparative assessment of his own skill at the piano alongside that of his songwriter colleagues:

> I can firmly but not boastfully claim that I am a better pianist than Irving Berlin, but as that superlative genius of light music is well known not to be able to play at all except in C major, I will not press the point.[16] Jerome D. Kern, to my mind one of the most inspired romantic composers of all, played woodenly as a rule and without much mobility. Dick Rodgers plays his own music best when he is accompanying himself or someone else, but he is far from outstanding. Vincent Youmans was a marvelous pianist, almost as brilliant as Gershwin, but these are the only two I can think of who, apart from their creative talent, could really play.[17]

Porter is notably absent in this general appraisal. Did Coward, whom Porter met in the mid-1920s in Venice and who knew him well, neglect to mention his friend in this candid, at times withering, description out of consideration? Porter certainly would not have been out of place among these songwriting luminaries, and one suspects that his playing would not have escaped Coward's unforgiving critique either. Nonetheless, his derogatory view of the pianism of his American colleagues is myopic. Comparing the playing of every songwriter to George Gershwin presents a distorted perception of their comparative musical skills by viewing the unique talents of these men through the narrow lens of virtuosity. Like comparisons with Shakespeare or Babe Ruth, this way of thinking ignores all aesthetic values but those that extol the virtues of the supreme master, making disparaging critiques on the rest of the field a convenient act of simple logic.

Porter enjoyed spending time at the piano with other songwriters. When George Gershwin visited Paris in 1928, he spent a long evening with Porter playing music together for hours.[18] Noël Coward was present when Porter met Richard Rodgers for the first time. The three composers played for one another, and the impression Porter made upon his American counterpart was strong enough to warrant a significant passage in Rodgers's memoirs. Rodgers was surprised in part due to the expectation that Porter's craft was limited by his wealth, since songwriting seemed to be merely a hobby for the rich American socialite living in Venice. By the time they met in 1926, Rodgers had worked on Broadway for six years, at first with little success, finally breaking in with his scores for the *Garrick Gaieties* and *Dearest Enemy*. He had confronted his share of doubt and hardship in the uncertain and competitive field of songwriting already and was therefore naturally predisposed to expect little in the way of craftsmanship from someone who enjoyed what he termed an "indolent" lifestyle on the Lido. His skepticism, however, seems to have been totally disarmed by Porter's music that evening: "As soon as he touched the piano to play 'a few of my little things,' I became aware that he was not merely a talented dilettante, but a generally gifted theater composer and lyricist."[19] What came as a surprise to Rodgers was well known to Porter's friends, since his art up to that time, which had been aesthetically and formally mature for years, was primarily expressed by entertaining at the piano at home and at parties. During the years when he was not composing for theatrical productions, he was the primary interpreter to convey the literate humor and elegant emotional appeal of his songs. The immediacy of Rodgers's response likely had as much to do with Porter's singing and playing as it did with his songwriting.

Some recollections of Porter's song demonstrations have been scathing, suggesting that he was not always able to show his music off in its best light. Bert Lahr played the roles of Louis Blore and Louis XV in *Du Barry Was a Lady* and recalled that he didn't like the score as he first heard it from Porter. He understood later that the problem was not the songs but rather Porter's rendition of them, giving this unvarnished assessment, as reported by his son, author and historian John Lahr: "Cole was a horrible piano player. Oompah, oompah. He played with a slow, wooden tempo. If you didn't know who it was, you'd have thought he was a learner."[20] In the same passage, the younger Lahr implies that Porter's infirmity might have accounted for his father's harsh, unforgiving response. In describing the comedic masterpiece "But in the Morning, No," the younger Lahr conjures the scene of Porter's dithyrambic exploits in Europe during the 1920s: "The song, with at least ten refrains, reached the epitome of stage ribaldry in this stanza, matched only by Porter's private performances in his early days at the Palazzo Rezzonico in Venice." Here he acknowledges that Porter's reputation as an excellent songwriter and performer went hand in hand during the period before his songs were routinely written and contracted for commercial productions. Thus, if we are to give the elder Lahr's assessment any credence whatsoever (his critique of Jerome Kern's playing is equally devastating), clearly Porter had lost his touch by the time he wrote the score for *Du Barry Was a Lady* in 1939. Or perhaps he was having a bad day, which was not uncommon after his injury. For his playing on the commercial recordings, made nearly ten years after Porter occupied the Palazzo Rezzonico in Venice, is anything but "slow" and "wooden." In fact, his careful manipulation of the tempo on several tracks reveals a tremendous flexibility of rhythm that he uses to enhance changes in dynamics and elucidate the lyrics. And the tempo he takes on "You're the Top" is brisk, faster than Ethel Merman's recording with Johnny Green and His Orchestra (Liberty Music Shop L-261).

Another Porter colleague, Arthur Schwartz, who was the producer of the Warner Bros. biopic *Night and Day*, was similarly disenchanted by Porter's music making. In a memo to Jack Warner listing suggestions to improve the movie's prospects, Schwartz writes of the need to relieve the audience of "the terrible monotony of Cole Porter singing and playing at the piano."[21] Schwartz's jaundiced view of Porter as a performer corroborates that of Bert Lahr and may have been the result of hearing him play at parties in the 1940s. After all, Schwartz himself was a superb pianist, and so it would not be unreasonable simply to take his opinion at face value. At the same time, his note could also have been a way to urge Warner not to press Cary Grant to attempt a portrayal of Porter singing at the piano without casting aspersions on Warner's star.[22]

Despite his naturally aristocratic demeanor, Porter maintained an unassuming, almost uncertain attitude about his work throughout his career. His modesty was as disarming as it was genuine to those who met him, given the extraordinary quality of his work. In a 1960 interview with Miles Kreuger for the radio program *Opening Night* on WBAI-FM, Jessie Matthews remembered Porter being astonished when she and her husband, Sonnie Hale, expressed their approval of Porter's music during rehearsals for *Wake Up and Dream* in 1929: "Sonnie and I went to the Savoy Hotel with Charles B. Cochran to meet Cole, and I remember him playing 'What Is This Thing Called Love?,' and Sonnie and I stood absolutely transfixed at this wonderful, wonderful tune. And Cole Porter turned and looked as if he couldn't believe we thought the music was so wonderful. I can only say that I was completely spellbound, and when he turned round and said, 'You really like it?,' as if he couldn't believe that we thought it was wonderful."[23] Miles Kreuger himself recalled meeting Porter for the first time in 1955 and being struck by his ingenuousness. Kreuger had arranged a meeting at the Waldorf Towers with Porter's secretary and was greeted in the living room by the composer.

> In a rather unattractive, high-pitched, flat, midwestern, Indiana voice, he said nothing like, "Hello, how are you?" He said, "Paul Cunningham [from ASCAP] says you like my songs." And he started walking slowly and tremulously to the piano and eventually sat down. And I said, "Yes." And he said, "What's your favorite?" And I said, "Gosh, I don't know that I have one favorite, but when I walk along the street, I find that, more than any other, I whistle 'Farming.'" And he did an Edward Everett Horton double take. And he said, "'Farming'! Nobody knows 'Farming.'" And I said, "Well, I know it." And he said, "Show me." And he started to play "Farming."[24]

The person who greeted this twenty-one-year-old aspiring theater historian in his living room was the same man whose music over the last several years had attracted thousands to events at the Hollywood Bowl and Grant Park in Chicago.[25] Porter's modesty, though seemingly disproportionate to his fame, enabled him to take delight in the admiration of someone who was born the year *Anything Goes* opened on Broadway. His lack of egotism was partly an authentic facet of his personality, and yet it may also have been fostered by years of work in a field where success can be fleeting and is often measured by your most recent hits and flops.

Songwriting for theater and film, particularly for those of Porter's caliber, was a multifaceted profession. Part artist, part dramatist, part salesman, part star, the songwriter on Broadway or in Hollywood had to be both versatile and charismatic to succeed in the years before television became a dominant force in entertainment. Name recognition among composers and lyricists was as important to the success of a production as it was among the principal actors. When M-G-M was promoting *Born to Dance*, the trailer announced "7 Big Song 'Hits' by America's No. 1 Song Composer." Besides the names of the actors, Cole Porter's was the only name the studio used to promote the movie. Coming off two consecutive hits on Broadway, by 1936 he had clearly become an audience draw nationwide. The craft of songwriting for stage and screen also generally involved some degree of integration within the dramatic situation, even in shows with the flimsiest of plots. These aspects of the songwriter's trade went hand in hand with the uncanny gift of transforming notes, harmony, rhythm, and words into memorable songs that could then become hits. Then, once a song was written, selling one's material to producers and leading players was necessary in order for the work to succeed. If the songwriter was not able to convey the potential of the song to win over an audience on a first impression to producers and directors (men who usually had little understanding of the mechanics of music), it generally would not make it into the production. Cole Porter's experience playing and singing his own songs in college productions and at parties in Europe equipped him well for this part of the job.

Porter kept a detailed diary over a period of six months (from 20 December 1935 to 9 June 1936) during the creative development of the film *Born to Dance*.[26] Numerous installments describe how he demonstrated his score for various members of M-G-M's production team as the film took shape and the reactions they gave. His rendition of the old-fashioned waltz "Hey, Babe, Hey!" on 19 March was considered by him "a thundering success." His performance of the rhythm number "Rap Tap on Wood" on 30 March was so well received that producer Sam Katz wanted to sign Porter to a contract for the following year. When on 14 April Porter played a trunk song for producers Sam Katz, Jack Cummings, and Max Gordon, writers Jack MacGowan and Sid Silvers, and dance director Seymour Felix that he had "resurrected" ("Easy to Love"), the reaction was immediate and overwhelming: "They all grabbed the lyric and began singing it, and even called in the stenographers to hear it, their enthusiasm was so great." When Porter played the entire score written up to 22 April for director Roy Del Ruth, he observed that though he is "supposed to be a very taciturn person, [he] was most enthusiastic and told us he thought we had a great picture." When Porter invited the entire music staff that was to work on the picture to his house on 19 May, served them drinks, and played them the score, "they left saying it was the greatest thing they had heard in years."[27] And when on 20 May he played the finale "Swingin' the Jinx Away," "it went with a bang." Only once did Porter meet with disappointment, when he played the song "Who but You," which was not used in the film. He wrote that "even as I was playing, they walked away from the piano and looked out the window, and at the finish of it they told me it was absolutely no good." There is likely no amount of musical skill that could have successfully pitched a bad song. But Porter's ability to convey the spirit and entertainment value of his songs for the film—some of them among his very best—is evident in the enthusiasm of most of his listeners' reactions.

The climax of the preproduction period came for Porter on 3 June, when he performed the entire score for studio bosses Irving Thalberg and Louis B. Mayer. It was a high-stakes showcase that took place at Mayer's office and filled Porter with such "dread" that he braced himself with a "stiff whiskey and soda" beforehand. In attendance were Sam Katz, Jack Cummings, Roger Edens, Sid Silvers, Eleanor Powell, Virginia Bruce, and Mayer's secretary, in addition to Mayer and Thalberg. The room must have been tense with anticipation, as there was already a lot of time and money invested in the picture. Within a short time, though, the audition went in Porter's favor.

> I passed out the lyric books and began. By the time "Rollin' Home" was over, I realized that the atmosphere was friendly. When I finished "Hey, Babe, Hey!" there was wild applause and L. B. began jumping around the room whispering to people. I attacked "Entrance of Lucy James" next, and it was during this that Thalberg suddenly became a different person and began smiling. Then the door opened and in walked Eddie Mannix (general manager of M-G-M) and L. B. said, "Cole, you've got to repeat 'Hey, Babe, Hey!' for Eddie," which I did, and they all sang it. From then on it was clear sailing and the moment I finished the finale, Thalberg leaped out of his seat, rushed over to me, grabbed my hand and said, "I want to congratulate you for a magnificent job; I think it is one of the finest scores I have ever heard."[28]

It is impossible to imagine this scene concluding as well as it did without Porter captivating everyone in attendance. Despite the intimidating audience he faced, he won them over by drawing on long experience playing for Broadway producers, not to mention his many friends among the songwriters, the smart set in New York, the expatriate social elite in Europe, going all the way back to his youthful exploits as the star of his college musicals at Yale.

Porter's fraternity—Delta Kappa Epsilon—and the Yale University Dramatic Association gave him an ideal training ground to develop his theater songwriting acumen. Not to be overlooked, though, during his sensational three-year tenure as Yale's resident composer of light music—where he composed at least eighty-eight distinct numbers for six musical shows—was the sudden maturation of his genius for delivering sophisticated comedy songs at the piano.[29] Newspaper reviews from a Yale Glee Club tour in the winter of 1912–13 provide a window into Porter's command of the stage during these concerts. His "singing pianologue act" received a rave notice from a Richmond, Indiana, newspaper that reflects a blossoming showmanship: "He is a born comedian. . . . [P]lays the piano very well and writes most of his own 'stuff,' which is unusually clever. . . . [H]e was made to sing six encores, all of them except one, presumably his own. . . . Indeed we rarely have a man in our vaudeville houses as good as this Yale junior."[30] Similarly, a Cincinnati, Ohio, reviewer reported that "when the audience had him there it wouldn't let him go until his stock of 10 or 12 encores was exhausted."[31] Another reviewer suggests that "he could make his fortune on the vaudeville stage, for his specialty consists of a running commentary on people and things while singing topical songs to his own accompaniment or giving imitations."[32] These accomplishments were also noted in the *New York Times*, where it was mentioned that Porter, "whose original ditties have made him well-known throughout the many cities where he has sung them in the last three years, was especially well received and forced to give encore after encore."[33] The reliability of these accounts lies in the fact that they are not reviews that reflect one person's opinion but rather news items that present the accomplishments of the Yale tour as facts. Lacking a description of Porter's playing, they nonetheless tell us clearly that his performances were not merely well received but show-stopping tours de force that had left audiences begging for more.

Anyone garnering this sort of response at a public performance at the age of twenty-one must have had a special gift to communicate with an audience, something that goes well beyond technical skill or even artistry. This evidence of Porter's early prowess as a performer calls to mind the comments Alan Jay Lerner made about him in a 1967 tribute at the University of Southern California: "He seemed to spring from nowhere. When the musical theater started in this country about 1919 or 1920, when Jerome Kern led the break from European operetta, you could follow a sort of progression from Jerome Kern to Dick Rodgers to Gershwin (of course, at the same time) down the line. But Cole seemed to spring like Jupiter from Minerva's head or something, all made. And what he did was so special and so unaccountable and so unexplainable that he is really of all, in a strange way, the most irreplaceable."[34] Lerner was undoubtedly referring to Cole Porter as a songwriter. But when considering this appraisal in light of the early reviews of Porter's performances, it is difficult to separate songwriting from song performance during his years at Yale or thereafter, for that matter. The same is true when we consider his work in Europe during his long apprenticeship to the professional theater.

The act of singing and accompanying oneself in original topical comedy songs in verse was, if not invented by Porter, perfected and lifted to the status of a high art by him at a remarkably early age. Porter's ability to combine the literary, musical, and comedic facets of popular song into the artistic expression of one performer was unique up to that time in the history of American popular arts and letters. Irving Berlin wrote both music and lyrics, but he almost always used an accompanist when he sang in public, as did Noël Coward.[35] Well into the mid-twentieth century, very few songwriters combined the allied arts of composing, lyric writing, singing, and playing the way that Porter did. Harold Arlen was a masterful performer of his own music, singing and playing at the piano, but he didn't write lyrics. Johnny Mercer was a fine singer who was equally prolific at creating sophisticated strophic poetry in song (and even occasionally wrote his own music), but he didn't play the piano. Frank Loesser was certainly an artist who amalgamated these skills, but his songwriting career as a composer only began in earnest during World War II. Comedy singer Tom Lehrer was equally adept as a songwriter and performer and should be counted in this specialized field, but again, he didn't begin performing at Harvard until the 1950s. When Bob Dylan came along in the 1960s, he also embodied all these diverse elements, albeit from a completely different realm of the American musical landscape.

The recordings Cole Porter made during 1934 and 1935, when he was at the zenith of his powers as a performer, confirm the impression left behind in the early anecdotal record of the composer as a gifted interpreter of his own music. The eight songs Porter recorded for RCA Victor over a three-month period beginning in October 1934 represent the pinnacle of his abilities as captured for posterity and thus provide far and away the best opportunity for us to appreciate and evaluate his artistry. They reveal Porter as a master of the form he invented—singer-pianist-songwriter—and prove that he could have made a career as a performer had he had the desire. His phrasing is elegant and sophisticated, articulated seamlessly with the ebb and flow of every lyric; his rhythm can be driving and infectious and at other times be deliciously gracious and limpid; his tempos in dance rhythm are solid and full of energy, though fluid and highly controlled in the slow passages and verses, fluctuating sometimes measure by measure as he navigates each turn of phrase. The selections he recorded may not all be the best-known or best-loved Porter songs, but they gave the composer perhaps the best chance to reveal his unique talents as an entertainer.

The private recordings are enlightening as well but reflect a different side of Porter's art. Here we can observe the composer in more casual, though certainly workmanlike, form demonstrating his songs for the purpose of conveying their basic outline for the production team. Not only is the quality of the performances less polished and even a little rough at times, but the songs themselves, including several ensemble numbers, are not consistently the type of material that was meant for public consumption in the format we hear. Accompaniments are less refined, and arrangements are usually brief or truncated, often featuring only a single chorus. Sometimes Porter simply interrupts himself, as in "Ev'rybodee Who's Anybodee" from the *Jubilee* demos, when he ends the instrumental solo abruptly saying "etcetera" and in "Montmart'" from *Can-Can*, when he simply stops to adjust the microphone and then continues. These blemishes are revelatory, though. Along with the many insights the recordings provide about the composer's skill set and interpretive intentions, the demos with all their imperfections offer anybody interested in the mid-twentieth-century songwriter's craft a view through the keyhole into the master's musical workshop. A significant anomaly presented by the demos is the gap of eighteen years between those made for *Jubilee* in the summer of 1935 and the set made for *Can-Can* in 1953. There is no evidence indicating the reason why Porter made private recordings for these shows but not for the twelve musical shows and five movies for which he contributed scores in the interim. Still, they yield much information as to how Porter wanted his music performed, though perhaps to a lesser degree than the commercial records due to their somewhat unrehearsed presentation and carefree delivery.

The demonstration discs Porter had produced of the six songs he wrote for the proposed Fox film *Adios, Argentina* were made at the Brunswick Studios in New York City sometime during the first week of January 1935. Each song was given at least two treatments, some as many as four in various arrangements for baritone Edward Nell, "The Foursome" Quartet (which appeared in *Anything Goes*), pianist Victor Piemonte, and the composer, who often played a second piano part. The twelve individual recordings are well produced and show Porter presiding over multiple studio sessions that required a high degree of organization in rehearsal and virtuoso execution.

Two weeks earlier, on 13 December 1934, he had made his first and only appearance as a performer on radio, headlining a bill on *Fleischmann's Yeast Hour* that Rudy Vallee claimed "comes closer to meeting our ideal requirements than any group we've brought together on this stage in recent months."[36] The program included Bea Lillie, Shirley Temple, Buck and Bubbles, William S. Hart, June Walker, and Henry Fonda along with Cole Porter, "the man of the hour in the songwriting world singing the song everyone is talking about, 'You're the Top' from *Anything Goes*, the biggest musical comedy hit of the year." The performance begins with Porter accompanying himself at the piano, but then he stops playing after the verse and goes on to sing four choruses with the studio orchestra. His singing is spirited and reflects the rhythmic freedom that came as a result of performing for a live audience without needing to accompany himself.

Cole Porter made enough recordings of various kinds to enable us to identify certain general traits in his performance style. The one constant that emerges from them all is his clear, impeccable diction. Intoning his lyrics with meticulous articulation so that each word could be clearly understood was his primary aim when singing. This was, after all, the same man who some remember would sit in rehearsals with a whistle and blow it every time he could not hear a lyric.[37] Careful attention to the proper weight of each syllable gives his delivery a speechlike quality, not natural speech but "heightened speech" in the Brechtian sense.[38] His pitches often wander intentionally in and out of the tune in the tradition of many of the finest singing comedians of the American stage, from Bert Williams to Robert Preston. When in his rendition of "The Physician" Porter intones the line "When I'd gaze up and see him there above me, looking less like a doctor than a Turk," the words are carried on indeterminate pitches unrelated to the melody (or harmony, for that matter) except in rhythm until the last three syllables. His clear elocution is evident in each tongue-twisting phrase—"He went thro' wild ecstatics when I show'd him my lymphatics" and "I know he thought a lotta my medulla oblongata"—as the cascading chromatics slip downward on the piano. Porter may have thought that the humor that comes in the iteration of each exotic medical name of the character's physiology is heightened when spoken over the accompaniment and thus only the last time gives a strict reading of the melodic line. Curiously, *Nymph Errant* star Gertrude Lawrence also speaks her way through the aforementioned line "when I'd gaze up . . ." but then does exactly the opposite of Porter in the chromatic sections of the chorus in her recording, singing the first two and speaking the last.

Sometimes Porter outdoes even the finest actors in characterization and comic timing. His mastery of the comedy song is nowhere more clearly in evidence than in "Thank You So Much, Missus Lowsborough-Goodby," possibly written for *Anything Goes* or for an unproduced musical, *Ever Yours*.[39] Written in the form of a sarcastic and all-too-candid "thank you" letter, the song was Porter's personal response to having been asked himself to take too many "weekends" in the country by matrons of the aristocracy. Recorded on 26 October 1934, along with "You're the Top," both recordings give us a view of Porter in top form.[40] The success of the record prompted Beatrice Lillie to take the song immediately into her repertoire, and little more than a month later she presented it during her appearance on *Fleischmann's Yeast Hour* (the same show on which Porter appeared). Lillie's singing is the work of a capable theater veteran, but her delivery also elucidates aspects of the composer's interpretation that make his version unparalleled. Her timing is excellent, diction is perfect, and characterization credible, but she somehow seems more amused than distraught by the memory of her weekend visit. By contrast, the moment Porter begins to sing "Missus Lowsborough-Goodby does weekends," one can sense his anguish. His words are sung with restrained bitterness at the thought of all the indignities and tedium he endured during "that infinite weekend." Thus, while Lillie is singing a song, Porter is telling a story, one intended to engender sufficient Schadenfreude to delight his audience. The emphasis he places on the word "bliss" ("But it would have been bliss, / Had I dared write her this") expresses a degree of pleasure at the thought of writing such a bitingly sarcastic letter that could only be felt by someone who has had the experience. His momentary outburst when recalling the "damp little room" is equally heartfelt, as is the abrupt tempo change and accelerando (marked *Più mosso* in the score) that mirror the anxiety with which he remembers the vapid socializing he was forced to endure. Each of the four fermatas (not in the score) at the end of the next four phrases enumerating his many sources of irritation (after "tinned salmon," "backgammon," "your dear, but deaf mother," "that bounder, your brother") lends emphasis to his complaints and pained exasperation. Porter then uses tempo to enhance extreme dynamic changes that shift abruptly from a near-operatic outpouring of emotion ("swear to myself there and then") to funereal tones that fade in a long *allargando* ("never to go for a weekend again"). Few of these interpretive choices are marked in the sheet music, suggesting that Porter did not insist upon other singers using his interpretation. As a result, these remarkable expressive liberties in his performance, particularly given their effectiveness, cast doubt upon the ability of his scores to reflect his intentions fully.

Observing the precise rhythm of a melody was never an obligation for Porter when singing his own tunes. In fact, it was a regular habit of his to vary the rhythm of his melodies according to the natural rhythmic scansion of a lyric. He was less inclined to alter the pitches of a melody, though, in keeping with his warning to Frank Sinatra: "Don't sing it if you can't keep to the line I composed."[41] But this admonition did not extend to rhythm, as long as the changes contributed to an even more natural delivery of the phrase. Though Ethel Merman claimed, "I don't tamper with the melodies or the rhythms," her recording of "I Get a Kick Out of You" shows her typical manner of interpreting a melodic line with rhythmic variation that accommodates the accents and syllabic patterns of the lyrics.[42]

In the score, Porter uses quarter-note triplets throughout the verse; but while Merman uses them too, she does not observe them in exactly the places he indicates. Instead, she applies her own rhythmic sense to the line "My story is much too sad to be told," converting Porter's syncopated figure to triplets in the first measure and syncopating in measure 2 where he wrote triplets (see ex. 1). She continues in this way, converting Porter's triplet setting of the words "when I'm out on a quiet spree" to quarter-eighth-eighth figures and his syncopated setting of the words "old ennui" to a simple quarter-quarter-half figure. Through the entire song, she never alters the melodic contour of the line, even while varying the rhythm all the way along.

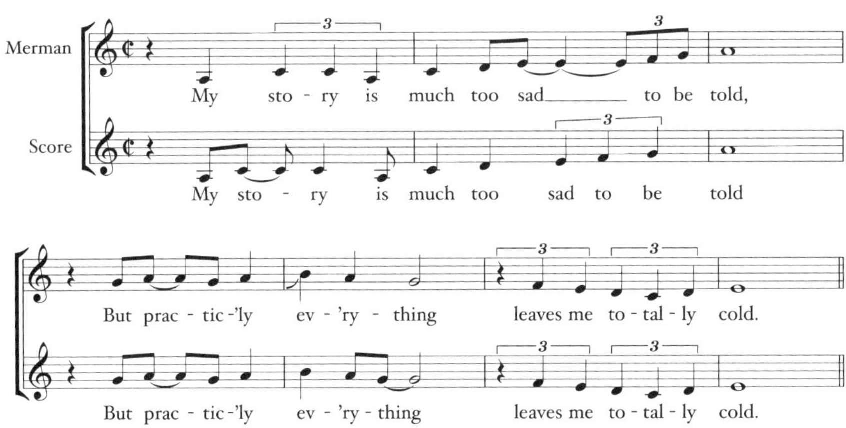

EXAMPLE 1. "I Get a Kick Out of You" (from *Anything Goes*), Ethel Merman and sheet music arrangement. Words and music by Cole Porter. Copyright © 1934 (renewed) WB Music Corp. All Rights Reserved. Used by permission of Alfred Music.

Although Merman's claim never to have changed the rhythm may seem false in this light, her statement should be read in the context of what jazz singers such as Billie Holiday and Louis Armstrong were doing interpretively at the time. Likewise, Sinatra's work as a band singer allowed him to feel free to make melodic changes in the late 1930s that Porter objected to, although certainly to a much lesser degree than the average jazz singer would make. Merman viewed herself instead as belonging to the camp of musicians who sing in the style of the composer as he intended the music to be performed in the theater. Porter, for his part, considered their musical relationship to be collaborative and claimed publicly that she was his favorite interpreter, noting in particular that "she has a sense of rhythm few can equal."[43]

EXAMPLE 2. "Anything Goes" (from *Anything Goes*), vocal and sheet music arrangement. Copyright © 1934 (renewed) WB Music Corp. All Rights Reserved. Used by permission of Alfred Music.

Not surprisingly, Merman's singing is totally in keeping with Porter's own practice of varying rhythm in style. In the recorded performances, he largely adheres to the score but always allows for a few tasteful liberties here and there in the rhythm. In his rendition of "Anything Goes," his departures from the score are almost entirely syncopations that attack a given note of a phrase in advance of the beat. Example 2 shows three phrases from Porter's recording of "Anything Goes" that include syncopations that deviate from the score on or within the following words: "God," "authors," "who," "night," "the," and "studios." Indeed, Porter's final iteration of the title phrase "anything goes" is so much more idiomatic than the one in the score that it makes one wonder whether the arranger simply copied the rhythm from earlier sections in the song. Since Porter's variants are a natural outgrowth of the lyrics, songs with multiple choruses tend in the sheet music to favor the rhythm of the first over successive ones. In Porter's rendition of "You're the Top," he sings the lyrics "you're the Colosseum" and "you're the Louvre Museum" with the rhythm as given in the score while offering variants in the second chorus that make a more congruent setting with the new lyrics.

Ordinarily, it would be difficult to say whether these variants were arrived at spontaneously or were worked out in advance and reinforced through repetition. Porter's appearance on the *Fleischmann's Yeast Hour*, however, gives us a unique perspective on his singing by allowing for comparisons to be made with his studio recording. The rhythm of his second chorus is fairly consistent in both versions, reinforcing the idea that he had merely hit upon the best rhythm for those particular words ("Mahatma Gandhi" and "Napoleon brandy") and stuck with it over time. Toward the end of the first half of the second chorus during his radio appearance, though, Porter clearly improvises the amusingly absurd superlative, "you're cellophane," in exuberant fashion, pausing momentarily on the downbeat and issuing the exclamation instead on beat 3 (see ex. 3). Studio recordings impose discipline upon performers to

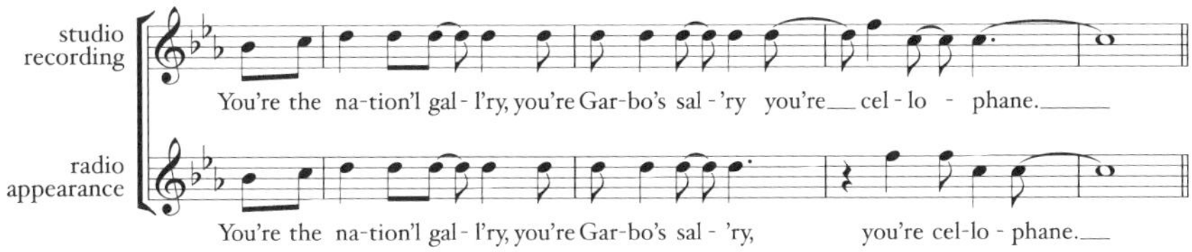

EXAMPLE 3. "You're the Top" (from *Anything Goes*), excerpts from two vocal performances. Words and music by Cole Porter. Copyright © 1934 (renewed) WB Music Corp. All Rights Reserved. Used by permission of Alfred Music.

make definitive interpretive statements, while live performances can encourage musicians to take risks. Singing without the encumbrance of having to accompany himself at the piano also allowed Porter a few momentary flights of improvisation beyond the rhythmic phrasing indicated in the score. Still, his rhythm, even when singing with a band, never strays far from the conventions deemed acceptable by tradition and good taste.

Porter's piano playing on the commercial recordings is deceptively facile. The effortlessness with which he plays on these records conceals the complexity of his art. It may seem on a first impression that he simply follows the sheet music in his performances, but closer scrutiny confirms what he once admitted in a radio interview when he said, "My accompaniments are usually too complicated for publication."[44] His sheet-music arrangements, often created by Dr. Albert Sirmay, were mostly simplified versions of the music rehearsal pianists, accompanists, and Porter himself would play. And though his technique was not comparable to that of other professional pianists, his accompaniments were nonetheless crafted meticulously and rendered with deftness and élan. Unlike George Gershwin, whose solo piano arrangements are virtuoso treatments of the musical material of his songs, Porter adheres closely to the formal skeleton of his scores to provide a framework for his singing. If we look at his accompaniments as if the simplified sheet-music version was the original arrangement, it appears that he expands the register, intensifies the rhythm, adds countermelodies and embellishments, and removes some doubling of the vocal line in his performances (although in reality his version always came first). Listening to the recordings while following along with the sheet music gives this inverted perspective and could explain the common misperception.

Porter's playing at its best was a mixture of apparent contradictions, combining an elegant lightness of touch with forceful dynamic changes and rhythmic vigor. His piano accompaniment to "You're the Top" embodies these diverse characteristics as well as any recording he ever made. To begin with, he takes the song at quarter note = 176, a livelier pace than one finds in most theatrical productions. In order to support this tempo, he leaves out some of the harmony in the verse, allowing the melody to move ahead unencumbered by the need to manage all of the chords the tune implies. The right hand generates harmony with foxtrot backbeats both gently and sparingly, usually when the melody rests between phrases (see ex. 4, mm. 12, 14, and 15). After allowing the voice to enter unobstructed by the piano, he proceeds with melody and bass in counterpoint. Throughout, Porter situates the bass in the low register (generally an octave lower than in the sheet music) and during the verse plays mostly staccato in the manner of a double bass in a dance orchestra.

EXAMPLE 4. "You're the Top," commercial recording piano accompaniment, mm. 8–16.

Typical of his style are the crescendos on the two anacruses preceding measures 11 and 15, which are accompanied by accelerandos that thrust energy toward the downbeat. In measure 15 he adds a chromatic descending bass line to compound the effect of the dynamic thrust, while the addition of an octave note in the right hand reinforces the downbeat and subtly displaces the melody to a lower register, providing increased interest and propulsion heading toward the second half of the binary structure of the verse.

Another strategy Porter employs to energize the downbeat is the coupling of a syncopated harmonic third on the last eighth note of the measure with an open fifth over the barline that occurs in the chorus (see ex. 5, mm. 36–37

EXAMPLE 5. "You're the Top," commercial recording piano accompaniment, mm. 32–41.

and 40–41). He uses this rollicking figure every four measures to mark the phrases as well as to propel the song forward rhythmically with the same robust energy as the anacrusis that jump-starts the chorus. The controlled explosiveness of Porter's rhythm brings to mind Diana Vreeland's perceptive comment about his sensitivity to the rhythms in nature, which she noticed during a gondola ride in Venice: "Everything with him is rhythm. That's why he's so contagious."[45]

Porter also integrates many idiomatic figures, phrases, and embellishments that enhance the musical interest and appeal of his accompaniments well beyond what is offered by the sheet-music arrangements. His recording of "Anything Goes" utilizes several such devices, beginning in the introduction, where he wraps up the buoyant syncopated melody with a variety of grace-note figures to achieve different ends. The three-note grace figures in the bass provide a decisive closing gesture to the phrase in measure 6, while the five single-note graces prepare the entrance of the voice that sustains the dominant cleverly with syncopated bell tones in different octaves (see ex. 6). Here Porter lends a dash of irony before proceeding to satirize the Pilgrims' plight in his tribute to his generation's triumph over Victorian mores by segueing with a figure that sounds at once sophisticated and quaint. The grace-note figure in the bass that energizes the dominant remains a constant feature of his accompaniment under the title phrase "anything goes" at the end of each A section, as well as in the turnarounds (note, in particular, the way it joins and reinforces Porter's rolled *R* in "Rockefeller"). His heavy rhythmic emphasis on beat 2 throughout the release section of the chorus ("The world has gone mad today") gives the faint impression of the bass notes being embellished with chromatic grace notes, although the quality of the recording makes this hard

EXAMPLE 6. "Anything Goes," commercial recording piano accompaniment, m. 1.

to confirm. The sheet music has the notes marked with an accent, suggesting that he may simply have been giving these notes extra weight and playing them slightly in advance of the beat. Yet Porter liked this accented dance figure, and when he used it again four years later in the sheet music of "My Heart Belongs to Daddy," he adorned it with grace notes.

Though most of the songs Cole Porter wrote were crafted for characters in musical comedies, his ability to play and sing them with panache made his performing a creative complement to his songwriting art. The early life of a Porter song was generally known to others only through his own interpretations. Though he insisted that he did not like to compose at the piano, a song would surely be honed and a suitable accompaniment crafted at the instrument once a melody was discovered.[46] Whenever possible, his wife, Linda, was the first audience for a new song, and inevitably his friends and acquaintances heard his songs long before they were rehearsed and staged in a production. Though few from his closest circle left their recollections on the subject, opening night of a Porter musical must have given his friends a chance to judge other performers in songs they already knew well from his interpretations. Recordings by original cast members from Porter's shows help to build an understanding that the rhythmic freedoms we find in his singing were part of a shared style that had its conventions and constraints. Understanding these limitations can lead to ideas and strategies about how to interpret Porter songs in the twenty-first century, when the musical style in which these songs were written is no longer entrenched in the vernacular of musical common practice.

Initially, the idea that recordings by a composer playing his own music can yield useful information for performers might seem obvious enough, particularly those by a composer of Cole Porter's stature. In the field of late nineteenth- and early twentieth-century performance practice, the technology of recording has given musicologists an enormous body of information with which to work. Recently, the recordings of Edward Elgar, Claude Debussy, Igor Stravinsky, and Sergei Prokofiev have been analyzed for what they can tell us about the tempo, dynamics, phrasing, period instrumental techniques, and general matters of style practiced (and presumably preferred) by these composers.[47] The effort to integrate information drawn from period recordings into a unified and persuasive "historically informed" performance practice for this period has admittedly been slow to gather momentum. Nonetheless, it seeks to engage a large mainstream of classical musicians whose tradition has been ostensibly dedicated to preserving the composer's intention. The interpretive tradition of American popular music in the twentieth century, however, has rarely been one in which the composer's original intention was sought, integrated, and preserved beyond the production for which the music was originally created—a practice that continues today. The fact is that most performers who have kept Porter's songs consistently before the public are influenced far more by evolving contemporary tastes and the commercial market than by questions of textual or interpretive authority.

This truism has a profound impact on the way the music of the so-called golden age of the American musical or the "Great American Songbook" is evaluated. For one thing, it suggests that one is more likely to identify aspects of the 1930s swing style in Lee Wiley's rendition of "I've Got You Under My Skin" with Victor Young and his orchestra or, say, of the 1950s big-band tradition in Frank Sinatra's interpretation of the same song with Nelson Riddle's orchestra than characteristics of Porter's music—characteristics, that is, that cannot be understood simply by studying the original vocal scores and sheet music.

In recent years, there has been a new trend emerging in musical theater performance to utilize original orchestrations in the revival of early Broadway shows. This effort to recapture the sound of original productions can also benefit from the interpretive ideas contained in period recordings of original cast members, particularly for scores where we know that composers expected singers to collaborate in the creative process by arranging or improvising melodic variants in style. Recordings help to fill the sizable gaps between what scores tell us about the music of a given show and what we know the musical and theatrical conventions of the day required of performers. Having several definitive performances on record by a composer brings us one step closer to the source. Listened to in this way, Porter's recorded legacy will undoubtedly "provide valuable insights" for years to come.

Notes

1. Robert Kimball, "The Cole Porter Collection at Yale," *Yale University Library Gazette* 44, no. 1 (July 1969): 8–15.

2. Ibid., 10.

3. Fortunately, at this writing there are still a number of friends and colleagues of Cole Porter among us who know his playing from personal experience: Patricia Morison, Miriam Nelson, Miles Kreuger, George Gaynes, Nanette Fabray, Anna Maria Alberghetti, Taina Elg, and Mitzi Gaynor among them.

4. On 26 October 1934 Porter recorded "Thank You So Much, Missus Lowsborough-Goodby" and "You're the Top" (both Victor 24766). On 27 November he recorded "Anything Goes" and "Two Little Babes in the Wood" (both Victor 24825). On 3 January 1935 he recorded "Be Like the Bluebird," "I'm a Gigolo" (both Victor 24843), "The Physician," and "The Cocotte" (both Victor 24859). These recordings have been reissued on *Let's Misbehave! A Cole Porter Collection, 1927–1940* (Naxos 8-120533, 2001, CD).

5. "Dr. Albert Sirmay, Composer, Editor," *New York Times*, 17 January 1967.

6. William McBrien, *Cole Porter: A Biography* (New York: Alfred A. Knopf, 1998), 151.

7. Interview with the author, 29 September 2012.

8. George Eells, *The Life That Late He Led: A Biography of Cole Porter* (New York: G. P. Putnam's Sons, 1967), 237.

9. Cole Porter, *Adios, Argentina*, private recordings, Cole Porter Musical and Literary Property Trusts.

10. McBrien, *Cole Porter*, 172.

11. Miriam Nelson (formerly Miriam Franklyn) appeared in *Panama Hattie* (1940) and *Let's Face It* (1941) with scores by Porter. Interview with the author, 1 October 2012.

12. One photo from this session can be found in *Cole Sings Porter: Rare and Unreleased Songs from "Can-Can" and "Jubilee"* (Koch International Classics 3-7171-2H1, 1994, CD). Another photo from the same session is reproduced in Robert Kimball, "Cole Porter, College Man," *Yale Alumni Magazine*, November 1992.

13. McBrien, *Cole Porter*, 161. During the 1920s Elisabeth Welch appeared in *Running Wild* and *Blackbirds of 1928*; she would have come in contact with Eubie Blake, James P. Johnson, Fats Waller, and Duke Ellington. Steven Bourne, *Elisabeth Welch: Soft Lights and Sweet Music* (Metuchen, NJ: Scarecrow Press, 2005).

14. Ethel Waters, *His Eye Is on the Sparrow* (Garden City, NY: Doubleday, 1951), 146–47.

15. McBrien, *Cole Porter*, 140–41.

16. Irving Berlin was, in fact, noted for only being able to play in the key of F-sharp major.

17. Noël Coward, *The Noël Coward Songbook* (London: Michael Joseph, 1953), 16.

18. McBrien, *Cole Porter*, 118–19.

19. Richard Rodgers, *Musical Stages: An Autobiography* (New York: Random House, 1975), 88.

20. John Lahr, *Notes on a Cowardly Lion: The Biography of Bert Lahr* (New York: Alfred A. Knopf, 1969), 204.

21. McBrien, *Cole Porter*, 290–91.

22. Grant does "perform" at the piano in *Night and Day*, although in an absurdly stylized and virtuosic rendition of the title song.

23. Jessie Matthews and Miles Kreuger, tapes made for the radio program *Opening Night*, 21–22 February 1960, Institute of the American Musical, Los Angeles.

24. Interview with the author, 20 December 2012.

25. Albert Goldberg, "Porter Tunes Provide Entertaining Evening," *Los Angeles Times*, 4 August 1952; Edward Barry, "50,000 Attend Park Program of Porter Airs," *Chicago Daily Tribune*, 21 August 1951.

26. Porter's diaries quoted in Eells, *The Life That Late He Led*, 134–51.

27. The staff that worked on *Born to Dance* was one of the best in the business. It included musical director Alfred Newman, musical arranger Roger Edens, and orchestrator Eddie Powell.

28. Eells, *The Life That Late He Led*, 150–51.

29. Robert Kimball, *The Complete Lyrics of Cole Porter* (New York: Alfred A. Knopf, 1983), 8–28.

30. McBrien, *Cole Porter*, 46.

31. Ibid., 47.

32. Ibid.

33. "Yale's Musical Clubs Had Fine Western Trip," *New York Times*, 5 January 1913.

34. The tribute occurred on 12 February 1967 and included Ethel Merman, Fred Astaire, Frank Sinatra, Gene Kelly, Jimmy Stewart, Garson Kanin, and Roger Edens on piano. It was recorded, and a transcript of the event was published shortly thereafter. Friends of the Library, *Cole Porter: The Life That Late He Led* (Los Angeles: University of Southern California, 1967). The recording of the event was subsequently issued on a CD entitled *You're the Top: A Testimonial* (Viper's Nest, UN-CD-180, 1995).

35. Berlin worked with many skilled musicians over the years, including Ted Snyder, Cliff Hess, Arthur Johnson, Frank Tours, and Helmy Kresa. One public performance where Berlin accompanied himself was the 3 August 1938 radio tribute he received during the promotion of Twentieth Century Fox's *Alexander's Ragtime Band*.

36. Rudy Vallee, *Fleischmann's Yeast Hour*, 13 December 1934, transcription of acetate record, private collection.

37. Patricia Morison has corroborated others in her recollection of the rehearsals for *Kiss Me, Kate* at the roof of the New Amsterdam Theatre: "You know how dirty that old theater was, dusty and dirty, and he would come in on the arm of a young man, impeccably dressed, having had lunch at Le Pavillon, and he'd put a little chair in the aisle, and he had a little whistle, and when he couldn't hear a lyric he would blow it and say, 'I couldn't hear that lyric.'" Interview with the author, 29 September 2012.

38. Bertolt Brecht and John Willet, *Brecht on Theatre: The Development of an Aesthetic* (New York: Hill and Wang, 1966), 44–45.

39. Kimball, *The Complete Lyrics*, 194.

40. Brian Rust, *The Complete Entertainment Discography* (New Rochelle, NY: Arlington House, 1973), 527.

41. McBrien, *Cole Porter*, 151.

42. Ibid., 166.

43. Cole Porter, "Notes on the Morning after an Opening Night," *New York Times*, 8 November 1936.

44. Ibid., 76.

45. McBrien, *Cole Porter*, 91.

46. At different times, Porter described his preference for writing music away from the piano. In an article for the *Journal American*, it was said that he "won't touch a piano while composing because you feel your fingers in the tune" (McBrien, *Cole Porter*, 173). In an article for the *Evening Journal*, he joked that "he would rather compose on a horse than on a piano" because "when I write at the piano it's always lousy" (ibid., 191).

47. For more information on historical recordings in relation to contemporary performance practice, see Robert Philip, *Early Recordings and Musical Style: Changing Tastes in Instrumental Performance, 1900–1950* (Cambridge: Cambridge University Press, 2004); Robert Philip, "The Twentieth Century: 1900–1940," in *Performance Practice after 1600*, ed. Howard Mayer Brown and Stanley Sadie (New York: Macmillan, 1989); José Bowen, "Finding the Music in Musicology: Performance History and Musical Works," in *Rethinking Music*, ed. Nicholas Cook and Mark Everist (New York: Oxford University Press, 1999), 424–51.

8

From "Young Bears" to "Three-Letter Words"

"Anything Goes," 1934–1962

JAMES HEPOKOSKI

Submitting popular songs from the Cole Porter era to musical and cultural analysis is no self-evident matter. This is especially the case with works that lingered in the repertory as popular standards. In the entertainment world and that of its commercial circulation, to perform or listen to a piece widely familiar as "that song" presents few if any difficulties. We recognize it to "be" that song, we enjoy it, and that's that. But what is it that we recognize? The question of identifying the more stable elements within a longer, much-varied tradition of individual song performances seems readily answered on superficial levels: reproducing or remembering the contours of a refrain-melody ("Yes! *That* song!") along with memorable aspects, perhaps, of a culturally settled text or some telling harmonic or rhythmic quirk or established performance mannerism. But the question becomes more difficult when we subject any such song to a deeper scrutiny, particularly when no early performance of it has come to be regarded as the touchstone of what it "is," its culturally classic version or foundational reference point.[1]

The challenge for scholars confronting these songs is to establish what it is that we claim to be studying. The philosophical problem of the ontology of the artwork—already a vexed issue in the analysis of art music (where does the "real" work reside?)—is multiplied many times over in this more fluid, unstable repertory. For all of the attractions that the seeming fixity of the notated scores or sheet music of the era might have to those trained in the study of Western "classical music," they are by no means definitive texts for these songs. Rather, they are mass-produced, commercialized arrangements kept at a limited level of generic standardization and performance challenge in order to maximize their attractiveness as items for sale. Even when a composer wrote down the music, or an early, skeletal, or preedited version of it, it was usually with this degree of standardization in mind, thinking always of the salable product down the road. There is little reason to claim that any autograph copy has more authority in defining the work than do initial (or later?) performances of it, recorded or otherwise. In this repertory it was understood by all parties that no performer was under an imperative to execute the score as printed; indeed, to do so would miss the point. At best, the printed representation of the song was only a rough-and-ready scaffolding or illustrative script (usually a collaborative product) to be rendered, arranged, or stylized as desired by the performers.

When reflecting, for instance, on Cole Porter's song "Anything Goes" (for which the composer's autograph materials, nonbinding in any case, seem now lost—or perhaps may never have existed at all), what is the "real" object for study? Is it the sheet music first printed by Harms in 1934—the commercial product of both Porter and a house editor bent on regularizing the musical text and modifying the original lyrics? Is it the first recording of the song, by Paul Whiteman and Ramona Davies on 26 October 1934 (perhaps recorded, as we shall see, with Porter present)? Is it the recording made by the composer himself a month later, on 27 November 1934? Is it the original arrangement for the Broadway stage concocted, it seems, by Robert Russell Bennett and Hans Spialek, among others, in 1934—or the piano reduction (conductor's score) and set of parts made of it and circulated for rental from 1935 onward? All of these differ from each other, as do many of the song's later recordings, printings, and arrangements. Yet all of them stake a claim to being genre-appropriate, marketplace realizations, perhaps equally legitimate realizations, of that song, with the sense that something relatively stable, though not literally producible, dwells behind the score or performance.

More important than any presumed deep-background stability of music and verbal text is the song's raison d'être: the intention of putting something generously reinterpretable into the fluidities of commercial circulation for whatever treatment it might get and profit it might gain. Under such conditions the supposed object under our eyes and ears blurs, becomes something mutable, a generous set of suggested options, even while some aspects of it are to remain the same. What such a song "is" is both what it originally was intended to be—in terms of its initial compositional production network (already a complex question)—and also what it became in its dissemination throughout the culture in multiple guises and performances, arrangements, updatings, and modifications. A song, qua an imagined, limited object, rapidly inflates to become the history of that song within the culture.

This is particularly true of certain Porter songs from the 1920s and 1930s that were to become standards by the 1940s and 1950s and then, from the 1960s onward, admired but reworked nostalgia curios. Even apart from questions about the music proper, Porter had originally fitted out some of these songs with clever lyrics that seemed to invite modifications in later, differing contexts. In some cases they sported local or insider-group references to celebrities or wealthy socialites of the day, including those in Porter's high-society circle (Lady Mendl, Elsa Maxwell, Monty Woolley, and others). In others the first-proposed lyrics contained slang for ethnic or national groups soon to be judged as over the line or unacceptable. (The touchstone case is found in the original opening lines of the refrain of the 1928 "Let's Do It, Let's Fall in Love": "And that's why Chinks do it, Japs do it, / Up in Lapland, little Lapps do it, / Let's do it, let's fall in love." The initial two lines were much later altered—abandoning the consistent, national-tour aspects of the first refrain—to "And that's why birds do it, bees do it, / Even educated fleas do it.")[2] In still others individual lines of Porter's original lyrics were assessed by some to be unacceptably sexual or too racy in their gleefully naughty double entendres. From this perspective, such lines needed scaling back or softening for a broader public.

As a result, the lyrics of some of Porter's most celebrated songs underwent a double process of *generalization* (away from the specifically local references) and *neutralization* (bowdlerization) as they made their way into the larger culture. This essay illustrates that process by looking at "Anything Goes" (from the 1934 musical of the same name) as an exemplary case study, tracing its path into broader consumption spheres from its sexually and socially mischievous original version through a series of differing, Porter-sanctioned alternatives in late 1934 and 1935 to its comfortable assimilation, by the 1950s, as an anodyne standard in the Great American Songbook to be interpreted by leading recording artists. To follow one important trail of this song is to recount a labyrinthine tale of texts. Reconstructing this complicated sequence of events tells us something significant about popular-song production and commercial distribution in the 1930s and subsequent decades. While at this stage of research the general outlines of the story seem clear, many details remain hidden. Much background documentary information is widely scattered or perhaps lost; more precise supplementary information, or even correction, may well turn up in subsequent years. What follows is grounded in work with the manuscripts in the Cole Porter Collection in the Irving S. Gilmore Library of Yale University; with materials from the New York Public Library; with currently published information concerning the 1934 show, *Anything Goes*; and with the evidence provided in the numerous recordings of the song.

The Suppressed Original Version (Early October 1934)

The earliest indication of the existence of the song "Anything Goes" stems from the period immediately running up to and including the (somewhat chaotic) rehearsals for the show. These began on 8 October 1934, less than a month before its 5 November Boston tryout run and about a month and a half before its 21 November Broadway premiere at the Alvin Theater in New York.[3] In May, June, and July of the preceding spring, as the shipboard comedy was being initially sketched out (under the auspices of Vinton Freedley) in England and France by Guy Bolton and P. G. Wodehouse (through at least one scenario and two early scripts), the enthusiastic Porter had proposed five possible (new) songs for the show, whose working title at the time varied from *Bon Voyage* to *Hard to Get*. "Anything Goes" was not one of the five songs.[4] While one cannot rule it out, no evidence suggests that "Anything Goes" had been written by even early or mid-September 1934.

In August and September Bolton and Wodehouse's second script was being substantially rewritten in or around New York by Howard Lindsay (the director of the show) and Russel Crouse, apparently still under the provisional but vulnerable title *Hard to Get*. But on 1 October the *New York Times* reported that it had been "made known yesterday" that Porter's forthcoming show, with the title *Anything Goes*, had been booked for the Alvin Theater for "sometime next month."[5] This title change must have occurred in mid- or late September, while Lindsay and Crouse's script was only half-baked at best. The two words "anything goes" have been variously attributed to an early (September?), casual remark of William Gaxton (contracted to play the role of Billy Crocker and willing to accommodate himself to a still-changing script; upon hearing the words, Porter is said to have replied, "Title!") or to Gaxton's doorman upon hearing that the show's title had not yet been decided.[6] However they initially surfaced, the two words stuck, and one might imagine that once the show's title had been determined, Porter must have set to work composing the related song.

One might therefore propose a provisional date for Porter's original version(s) of the song and its text around late September or early October 1934. The earliest mention of the song comes from a draft of Lindsay and Crouse's script for the show that is available in the New York Public Library for the Performing Arts.[7] This working script, which includes numerous deletions and alterations, probably dates from the late September–October period. It places the song, by title only (not including its text), in its proper spot (for Ethel Merman as Reno Sweeney, saucy nightclub singer and former evangelist), shortly before the closing curtain of act 1. An obvious interpolation, the song-and-dance Merman vehicle has little to do with the plot of the show at this point. It is artificially triggered as the brassy Reno explains why it is possible to imagine that the hypereffete English lord, Sir Evelyn Oakleigh, might actually marry her ("Don't worry, in this day and age, anything can happen").[8]

Porter's initial task was to produce a sketch-outline of this new song, which at this point necessitated a verse ("Times have changed . . .") and at least one refrain ("In olden days . . ."). Whatever Porter jotted down (now lost)—or perhaps dictated—may have been fleshed out by his loyal editor (Albert Sirmay) and then copied by another, more professional hand into a piano-vocal score—a master document of sorts that was probably also conceived as a model to be sent out (or recopied) at some later point for sheet-music printing. One such cleanly prepared ink copy of "Anything Goes" is housed in Yale's Cole Porter Collection.[9] It consists of the verse (unprepared by a piano introduction) and a single refrain, subjected to a first ending (which features a turnaround probably composed by Sirmay, not Porter) and subsequent repeat—which was, of course, how the song was to be printed for sale, not sung in the show. This six-page manuscript (preceded by a title page) presents the song, marked *Moderato*, with a B-flat minor verse that leads to a B-flat major refrain. Apart from its key and lack of an introduction, the music of this manuscript version is essentially that found in all editions and printings of the song. What differs from later versions is a portion of the refrain text.

From the beginning—and in all subsequent versions of the text—the two complementary (contrasting) quatrains of the verse text were invariant, never subjected to revision. The Yale ink score provides them as follows (and here I have regularized the punctuation, separated the quatrains, and supplied a bracketed addition to emend either a copyist error or a slightly differing, early version of the text):

> Times have changed,
> And we['ve] often rewound the clock
> Since the Puritans got a shock,
> When they landed on Plymouth Rock.
>
> If today
> Any shock they should try to stem,
> 'Stead of landing on Plymouth Rock,
> Plymouth Rock would land on them.

Playing on the topic of reversals and dissimilar eras, these lines introduce the image of an American-puritanical tradition of tight-laced decorum now shattered and overturned in modern times. (One might note en passant that it was the Pilgrims, not the Puritans, who "landed on Plymouth Rock.") The rhythmically emphasized "clock/shock/Rock" end rhymes convey an abrupt bluntness (ship against rock), just as the shifting of the repeated "Plymouth Rock" to the initial position of the final line also reinforces the idea of modern reversals. Because neither Porter nor anyone else altered this verse in any subsequent version, we shall leave it behind here, noting only that Porter's musical setting (two minor-mode, complementary phrases, each four lines long, ending in a half-cadence) colors these words to amusing effect: the initial, time-marches-on bass impulses; the bluesily smeared, nightclubbish opening declaration ("Times have changed"); the bass-triplet jolts into lines 3 and 4; the clock-winding Neapolitan harmony ("Since the Puritans got a shock"); the pseudo-parallel-major complement launching the second quatrain ("If today," functioning now as V^7 of iv and thus still in the tonic minor); the similarity of the final taunting figure, "on them," to the first line's "Times have changed" and the second quatrain's "If today."

It is once the song's AABA' refrain space is entered, however, that the textual history of the song becomes problematic. The music sets four lines of text for each A section and seven for the contrasting B section. The Yale ink-copy score from early October contains seven B-section lines ("If saying your pr'yers you like") that Porter, by the last week of that month, would alter. This earlier text reads (presented here, again, with editorial regularizations and formatted spacing to make the AABA' structure clear):

In olden days a glimpse of stocking
Was looked on as something shocking,
But now, God knows,
Anything goes.

Good authors too who once knew better words,
Now only pick [*sic*] four-letter words
For their prose,
Anything goes.

If saying your pr'yers you like,
If green pears you like,
If old chairs you like,
If backstairs you like,
If love affairs you like
With young bears [you] like,
Why, nobody will oppose.

And ev'ry night the set that's smart is
Indulging in nudist parties
In studios,
Anything goes.[10]

Triggered by the verse's final-line taunt (and set-up dominant chord), the refrain, initiated by the mock-antique "in olden days," seeks an even more droll irony, a witty posture of faux amazement addressed to sophisticates in the know. It unreels a list of much that is supposedly now legitimized beyond reproach in urban-modern times, and especially in Porter's fantasy worlds of entertainment, wealth, and high society—brazenly secular, irreverent, and sexually unrepressed. The poetic tone unfolds in the ultraclever, Porterian style of vers de société, "crisp and sparkling," "playfully malicious," "elegantly naughty"—lines that sport an air of "insouciance" or "bemused sophistication."[11]

The refrain's progressively heightened imagery begins with back references to the verse ("olden days" and the echo of "shocking" with the verse's "shock"—the key image behind the entire song) and casually sweeps away lingering residues of the puritanical value system with the flippantly profane "But now, God knows" in order to hammer out the first appearance of its subrefrain, "Anything goes." From this initial quatrain the refrain branches out in progressively eroticized ways, from the mockingly demure "glimpse of stocking" to the next quatrain's "four-letter words" (upping the profanity ante from "But now, God knows") to the B section's "backstairs" assignations to "love affairs with young bears" to the climactic image in the final A section, the smart set's "indulging in nudist parties"—the striptease other to the initial "glimpse of stocking."

In the energetically accumulative B section, though—an intensifying series of "shocks"—Porter's original text may have crossed the line. It seems possible that "love affairs . . . with young bears" referred to gay-male sex, an allusion slipped into the rapidly mounting text that uses what might have been part of the urban-underground slang of the time. But was this its connotation? To claim that securely requires one to recover features of American gay slang of the 1920s and 1930s, but the problem is that the word "bears" to characterize certain categories of gay men surfaced more publicly only in the post-Stonewall era in the 1970s and 1980s and is difficult to document before that time.[12] Yet it was precisely this line of the B section, taking the preceding five lines with it (since their rhyming purpose—"pr'yers," "pears," "chairs," "backstairs," "affairs"—was to drive to the climactic "bears" image), that would be suppressed in the original text of Porter's song. Somebody must have objected to it; otherwise, why revise it?[13]

Moreover, we also know that another Porter song originally slated for *Anything Goes* and with a passing same-sex reference—this time a lesbian one—was dropped during the October rehearsals for that reason. That song was "Kate the Great":

> Catherine of Russia, that potentate,
> Knew that her job was to fascinate . . .
> And think of the history she made.
> Why, she made the Congress,
> She made the Premier,
> She made the clergy . . .
> She made the butler,
> She made the groom,
> She made the maid who made the room.

Merman is reported to have feared that "she couldn't sing such a line in front of her mother on opening night."[14] In the role of Reno Sweeney she was also the one assigned to sing "Anything Goes"—which was doubtless written for her—and it is conceivable that the presumed objections to "love affairs with young bears" could initially have been hers. Apparently, the double entendres of "You're the Top" and "Blow, Gabriel, Blow" passed muster, and Porter's immediate rewriting of the B-section lyrics of "Anything Goes" to feature (as we shall see) an even more explicitly randy heterosexuality prompted no similar protestation (not to mention the "even one sniff" of cocaine sung in her "I Get a Kick Out of You").

While the AABA' refrain music of "Anything Goes" is not difficult to characterize, one should notice its idiosyncratic framework of registral, rhythmic, accentual, and intensification-and-release patterns. This is an individualized schema capable of being synchronized only with poetic patterns devised to match its antically jagged contours. As with "Let's Do It," "You're the Top," and several other Porter songs, one might imagine the song as an invitation to a refrain game of generating new, witty lyrics to match the music's quirks—which in fact is what was soon to happen with this melody. Its A and A' sections (music heard thrice, though with an emphatic, concluding variant at the end of A') are confined to the melodically pentatonic, in this context an "American pentatonic" readily synchronizable with the minstrel-show, parlor-song, and vaudeville strains of American music.[15] Much of its appeal lies in its playfully infectious, prancing rhythm, carving out individual words of text. The dance syncopations that rhythmically twist the end of line 1 ("glimpse of stocking") are immediately multiplied in the spring-loaded, pirouetting syncopations of the second ("Was looked on as something shocking"). In turn, these vault the vocal line upward into the melodic apex ($\hat{10}$) to set in high relief the irreverent "*God* [knows]." The sudden vocal prolongation of "knows" over a bar and a half both sets up the decisive end rhyme ("knows"/"goes") and, like a held breath, rhythmically prepares the declaratively accented, rat-a-tat-*tat* pronouncement finally released with a parodic, quasi-plagal cadence in the fourth line: "Anything goes." With different words, the same succession recurs in the second A and final A' sections.

By way of contrast, the seven-line B section leaps at once onto the bright major mediant (III, "If saying your pr'yers you like," a fast-fading residue of lingering puritanism) to begin a chain of compressed, rapid-fire reiterations (more illustrative shocks) that hammer the vocal line chromatically upward to the apex pitch once again, on the second syllable of the crucial word "af-*fairs*." At that (taboo?) apex point, the major mediant darkens into the minor (iii, "af-*fairs* you like"), and the melodic line plunges downward into the lower shadows ("With young bears *you like*"), only to end by producing a jack-in-the-box dominant seventh of the original tonic at the end ("[op-]*pose*," which also reactivates the song-anchoring "-ose" rhyme), harmonically interrupted, to set up the return of the pentatonic A'.[16] No wasted gestures. In "Anything Goes" everything counts.

The First Revision: Finalizing the 1934 Theatrical Text (Mid-October 1934)

By mid-October 1934 Porter had decided—or had been advised—to change the words to the (first) refrain's B section. The "young bears" text would hibernate for the next four or five decades, when it would be discovered and printed as an "original," supplementary text in Robert Kimball's *The Complete Lyrics of Cole Porter* (1983).[17] Four years after this publication this B-section text was interpolated into the end of the "Anything Goes" sequence in the 1987 Lincoln Center revival of the show, as well as into the 1989 London production of the musical and all Broadway and London productions thereafter. Whatever Porter's original intention might have been, in its revived, 1987 context, "bears" could be construed more unmistakably as gay slang.[18]

In October 1934, as Porter mapped out a revised text for "Anything Goes," he also wrote (or had written) lyrics for a second and third refrain. This was the multiple-refrain text destined for the Broadway stage: an initial verse and three game-like "list" choruses (a complement to "You're the Top"). It is the verse-and-three-refrain version that Cole Porter himself recorded on 27 November 1934—a promotional recording made six days after the New York premiere of the show—and it is the version that would appear (with some inadvertent errors and accidental omissions) in the 1934–35 Tams-Witmark promptbook (libretto) prepared for rental purposes.[19] This is surely the text that Merman sang onstage toward the end of act 1, and it is the one reproduced in Robert Kimball's *The Complete Lyrics of Cole Porter* and performed on John McGlinn's 1988–89 restoration of the 1934 musical.[20] We shall refer to it as the 1934 Theatrical Text. Before considering the evidence for its mid-October dating, let us consider its three refrains (which follow the invariant verse, "Times have changed"). I furnish them here as they are found, primarily, in the 1934–35 Tams-Witmark promptbook.[21] Footnotes within the text indicate the variants heard in Porter's 27 November recording. Once again I have regularized punctuation, capitalization, and line lengths and interpolated separations to indicate the AABA' structure.

REFRAIN 1
In olden days, a glimpse of stocking
Was looked on as something shocking,
But now, God knows,
Anything goes.

[Good authors too who once knew better words
Now only use four-letter words
Writing prose,
Anything goes.]

If driving fast cars you like,
If low bars you like,
[If old hymns you like,]
If bare limbs you like
If Mae West you like
Or me, undressed, you like
Why, nobody will oppose.

When ev'ry night the set that's smart is in-
Dulging[22] in nudist parties in
Studios,
Anything goes.

REFRAIN 2
When Missus Ned McClean [*sic*] (God bless her)
Can get Russian Reds to "yes" her
Then I suppose
Anything goes.

When Rockefeller still can hoard en-
Ough money to let Max Gordon
Produce his shows,
Anything goes.

The world has gone mad today
The good's bad today
And black's white today
And day's night today
And that gent today
You gave a cent today
Once had several châteaux.

When folks who still can ride in jitneys
Find out Vanderbilts and Whitneys

Lack baby-clo's
Anything goes.

REFRAIN 3
If[23] Sam Goldwyn can with great conviction
Instruct Anna Sten in diction
Then Anna shows
Anything goes.

When you hear that Lady Mendl, standing up
Now turns[24] a handspring landing up-
On her toes,
Anything goes.[25]

Just think of what[26] shocks you've got
And what knocks you've got
And what blues you've got
From that news you've got
And what pains you've got
(If any brains you've got)
From those little radios.

So Missus R,[27] with all her trimmins
Can broadcast a bed from Simmons
'Cause Franklin knows
Anything goes.

Each of the three "list-song" refrains pursues a different strategy of allusions. The first capitalizes on the currency of profanity and sex; the second on 1934 gossip of the American superwealthy; the third, mostly, on similarly recent chatter about media and political celebrities. In the first refrain, it is the newly written (and, for 1934, audacious) B section that catches our attention. With the decision to delete "love affairs with young bears" came a set of new lines that, while more explicitly titillating, are more normatively housed within the realm of heterosexuality. Moreover, Porter took care to ensure that the new, rapid-fire B-section lines were equally coordinated with the musical drive to that section's melodic high point, which also sets off its roguish collapse of major III into minor iii and its concomitant plunge downward. Thus the revised text loses none of the original words/music synchronization. Instead of peaking on "young *bears*," the apex pitch and modal shift now occur with the image of the bawdy and bosomy "Mae *West*." (With this B-section alteration we have yet another connection to Merman and Gaxton's "You're the Top," which includes the line "You're the moon over Mae West's shoulder.") This leads directly to (Reno/Merman's) descending line "Or me, un-*dressed*, you like," whose exuberantly risqué new words provide a conceptual, more appropriate bridge-link to the climactic "nudist parties in studios" of the final A'. In this revised first refrain, the mischievous sparkle of Porter's new B-section text continued to push the limit of what was acceptable at the time.

The second and third refrains are equally well matched with the musical schema.[28] In them Porter produced abundant strings of references to 1934 celebrities and high society, a feature anticipated by the mention of "Mae West" in the revised first refrain. These were temporally localized lines that potentially bore a built-in expiration date with regard to their relevance or comprehensibility. These references have been clarified a number of times (most conveniently by Miles Kreuger) and are easily enhanced by simple Internet searches.[29] The wealthy Mrs. Ned McLean, owner of the Hope Diamond (once owned by Catherine the Great), had just returned from a bejeweled, flamboyant, and controversial trip to the Soviet Union. Max Gordon had just converted Rockefeller's "mammoth movie palace," Radio City, "into a mammoth legitimate theatre." The Vanderbilts and Whitneys, it appears, had been grousing about financial losses during the Depression. Anna Sten was a Ukrainian actress known in German films now trying to break into American productions under the aegis of the Polish-born Sam[uel] Goldwyn. Lady Mendl (Elsie de Wolfe, "adventuress, interior decorator, and international hostess") had been part of the Cole and Linda Porter circle for some time—and was known for eccentric behavior, which included (at age sixty-eight in 1934) such vigorous exercises as headstands, walking upside down on her hands, and yoga.[30]

But it was of course the final quatrain of refrain 3, the reference to "Missus R," Eleanor Roosevelt, that provided the capper to the whole song, a capper elegantly prepared by the third refrain's B-section allusions to the brain-draining "shocks" provided "from those little radios." In early 1934 the ever-colorful and enterprising first lady had resumed her radio broadcasts. At least five of them, it seems, were sponsored by Simmons Mattresses.[31] Needless to say, in the free-wheeling context of "Anything Goes," the eye-winking charge lay in the association of "Missus R" (and Franklin) with the bedroom, all delivered with good cheer via Porter's sporty music.

The new, three-refrain text had been available since mid-October 1934, the period of the rehearsals. How do we know this? On 26 October, about a week and a half before the Boston tryout for the show, Porter agreed to record two of his own songs at the Victor Studio. This was the first time that Porter's voice and piano styling were to be captured on disc, and for this occasion (Victor 24766) he recorded one song from the upcoming *Anything Goes*, "You're the Top," along with a dyspeptically mordant song not included in the show, "Thank You So Much, Mrs. Lowsborough-Goodby."[32] In the same studio and on the same day, Paul Whiteman recorded dance-band arrangements of four Porter songs from the forthcoming *Anything Goes*, destined for two 78 rpm discs. It is not unreasonable to suppose that Porter was present for these Whiteman recordings. (At the very least he must have approved of them as part of the initial or advance promotion for the musical.) Whiteman's first 78 rpm pairing on that day was "I Get a Kick Out of You" and "You're the Top"; this was immediately followed by "All through the Night" and "Anything Goes," destined for a second disc.[33]

Whiteman's 26 October "Anything Goes" is a fox-trot arrangement that, midway through, features Ramona (Davies) as the vocalist.[34] Ramona's lyrics are those of the revised first refrain, complete (thus including the B section that leads to "Mae West" and "me undressed"), albeit with a softening of the third line of refrain 1 ("But now, God knows" becomes "But now, Lord knows"—surely with the composer's knowledge), followed by (after a return to an instrumental AA) refrain 2's full B section ("The world has gone mad today") and concluding A' quatrain (delivered here as "Folks who can still ride in jitneys"). Since refrains 1 and 2 are in evidence, Porter must have revised the text sometime before 26 October—enough beforehand for Whiteman's arranger to have pulled together a score and set of parts for the recording session. Since refrain 2 had been devised by this time, refrain 3 is likely to have been as well, even though it is not heard on Whiteman's recording.

The Harms Sheet-Music Text (1934)

As the October rehearsals were proceeding, the production team's thoughts were turning toward the various ways in which the musical's songs would be made commercially available for sale to a broader public. One of these was the production of the sheet music of individual songs from the show, contracted with Harms, Inc., of New York. This process must have begun in time for the songs to be ready for sale by the time of the premiere, if not earlier. Harms's primary models for publication would probably have been the neatly prepared ink copies of the individual songs for the rehearsals, most of which still exist in Yale's Cole Porter Collection. The resulting sheet music would be the first printed version of each of the songs. By at least mid-November, if not earlier, Harms had printed eight selections from *Anything Goes*: the title song, "Anything Goes," along with "Buddie [*sic*] Beware," "You're the Top," "All through the Night," "I Get a Kick Out of You," "Blow, Gabriel, Blow," "The Gypsy in Me," and "Waltz down the Aisle." That the last of these was a song cut before the 5 November Boston premiere suggests that Harms had been preparing this music in late October or very early November. Each song was published with identical front-cover illustrations of the smiling stars of the musical, William Gaxton, Ethel Merman, and Victor Moore.

The 1934 Harms version of "Anything Goes" transposed the B-flat minor-major of the rehearsal ink copy into C minor-major. It was also furnished with a new four-bar introduction (probably by Albert Sirmay). What follows is the C minor verse (the invariant "Times have changed") and, as was the sheet-music norm (and as is found on the earlier ink copy), a single refrain marked with first and second endings and a repeat sign, with the notational implication that one was to sing the same refrain twice. The sheet-music repeat norm, though, meant little. It was surely nonbinding. For the 1934 Harms version, it was decided to print only one refrain text that conflated aspects of refrains 1 and 3. The AA sections were furnished with the opening foundational text from refrain 1: "In olden days" (including "But now, God knows") along with "Good authors too" and their "four-letter words." Instead of moving into the remainder of refrain 1, however (steering clear of "Mae West," "me undressed," and the "nudist parties"), it was deemed more prudent to shift into the BA' sections of refrain 3 with its timely reference to Eleanor Roosevelt: "Just think of those shocks you've got,"[35] "those little radios," and "So Missus R with all her trimmins." Harms's telescoped version of the text was used by the Dorsey Brothers in their recording from 27 November 1934, the same day, coincidentally, as Porter's own recording of the song. The Dorseys' only deviation from the Harms text was their modification of "But now, God knows" to "But now, Lord knows" (as in Whiteman's October recording).[36]

As we shall see, the 1934 Harms sheet-music text remained available for only about a year, if even that long. By late 1935 or early 1936, the company would outfit new printings of their single-refrain sheet music with a different text for the end of the B section and all of the concluding A' section. This differing, "neutralized" text would have the longest life of them all.

The Neutralized Text: "Finale Ultimo," Act 2 (1934)

In the song's reprise at the end of act 2, where it recurs as the final section of the "Finale Ultimo," there is an exuberant *lieto fine,* in which, to bring down the curtain, the entire company and chorus sing in celebratory fashion the first refrain of "You're the Top" followed by a single refrain of "Anything Goes."

What were the lyrics sung in the latter song's reprise? The earliest evidence of which I am aware is the 1935 Tams-Witmark conductor's score for rental, to be discussed below. For the present we need only observe that in that score (and also in John McGlinn's 1987 recording of the show's restoration, which may have been grounded in even earlier materials),[37] we find a revised refrain 1 text that retained only its first half: the BA' portions of the AABA' structure are now fitted out with new words. It seems likely that this new text, with its revised lyrics, had also been sung in New York performances in 1934–35.

But why was a revised text called for at all? By November 1934, quite apart from the "Finale Ultimo" question, it may already have become clear that the song "Anything Goes" could have considerable lasting power as a single song extracted from the context of the show. The Harms text's awkward condensation was hardly optimal for this purpose: with its inclusion of the reference to "Missus R" and the "bed from Simmons," that text was likely to become dated, losing its original, mischievous punch. Pursuing such thoughts, it must have occurred to Porter or the larger production team that it would be prudent to devise a more neutralized version of refrain 1 to give the song a longer shelf life as a detached, single-refrain number. (He had learned, perhaps, from his experience with the radio-censored "Love for Sale" from 1930—discussed in Buchler's chapter in the present volume—that in the world of practical commerce it was not the case that "anything goes.")

The vulnerabilities of the Theatrical Text of refrain 1 for a broader American audience were twofold: the profane single line "But now, God knows" in the first quatrain, which Whiteman and Ramona had already softened to "Now, Lord knows" in their 26 October recording, and, more broadly, the erotic bite of refrain 1's second half (BA': "Mae West," "me undressed," "nudist parties"), which text Harms had already replaced with refrain 3 extracts—hardly an elegant solution. In part to suit the purposes of a more widespread distribution, Porter must have agreed at some point to tone down "But now, God knows" to "Now, Heaven knows" and also to craft a new, milder BA' text for refrain 1, one that also avoided the temporally circumscribed reference to "Missus R's" radio broadcasts. From this perspective, the logic of this BA' revision seems clear. Once the "Missus R" quatrain was marked for replacement, the end of the B section also had to be rewritten, since the whole point of the Theatrical Text's clause "And what pains you've got / (If any brains you've got) / From those little radios," was to set up Missus R.

Toward that end Porter crafted what I call refrain 1's 1934 Neutralized Text. He wrote it at some point before 23 November 1934 (two days after the New

York premiere of the musical), for it was sung in a recording made on that day by the Leo Reisman Orchestra with Sally Singer as the vocalist (Brunswick 7332).[38] Identifiable as such by "Now, Heaven knows" in the first A section and its new B section and final A' quatrain, this text, or ad hoc, negligible variants of it, would appear in a number of later manuscripts, printed editions, and recordings. As such it is a crucial text in the reception history of "Anything Goes." I present here the version of the Neutralized Text of refrain 1 as it appears in the "Finale Ultimo" of the 1935 Tams-Witmark conductor's score. (Sally Singer's version, in F major, tweaks two words of what must have been provided to her, and I have relegated those two small deviations to the endnotes.)

In olden days a glimpse of stocking
Was looked on as something shocking,
Now, Heaven knows,
Anything goes.

Good authors too who once knew better words
Now only use four-letter words,
Writing prose,
Anything goes.

The world has gone mad today,
And good's bad today,
And black's white today,
And day's night today,
When most guys today,
That women prize today,
Are just silly gigolos.[39]

So though I'm not a great romancer
I know that you're (I'm) bound to answer
When I (you) propose,
Anything goes.[40]

Whatever other ("Finale Ultimo") factors might have lain behind it, Porter must have devised this text also for toned-down, primarily single-refrain performances of the song, perhaps even as an emended alternative to the first printing of the Harms sheet music. Obviously, these lyrics could not be followed by the Theatrical Text's refrain 2, for this new B section's first four lines ("The world has gone mad today") import those of that second refrain, and to hear them again en bloc immediately afterward would be inelegantly redundant. The Neutralized Text's last three B-section lines are new, beginning with "When most guys today," cleverly attaining the apex pitch and fleeting shift to the minor mode on the word "guys." While effective as a text setting on its own terms, these new lines retain only a faded memory ("silly gigolos") of the formerly naughty tone. The original B-section's tang, whose raciness was a central aspect of the song as first conceived, is now served up as less spicy fare.

Still, it may be the new final quatrain that most captures our attention ("So though I'm not a great romancer"). Here the newly written lines whitewash over the Theatrical Text's "nudist parties in studios," a slippage into the self-deprecatingly coy to cover over the original Porterian zingers. The poetic principle in all earlier versions of each refrain had been to intensify from their openings to their most playfully outrageous images in the final quatrain. But this new stanza is deflationary. The subrefrain "anything goes" had been consistently produced to register the "shock" of once-unthinkable practices now considered acceptable, even regarded as modern norms, now that "times have changed." Not here. In this context the last four lines are given over to a domesticated sentiment that undercuts—or perhaps only mildly sustains—the consistent impertinence that the song had originally delighted in conveying. And yet Porter might have regarded the creation of the November 1934 Neutralized Text as a prudent commercial move.

Such considerations need not have been the only ones in play. This returns us to the question of the text used for the reprise in the show's "Finale Ultimo," where it follows an unaltered stanza of "You're the Top." As mentioned above, the 1935 rental score provides the Neutralized Text at this point. That this text begins with the two foundational quatrains of refrain 1 ("In olden days"; "Good authors, too") makes sense: those incipit lyrics are the ones most associated with the song. But it is easy to imagine that Porter (and others) might not have wished to ring down the curtain with the image of "nudist parties in studios." This would have ended the show on a licentious note at precisely the point at which the comedy's denouement had led to reconciliation and a promise of marriage ("you're bound to answer / When I propose"). It may be, then, that in or around early November (but after Harms's first printing of the sheet music) Porter might have decided that a more generously good-hearted text, relocated within a more conventional morality that the earlier portions of the show had been devoted to tweaking, would be more appropriate at the show's end and would also be a text that would solve the problem of the song's single-refrain dissemination into the larger culture.

"Anything Goes": Differing Tracks of Dissemination (1934–1935)

By the evening of the musical's gala premiere in New York, 21 November 1934, Porter had sanctioned three different texts for "Anything Goes" (not counting the original, suppressed text with "young bears"): the impertinent, three-refrain Theatrical Text; the single-refrain, somewhat clumsy Harms Sheet Music Text (soon to be discarded); and the apparently single-refrain (or "Finale Ultimo") Neutralized Text. As we have seen, on 23 and 27 November, two and six days after the premiere, three recordings were made of this song, and all three versions of the lyrics were represented in them: Leo Reisman and Sally Singer's 23 November recording (the Neutralized Text)—the second ever made of this song; Cole Porter's 27 November recording (paired with "Two Little Babes in the Woods"); and, on the same day, the Dorsey Brothers recording (the 1934 Harms text).

So far as current evidence tells us, we have reached the end of the refrain variants of the lyrics written by Porter himself, but we are by no means at the end of our story. What has emerged thus far, though, is central to our understanding of what the earliest conceptions of this song were. This brings us back to one of the ramifications of the issues posed at the opening of this essay: the question of where the "real work" resides or, in this case, the question of what the "real lyrics" for this song are. But these are the wrong questions, reductive in how they are posed and in any presumed conclusive answer that they might expect. As was (and would continue to be) the case with other Porter songs as well, "Anything Goes" was splitting its identity to follow at least two early, separate tracks of American dissemination and reception, neither of which can be discounted. On the one hand, there was the higher-voltage, theater-oriented song with its three refrains but obviously short shelf life because of its specifically localized references. On the other hand, Porter and others were also envisioning a more compact, durable, and standardized single-refrain version detached from the show and suitable for commercial distribution or private performance. By November 1934 "Anything Goes" was on its way to becoming two different things, existing under at least two different, equally authorized conceptions.

As for the words of the Theatrical Text, they were less permanently fixed than they were grounded in a cluster of text-construction rules, of which Porter's three refrains served as the classic, composer-authorized exemplars. Anchored in its American high-society, late 1934 world, the Theatrical Text established the underlying *idea* fueling the song's lyrics.[41] On this multiple-refrain track the song's idea (a schema, a set of guidelines, a verbal challenge) was to follow a proclamatory, invariant verse ("Times have changed") with a string of witty refrains, a feature characteristic of the theatrical Porter. The successive refrains were to be constructed as participants within a flexibly construed refrain game. They were to move from a risqué initial refrain (that attention grabber) to ones whose impishly wrought barbs were locally relevant to the performance's time and place, dishing out a snappy contemporaneity that capitalized on current contexts or celebrities' quirks and foibles.

The "Anything Goes" game had a number of additional, implicit rules. The opening two quatrains of the first refrain ("In olden days" and "Good authors, too") were the requisite entry ticket for any otherwise altered performance of the song—they had to launch it—and any non-Porter version was obliged to include the invariant, punch-line pop-ups of the subrefrain, "Anything goes," to end each A or A' section. Newly written stanzas not only had to feature the properly slotted "ose" rhymes ("knows," "prose," "studios," "suppose," "shows," and so on) to underscore the jabbing repetitions of "Anything goes" but also had to coordinate any new text with the idiosyncrasies of Porter's music in terms of rhythm and accentual emphasis, along with its musical drives to apex pitches, temporary tonicizations, modal switches, and approaches to cadence.

Another essential part of the game was that of reveling in the delight of textual "shock" and hyperclever unconventionality pushed to the limit of sophisticated taste. In order to remain true to the song's spirit or underlying idea, any new, non-Porterian lyrics should strive to match the originals in terms of cheeky audacity. Porter's 1934 words were not only an exemplary realization of the game but also the lyrics closest to the composer's original concept of the song. Still, as we shall see, there is little reason to think that he actively discouraged other combinations and realizations within the context of the show.

The Neutralized Text—the second, all-purpose dissemination track—proved to be more long-lasting, especially after Harms, probably in 1935, replaced the earlier-printed conflation text with it. Although it is a softened revision of the Theatrical Text's refrain 1—and in this respect tones down the foundational "shock" principle of that text—it may be considered Porter's fourth, socially compromised exemplar of the "Anything Goes" game, initially to be used, it seems, for the song's single-refrain reprise in the show's "Finale Ultimo" and thereafter in various other, broader contexts as the occasion demanded. Nonetheless, even as its initial raison d'être appears to have been to provide a verse and single refrain for stand-alone performance, it would at times be used (as in the Reisman-Singer recording) as the first refrain followed by some or all of a second—or perhaps even a third. Before long, after memories of the Broadway show and its more involved text faded, purchasers of the sheet music or later Porter song anthologies would naturally assume that they owned the single-refrain, finally authorized text for the song. And in this second-track sense, they did. By and large, this was the way that the song would filter into the larger marketplace, displacing the more localized 1934 Theatrical Text until its more complete recovery in the 1980s. But of course things are not that simple. While the Theatrical and Neutralized Texts persist as two early, essential nodes in this tale of texts, new refrain mixtures, seeming accidents, and still other non-Porter texts would follow.

Mix and Match: The Tams-Witmark Rental Score (1935)

After opening on 21 November 1934, *Anything Goes* closed a year later, on 16 November 1935, having presented 420 performances. By this point Tams-Witmark was ready to make it available for rental to American theater companies outside of New York. Their rental materials consisted of a promptbook (libretto), a conductor's score,[42] and a set of parts. Curiously, when the song is introduced in act 1, the texts of the promptbook and the conductor's score differ. The promptbook provides the verse and three refrains of the 1934 Theatrical Text—the wittier, more pointed lyrics also heard on Porter's recording. While the 1935 rental score also provides three refrains (separated by dance interludes, as in the show itself), it reproduces the 1934 Neutralized Text for the first of them (B-section "gigolos"; A'-section "great romancer"), albeit reinstating "But now God knows" in the first A section. In other words, the conductor's score not only presents a softened text for refrain 1 but also wades directly into the redundancy problem, for the first four lines of the B section of refrain 1 ("The world has gone mad today") are now identical to those also prescribed for the same spot in refrain 2. Is this the result of a copyist's blunder—mistakenly importing the text from the one that would be sung in the "Finale Ultimo," even though the promptbook provides the differing Theatrical Text—or was it an intentional mollification of the refrain 1 text for non–New York performances? It's difficult to know. Nor is this the end of our tale of textual volatility. By late 1935 yet another factor had entered into the mix: the transferal of the show over to London.

The London Production (1935)

On 28 November 1934, only seven days into the New York run of the show, the *New York Times* reported that plans were under way for "G. B. Cochran's London production of 'Anything Goes!' in full flower here at the Alvin."[43] This was to be a reworking of the New York show in which characteristically American gags in the promptbook were to be refashioned into English ones and new, British-appropriate lines were to be written for the two refrain-game songs, "You're the Top" and "Anything Goes." P. G. Wodehouse, who had had a hand in the original, rejected script, was entrusted to this task. After some delays the London version of *Anything Goes* opened at the Palace Theatre on 14 June 1935. Its cast, of course, had changed, and the Merman role of Reno Sweeney was given to the French-born Jeanne Aubert. The English "Anything Goes" combined some of Porter's lines with many more by Wodehouse, who apparently had Porter's blessing to devise new words for later refrains of the song. Confusing the matter further is that we currently have two printed sources for these texts. The earlier one is a shorter, typescript version with only two refrains found in the London promptbook—or at least the rental version of it for "representation by amateurs . . . in the British Empire (excepting Canada)," marked "Copyright 1936 by Harms, Incorporated / New York / Copyright 1936, by Samuel French, Ltd."[44] A longer version has been recently published (presumably on the basis of an authoritative but uncited Wodehouse document) in a 2004 anthology edited by Barry Day, *The Complete Lyrics of P. G. Wodehouse*.[45]

Let's first consider the longer version printed in the Day anthology, which sports four refrains—one more than those in the 1934 New York text and two more than those in the London promptbook. (Day, at least, reports that Wodehouse's "revisions . . . were done 'with Porter's enthusiastic approval.'")[46] Here the lyrics start with Porter's verse and first refrain ("In olden days," proceeding through the 1934 theatrical version, with "Mae West," "undressed," and "nudist parties").[47] Following refrain 1 the text veers off into new, London-oriented lyrics. Refrain 2 seems to have been written entirely by Wodehouse. Perhaps reflecting his burdensome tax complications of the time, it takes a pointedly political turn with a concluding poke at the Conservative Party figure Neville Chamberlain, then chancellor of the exchequer:[48]

When maiden aunts can freely chuckle
At tales much too near the knuckle
The facts disclose
Anything goes.

When in the House our Legislators
Are calling each other, "Traitors"
And "So and So's"
Anything goes.

The world's in a state today
Like Billingsgate today
We are each today
For free speech today
Nothing's blue today
Or taboo today
Or meets with scandalous "Oh's"

But while we hope for days more sunny,
The Government gets our money
'Cause Neville knows
Anything goes.

The third refrain—which was the second and final one printed in the rental promptbook—was also apparently mostly Wodehouse. It is possible, however, that Porter might have had a hand in it or at least approved it for at least two reasons: it retains four lines from the B section of Porter's 1934 New York refrain 2 (italicized here); and this is the only new London refrain that included lines destined to make it into some subsequent American performances (including the 1936 Harms vocal score—discussed below—and the 1962 and 1987 revisions of the show). In this version I have changed one word from Day's 2004 anthology to match the racially charged one, "coons," found in the 1936 London promptbook:

When Grandmamma, whose age is eighty
In night clubs is getting matey
With gigolos
Anything goes.

When mothers pack and leave poor father
Because they decide they'd rather
Be tennis pros
Anything goes.

The world has gone mad to-day
And good's bad to-day
And black's white to-day
And day's night to-day,
In Colney Hatch to-day[49]
We ought to snatch to-day
A little rest and repose.

When ladies fair who seek affection
Prefer coons[50] of dark complexion
As Romeos
Anything goes.

Day's printing of Wodehouse's fourth, final refrain turns once again toward political questions of money, the economy, and the rich. Its unimaginative opening leads to unexpectedly tendentious lines that can strike one as out of place in this game-like text:

The dogs chase fleas, the bees chase honey
And we all are chasing money
And when it shows
Anything goes.

The Duke who owns a moated castle
Takes lodgers and makes a parcel
Because he knows
Anything goes.

It's grab and smash today
We want cash today
Get rich quick today
That's the trick today
And the Great today
Don't hesitate today
But keep right on their toes

And lend their names, if paid to do it
To anyone's soap or suet
Or baby clo's
Anything goes.[51]

But what was the text sung on the London stage in 1935? This is unclear. The two refrains given in the British promptbook indicate that the text of refrain 1 was the Neutralized Text ("silly gigolos"; "great romancer"), while that of the second was that of Wodehouse's "third" refrain cited above: "When Grand-mammas [*sic*] whose age is eighty / In Night Clubs are getting matey / With gigolos." By any standard this is a clumsy solution. Not only do we get the redundancy of the repeated four B-section lines in each stanza (beginning "The world has gone mad today") but the word "gigolos" also appears in both refrains. Additionally, of course, that refrain climaxes with the regrettable juxtaposition of "ladies fair" with "coons of dark complexion."

It seems unlikely that London's Reno, Jeanne Aubert, led off with the promptbook's Neutralized Text. Sometime in 1935, but probably after the London premiere, while the musical was still holding the London stage, Aubert made a recording that began with "I Get a Kick Out of You" and concluded with "Anything Goes" (Aubert and the Four Admirals, with Francis Collinson conducting the Palace Theater Orchestra).[52] The medley is vocal throughout (it is not a separate, dance-band arrangement) and gives every indication of being a recorded document of the 1935 version being then presented at London's Palace Theatre.

For "Anything Goes," Aubert's version of refrain 1 is essentially identical with the 1934–35 New York Theatrical Text (and not the version printed in the London promptbook) with two alterations: Aubert softens Porter's "But now, God knows" to "But now, Lord knows" (but not as softened as the London script's "Now Heaven knows"); and "Good authors" is sung as "Good writers." This may well be what she was singing in London in 1935—which version includes the New York B- and A'-section lines beginning with "If driving fast cars you like" and proceeding to "Mae West," "me undressed," and "nudist parties in studios," all of which are heard in her recording. Aubert's refrain 2, though, matches most of the text printed in the 1936 British-rental promptbook ("When Grandmammas whose age is eighty"). What does not appear in the Aubert recording, though, is its racially objectionable final quatrain ("When ladies fair who seek affection / Prefer coons of dark complexion"). Instead, Aubert sings the final quatrain of what Day later printed as Wodehouse's second refrain: "And while we hope for days more sunny / The government gets our money / 'Cause Neville knows / Anything goes." As was the case in America, the evidence that remains from the London production suggests that the text of the song was continuing to be unstable, with numerous versions available to be assembled in different, personalized combinations. In all of this, little was at stake besides the demands of immediate entertainment and a hoped-for marketing success.

The Harms Vocal Score (1936)

By early 1936, following the closings of the New York and London productions of the show and the shift into rental productions beyond those cities, the song

"Anything Goes" had acquired no fewer than eight authorized refrains (again, disregarding the early "young bears" refrain), ranging from the racy to the political to the bland. Following the invariant verse ("Times have changed"), the only constant in all of this seems to have been the principle that, however the initial (or perhaps only) refrain was to continue, it was to begin with its two foundational quatrains to anchor the song: "In olden days" and "Good authors too." In that year, hoping to capitalize on the show's success, Harms published a 108-page vocal score of it that claimed to include all of the music, including the overture, various sets of incidental music, and music for scene changes, reprises, and so on.

For our purposes, it need only be observed that for "Anything Goes," toward the end of act 1, Harms replaced what had actually been sung on the New York stage and what was available in the rental score (three refrains with interpolated dances) with what is surely Harms's final (re)printing and revision of the three-page sheet music for it (on pp. 53–55). Its key, for instance, is the same C minor-major as the 1934 first printing of the sheet music, and it features the telltale, sheet-music-style first and second endings following a single refrain, inappropriate in an actual stage performance. The text printed here, though, is no longer what one had found in the earlier, 1934 Harms printing (whose last half had jumped to "Just think of those shocks you've got," "those silly radios," and "Missus R"). By 1936 the refrain text, following its two invariant quatrains (albeit here with "Now, Heaven knows"), had now been altered into the Neutralized Text ("The world has gone mad today"; "silly gigolos"; "So though I'm not a great romancer"). This synchronized it with the first refrain of the Tams-Witmark rental score while, at the same time, omitting the latter's second and third refrains along with their interpolated dances. Obviously, by 1936 Harms's 1934 sheet music for the song had been silently corrected to incorporate this new text. Airbrushing away much of the song's original bite, the Neutralized Text would now become the song's most generally available published lyrics. As a result, Harms's 1936 printing—now found in both the sheet music and the vocal score—was destined to become the song's normative text when it resurfaced as a standard in the 1950s.

Harms's 1936 vocal score, however, did provide a different text for what immediately followed on the succeeding pages, now under the indication "ENCORE.—Reno and QUARTETTE. Anything Goes." (No such "encore" is found in the Tams-Witmark rental score.) As if to complicate textual matters further, the text for that printed encore (and the most curious feature of this score, pp. 56–59) is that of Wodehouse's (?) refrain 3 from the London production, only slightly emended: "When grandmammas, Whose age is eighty in nightclubs are getting matey with gigolos," "When mothers pack and leave poor fathers," "The world has gone mad today," "Colney Hatch," and "coons of dark complexion"—a text not available in the single-refrain sheet music. In short, any purchaser of the 1936 vocal score would have found only two refrains for the song (New York Neutralized and London refrain 3) and assumed that they were its two authoritative texts. And what about the reprise of the song at the end of the show ("Finale" [Ultimo])? Here the 1936 Harms score agrees with the rental Tams-Witmark score, rounding out the musical by bringing back the Neutralized Text.

The Hollywood Film (1936)

In 1936 Paramount Studios brought out a much-altered film adaptation of *Anything Goes*—under that title—starring Ethel Merman and Bing Crosby.[53] Notwithstanding its substantial alteration of the plot, coupled with the suppression and replacement of many of the show's songs, this film sought to ride the wave of the musical's success. Since the title of the film is that of the musical—and the song—one might have expected that Merman would provide a more or less complete performance of it (as she does with "I Get a Kick Out of You" and a textually altered "You're the Top"). But that is not the case. Paramount must have decided that *any* texted version of this song—even the Neutralized Text—was too spicy for Hays Code–regulated American cinema. And yet the song had to be presented in some way to match the film's title. The solution was to have Merman present only a fragment of the song at the very opening. Following the initial announcement, "Adolph Zukor Presents," the screen dissolves to Ethel Merman on a stage with Hollywood-style background dancers. Merman is allowed to sing only three lines: "In olden days a glimpse of stocking / Was looked on as something shocking / Now, Heaven knows." And at this point, now unsung, the title appears on the screen, *Anything Goes*—and the music immediately shifts into an instrumental version of "All through the Night." Apart from its refrain's initial three lines, "Anything Goes" was censored out of the 1936 film, *Anything Goes*.

Becoming a Standard (1950–1959)

Following its initial flurry of 1934–36 popularity, the song "Anything Goes," along with several others from the show, entered a fourteen-year fallow period in which few, if any, notable recordings of it were made. Its vital moment had come and gone. Broadway—and American culture (not to mention Porter himself)—had moved on. By 1949—the full calendar year of the *Kiss Me, Kate* run, along with the premiere of Rodgers and Hammerstein's *South Pacific*—a show like *Anything Goes* would have been remembered, if at all, as a smart, once-loved relic of an earlier theatrical and political era.

This was now the age of the emerging 45 rpm disc and LP and that of recording "original cast" albums of major Broadway musicals. This endeavor was spearheaded by Goddard Lieberson of Columbia Records. By 1949 Lieberson had hit upon the idea of producing "studio cast" (not "original cast") Columbia Masterworks recordings of newly scored (hence updated) shows from earlier decades, among them selections from *Anything Goes* and Arthur Schwartz and Howard Dietz's *The Band Wagon* (1931).[54] For *Anything Goes* Lieberson managed to sign Mary Martin to perform the Reno Sweeney songs. (At that time Martin was enormously successful as Nurse Nellie Forbush in *South Pacific*.) The recording was made in late August or early September 1950, and Columbia released it in two formats: a box of four 45 rpm discs and a ten-inch LP.[55] Rather than re-creating the 1934 *Anything Goes*, the album offered an array of new arrangements (by Ted Royal) of individual numbers selected from the musical, and the whole was conducted by Lehman Engel. The liner notes on the back of the LP proudly crowed, "Here are the wonderful songs . . . sung precisely as they should be with relish and fine romantic feeling and intimacy by America's greatest comedy star, Mary Martin." As a cultural document of its time this album tells us a great deal, both in its packaging and in the recorded performances that it conveyed. The 1950s reentry of the song "Anything Goes" was one into a much-changed world, a world of retrospective memory and Broadway commemoration ("Columbia Masterworks") that invited listeners to frame the song and its text in new ways.

Sweet, smooth, homogenized (in the style of "Nellie Forbush"), and underpinned by an equally processed orchestration, Mary Martin's two-minute-plus recording is leagues away both from what must have been Merman's original delivery of it and from the flippant wit that had characterized the song some sixteen years earlier.[56] Martin's version tracks dutifully through what was printed in the 1935–36 Harms version, that is, the now-standardized Neutralized Text (with "Now, Heaven knows," "silly gigolos," and "great romancer"), even to the point of taking the notated repeat and singing through the same lyrics twice (a solution completely at odds with the 1934–35 practice of multiple, differing refrains). But in Lieberson's, Royal's, and Engel's hands (or perhaps Martin's?) even that Neutralized Text, in 1950, was thought to carry a problematic line. It is at this point that the phrase "four-letter words" gets replaced with the prim "three-letter words" ("Good authors too who once knew better words / Now only use three-letter words")—which seems to be nonsense ("God"?) in just about any context that one might imagine. This was less the song as a now-recovered representative from the 1934 musical than it was a pleasant, slow-paced Mary Martin vehicle. In this respect, the song was no longer a saucily clever social intervention but rather a musical object notationally preserved in the generically formatted Harms sheet-music script, now to be regarded as the starting point for subsequent reworkings. In short, it was becoming a neutralized, nostalgic curio or classic oldie made publicly available for relaxed consumption: a "masterwork" on its way to becoming an honored fixture in the Great American Songbook.

While one or two more bracing recordings of the song also appeared in the early 1950s (notably that of *Pal Joey* Broadway star Helen Gallagher in 1953),[57] its lyrics' dilution into inoffensive pabulum reached its furthest point with Mitzi Gaynor's rendition of it in Paramount's 1955–56 song-and-dance film, *Anything Goes* (whose plot bears no resemblance to the 1934 musical). This was the Hollywood transformation of the song into winsome cuteness. What the film offered was a big-screen production number—Gaynor, chorus, and dancers—built around a presumably now-familiar American standard—"Anything Goes" as the backdrop source of nightclub arrangements, Las Vegas reviews, and Hollywood films. Martin's "three-letter words" resurfaces here, as does most of the Neutralized Text.[58] The verse is gone altogether, though, and after a half-minute of Hollywood-glamour lead-in, Gaynor launches into the "three-letter words" refrain, though the Neutralized Text's final quatrain ("So though I'm not a great romancer") is replaced with what those in control must have regarded as harmless, further-sanitized, and button-bright final lines:

> So if romance is what you're cravin'
> Don't sit on your hands behavin'
> Like Eskimos,
> Anything goes.

The strangely out-of-place "Eskimos" quatrain (not to mention its unsettling, happy-talk assumptions undergirding the proffered image of freezing, immobile Inuits) functions here as a New World *Aufforderung zum Tanze* directed to all listeners, and with it the music turns to a glitzy celebration of

Hollywood dancing. When the time comes to begin a second refrain, we hear refashioned, 1950s-appropriate words delivered intermittently, its sections separated by more dancing:

When wrestlers go to drama classes
To learn how to please the masses
On T.V. shows,
Anything goes.

. . . .

And when the craze for dancin's spreadin'
Until even Grandpa's treadin'
On Grandma's toes,
Anything goes.

. . . .

Consider those books we've got,
The new looks we've got,
The fool fads we've got,
The mad ads we've got,
The crazy games we've got,
The ladies' names we've got
For each hurricane that blows.

And the song's concluding lines—when they finally do appear—leave behind Porter's A' music, now pushed to the sidelines, replacing it with a grandly climactic close, new music and new words cloaked in a jazzy, minstrel-show affectation:

Hey all you Jills 'n' you Joes,
Get yo'self off o' yo' toes,
'Cause I propose,
You know anything goes!

By the mid- and later 1950s, now marketable as a fondly remembered Cole Porter classic from an earlier era of Broadway, "Anything Goes" had reentered the popular-music world as a comfortably defused standard. The "shocks" of its originally mischievous lines having long since dissipated, the song had ossified into a repertory number for star-singer personalization and "easy-listening" processing, offered up as a suave, adult alternative to the ever-swelling tidal wave of teenage rock 'n' roll and Brill Building culture. This was the case with the major-studio recordings of the song at that time by four big-name vocalists:

Ella Fitzgerald (on the 1956 Verve album, *Ella Fitzgerald Sings the Cole Porter Songbook*, a two-disc set of LPs with orchestrations by Buddy Bregman); Frank Sinatra (on the 1956 Capitol LP, *Songs for Swingin' Lovers*, with Nelson Riddle orchestrations); Jo Stafford (on the 1958 Columbia LP, *Swingin' Down Broadway*, with arrangements and orchestrations by her husband, Paul Weston); and Tony Bennett with Count Basie (on the 1959 Roulette album, *Basie Swings, Bennett Sings*, also released as *Strike Up the Band*).

All four recordings projected the song at a relaxed, casual-swing tempo, backed up by high-style orchestrations; each of the singers delivered only the Neutralized Text, including "Now, Heaven knows"; and each of them restored the Martin-and-Gaynor suppressed letter and sang the relevant line as "four-letter words." Fitzgerald's recording was the only one to include the verse ("Times have changed"): at least on disc, the song was more often pared down to its refrain. All four recordings featured what amounted to two runs through the Neutralized Text, as had Mary Martin's in 1950. On three of them—Fitzgerald's, Stafford's, and Bennett's recordings—the problem of textual redundancy was partially alleviated by following the first round of the Neutralized Text by an instrumental sounding of the first two sections of the refrain, AA, after which the singer reenters to restate the texts of B and A': "The world has gone mad today" and "So though I'm not a great romancer." Only Sinatra resorted to two complete, back-to-back statements of the same words, although the second run-through was pitched a half-step higher, up from A-flat major to A major. Sinatra also concluded the song with a personally texted extension to the refrain, "May I say before this record spins to a close, I want you to know, anything goes."

The Television Production: Ethel Merman Returns (1954)

Somewhat exceptional to all of this—and yet essentially similar to it—was NBC's 27 February 1954, fifty-two-minute television production (by Jule Styne for *The Colgate Comedy Hour*) of what was billed as *Anything Goes*. The show starred Ethel Merman, reprising several of her songs from 1934, Frank Sinatra, and Bert Lahr.[59] Its plot was altered and slashed back to become the flimsiest of frames for the main items of interest: celebrity renditions of seven songs from the musical, newly orchestrated by Buddy Bregman and Nelson Riddle, along with accompanying chorus and dancers. As one of the few available recordings of Merman singing "Anything Goes"—some two decades after she had introduced it in New York—this is a significant document, and Merman's high-energy performance of the song is typically effusive and Broadway-brassy.[60]

"Anything Goes" appears three times in this production, but the third is only a postshow encore in which Merman, on Sinatra's request ("seeing as we have a little time"), reprises her initial delivery of it.[61] In these two performances Merman sings the verse ("Times have changed") and the AAB portions of the now-standard Neutralized Text (including "Now, Heaven knows" and "four-letter words"). Its rollicking final A', however, is given a new, ad hoc text that is even blander than the neutralized one—"So even out in high society / You can't forget propriety, / Goodness knows / Anything goes." (Does this mean *anything* in the context of this song?) And instead of closing cadentially, this substitute quatrain leads to a newly written, non-Porterian epilogue ("The world is topsy-turvy, nonconventional, Technicolor, hypertensional . . . Love, love, love is here to stay . . . and anything . . . anything . . . anything . . . goes"). For the middle performance, now without verse, Merman and the chorus again deliver the Neutralized Text's AAB, but then, leaving Porter's music and words behind, Merman veers elsewhere, replacing Porter's final A' music (and text) and merging instead into a recomposed ending to the song.[62] While it is of interest to see Merman singing this and other songs from the musical, as an ephemeral, one-off special event, the television production did nothing to advance the question of the lyrics and had little impact on the main recording history of the song in the 1950s.

The Revision of "Anything Goes": Mix and Match as Creative Nostalgia (1962)

Our tale of altered texts and performances of "Anything Goes" through the late 1950s—its standardization and neutralization—has come to an end, although we might conclude with a few words about the substantial overhauling and re-presentation of the whole musical that appeared as an off-Broadway revival at the Orpheum Theater on 15 May 1962. While yet later, textually bolder revisions would appear in 1987 and, slightly altered again, in 2011, it is the 1962 version that has commonly been the basis of most local or amateur productions since that time.[63]

The thorough revision of the script was undertaken by the now-seventy-eight-year-old Guy Bolton, who had had a major hand in the earliest 1934 plans for the musical. For updated changes in the lyrics of "You're the Top," he initially solicited, by mid-October 1961, new lines from his old colleague P. G. Wodehouse (who on 28 October wrote to Bolton that "I have always disliked [the show] *Anything Goes* heartily" and was only too eager to detail the reasons why).[64] Whether Wodehouse had any influence on the selections of lines for the New York 1962 version of "Anything Goes" is currently unknown. In any case, "Anything Goes" called for little by way of freshly created lyrics. It is clear, though, that by late October 1961, on Bolton's request, he was fashioning at least some new lines for the song, most likely for the projected London adaptation of the 1962 show.[65] (So far as we know, the ailing Porter was uninvolved with any of this.) For the 1962 revival Bolton dropped several of the original songs from the 1934 musical and inserted into it several other Porter hits, including, among other songs, "It's De-Lovely," "Heaven Hop," "Friendship," and "Let's Misbehave." As for "Anything Goes," it was now shifted forward to become the concluding number of act 1. Bolton knew that he had to retain the idea of multiple stanzas for the refrain (separated by dances), as befit a nostalgia-oriented, period-piece revival. His problem was, which lines were to be chosen among the variously available texts for the song? Clearly, he wished to restore touches of the original spicy Porterian lyrics ("me undressed" and "nudist parties" were now to make a comeback), and yet he must have assessed most of the 1934 references to notable individuals to be too obscure or dated to revive.

Bolton's solution was a curious one. Following the verse, we are given two full refrains (expanded with dances) and, following a full close and applause (noted in the promptbook and score), an "encore," of the second half only, BA', of a third. Refrain 1 is our now-familiar Neutralized Text (including the softened "Heaven knows"), the lyrics that had become the standardized text in all major recordings from 1950 to 1962. Bolton then refashioned refrain 2 into a composite of two different texts. The first two sections, AA, relied not on Porter at all but restored the first eight lines of Wodehouse's 1935 London text (doubtless prompted in this respect by the 1936 Harms vocal score): "When grandmamma whose age is eighty" and "When mothers pack and leave poor father."[66] But Bolton was not about to lead those lines to their original conclusion, which featured the (to Americans) cryptic reference to "Colney Hatch" and the impossible-to-revive reference to "coons of dark complexion." Instead, for the B and A' sections of refrain 2, the 1962 script switches to the "naughty" lyrics of the 1934 Theatrical Text's refrain 1: "If driving fast cars you like," "Mae West," "me undressed," and "nudist parties in studios." With this cobbled-together refrain 2, the song proper ends. Following the applause, a brief encore brings down the curtain to act 1. This begins with the music of a single A section played by the orchestra. The chorus then enters with the B section from refrain 3 of the 1934 Theatrical Text: "Just think of what shocks you've got." This of course led to the evoking of "those little radios," which in turn had originally been the trigger for the 1934 concluding reference to "Missus R" and the "bed from Simmons." Apparently the reviser(s) judged that Roosevelt reference to be too arcane for 1962 audiences, even in an explicit period piece. Audiences would have to wait until 1987 to hear that reference (and several others) restored, and instead we find a new (and astonishingly lame) plot-referring quatrain to end the song:

> They think he's Gangster Number One,
> So they've made him their favorite son
> And that goes to show,
> Anything goes.[67]

The year 1962—two years before the death of Cole Porter—marked a major moment with regard to the fortunes of "Anything Goes" and the musical itself. On the one hand, from this point onward the song, or at least one version of it, became reattached to theatrical practice. The 1962 version of the show *Anything Goes* went on to become a staple of amateur, college, and high-school productions. On the other hand, as one of many standards being rapidly eclipsed by the rock, youth, and folk cultures of the 1960s, the song "Anything Goes" was relegated to the "easy listening" shelves, to nightclub acts, or to campy or nostalgic re-creations by new generations of singers hoping to keep the old torch alive through creative reinterpretation. As for the original 1934 show, it was now erased from memory—only to be rediscovered and restored to documentary life in 1987 (albeit with a generous glaze of 1980s performance style) by John McGlinn's recording of 1987, with original texts and orchestrations. Broadway, meanwhile, was moving elsewhere, with new stylizations and updated, high-tech rethinkings of the musical in the 1987 and 2011 revisions of *Anything Goes*. But all this is far removed from the crackle and flavor of 1934 Broadway. Very far removed indeed. That era had passed—forever.

Notes

1. As is the case, arguably, with Judy Garland's performance of Harold Arlen and E. Y. Harburg's "Over the Rainbow" in the 1939 film *The Wizard of Oz*. It may be that most subsequent performances were delivered and heard with Garland's classic performance as the central reference point. The sonic and visual image of the Garland performance is more the "real song" for later generations than the mute, sterile sheet music produced for home consumption, among whose tasks it was to call to mind Garland's realization.

2. Several recordings from 1928 well into the 1940s contain the original text—from Irving Aaronson's (with Phil Saxe), The Georgians', Rudy Vallee's, and Paul Whiteman's recordings (1928) through at least those of Mary Martin (1940), Rudy Vallee once again (1940), Benny Goodman (with Peggy Lee [1941]), and Billie Holiday (1941). Recordings

from the 1950s generally substitute the altered text, suggesting that the original lines had become problematic in the post–World War II years.

3. The onset of rehearsals "under the direction of Howard Lindsay" was noted in the *New York Times*, 8 October 1934, 15.

4. See Lee Davis, *Bolton and Wodehouse and Kern: The Men Who Made Musical Comedy* (New York: James H. Heineman, 1993), 329–36; and George Eells, *Cole Porter: The Life That Late He Led* (New York: Putnam's, 1967), 118–20. A copy of Bolton and Wodehouse's early scenario (unknown to Davis) is available in the Howard Lindsay and Russel Crouse Papers, 1909–1980, Wisconsin Historical Society Archives, Wisconsin Center for Film & Theater Research, Theater Collection, Madison.

5. *New York Times*, 1 October 1934, 14.

6. Eells, *Cole Porter*, 124.

7. RM 7446, Billy Rose Theater Division, New York Public Library for the Performing Arts.

8. NYPL script RM 7446, act 1, p. 14. (Reno's trigger words were only slightly changed in the 1934/35 script, 1 June 1978.)

9. Folder 196, box 26, MSS 82, Cole Porter Collection, Irving S. Gilmore Music Library, Yale University. It may be that an earlier ink copy was prepared during the rehearsal period, although that would have been an unusual procedure. Robert Kimball reports that "the lyric for an earlier version of the first refrain was found in a copyist ink score at Warner Brothers Music warehouse, Secaucus, New Jersey, [in] February 1982" (*The Complete Lyrics of Cole Porter* [New York: Knopf, 1983; reprint, New York: Da Capo Press, 1992], 171). The Secaucus Cole Porter material, however, is reported to have been given to Yale's Cole Porter Collection in November 1984 (Richard Warren, Curator of Historical Sound Recordings, to Florence Leeds, 20 November and 7 December 1984, acknowledging receipt). It is unclear whether the copy that Kimball saw a year or two before this is the same "Secaucus" one currently available at Yale and discussed in the text above: Kimball's transcription of its text differs slightly from the Yale version. See note 10.

10. Kimball, *Complete Lyrics*, 172, prints slightly different lyrics attributed to the Secaucus-warehouse version of the ink copy that he consulted before 1983 (see note 9). In Kimball's transcription, the text of the final BA' section—the central aspect of the textual question considered here—is identical to that of the Yale copy. Kimball does transmit, however, a different version of the initial AA section, which, if accurately transcribed, would obviously precede the version found in the Yale copy:

> In former times a glimpse of stocking
> Was looked on as something shocking,
> But now God knows—
> Anything goes.
>
> Novelists who once knew better words
> Now only use four letter words for their prose—
> Anything Goes.

"In former times" would have been altered definitively to "In olden days"; "novelists" does not suit the rhythm of the eventual melody well; and so on.

11. On vers de société as a model for popular-song lyrics of the day, see Philip Furia, *The Poets of Tin Pan Alley: A History of America's Great Lyricists* (New York: Oxford, 1990), 6–7 ("crisp and sparking," "playfully malicious," a discussion drawn from an anthology of such verse by Carolyn Wells). "Elegantly naughty," "insouciance," and "bemused sophistication" are taken from Furia's treatment of Porter (160, 153, 169).

12. On the possibly unstable meanings of this term and its more public surfacing from the mid-1960s onward, see Les Wright, "Introduction: Theoretical Bears" and "A Concise History of Self-Identifying Bears," in *The Bear Book: Readings in the History and Evolution of a Gay Male Subculture*, ed. Les K. Wright (New York: Haworth Press, 1997), 1–39. Wright notes that the earliest documentable mention of "bears" in this context stems from Los Angeles "bear club" minutes from 1966 (21) but also observes, more generally (in the early post-Stonewall years), that "an idea of bears was clearly circulating in the gay communities (whether urban enclaves, private network of friends, or organized social clubs) at the same time" (22). The question of whether a similar sense of the word was in circulation in Porter's world of the 1920s and 1930s may at this point be impossible to confirm. With regard to gay-slang imagery referring to animals, George Chauncey, *Gay New York: Gender, Urban Culture, and the Making of the Gay Male World, 1890–1940* (New York: Basic Books, 1994), cites the earlier twentieth-century prevalence of the term "wolf" for a sexually aggressive gay man (e.g., 65, 67, 86, 88, 90, and many other places) and "lamb" (or "kid" or "punk") for more passive types (90, 397)—though the term "bears" does not appear in his book. (In a personal communication Chauncey has indicated that, while not ruling out the possibility of the Porterian "bear" double entendre, he has been unable to uncover unambiguous instances of that term's usage in the 1920s and 1930s—and could only speculate that if it carried any such connotation at the time, it could have been used as a substitute for "lamb" or "kid.")

13. If the line is construed to mean the love affairs of women with men, there would have been no reason to censor the text. Porter's erotic wit, when interpretable heterosexually, typically (at least within his shows) survived the censor's pen. Porterian bears have a history. In "Let's Do It" from 1927–28, the concluding lines of the final refrain, refrain 5, are "The world admits bears in pits do it, / Even pekineses in the Ritz, do it, / Let's do it, let's fall in love." Innocent enough, one might conclude, within a list-song trotting out, seriatim, numerous types of zoological species. But when that song was dropped from *Paris*, the bear image found its way into its replacement, "Let's Misbehave," whose concluding lines, in the published text, read:

> They say that bears
> Have love affairs
> And even camels;
> We're merely mammals,
> Let's misbehave.

Curiously, those lines were not included in Irene Bordoni's 1928 recording of the song. Were they suppressed? One of Bordoni's replacements, also echoing "Let's Do It," seems naughtier:

I always squeeze
My pekinese
Whenever he's good;
Your pedigree's good,
Let's misbehave.

Proceeding onward, it is fairly easy to draw imagery connections between "Let's Do It," "Let's Misbehave," and "Anything Goes"—as if each were a substitute for or over-writing of the other, with fleeting allusions to what it had replaced. "Let's Misbehave" disappeared from view after 1928 (why?) only to resurface in the 1962 revision of the show *Anything Goes*, where it is to be foppishly sung, perhaps with gay connotations, by Sir Evelyn Oakleigh. In the 2004 biopic of Porter, *De-Lovely*, Elvis Costello's campy performance of the song altered the final quatrain in a way that might have meant to underscore its same-sex implications:

They say that bears
Have love affairs
And even camels;
We're men and mammals,
Let's misbehave.

14. McGlinn, "The Original 'Anything Goes'—a Classic Restored," program booklet accompanying the McGlinn recording of the original orchestration and lyrics of the 1934 *Anything Goes* (EMI Compact Disc 7 49848 2, 1989), 33. Eells had hinted at much the same thing, citing "[Porter's] willingness to submit the score of his show for [Merman's] father's and mother's approval. And when they vetoed two numbers, he discarded them without protest" (*Cole Porter*, 122). Merman's *An Autobiography* (New York: Simon and Schuster, 1978), written in collaboration with George Eells, mentions nothing about these incidents. Cf. Raymond Knapp's view of the gay subtexts of *Anything Goes* (and "Kate the Great") in *The American Musical and the Formation of National Identity* (Princeton, NJ: Princeton University Press, 2005), 88–97.

15. In this respect, cf. the similarly pentatonic Reno Sweeney's (Merman's) "Blow, Gabriel, Blow."

16. The I–III (iii)–V arpeggiation through the AAB portion of the song is too obvious to require extended comment.

17. See notes 9 and 10 above.

18. I call this newly cobbled-together version (which goes out of its way to interpolate the "young bears" B section as a final add-on) the 1987 Theatrical Text. It may be heard on compact disc, sung by Patti LuPone, on the recording *Anything Goes: The New Broadway Cast Recording* (RCA Victor 88697 90254 2, 1988) or sung by Elaine Paige on *Anything Goes: London 1989 Cast Recording* (First Night Records, OCRCD 6038). A 1990 video of the song in this latter production—with Elaine Paige and accompanying dancers—may be seen on YouTube at http://www.youtube.com/watch?v=ZCFJyJa01xI. The 1987 Theatrical Text also appears, with only small alterations, sung by Sutton Foster in the 2011 Broadway production, *Anything Goes: New Broadway Cast Recording* (Ghostlight

Records, 8-4452, 2011). See note 67 below for an outline of the 1987 Theatrical Text (which also includes lines from the 1935 London production).

19. The 27 November 1934 recording is Victor 24825, mx BS 86065-1. Unless otherwise specified, the dates of the many early recordings cited in this essay can be verified on the Online Discographical Project, http://www.78discography.com. Additional confirmation may often also be found at http://www.sondheimguide.com/porter/cole.html. The promptbook consulted here is that found in box 26 of the Cole Porter Collection (the box containing the *Anything Goes* materials) in Yale University's Irving S. Gilmore Library. Other copies may be found elsewhere.

20. For the documentation of McGlinn's compact disc, see note 14 above.

21. See note 20 above. Since the various sources differ in small details, the text is not a stable one. Moreover, the promptbook of 1 June 1978–79 inadvertently omits the first-refrain quatrain, "Good authors too," and its B-section line "If old hymns you like," lines that I have restored here in brackets.

22. Porter's 27 November 1934 recording (Victor 24825), variant: "Intruding" (introducing a subrhyme with "nudist"), which is also the version printed in Kimball, *Complete Lyrics,* 171.

23. Porter recording: "When."

24. Porter recording: "does."

25. In the promptbook these last two lines were printed as a single line.

26. Porter's recording of refrain 3 substitutes the word "those" for "what" in the first line and in the second word of the next four lines:

> And those knocks you've got
> And those blues you've got
> From those news you've got
> And those pains you've got.

Kimball transcribes Porter's sung lyrics, not those of the promptbook, but alters the awkward "those news" to "that news" (*Complete Lyrics*, 172). As will be seen, the 1934 Harms sheet music includes all of Porter's "those" variants.

27. The line is misprinted [?] in the promptbook as "So Missur . . . with all her trimmins."

28. One might note the apex pitch in the B sections of refrains 2 and 3, setting, respectively, "that *gent* today" and "what [or those] *pains* you've got."

29. Kreuger, "The Annotated 'Anything Goes,'" in the program booklet for the John McGlinn 1988–89 recording of the show (68–69)—one source of the information in this paragraph and the source of the immediately quoted material.

30. Elsie de Wolfe called attention to the value of her exercise routines in her autobiography from 1935, *After All* (London: William Heinemann), 233–35. A photograph facing page 234 identifies "Elsie de Wolfe [standing] on her head at Maxine Elliot's villa at Golfe Juan." Another image of de Wolfe's exercises may be found at http://habituallychic.blogspot.com/2011/01/lets-get-physical.html.

31. Maurine H. Beasley, *Eleanor Roosevelt and the Media: A Public Quest for Self-Fulfillment* (Urbana: University of Illinois Press, 1987), 72–73. In addition, an Internet

image search ("Eleanor Roosevelt Simmons") readily turns up two of her printed-advertisement endorsements for Simmons (a company that marketed itself as a merchant in upscale luxury): "Mrs. Franklin D. Roosevelt says, 'I've never known such comfort'"; and "In my opinion the PERFECT GIFT is one that fills a real place—Luxuriously."

32. The Online [78 rpm] Discographical Project (note 20 above) at http://www.78discography.com/vic24500.html. "Thank You So Much" bears the earlier matrix number (BS 84900-1 as opposed to BS 84901-1) and was thus recorded first. Robert Kimball comments, "Published December 1934. A typescript of the lyric was found among the unused lyrics of *Anything Goes,* indicating that Porter might have contemplated using it in the show" (*Complete Lyrics*, 274).

33. One notices the closeness of the Victor-disc numbers for the Porter and Whiteman recordings (Victor 24766, 24769, and 24770). The two 78 rpm numbers in between (24667-8) were unrelated recordings made the day before by Enrique Madrigera & His Orchestra. Hence the next available numbers, after Porter's, were Whiteman's two 78s, four songs. This suggests that Whiteman recorded his songs immediately after Porter had completed his own.

34. The Whiteman recording may be heard on YouTube at http://www.youtube.com/watch?v=zrWrKmvspGw.

35. The 1934 Harms sheet-music text differs from the Tams-Witmark promptbook text in printing the word "those" in this and succeeding lines where the promptbook reads "what." "Those" corresponds also to the lyrics that Porter sings on his 27 November 1934 recording. See note 26 above.

36. The Dorsey Brothers recording, whose vocalists included Bob Crosby, may be heard both on Spotify and on YouTube at http://www.youtube.com/watch?v=MCjhFru6m7g. Once again, my source for the recording date is the Online [78 rpm] Discographical Project, in this instance at http://www.78discography.com/Dec100.htm.

37. McGlinn notes that his reconstruction of the "Finale Ultimo" was "rebuilt from parts and [orchestrationally] restored [in the 1980s] by Spialek" ("The Original 'Anything Goes'—a Classic Restored," 33).

38. This recording may be heard on YouTube at http://www.youtube.com/watch?v=ZwJ9uktauaE. Again, my source for the recording date is the Online [78 rpm] Discographical Project, in this case at http://www.78discography.com/BRN7300.htm. The 1934 Neutralized Text was also sung in the 1935 British recording by Ambrose and His Orchestra (Decca ACL-1186).

39. Singer omits the word "just."

40. Singer adds the word "'Cause," rendering the final line as "'Cause anything goes."

41. One might add that the piano-vocal Harms version of the music was likewise only one scripted realization of that music's idea—or schema—that played into an implicit, genre-specific set of guidelines for how it might be subsequently recast. It was understood that later arrangers would reconceive central aspects of its layout, harmony, style, and tone. The point behind all of these realizations was to present the schema directly and recognizably, colored by a personalized stylization by the arranger or performer, who was then considered to be the immediate bearer or carrier of the musical schema—or game.

42. A cardboard-bound ozalid print of a manuscript copy for piano and voice; one such copy, identified as "*Anything Goes* Orig.," is available in Yale's Cole Porter Collection. While its cover proclaims it to be a conductor's score for the "original" version, the Yale copy of "*Anything Goes* Orig." does not bear a date. It is clearly a rental score, not the score used in the first 1934 performances of the show: so much can be told from its various inclusions and omissions. (It also contains a number of copying errors throughout.) Still, it probably represents the state of the show by the time of the initial availability of the off-Broadway rentals in late 1935.

43. *New York Times*, 28 November 1934, 25.

44. Samuel French was the London rental outlet for the production of musicals. The company's name and address, along with its claim of "the rights of representation . . . in the British Empire (excepting Canada)," appear on the verso of the title page. I am grateful to Geoffrey Block for providing me with a photocopy of this script.

45. Barry Day, ed., *The Complete Lyrics of P. G. Wodehouse* (Lanham, MD: Scarecrow Press, 2004), 408–15.

46. Ibid., 409.

47. The London promptbook, however, substitutes "Now, Heaven knows" for Porter's "But now, God knows."

48. This refrain also appears in Robert McCrum, *Wodehouse: A Life* (London: Viking; New York: Norton, 2004), 228–29. McCrum also devotes much attention to Wodehouse's tax problems.

49. "Colney Hatch" refers to the Colney Hatch Lunatic Asylum, by that time a generalized reference for madhouses within England. The term may have been one of the sources for the more recent, general slang words "booby hatch." See the collection of etymological references summarized at http://www.wordwizard.com/phpbb3/viewtopic.php?f=5&t=4458.

50. Day, *Complete Lyrics*, 410, perhaps censoring out the offending, racialist word, reads "Prefer gents of dark complexion." Day's system of italics and nonitalics suggests that this line, along with a few others, might have been Porter's, although until one is presented with the evidence, one should remain skeptical.

51. In Day, *Complete Lyrics*, two lines of this refrain are nonitalicized, suggesting that they could be of Porterian derivation: "The Duke who owns a moated castle" and "And the Great today." As was the case in refrain 3, it is unlikely that Porter parachuted in for these two internal lines. It is more likely that they were Wodehouse's. All four refrains (probably taken from Day's anthology), though without "coons," may be heard in the 2000–2001 recording by Hal Cazalet and Sylvia McNair, *The Land Where the Good Songs Go: The Lyrics of P. G. Wodehouse* (Harbinger Compact Disc, HCD 1901). (The track is also available on Spotify.)

52. Columbia DX 697. This recording, along with its companion, "I Get a Kick Out of You," may be heard on YouTube at http://www.youtube.com/watch?v=QJXBJvL51pQ. Also available is "You're the Top," sung by Jack Whiting and Jeanne Aubert (with its curious inclusion of a reference to "Mussolini"): http://www.youtube.com/watch?v=x6S-7Bd5k_I.

53. A second release of the film was retitled *Tops Is the Limit*—suggesting that even the title, *Anything Goes*, was eventually assessed to be excessively provocative.

54. The account in this paragraph is drawn from two online sources. The first is found at http://www.allmusic.com/album/anything-goes-mw0000988945: "At the time of its release [1950], this album was the only collection of music from *Anything Goes* available, which made it particularly valuable." The second is http://www.sondheimguide.com/porter/anythingrec.html. The still-uncataloged Goddard Lieberson Papers in the Irving S. Gilmore Library (MSS 69) contain Lehman Engel's enthusiastic plans (beginning 28 April 1950) for the *Anything Goes* and *Band Wagon* projects. Mary Martin was on board by June or July 1950. The Engel-Lieberson correspondence indicates that the album was apparently recorded in late August and early September 1950.

55. The ten-inch LP was released as Columbia CL 2159. Paired with arrangements from *The Band Wagon*, it is now available on compact disc, DRG B000060PC6.

56. The Mary Martin / Ted Royal / Lehman Engel recording of the song may be heard on Spotify.

57. This was released on an RCA ten-inch EP, LPM-3157, with Broadway conductor Milton Rosenstock leading the orchestra. Here we find the invariant verse ("Times have changed") followed, first, by the complete Neutralized Text (with "Now, Heaven knows" and "four-letter words") at a bouncy, upbeat tempo. The orchestra continues with a nontexted arrangement of the first half of the next refrain, AA, whereupon Gallagher reenters at a radically scaled-back tempo to underscore the now-lurid return of the "original" refrain 1 B-section text, "If driving fast cars you like," and so on. Most notably—at hyperslow tempo and delivered with unalloyed sexual suggestion—she alters the reference to "Mae West" to sing, "Or the *best* you like / Or me un*dressed* you like / . . . *Well* . . . Heaven only knows." For the final A' quatrain the "nudist parties" are banished. The up-tempo returns for Gallagher to conclude the song with one of Wodehouse's quatrains, "When mothers pack and leave poor fathers."

58. The 1955–56 Paramount film led to the Decca soundtrack LP, 8318. The film is available on DVD (Paramount 05513), and its soundtrack may be heard on compact disc (Decca B-0001933-02). Gaynor's film performance of "Anything Goes" is also viewable on YouTube at http://www.youtube.com/watch?v=Hqo_OgAANgM. The soundtrack recording is clearly a different performance from that seen in the film. Gaynor, it seems, rerecorded the song for the LP over the original orchestral track. On the soundtrack recording, Gaynor's "stocking" and "shocking" are delivered as "stockin'" and "shockin'." Cf. the dropping of the g's in the final quatrain of both the film and the soundtrack version. In addition, some of the lines assigned to the chorus in the film are sung by Gaynor alone on the soundtrack.

59. This production is viewable on YouTube at http://www.youtube.com/watch?v=QKkPb8uhPZo and is also available as a DVD from Entertainment One.

60. There also exists a clip of a 1979 (!) performance of the song by a seventy-one-year-old Ethel Merman on the television special *Musical Comedy Tonight*. This includes the complete Neutralized Text and, at the end, the 1934 refrain 1 B section ("If driving fast cars you like," "Mae West," "me undressed") but provides a new text

entirely for the final A quatrain. It is viewable on YouTube at http://www.youtube.com/watch?v=4zJ3vqkXqRU.

61. On YouTube this occurs at 4:52, 12:05, and (for the encore) 48:16. The encore is preceded by a very brief "finale" presenting only a fragment of the song.

62. For the second quatrain, A ("Good authors too"), the chorus may be altering the text to "two-letter words" (!).

63. See the Tams-Witmark web page at http://www.tamswitmark.com/musicals/anything62.html. On some aspects of the 1987 and 2011 versions, see notes 18 above and 68 below.

64. The litany of complaints alluded to here appears in Wodehouse's first letter (of two) to Bolton on 28 October 1961, which also enclosed his proposal for "the revised 'You're the Top' lyric," apparently for New York. Apart from disparaging Porter's original text for "You're the Top" ("The poor devil got very exhausted after doing five refrains"), Wodehouse faulted the show's overly heavy reliance on Reno/Merman ("The wrongness of the balance offends my artistic soul") along with its music ("The score is so thin. Apart from the three song hits we have almost nothing"). This letter is printed in Sophie Ratcliffe, ed., *P. G. Wodehouse: A Life in Letters* (London: Hutchinson, 2011), 504–5. See also note 66 below.

65. Wodehouse's advisory role, if any, in the New York 1962 version of the song "Anything Goes" remains unclear. In a second 28 October 1961 letter to Bolton, Wodehouse boasted of having created a "masterly couplet" for (the London version of?) "Anything Goes": "When the courts decide, as they did latterly, / We could read *Lady Chatterley* / If we chose, / Anything Goes"—and followed it up with more self-praise: "(Darned sight better than anything old King Cole ever wrote)" (Ratcliffe, *P. G. Wodehouse*, 505).

66. Again, this claim presumes that Porter had no hand in the production of these lines for the 1935 London production.

67. We are now at the moment when it is possible also to summarize what I call the New 1987 Theatrical Text—the standard text in revised major productions of *Anything Goes* from the 1987 Lincoln Center version onward. This is the text that, among other things, restores the originally suppressed line about "young bears" (see note 18 above). The first two refrains are essentially taken over from those in the show's 1962 revision. In brief, the sequence of events in this highly composite 1987 text is verse; first refrain (Neutralized Text); dance; composite second refrain (AA sections, London refrain 3, "When grandmamma," "When mothers pack"—followed by BA' of the 1934 Theatrical Text's refrain 1, "If driving fast cars," "Mae West," "me undressed," "nudist parties"); longer dance, preparing the entrance of two versions of BA' only (chorus sings BA') of the Neutralized Text—thus heard now for the second time—followed by Reno alone singing the suppressed, original B section, "If saying your pr'yers you like," "if love affairs with young bears you like," followed by yet another, third statement of the Neutralized Text's final A' section ("And though I'm not a great romancer").

9

Keeping Faith with John Q. Public

Cole Porter, Billy Rose, and *Seven Lively Arts*

JAMES O'LEARY

For sumptuousness, for expense, and for hype, few shows rivaled Cole Porter's *Seven Lively Arts* (1944). Photographs, written accounts, and anecdotal evidence from the time have all suggested that this revue was huge in every respect. Norman Bel Geddes's glittering sets were mammoth—much bigger than what could have fit in most theaters, requiring a convoy of ten train cars to move.[1] Contemporary reports marveled at the "acres" of scenery, and when the show opened for its out-of-town tryout in Philadelphia, two full trucks had to be sent back to New York because their contents could not fit on the stage.[2] Supernumeraries, coryphées, and choristers populated the sets, amounting to a veritable army of singers and dancers who wore couture costumes that glittered under the "couple million candlepower" of lighting arranged on the grids by director Hassard Short.[3] The sequence closing the first act featured so many performers that Jumbo, the bejeweled model elephant and scenic coup de grâce, almost did not fit onstage.[4] As one critic remarked, "Into [this revue is] piled a little bit of everything but the kitchen sink—and if that could dance or were pretty, it probably would be there, too."[5]

Just as notable as the spectacle was the eclectic roster of people who contributed to it. George S. Kaufman, Moss Hart, and Ben Hecht furnished the sketches; Porter supplied the music and lyrics (of which "Ev'ry Time We Say Goodbye" is the only song that remains in the regular performance and scholarly repertories).[6] World-renowned comedienne Beatrice Lillie, famous for her improvisation and slapstick, returned to the New York stage for the first time since 1939 to perform in *Seven Lively Arts*.[7] She shared the boards (and the top of the marquee) with Burt Lahr, known for his "acrobatic eyes" and "twisting face," and comedian Doc Rockwell, known for his "prominent teeth and the gift of gab."[8] The show also featured, however, a number of performers who were relative strangers to the Broadway stage. Most prominent in this coterie were Anton Dolin and Alicia Markova, two dancers from England via Diaghilev's touring Ballets russes who shared above-the-title billing with Lillie and Lahr.[9] Dance music was furnished not by Porter but by William Schuman and Igor Stravinsky.[10] In charge of the pit was Maurice Abravanel, a conductor at the Metropolitan Opera, and in charge of the singers was Robert Shaw, then famous as the Collegiate Chorale conductor. In charge of the lobby was Salvador Dalí, who decorated the walls with murals depicting each of the seven lively arts for the premiere.[11] The talents of famous bandleader and clarinetist Benny Goodman were employed twice during the show: he ended the first act with a burst of swing and played Carl Maria von Weber's Clarinet Concerto at the top of the second act.[12]

Given the attention the show received at the time, its subsequent obscurity in the scholarly literature may seem surprising. Nevertheless, most historians have described this revue as a disappointment, as if the combination of creators promised "something that may have been wonderful, but wasn't," resulting instead in a "conventional," "pedestrian" "debacle," "top-heavy with talent."[13] In the words of Gerald Bordman, "The show's 'artiest' moments, such as the Stravinsky ballet, were dismissed by highbrows as trite and by regular playgoers as pretentious."[14] For many, the show remains noteworthy as an oddity, an unusual concatenation of material from far-flung, even incongruous, genres and repertoires.

This distinction between highbrow and lowbrow, however, was not limited to critical reaction. (For our purposes, words such as "arty" and "serious" will be synonyms for "highbrow," and "lively," "commercial," "middlebrow," and "popular" will stand in for "low.")[15] In fact, Billy Rose, the show's producer, referred to it often, and early on in the rehearsal process seemed convinced that "music, ballet, theater, opera, movies, radio, and modern painting were arty and lively enough for a good show theme."[16] But as opening night approached he changed his mind, saying to the press only a few days before the premiere, "My principal concern . . . is that the public and the play reporters will come on Thursday night with their imaginations occupied by the 'arts' and that they will have buried in their consciousnesses the adjective 'lively.'"[17] Confidence became apprehension: it was as if he realized that *Seven Lively Arts*, under a veil of comedy and spectacle, toyed with some kind of taboo by crossing between high and low. For Rose, "lively" *and* "arty" became "lively" *or* "arty." Why did he have to choose?

What follows is the story of this unusual collaboration between high and low artists. Rather than view the high-low crossover in this revue as a sign of cultural tone deafness or as a bizarre cultural oddity, I will describe the nature of the collaboration between Billy Rose and these artists, focusing especially on Cole Porter. No record survives that would suggest any direct communication between Stravinsky, Schuman, Porter, the librettists, and the arrangers. Instead, it appears that they were given their directive from Rose himself, not in terms of a strict plot outline per se, but in terms of a general theme of high and low. The result was a show that straddled the line between a so-called integrated musical and a musical revue. Although the show consisted entirely of sketches, and even though there was no real story to follow in the show, most of the sketches dealt with the theme of artistic prestige in some form or another. Thus, whether Porter was producing music that was directly related to the general theme of lively arts, or whether he was writing for a specific sketch, most of the songs addressed artistic prestige in some way. This chapter, then, will focus on the larger collaboration into which Porter and Rose situated the musical material. First, I examine the manner in which Porter's music specifically undermined the "lively"/"arty" divide. Then I analyze the critical reaction to the show, revealing not only some of the ways in which postwar composers and critics negotiated these cultural territories but also what was at stake in crossing between them.

Oompah Polyglot: Cole Porter and *Seven Lively Arts*

Seven Lively Arts was not Rose's first attempt to straddle the line between classical music and Broadway. Less than a year earlier he had produced *Carmen Jones*, Oscar Hammerstein II's 1943 adaptation of Bizet's *Carmen*, set in a contemporary South Carolina parachute factory with an African American cast. Although a complete investigation of Rose's theatrical career lies beyond the scope of this essay, to understand exactly how Porter's music was to be situated into the larger concept of *Seven Lively Arts* it is instructive to compare Rose's rhetoric during his collaboration with Porter to his rhetoric with Hammerstein on *Carmen Jones*.

From the earliest announcements in the press, Hammerstein was clear that *Carmen Jones* would not be a "swung," "jazzed," "boogie-woogie," or "hepcat" *Carmen* with "Tin Pan Alley twists" but rather would simply "translate" the original while keeping the essence the same.[18] The purpose of these announcements was not only to tap into the prestige associated with Bizet's opera but also to distance *Carmen Jones* from a kind of Broadway musical that had been popular in the late 1930s and early 1940s, one that took classic texts and updated them with African American casts and modern Broadway or jazz music. Such extravaganzas included *Hot Mikado* (Michael Todd's popular 1939 adaptation of Gilbert and Sullivan's *The Mikado*) and *Swinging the Dream* (the 1940 musical adaptation of Shakespeare's *Midsummer Night's Dream*).[19] Even though he modernized *Carmen*, Hammerstein went to great lengths to convince the press that he was not trying to efface the boundary between high and low. He explicitly maintained that *Carmen Jones* was "not grand opera."[20] He "dared not toy with tradition" but instead "[bowed] in humble supplication to his posthumous collaborators, Henri Mielhac and Ludovic Halévy."[21]

At first, Rose echoed Hammerstein, and in the weeks leading to *Carmen Jones*'s opening, the producer conspicuously played down his typical Broadway bravado: "I am . . . deliberately embarking on a theatrical venture which is not a good financial risk. For this first time in my life I am about to toss a couple hundred thousand dollars into the air with the gesture of a man who doesn't care what happens to it. I am about to produce 'Carmen Jones' in as honest and sincere a production as I am capable of managing."[22] He claimed to be forsaking financial concerns, thereby distancing himself from the commercial entertainment that made him famous. No matter that it was not true—*Carmen Jones*'s price tag was well publicized. Rather, Rose's conversations with the press constituted a public performance in which he ostentatiously claimed to be "honest and sincere," pledging allegiance to what he called "art for art's sake" with no tangible rewards other than aesthetic interest.[23]

This rhetoric did not last. Once Rose turned his attention to *Seven Lively Arts*, his demeanor began to change. Rose bragged that *Carmen Jones* was "real opera" because "in a year it will play to 800,000—more people than will hear 'Carmen' at the Metropolitan in a century."[24] Although few words survive from Porter about his work on *Seven Lively Arts*, the essential difference between the two lyricists is clear from the material Porter wrote for the show. If Hammerstein was deferential (even obsequious) toward the boundaries between opera and musical theater, Porter was the opposite. For example, the song "I Wrote a Play" (cut from the show before it opened in Philadelphia) follows a young, ambitious playwright as he shops his play *Boy Meets Girl* from producer to producer. The young writer's first verse describes the toil he endured writing this play. The homophonic texture and the unadorned diatonic harmony in the accompaniment suggest simplicity, as if the young man's motives are somehow "pure," dedicated to his art above all—a mood underscored by a hint of piety from the amenlike $\hat{4}$–$\hat{3}$ suspension at the cadence (ex. 1).

During the course of the song, the protagonist visits the prestigious Gilbert Miller's office, then the equally prestigious Theatre Guild, both of which would have been recognized at the time by contemporary audiences for importing European plays and producing the avant-garde works of such a writer as Eugene O'Neill. Next follows his visit to the infamous Mike Todd, known for his Broadway spectacles. Each producer suggests changes to his play that, one supposes, offend the young man's artistic sensibilities. Todd, for example, tells the playwright that his play is "being rewritten by Gypsy Rose" and that Todd is "hiring a nudist to do the clothes." At last the playwright sends the play out to Samuel Goldwyn in Hollywood, who tells the young protagonist that he "read part of it all the way through" and who ultimately has no interest in the text itself. Nevertheless, Goldwyn mentions that he recently bought

> A play that was tough to get
> Called *Romeo and Juliet*
> But if the title was "Boy Meets Girl"
> What a hell of a picture for Milton Berle.

Of course, the young man sells. What the listener assumed was a song about this young playwright's highbrow artistic integrity was actually a song about holding out for a windfall. The critical aspect of the comedy was that the scruples of the former could appear identical to the opportunism of the latter,

EXAMPLE 1. Cole Porter, "I Wrote a Play," mm. 8–14. Irving S. Gilmore Library, Yale University. Used by permission of the Trustees of the Cole Porter Trust.

a critique played out in the accompaniment. As the main character ventures further into the production side of theater, the pitch content of the melody remains largely the same, but, as can be seen in the Sam Goldwyn verse in example 2, the rhythm becomes gradually more syncopated, the accompaniment takes on conspicuous dance patterns, the harmony increasingly features altered chords and chromatic passing tones, and the simple diatonicism of the first verse is replaced by abrupt, Broadway-style key changes.

To mark the musical distance between the first and final bars of the song, the original $\frac{6}{8}$ homophonic texture returns suddenly when the young playwright finally sells out, but this time adorned with chromatic chords and, instead of an "amen" cadence, an ornamental trill (ex. 3). Is this trill operatic?

EXAMPLE 2. Cole Porter, "I Wrote a Play," mm. 32–41. Irving S. Gilmore Library, Yale University. Used by permission of the Trustees of the Cole Porter Trust.

Is it "arty"? Ostentatiously so, but here such "operaisms" stand in not as a symbol of high art but as an ironic commentary on purely commercial art. Porter's music, like the protagonist, crossed easily between high and low, and this very promiscuity (recognized as such) provides the song's humor.

Although many of Porter's most famous songs were episodic and essentially strophic, the most conspicuous aspect of this particular song was its gradually changing accompaniment, which underlay a relatively fixed melody. Porter used this strategy elsewhere in the show, as in Lahr's song "Drink" (act 1, scene 9, labeled "Drink, Drink, Drink" in some of the scores), for similar wink-wink-nudge-nudge jokes about show business:

> Drink to the *Desert Song* and *Rose Marie*,
> Drink to Moselle, to hell with Burgundy,
> Drink to Sigmund Romberg, our greatest prize,
> But "Don't fire before you see the whites of his eyes."
> Drink to *The Student Prince*, that show sublime
> And please don't forget Jeanette in *Blossom Time*,
> Drink to Nelson Eddy before you faint
> And here's to J. J. Shubert, our patron saint.[25]

EXAMPLE 3. Cole Porter, "I Wrote a Play," mm. 197–203. Irving S. Gilmore Library, Yale University. Used by permission of the Trustees of the Cole Porter Trust.

There are a few levels of critique in this piece. First, there is the insider's reference to Sigmund Romberg, whose own "Drink, Drink, Drink" from *The Student Prince* (1924) had been seen on Broadway only a year earlier in a revival directed by J. J. Shubert. Members of the Shubert family, in addition to producing shows, were also powerful because they owned a national network of theaters, including many in New York City. Given Rose's longstanding problems in finding theaters for his shows, the line "patron saint," sung slowly with sudden mock reverence, would have been especially flippant considering *Seven Lively Arts* was playing in the Ziegfeld Theater, which Rose, not the Shuberts, owned.

There may have been an additional dig at the Shuberts: Romberg's original song from *The Student Prince* was a Prohibition Era paean to Heidelberg, beer, and love. In Porter's version, the sailors' praise of German wines (Moselle) over Allied French wines (Burgundy), along with their love of an operetta set in Germany by an Austro-Hungarian composer, may have been seen as being in bad taste during the war. Perhaps this was an oblique commentary on the Shuberts' choice of producing an operetta that romanticized Germany during World War II.

But there was, in fact, still another level of critique in this song, one of the division between high and low art. The first section of "Drink" (labeled as the first and second "refrain" in the score) is in a $\frac{6}{8}$ "Tempo di Marcia," but for the rest of the piece (called "patter" in the score) it subtly switches to $\frac{2}{2}$ (ex. 4). While the first section seems like a pastiche of operetta, the new meter would have been conspicuously popular, which, combined with ragtime rhythm on the words ending each line (such as "slick and sleek"), suggests a Broadwayesque sound. Additionally, when these rhythms align with the punch line of a joke (usually every sixteen bars), there is often an orchestral interjection that sounds far removed from the previous pastiche, often with muted brass.[26] However, even though on paper the difference between the two sections may seem striking, the aural effect of switching between a militaristic $\frac{6}{8}$ oompah and Broadway $\frac{2}{2}$ oompah was subtle, as if the oompah accompaniment could become polyglot, a dialect whose basic syntax was comprehensible, though marked, on both sides of the high-low divide.

The subversive aspect of *Seven Lively Arts*' music was how easily it could travel from high to low and back. First, the cross from low to high: in act 2, scene 5, an "east-Asian" novelty song called "Frahngee-Pahnee," performed at the "Tempo of 'Begin da Beguine,'"[27] led directly into Beatrice Lillie's song "Dancin' to a Jungle Drum," in which she intoned on a single pitch, "But the

EXAMPLE 4. Cole Porter, "Drink," mm. 64–78. New York Public Library. Used by permission of the Trustees of the Cole Porter Trust.

thing that leaves me completely numb is the beat, beat, beat, and the tick, tick, tock, and the drip, drip, drip of a jungle drum."[28] "Night and Day," one of Porter's most popular songs, here comes across as blunt, vapid—a typical critique of commercial music. Porter's lyrics, in a highbrow vein, spoofed the composer's own success.

More common was the cross from high to low. For example, the Philadelphia program lists act 2, scene 1 (immediately following Schuman's ballet) as "I Waver Twixt Madness," a song for Lillie from the 1907 opera *Tom Jones* by English composer Edward German. Although the surviving full score for *Seven Lively Arts* gives only sketchy details about its orchestration, the trend of juxtaposing serious art and pure silliness is nonetheless evident: moments of "serious" singing, such as an elaborate trilled cadenza, were set off against moments of pure slapstick comedy, such as a scored coughing fit.[29] In each case, opera and "operaisms" were pegged as the hallmark of high. But the most conspicuous opera/Broadway juxtaposition was first-act closer "Billy Rose Buys the Metropolitan Opera House!" For this sequence, a whole team of arrangers and orchestrators, including Hans Spialeck, Ted Royal, Fred Waring, and Robert Russell Bennett, created a musical montage of operatic scenes (selections from *Aida*, *Carmen*, *Das Rheingold*, *Die Walküre*, and the Barcarolle from *Les contes d'Hoffman*) that slipped into Tin Pan Alley and jazz songs (such as Dana Suesse's "Yours for a Song" and Rodgers's "The Circus Is on Parade"). The final section of this sequence was particularly striking. Following Goodman's performance, there was an elaborate reprise of Porter's "Only Another Boy and Girl" to bring down the first-act curtain, superimposed over a mélange of operatic quotations (ex. 5). Was this supposed to be an example of a musical world without boundaries? Or instead was the prominence of the Porter melody over the fragmented, accompanimental, operatic quotations supposed to signal Broadway's supremacy over highbrow opera? Either way, it did not matter; the sequence undermined the very cultural distinctions that made it funny in the first place.

Failure versus Flop: The Reception of *Seven Lively Arts*

Many critics welcomed Rose's production as a critique of the Metropolitan Opera. Henry Simon, for example, declared, "The imagination, handsome staging, the skillful orchestration for reduced numbers and the careful direction give just a hint of how opera *might* be produced if our American companies stopped aping 19th-century European traditions of large, under-rehearsed

EXAMPLE 5. Cole Porter, "Closing Theme: Opera Finale," mm. 32–64. New York Public Library. Used by permission of the Trustees of the Cole Porter Trust.

repertoires." For him, as for many other critics, highbrow arts were not beyond reproach in practice. But Simon continued: "On the whole, though, the impresario shows more interest in liveliness than in art."[30] The word "though" suggests his reservations. Ultimately he had no intention of blurring "lively" and "arty," even if he criticized the quality of the Metropolitan Opera's productions.

Most critics agreed, and therefore it should not be surprising that many seemed confused by the antihierarchical aspect of *Seven Lively Arts*. Dismantling the borders between the artistic categories never even seemed to be an option for them. The *Herald Tribune*, for example, contended that "the notion of playing a serious Stravinsky in a show or of asking Markova to dance seriously in one is a mistake anyway. Their talents need a more intense concentration, a more sincere curiosity than a show audience cares to give."[31] Another critic wrote: "Mr. Rose's intentions are, of course, strictly honorable in a cultural way, and maybe the 'Scene [*sic*] du Ballet' wasn't actually as it seemed when set before an audience palpitantly waiting for Beatrice Lillie to make her next entrance."[32] For these reviewers, highbrow and lowbrow venues were coded with appropriate behaviors (highbrows wanted Stravinsky, the masses wanted Lillie), and the kind of art offered in each cultural territory was thus incommensurable, no matter how well it was mounted.

Even though critics rejected *Seven Lively Arts* on highbrow terms, the revue was by no means a "flop." Most may have been ambivalent about the "high culture" components of *Seven Lively Arts*, but many enthusiastically praised the production in distinctly different terms. R. E. P. Sensenderfer's review in the *Evening Bulletin* literally handed off the highbrow aspects of his column to somebody else in order to praise the middlebrow aspects of the show.

> Getting around to a more serious side, we'll begin with "Sideshow for Orchestra" a new work by the young American composer William Howard Schuman. As this is a little out of my line let's turn it over to the music critic. (Go ahead, Max.)
>
> "The musical form of this composition is actually a rondo in that the opening statement of the theme constantly reoccurs in alternating forms throughout, moving from the tonic to the dominant or sub theme, and, developing with ornamentation, figuration and . . ."
>
> That will do—thank you, Max. Most of us had better string along with Mark Twain who assured that this classical music is really much better than it sounds.[33]

After Sensenderfer dismissed the music critic's paragraph of almost nonsensical jargon—jargon meant to sound like jargon, meant to implicate, and then dismiss, highbrow appreciation—he quipped that for all its theorizing and abstraction, the music is simply not very entertaining, as if the air on this mountaintop of highbrow appreciation was indeed rarefied but awfully thin. In this case, the reviewer certainly identified himself: he was not highbrow at all and had no qualms about being popular.

In fact, the positive reviews of this show tended to deploy a distinctly middlebrow critical language. So stunned, so overwhelmed were the theater reviewers by its visual splendor that many of them seemed unable to describe the spectacle. Their writing grappled with the edge of the English language. Searching for appropriately effusive adjectives, they peppered their columns with phrases like "wowser," "tops," "super-whooper," "splendiferous," "hippodromic," "Scheherazadian," "whopping," "melliferous," "smash hit," "mastadonic," and "boff," all in praise of the show's "gorgeousity."[34] One critic waxed poetic: "Fragonard pastorals and Guerin visions of ancient Balbec are reproduced in heroic size on the stage, peopled by exquisitely beautiful girls wearing such fabrics as you can associate only with Marco Polo's tales of the pleasure dome of Kublai Kahn."[35] This was enthusiastic, onomatopoetic language in which the effect of the sound as it fell on the ears took precedence over its signifying capabilities—in other words, this critical language was "lively," not "arty."

The kind of praise this show did receive has been all but ignored by subsequent commentators. There are two reasons for this. First, the historiographical tradition of the Broadway musical tends to prioritize "art" over "lively," usually tracing the development of abstract formal constructs such as the "integrated musical" or the "concept musical" throughout time.[36] Recognizing, however, that there was more than one style of critical language seems especially important for 1944, when *Seven Lively Arts* opened: it was, after all, only a year after *Oklahoma!* brought the discourse of formal integration to new levels of intensity. Second, a number of cultural critics have decried such terms as "highbrow," "middlebrow," and "lowbrow" as "essentializing categories." Robert Walser, for example, has written that "the social function of distinctions such as 'highbrow' and 'lowbrow' is precisely to stabilize signs, prop up automatic dismissals, and quash dialogue and debate."[37] This was certainly true, especially in the heated cultural discourse of the 1940s. Yet a historiographical eye averse or insensitive to high/low distinctions may pass over the effusive language either as indistinct from other critical language or as mere fluff. Rose and Porter, however, were calculated and deliberate in choosing the register of music and language for *Seven Lively Arts*, and they deployed this register aggressively. Far from vapid, Rose's production was principled, and with *Seven Lively Arts* he saw himself as opening highbrow art to the general public: "You can bet your bottom dollar that I'm keeping faith with Mr. John Q. Public. The fancy-pants set has never been important in my scheme of things. The money to buy the Ziegfeld Theatre came from the 11,000,000 who saw the *Aquacade*. They're my people and I want to be their boy."[38] Of course, the man who charged $24.50 for tickets to *Seven Lively Arts* could not have actually been interested in opening the aisles to just anybody who came along, but this is only paradoxical if one takes Rose's words literally. They were rhetoric—but even if it was not literally true, the rhetoric itself was ideologically charged. In an era of the burgeoning mass culture critique, when commercial, popular art was riddled with political overtones, and in an era when *Oklahoma!*'s success had elevated talk of "integrated form" and American opera to a fever pitch, Rose's and Porter's spoof of the exclusivity of highbrow art was more than an expression of taste. Keeping artistic faith with John Q. Public was controversial. Recognizing "lively" language as a distinct, self-conscious, and intentional cultural performance would allow "lively" art to emerge as a category that was just as principled, ideological, and aggressive as its highbrow counterpart.

Notes

I would like to thank Richard Warren and Emily Ferrigno for their invaluable advice and assistance in the Cole Porter Collection. I would also like to thank James Hepokoski, Nicholas Betson, Karen Leistra-Jones, and Daphne Tan for their feedback on early versions of this chapter. In the notes that follow, press material taken from the *Seven Lively Arts* scrapbook, reel 2, MSS 82 in the Cole Porter Collection in the Irving S. Gilmore Music Library of Yale University has been designated CP. Press material from the New York Public Library *Seven Lively Arts* Scrapbook NYPL, MWEZ + n.c., box 25,491 has been labeled NYPL.

1. Contemporary reports all emphasize that the spectacle was unusually large, but the exact number of trucks (nine or ten) differed from critic to critic. See William Du Bois, "Erstwhile Mahout Captures Sixth Avenue," *New York Times*, 10 December 1944; Edwin H. Schloss, "Billy Rose's 'Seven Lively Arts' Has Premiere," *Philadelphia Record*, 25 November 1944 (CP); and Maurice Orodenker, "Seven Lively Arts," *Billboard*, 2 December 1944 (NYPL).

2. Wolcott Gibbs, "The Theatre," *New Yorker*, 16 December 1944.

3. Lewis Nichols, "Ring Out Wild Bells," *New York Times*, 17 December 1944. Details about the costumes (and gowns) can be found in Virginia Pope, "Design—a Lively Art," *New York Times*, 3 December 1944.

4. Nichols, "Ring Out Wild Bells."

5. Lewis Nichols, "The Play," *New York Times*, 8 December 1944. A similar review was written after the Philadelphia premiere: "Well, what have you? The answer is: such a superlative show as we haven't seen in seasons, a show that includes everything but the well-known kitchen sink—and even that is mentioned somewhere" (Linton Martin, "'Seven Lively Arts' Opens at Forrest," *Philadelphia Inquirer*, 25 November 1944 [CP]). The sink was mentioned in act 1, scene 9, "Drink." See NYPL Mu 784, 8.

6. Other writers included Charles Sherman and Norman Corwin, as mentioned in Sam Zolotow, "News of the Stage," *New York Times*, 19 June 1944; as well as Robert Priosh and Joseph Schrank, as mentioned in the Philadelphia Program.

7. Stage Notes, *Chicago Daily Tribune*, 13 July 1944; S. J. Woolf, "Beatrice Lillie's Recipe for Laughter," *New York Times*, 26 November 1944.

8. Richard P. Cooke, "The Theatre: Lively Lillie," *Wall Street Journal*, 9 December 1944; Nichols, "Ring Out Wild Bells"; Nichols, "The Play."

9. Dolin was also involved in Porter's *Within the Quota* (1923). See chapters in this volume by Morrison and Weiss. See also M.L., "Alicia Markova, Anton Dolin Partners of Long Standing," *Christian Science Monitor*, 20 September 1945.

10. His music was described as "serious" by R. E. P. Sensenderfer, "Billy Rose in Bloom in New Revue," *Evening Bulletin*, 25 November 1944 (CP); Martin, "'Seven Lively Arts' Opens." Schuman's contribution was cut before the New York opening. See Henry Simon, "Don't Be Serious," *P.M.*, 17 December 1944 (NYPL).

11. "'Seven Lively Arts' Is Launched by Billy Rose with Champagne," *New York Herald-Tribune*, 8 December 1944 (CP); Robert Garland, "'Seven Lively Arts' at Ziegfeld Theater," *Journal American*, 8 December 1944 (CP). A fire at Rose's mansion has since destroyed these paintings, but Dalí created a set of replacements for the impresario that have been photographed in NYPL 8-MWEZ + n.c., box 26,293, "Revue and Production Records, 1952–1954," folder 14, "Seven Lively Arts (1944)." For information about Maurice Abravanel, see Sensenderfer, "Billy Rose in Bloom."

12. Critics disagree about the identity of this piece, and no clues survive in the archives to shed light on what it may have been. Some thought it was the Weber Clarinet Concerto: John Chapman, "'Seven Lively Arts' Crowds Laugh at Gags and Not Critic," *Daily News*, 3 March 1945 (CP); Seymour Peck, "The King of Clarinetists," *P.M.*, 6 December 1944. Others said it was the Mozart Clarinet Concerto: Sensenderfer, "Billy Rose in Bloom" (CP).

13. These quotations come from, respectively, Cecil Smith, *Musical Comedy in America* (New York: Theatre Arts Books, 1950), 184; Gerald Bordman, *American Musical Revue: From the "Passing Show" to "Sugar Babies"* (New York: Oxford University Press, 1985), 130; Steven Suskin, *Show Tunes 1905–1991: The Songs, Shows and Careers of Broadway's Major Composers*, 4th ed. (New York: Oxford University Press, 2010), 225; Gerald Bordman and Richard Norton, *American Musical Theater: A Chronicle*, 4th ed. (New York: Oxford University Press, 2010), 544; William McBrien, *Cole Porter: A Biography* (New York: Alfred A. Knopf, 1998), 282.

14. Bordman, *American Musical Revue*, 127.

15. This bipartite division is an oversimplification. Cultural critics since at least Gilbert Seldes (as discussed in note 33) have devised a third category in which art appears high or low but is not. Consider, for example, folk art, which, though perhaps crude, nonetheless struck many highbrows as worthy of esteem. On this subject, see, for example, Victoria Grieve, *The Federal Art Project and the Creation of Middlebrow Culture* (Urbana: University of Illinois Press, 2009). On the other hand, there could be art that appeared high but was merely "orotund," in the words of Dwight Macdonald, who was particularly vehement in condemning this kind of art in *Against the American Grain* (New York: Random House, 1962). For a more in-depth discussion, see James O'Leary, "Lousy Publicity, *Oklahoma!*, and the Politics of Formal Integration," *Journal of Musicology* 31, no. 1 (Winter 2014): 139–82. For the purposes of this essay, however, the subtle distinctions between "middlebrow" and "lowbrow" that arose in the late 1930s and early 1940s need not concern us.

16. Donald Heritage, "Seven Lively Arts? Billy Rose Is Eighth," *Philadelphia Record*, 12 November 1944 (NYPL).

17. Lucius Beebe, "Stage Asides: Billy Rose Fears Public Will Think Him Artistic," *Herald Tribune*, 3 December 1944 (CP). Rose continued:

> Just to show you how much of the program is devoted to serious contemplation of the arts: the Stravinsky music rates just nine minutes at the opening of the second act, and Benny Goodman appears only twice, once alone and once with his band for a total of eleven minutes. By and large there is about as much grave genuflection in the direction of the muses as there is, say, in the floor show at the Diamond Horseshoe [his popular nightclub], and you know how much that is! . . . All I hope for on Thursday night [opening night] is that the boys come looking for fun and foolishness and nothing else. . . . Just remember, though, when you come to the Ziegfeld under its new management you aren't coming to Carnegie Hall!

This represented a marked change in Rose's rhetoric.

18. Rialto Gossip, "Theatre Guild Makes Plans for Its Season Here and on the Road," *New York Times*, 9 August 1942; "Gordon to Offer All-Negro Opera," *New York Times*, 13 July 1942; Nichols, "About 'Carmen Jones,'" *New York Times*, 12 December 1943; Sam Zolotow, "Opening Tonight of 'Carmen Jones,'" *New York Times*, 2 December 1943; "Carmen Gone Broadway," *Newsweek*, 13 December 1943, 91.

19. "All-Negro Cast Will Present New 'Carmen,'" *Chicago Daily Tribune*, 6 September 1942; Mark Barron, "New York Notes: Hammerstein Will Make 'Carmen' Over into 'Carmen Jones,'" *Los Angeles Times*, 30 August 1942. See also Annegret Fauser, "Dixie Carmen: War, Race, and Identity in Oscar Hammerstein's *Carmen Jones* (1943)," *Journal of the Society for American Music* 4, no. 2 (May 2010): 127–74.

20. Oscar Hammerstein II, *Carmen Jones* (New York: A. A. Knopf, 1945), xvii. He wrote,

> *Carmen Jones* is an indication, if not positive proof, that opera in English may be popular if the lyrics are singable, understandable, and dramatic. A more complete proof would be an adaptation of the original, keeping the scene in Spain and all the details the same except for the exigencies of translation. Some day someone who understands music and the theater will write a straight English version of some opera and some courageous director will force the singers to act in a sensible manner—and the result will be astounding!
>
> *Carmen Jones*, however, does not blaze this trail. *Carmen Jones* is designed to play eight performances a week, for as many weeks as the public will come. It is designed for the same theaters that play musical comedies. Therefore there is not room for ninety men in the orchestra pit. Our chorus is not so large as a grand-opera chorus. We have moments of dancing integrated into the performance throughout the evening. It is lavishly produced by Billy Rose, and in a modern manner.

21. Irving Spiegel, "Negro Cast Will Sing Carmen," *New York Times*, 23 August 1942; Nichols, "About 'Carmen Jones'"; Rialto Gossip, "Theatre Guild Makes Plans." At times, their writing takes an almost religious stance toward *Carmen*. For example, Bizet's score was "pure and undefiled . . . with no sacrilege," appears in "'Carmen Jones': An All-Negro Cast Makes Oscar Hammerstein II's Modernization of Bizet's Opera Memorable Theater," *Time*, 13 December 1943, 111.

22. Quoted in Chapman, "N.Y. Stage Suffers Acute Real Estate Shortage," *Chicago Daily Tribune*, 3 October 1943. Journalists were quick to repeat Rose's language. For example, "Mr. Rose offered Thespis (and Broadway) his 'Carmen Jones.' Friends and

bookkeepers were both against it; but Mr. Rose could now afford to ignore his bookkeepers—and silence his friends with the dictum of art for art's sake" (Du Bois, "Erstwhile Mahout," X5).

23. Kyle Crichton, "Carmen Jones," *Collier's*, 15 January 1944, 60.

24. John Desmond, "Broadway's Barnum Looks at the Opera," *New York Times*, 26 March 1944.

25. NYPL Mu 784 P, 19–22.

26. NYPL JPB 82-75 no. 10, box 1, folder A.

27. NYPL Mu 784 P, 52, 54.

28. CP, box 37, folder 244.

29. NYPL JPB 82-75, box 1, folder e, 25.

30. Simon, "Don't Be Serious."

31. Edwin Denby, "'Scene De Ballet' at Billy Rose's," *Herald Tribune*, 24 December 1944 (CP).

32. Schloss, "Billy Rose's 'Seven Lively Arts' Has Premiere."

33. Sensenderfer, "Billy Rose in Bloom."

34. Ibid.; Martin, "'Seven Lively Arts' Opens"; Linton Martin, "'Seven Arts,' Rose Revue, Super-Show," *Philadelphia Inquirer*, 26 November 1944; Garland, "'Seven Lively Arts' at Ziegfeld Theater"; Thomas R. Dash, "The Week in the Theatre: Seven Lively Arts," *Retailing Home Furnishings*, 18 December 1944; "Billy Rose Is Now a Different Rose but Same Gay Lillie Guilds His 'Arts,'" *Newsweek*, 18 December 1944 (CP); Ward Morehouse, "'Seven Lively Arts' Big and Beautiful—and It Has Beatrice Lillie," *New York Sun*, 8 December 1944 (CP); Orodenker, "Seven Lively Arts"; Heritage, "Seven Lively Arts"; Robert Coleman, "The Theatre: Rose's $24 Show Is Well Worth It," *Daily Mirror*, 8 December 1944 (CP); Douglas Hawley, "Billy Rose as Modern Ziggy," *Dallas (TX) Times-Herald*, 8 December 1944 (CP); Elsa Maxwell, "Elsa Maxwell's Party Line: 7 Come 11 Lively Arts," *New York Post*, 14 December 1944 (CP).

35. Burton Rascoe, "'The Seven Lively Arts'—New Era in Magnificence," *World Telegram*, 8 December 1944 (CP).

36. Many scholars have questioned this view. For a summary of this debate, see O'Leary, "Lousy Publicity."

37. Robert Walser, "Highbrow, Lowbrow, Voodoo Aesthetics," in *Microphone Fiends: Youth Music and Youth Culture*, ed. Andrew Ross and Tricia Rose (New York: Routledge, 1994), 235, 244. Such commentaries are common, and one of the most cited comes from Lawrence Levine, *Highbrow/Lowbrow: The Emergence of Cultural Hierarchy in America* (Cambridge, MA: Harvard University Press, 1988), 1–9.

38. Advertisement for *Seven Lively Arts*, *New York Daily News*, 21 November 1944.

10

"The Beat Beat Beat of the Tom-Tom"

Cole Porter and the Exotic

JOSHUA S. WALDEN

In the songs of Cole Porter, love has a potent but mysterious agency. It arrives unannounced and departs just as suddenly, and while it lingers it can change one's perception of the world. In "What Is This Thing Called Love?" (1929), love flies in through the window and alters the singer's "humdrum" existence. When it departs, leaving a wintry chill in its wake, the singer feels its effect linger on. But what *is* this thing called love? Porter never answers the question, though he asks it repeatedly; in his refrain, five of the seven sentences are questions about "love's mystery." In the musical setting and the original staging of this number in the revue *Wake Up and Dream*, the enchantment of "this thing called love" was evoked by sonic and visual elements of the exotic. Porter claimed the song was inspired by ritual drumming patterns he heard in Marrakesh, and the piano-vocal sheet music edition incorporates a simple drumlike oompah ostinato with heavy downbeats and dotted rhythms.[1] A 1929 recording by Leslie Hutchinson extended the eclecticism of the song's exotic reference, preceding the "African drumbeat" with four strokes of a Chinese gong. Produced in London and on Broadway, *Wake Up and Dream* featured the song in a dance sequence that similarly associated love's enigma and ineffability with the wonders of distant landscapes. In the show, a singer leaned against the edge of the stage and performed the song as three dancers, choreographed by George Balanchine, enacted an interpretation of the text to the persistent beat of a tom-tom, dancing around a statue designed by Oliver Messel to resemble an African idol.[2] The sheet music of "What Is This Thing Called Love?" had its own curious amalgam of exotic references on the art deco cover, which depicted a dance between the commedia dell'arte character Pierrot and a girl in a flapper dress before a modernist reinterpretation of Hokusai's *Under the Wave off Kanagawa*.

In its multiple allusions to sounds and images from across the globe, "What Is This Thing Called Love?" joins many other songs by Porter that correlate the mysteries of love with the curiosity and wonder of the music, dance, costumes, and landscapes of cultures and places that Porter considered exotic. Porter incorporated a broad range of musical references into his works throughout his career, often to depict the powerful passions that overwhelm the characters in his songs. In his music and lyrics, he invoked sounds he considered exotic—including instruments, rhythms, and elements of song and dance genres from around the world—as metaphors for love's transformative powers, which he depicted as universal and unpredictable. He thus looked outward, searching for unfamiliar musical techniques to evoke his characters' interior passions. He encountered these eclectic sources of inspiration in his musical training, during his varied career in America, and throughout his extensive world travels. His aim was never ethnographic authenticity, however, and far from precisely imitative of their musical models, his adaptations were instead evocative of the exotic in a manner that would be immediately familiar to his American listeners. In an interview for the *New York Times*, Porter jokingly described the imprecise nature of the mambos so popular in the United States during the 1950s: "There is an actual, distinctive form of music in Cuba called mambo . . . but the craze here is such that people write songs in any tempo and call them mambos. I fully expect the next will be called 'The Waltz Mambo,' just so that people of middle age will have a new step to do."[3] Porter's tongue-in-cheek mocking of such vague musical borrowing in popular song in fact comes close to describing the imprecision of many of his evocations of international dance styles in his works.

This chapter explores the extensive range of musical references in Porter's songs to view the meanings that emerge out of this eclecticism, with particular focus on "Begin the Beguine" and its history of varied interpretations in sound recording and cinema. Throughout Porter's works, the exotic, something one dreams of from home and experiences only on a rare voyage abroad, is a metaphor for the true love that is passionately desired but ultimately elusive.

This metaphor appears to reflect an ambivalence that likely characterized Porter's own experience as a gay man in a heterosexual marriage in early and mid-twentieth-century America. In "Begin the Beguine," the link between the tropical vacation and the fleeting romance, reflecting an exotic milieu and an impassioned love that are unattainable at home and cannot be made to last, is rendered explicit in the lyrics about the singer's distant memories of an irretrievable love "under the stars" as a band played the beguine. The chapter concludes by reconsidering the question of the persistent reception of the so-called Jewish nature of Porter's works, a notion raised first by Porter and Richard Rodgers. It suggests that this common interpretation of songs including "What Is This Thing Called Love?" and "Begin the Beguine" was rooted not in their use of the minor mode, as is commonly proposed, but in their rich diversity of references to a broad range of musical traditions, an eclecticism that reflects the hybrid nature of Yiddish theater and other forms of early twentieth-century American Jewish entertainment.

"There's a Little Bit of Gypsy in Me"

In 1917, following the disappointing response to his first Broadway musical, *See America First*, Porter moved to France, where he studied composition briefly at the Schola Cantorum in Paris.[4] The scores of his songs appear to demonstrate the skills gained during his formal studies, as well as the influence of Gilbert and Sullivan, whose operas had inspired him since his time at Yale. They also show the influence of the jazz and blues he encountered in *boîtes de nuits* he visited in Paris.[5] He often paired techniques of these genres with unlikely subjects in songs such as "The Blue Boy Blues" (1922), a comic retelling of railroad magnate Henry E. Huntington's purchase of Gainsborough's *Blue Boy*, in which the boy in the painting sings the blues about his transatlantic move. Jazz inspired Porter's composition and subject matter throughout his career in numbers from "Broadcast a Jazz" (ca. 1924), a song Porter called "a knockout" with "an entirely new rhythm, which only the blacks have used so far," to "Now You Has Jazz" (1950), which became a hit for Bing Crosby and Louis Armstrong, who performed it in the film *High Society*.[6] Both songs celebrate the global popularity of jazz's uniquely American sound. In "Broadcast a Jazz," the text states that jazz allows "old Yankee land" to "show what she has" to the rest of the world, and the singer calls on a "syncopatin' band" to play "until Calcutta / Cries, 'Enough,'" Turkey is driven insane, Europe is thrilled, and Brazil is shocked. In "Now You Has

Jazz," likewise, listeners as far-flung as Siam, Bangkok, and the Amazon all adore American jazz. The singer states:

> They're all molto hip
> In Italy. . . .
> Frenchmen all
> Prefer what they call
> "Le Jazz Hot."

Porter borrowed elements from Latin American dance in songs including "I've Got You Under My Skin" (1936), "So Near and Yet So Far" (1941), and "Sing to Me, Guitar" (1944).[7] "Begin the Beguine" was supposedly inspired by the eponymous dance genre from Martinique, and Porter claimed that "Night and Day" (1932) reflected his effort to evoke the sounds of religious chant and the rhythms of traditional drums that he heard during a visit to Morocco.[8] The scores of Porter's musicals also exhibited a vibrant hybridity, with changing references from one number to the next. Among the varied stylistic sources in *Anything Goes*, for instance, Porter imitated revivalist songs in "Blow, Gabriel, Blow," hymns in "Public Enemy No. 1," flamenco in "The Gypsy in Me," and sea shanties in "Lady Fair." In *Kiss Me, Kate*, he evoked musical styles as diverse as Italian Renaissance song genres, Verdi's operas, blues, the Viennese waltz, and, in "Brush Up Your Shakespeare," the turn-of-the-century hybrid of the "Bowery waltz."[9]

In these songs and others, the melodic and harmonic techniques, and especially the rhythmic patterns that Porter adapts from African American genres, Latin American and Caribbean dance, art music, and other genres he encountered in his travels, are grafted onto the idiom of American popular song in which he worked in a stylistic conflation Matthew Shaftel associates with the "colonial mentality of [Porter's] time."[10] These eclectic references operate in a context that remains comfortably within the realm of American popular music; his songs experiment with other forms and genres in the manner of pastiche. Rather than exhibiting the smooth assimilation of musical techniques and genres, many of the songs foreground their hybridity, so that the exotic, the "highbrow," and the homegrown genres of jazz and blues are marked as different even as they are invoked. Porter leaves the seams between disparate styles audible, implying a distance between his characters' exterior social performances and their internal passions.[11]

In addition to adapting techniques from varied genres in his musical arrangements, Porter invokes song and dance styles from around the world in his lyrics, firmly identifying exotic musical sounds, traditions, and scenarios. Such references are often incorporated as signifiers of place, alongside descriptions of costume, landscape, or food. Lyrics about the guitar set the scene in "My Spanish Shawl" (ca. 1922), "I Dream of a Girl in a Shawl" (1929), and "Hasta Luego" (1942), while the Tahitian "Twin Sisters" (1922) strum the ukulele; the banjo signifies regions of the United States in "My Georgia Gal" (1913) and "The Banjo That Man Joe Plays" (1929), a song about San Francisco; and saxophones play in "The Heaven of Harlem" (ca. 1929). These allusions to musical instruments and genres are analogous to the incorporation of exotic instruments in operas to conjure distant landscapes, such as onstage "Janissary" percussionists in Mozart's *Die Entführung aus dem Serail* and Carmen's castanets in Bizet's opera.[12] A Spanish dance genre marks nationality in "Barcelona Maid" (1912): "Her charms were cleverly displayed, / Fandango dancing." Similarly, in "Entrance of the Indian Maidens" (1916) from *See America First*, the maidens sway to a "simple but effective dance, / Singing slowly melancholy tribal chants." Tourists dance "'neath the stars . . . to a fancy orchestra" in "Visit Panama" (1940), and "a little rumba numba" is heard, in the eponymous 1941 song, by a visitor to Argentina.

"The Good-Will Movement" (1943), from *Mexican Hayride*, stages U.S. political and cultural outreach to Latin America as a dance routine devised by Vice President Henry A. Wallace to "promote back-pattin' / 'Twixt ourselves and our neighbors Latin" through the creation of hybrid forms of music and dance. The music is "'Oklahoma' / Plus a rumba beat, / 'La Paloma' / But in Basin Street," the lyrics explain; it is

> muy catchy
> If you care for corn,
> Mariachi
> Plus a Harlem horn. . . .
> The rhythm comes from Taxco,
> But the tune's Berlin.

This comic song ultimately fails to extend a genuinely friendly hand across the border, with its line about "spics and gringos" and stereotypes about Latin American cultures, but what it does accomplish is to describe the popular hybrid fusion of rhythmic techniques from Latin American music into popular song and to identify New Orleans and New York jazz and Broadway songs—works by Rodgers and Hammerstein, Irving Berlin, and, with this number,

Porter himself—as the national music of the United States, corresponding to Mexican mariachi and Afro-Cuban rumba.

When Porter composes his own faux "folk songs" in imitation of traditional genres, he frequently introduces the exotic setting of the music in an opening verse. In his introduction to the 1913 "Maid of Santiago," Porter describes the story of a cavalier who emerged nightly beneath a young woman's window to strum his guitar and sing an ardent love song, which makes up Porter's refrain. The Italianate refrain of "Cazanova" (1933) is described in the song's introductory section as a "phony canzone" that "a certain gal / Sang in soprano, / And not in piano" on the banks of the canal in Venice. In "Be Like the Bluebird" (1934) from *Anything Goes*, the "folk song," an allegory about a bluebird that sings in the face of trouble, is described in the first verse as "an old Australian bush song / That Melba used to sing." Similarly "Carlotta" (1944), a number from *Mexican Hayride* about Emperor Maximilian I and Empress Carlotta of Mexico, features a love serenade in its refrain that is introduced in the preceding verse as a song performed by an "enchanted little native" who "fell in love with the Empress fair." By presenting these comic imitations of disparate genres—the Venetian canzone, the Australian Aboriginal song, and the Chilean and Mexican love serenades—Porter sets his works apart from the music of Broadway that surrounds them, marking them as echoes of imagined distant times and exotic landscapes.

National and regional songs, dance rhythms, and instruments also have the power to elicit strong feelings of geographic belonging in Porter's music, as in the 1916 numbers "See America First," in which the listener is told to "get that grand old strain of Yankee Doodle / In your noodle," and "Pity Me, Please," whose impressionable narrator was "incurably stung / By the microbe of Anglomania" upon hearing "God Save the King." And in "Since Ma Got the Craze Espagnole" (1919), we learn that the mother's fascination with Spain involves a study of Spanish song and dance: "O'er the Fandango she's gone so silly, / That the parlor floor's getting all hilly."

This last song associates a foreign dance not only with patriotic fervor but also with the awakening of a previously undiscovered inner passion. In some of the most intriguing references to eclectic musical styles in Porter's works, the singers invoke exotic sounds to express the feelings that well up within their characters but remain outwardly stifled until they finally burst forth. In "Night and Day," written for the 1932 musical *The Gay Divorce* and reprised two years later in the film version, *The Gay Divorcee*, Fred Astaire's character declares his love for the leading lady (Claire Luce onstage and Ginger Rogers onscreen), suggesting "the beat beat beat of the tom-tom / when the jungle shadows fall" as a simile to describe the "hungry yearning burning inside of me" because "night and day, you are the one." In the song "Sing to Me, Guitar" (1944), the instrument's timbres are a metaphor for the hopeful memories and sadness of a young woman separated from her lover. She entreats the guitar to transport her back to the time of forceful emotions when, on an "evening divine . . . his lips pressed to mine / As we kissed and we kissed and we kissed," and also to foretell when they might reunite. "Don't Tell Me Who You Are" (1920s) tells the story of a singer and a fiddler who engage in a moonlight fling but do not reveal their names so that their passion can remain a dreamy memory fed by music. The singer implores:

> I want to think, all through life, it's
> Been Jascha Heifetz
> Playing to me from afar.
> But if I knew your name,
> It would spoil the whole game,
> So don't tell me who you are.[13]

No song by Porter better expresses this musical metaphor for the hidden passion waiting to emerge from within than "The Gypsy in Me." This song was written for the character Hope Harcourt, a young American debutante under the thumb of her strong-willed mother; in later productions the song was given to Hope's fiancé, the older British gentleman Sir Evelyn Oakleigh. In the case of both characters, depicted in their own ways as naive and repressed early in the musical, it comes as a surprise when they later confess: "I can't wait to get the stage all set / So I can let the gypsy in me out." As the tempo increases and a syncopated dance beat settles in, the singer begins the refrain with the words, "Hiding away / There's a little bit of gypsy in me / That's never been found," signifying a simmering passion that will break free on a "magical night":

> While the tinkling guitar
> Not too near, not too far,
> Gaily strums away,
> Hums away,
> A titillating tune.

This mysterious star-lit music will mark her (or his) reunion with a true love: "When I'm there in that dream / With the one in the world I worship passionately." This number is situated within a common genre of popular song in Europe and America in which stereotyped visions of Rom music and culture were invoked to describe impassioned, often fleeting feelings of love, frequently beneath a "Gypsy moon."[14] Porter had already used the phrase "the gypsy in me" in "Find Me a Primitive Man" (1929), in which a singer remarks, "The only man who'll ever win me / Has gotta wake up the gypsy in me." These songs owe their imagery to the popular mythology, originating in eighteenth-century German anthropology and drawn upon by Franz Liszt in his Hungarian Rhapsodies and book *Des Bohémiens et de leur musique en Hongrie* (1859 and 1881), that characterized Rom music as expressive of a particularly authentic and spontaneous emotion dwelling deep within the soul.[15] Porter employs this notion to indicate a hidden passion within the archetypes of the earnest, naive debutante or respectable British gentleman.

Porter's references to eclectic musical forms in his songs typically involved exotic stereotypes, but they also went beyond mere exoticism to achieve a unique, multidimensional notion of character. These numbers sketch out a divergence between inner feeling and external behavior: they reflect a belief that passion, spontaneity, and desire reside behind the facade of modern social respectability. Evocations of other genres, self-consciously incorporated in the manner of musical collage, operate as signs of difference, of what makes people individuals despite social pressure to conform. This might help to explain why Porter's songs have been so popular with singers associated with widely divergent styles. Terry Castle observes that Porter's "most humanizing talent . . . was his power to make others human" and that his songs allow their performers "to sound more fully alive in the singing and playing of them."[16] In its broad range of musical reference, Porter's repertoire permits performers to represent the friction between inner and outer modes of expression and to embody richly complex characters.

"When They Begin the Beguine"

"Begin the Beguine," like "What Is This Thing Called Love?," incorporates eclectic musical techniques to characterize love as a mysterious force that changes the singer's perception of the surrounding world. And as in "Night and Day," the song's text invokes musical sounds that Porter considered exotic to initiate a cascade of nostalgic recollections. According to Porter, "Begin the Beguine," written in 1935 for the show *Jubilee*, was of truly international inspiration, incorporating a rhythmic scheme he jotted into his notebook at a performance of dancers from Martinique in a Parisian nightclub in the 1920s with a melody inspired by the opening of a dance he witnessed ten years later in Kalabahi, Indonesia. He interpreted the beguine rhythm as an up-tempo alternative to the popular rumba and observed, "For some reason, the melody that I heard and the phrase I had written down seemed to marry. I developed the whole song from that."[17] In Martinique the two forms of beguine—the rural *bigin*, played on the *bélè* drum with text in call and response, and the urban orchestral beguine—are hybrid genres themselves, the former with West African roots and the latter based on the music of French colonists. They share a syncopated rhythmic foundation in $\frac{2}{4}$ time, with accents on downbeats and the fourth and eighth sixteenth of each measure, and a tie between the end of the first beat and the start of the second (ex. 1).[18] Porter's score to "Begin the Beguine" does not follow the beguine's rhythmic scheme but suggests it with almost perpetual alternations of offbeat chords, syncopations, and occasional triplets in the piano's right hand (ex. 2).[19] An ostinato in the left hand built of a half and two quarter notes repeats through most of the score, contributing a sense of primitive simplicity.

"Begin the Beguine" is built of unusually expansive phrases of sixteen measures in $\frac{4}{4}$ time, with a final section of twenty-eight measures, creating an appropriate musical setting for the wistfully introspective and nostalgic tone of the lyrics. The structure follows the scheme AABACC', with sections A and C in major and the contrasting B section beginning in minor. The length of the phrases also permits gently building undulations in the melodic contour that operate on both lower and higher levels of the phrasing at once. The

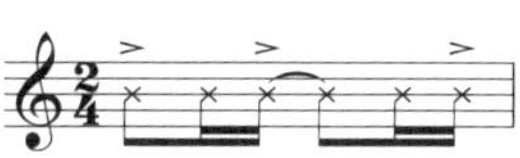

EXAMPLE 1. Beguine rhythmic scheme.

EXAMPLE 2. "Begin the Beguine" (from *Jubilee*), mm. 1–4. Words and music by Cole Porter. Copyright © 1935 (renewed) WB Music Corp. All Rights Reserved. Used by permission of Alfred Music.

melody rises and falls in an arc in each four-measure subphrase of the A and B sections, while over the course of the sixteen measures the apex of each subphrase reaches increasingly higher from the first to the second and third, falling back downward in the fourth subphrase. In the C and C' passages, which set a new, more plaintive section of the text, this pattern is inverted: the melody forms a downward arc in each four-measure subphrase, while the nadir of each subphrase reaches lower in the second and third, returning upward in the fourth. The lyrics narrate nostalgia for the loss of a passionate love affair and the narrator's internal struggle over whether it is preferable to forget or remember.

In the first and second sections of the text, the sound of a beguine initiates the singer's "memory evergreen," an undying reminiscence of a starlit night of "tropical splendor" with a beloved, the palm trees swaying to the music of an orchestra. The B section opens briefly in the parallel minor on the sorrowful acknowledgment that this romantic night is irrevocably in the past, "except when that tune clutches my heart." As the melody reaches upward, the singer describes being transported by the music back to a distant time and place where the permanence of the relationship seems possible again and where the lovers promise never to part. The third A section brings regret that the "moments divine" and "rapture serene" dissipate suddenly, leaving only the regret of wasted opportunity when the clouds come along, recalling the "winter's chill" that accompanies the loss of love in "What Is This Thing Called Love?" In the C passage the singer, wishing to avoid the bittersweet memories, implores, "So don't let them begin the beguine," the high opening tessitura representing the yearning tone of this request. In the final section, the singer poignantly reconsiders, favoring recollection over resignation and forgetting: "Oh yes, let them begin the beguine, make them play / Till the stars that were there before return above you, / Till you whisper to me once more, 'Darling, I love you!'" The beguine, like so many musical sounds in Porter's songs, is a trace from another, more impassioned time in the singer's life and a reminder of past love. It is also an extended metaphor of love's overwhelming influence in both the text and the driving syncopations and throbbing melodic contours of the music.

Despite the failure of *Jubilee*, "Begin the Beguine" inspired a host of later interpretations that drew upon a variety of dance forms, orchestrations, and performance styles.[20] The song has been performed in genres from jazz to disco and opera by artists as disparate as the Andrews Sisters, Julio Iglesias, Thomas Hampson, and the Malian singer Salif Keita, who altered the music and translated the text in his recording on the 1990 Porter tribute album *Red Hot + Blue*.[21] The Spanish-born, Cuban-bred band leader Xavier Cugat released one of the first recordings in 1935; his band features the accompaniment of perpetual rhythms in the percussion that turn Porter's beguine into a rumba. Clarinetist Artie Shaw helped to popularize the tune, releasing it in 1938 on the B side of a disk featuring "Indian Love Call." Shaw rejected an early arrangement that more closely resembled the traditional rhythmic scheme of the Martinican beguine in favor of a straightforward swing arrangement.[22] In Bing Crosby's recording the ensemble performs a rhythmic scheme of 3 + 3 + 2, the tresillo pattern associated with rumba, as the strings play their melodies languorously in shimmering tremolos. Ella Fitzgerald, by contrast, favored a swing interpretation in $\frac{4}{4}$ time, with the backing of a big band arrangement supported by perpetual dotted rhythms played on offbeats on the hi-hat, occasionally alternating with syncopated passages. But her version also merges techniques from contrasting dance genres: her band arranger, Marty Paitch, annotated the word "(Charleston)" in the drum part in the final stanza, when she sings "What heaven we're in"; this is followed a few measures later by a phrase accompanied by a syncopated vamp of 3 + 3 + 2, perhaps a nod toward the Caribbean origins of the beguine, as she ad libs the closing words, "Let them begin the beguine."[23]

"Begin the Beguine" also appeared in contrasting interpretations in two biopics about Porter, *Night and Day* (1946) and *De-Lovely* (2004). In these renditions of the song, filmed in both movies as stage performances that Porter hears or watches, the text's invocation of the beguine and the syncopated rhythmic scheme inspired the filmmakers to create fanciful settings for the song that incorporate techniques from different Latin American music genres. In the earlier film, Porter is shown composing the song as a soldier with the French army, at the front in World War I, as he listens to the rhythmic sounds of the battle and the beating drums of African soldiers. Later, having suffered injuries from a horse-riding accident that would torment him the rest of his life, Porter listens over the telephone from his sickbed to a rendition by the Colombian singer Carlos Ramírez, who performs the song on a tropical set of palm trees and lagoons, surrounded by exotic dancers and shirtless male drummers. Emerging from the crowd of this fantastical landscape is a dancing couple dressed in white who wreathe and turn in an interpretive depiction of the lovers described in the text. Separated in space from the performance, just as the song's narrator is in time from the experience that occupies his memory, Porter hears the song through the telephone receiver as a trace of a happier period, a "memory evergreen," and smiles broadly.

In *De-Lovely*, by contrast, Porter attends a stage performance in which Sheryl Crow, on a night-blue stage framed by glittering palms, sings a slow, minor-mode version of the song as her band plays a syncopated bossa-nova beat with stammering guitar, muted trumpet, and drum played with a brush mallet. Her voice glides longingly and sultrily between notes with a lilting sense of melancholy. Crow omits the final verse, with its ultimately celebratory treatment of nostalgia in which Porter's lyrics double back on the previous verse with the words, "Oh yes, let them begin the beguine, make them play!" Instead, she concludes with the desperate exhortation in the penultimate stanza, "So don't let them begin the beguine! / Let the love that was once a fire remain an ember." At this point in the film, Porter's marriage has begun to unravel, and he watches Crow's performance alone, Linda's seat empty beside him. The lyrics "To live it again is past all endeavor, / Except when that tune clutches my heart" take on poignant significance: the beguine, reinterpreted as a mournful bossa nova, heightens the fault lines in their relationship by emphasizing the impossibility of a return to their earlier harmony. The song becomes a plea to suppress the painful memories of a lost romance.

But the most inventive and stylistically eclectic rendition of "Begin the Beguine" preceded these others: in the backstage musical film *Broadway Melody of 1940* (also discussed by Shaftel), the song is heard in the movie's final number, an extended sequence featuring Fred Astaire, Eleanor Powell, and a cast of singers and dancers. This number opens in an amalgam of two age-old exotic stereotypes, the Turkish harem and the tropical island. At the start, Carmen D'Antonio dances sensually in a close-fitting gown. Dubbed by mezzo-soprano Lois Hodnett, D'Antonio appears to sing "Begin the Beguine" in a low, sultry voice. The camera pans back to reveal a group of women in various states of repose, wearing turbans and flowing dresses, lounging in the manner of odalisques in Ingres's orientalist paintings. They harmonize on the syllable "ah" across high melismas, a common trope of exoticist numbers in opera and other genres. The camera pans upward to a raised portion of the stage, revealing a set that evokes a small isle of white sand before a starry sky, surrounded by a reflective floor like a still lagoon. Women wearing belly-dance garb with flowers in their hair sway in imitation of tropical dance.

This dual world of lounging harem girls and tropical-island dancers elides with the start of the second section, which incorporates movements and sounds resembling flamenco, implying the quality of passion long associated with Rom music that Porter invoked in "The Gypsy in Me." As the dancers continue their fluid movements over the island set, Eleanor Powell enters with erect posture and arms held out to her sides. She taps forcefully, her heavy tread mimicking flamenco as her rhythms, alternating heavy downbeats with offbeat triplets, recall the patterns of Spanish bolero. Hodnett's singing comes to an end, the other dancers leave the stage, and Astaire enters, dressed as a bullfighter. The two continue to dance in a tap style inspired by flamenco, with heavy steps and arms held alternately at their sides, behind their backs, and overhead, as though holding castanets. The orchestra plays an instrumental version of "Begin the Beguine" in a "Spanish" style, transposing the music to the minor and incorporating chromaticism, ornaments, glissandos in the harp, and stammering offbeat syncopations in the low strings. As this section approaches its conclusion, a compound rhythm of 3 + 3 + 2 is heard in trumpets, timpani, and dance steps before Astaire and Powell leave the stage in a flourish of turns.

The final section takes the dancers back across the world to their musical "home" on Tin Pan Alley in an urban, jazzy interpretation of "Begin the Beguine." A percussionist plays dotted rhythms on the hi-hat, and the brass section blares, accompanying the entrance of four women from the vocal group the Music Maids, an ensemble that appeared in a number of movies and often recorded background vocals for popular singers of the standards. A reflective backdrop shows the mirror image of the band, as the Music Maids perform in close harmonies and interpolate a patter of scat syllables and additional text in a style that recalls the Andrews Sisters. When they reach the "night of tropical splendor," they add the words "In the merry land of Oz"; here the passionate memory conjured by the beguine's rhythms is of the colorful cinematic fantasy world of the Emerald City and the Yellow Brick Road. Invoked from this black-and-white vaudeville stage one short year after the marvels of Technicolor in *The Wizard of Oz* and in the wake of the Great Depression, the land of Oz is a world as exotic to the denizens of Dorothy and Auntie Em's farm as the tropical island, the Spanish bull ring, and the swanky urban nightclub were for many of the viewers of *Broadway Melody of 1940*. The seemingly limitless mirrored set also stands for a fantasy world, the Olympian dream of so many backstage musical characters, and onto this stage Astaire and Powell reemerge, in aristocratic and stylish white formalwear, for a final tap-dance routine to the accompaniment of the big band that can be seen reflected behind them. After their performance, Astaire and Powell meet their erstwhile dance partner backstage, and the three return to their audience to tap in synchrony to a reprise of Porter's "I've Got My Eyes on You." The references to global musical genres and fantastical exotic spaces in this number evoke the love in the characters' hearts and permit a joyous dénouement, with the dissipation of the previous tension between the movie's three stars.

"I'll Write Jewish Tunes"

On a trip to Europe with Lorenz Hart in 1926, Richard Rodgers was strolling the shore of the Venice Lido when he ran into Noël Coward, who introduced him to Porter. Porter invited them to dinner at the ornate palace he was renting, the Ca' Rezzonico, where he impressed Rodgers with his "remarkably keen knowledge of both classical and popular music," as well as his detailed familiarity with Rodgers's own work.[24] Porter described his middling success on Broadway up to that point, stating that he was happy to remain in Europe but confessing that he hoped for the chance to return to Broadway. In an anecdote in his autobiography that would be frequently repeated in later writings on Porter, Rodgers recalled that Porter told him that "he had discovered the secret of writing hits. As I breathlessly awaited the magic formula, he leaned over and confided, 'I'll write Jewish tunes.' I laughed at what I took to be a joke."[25] But Rodgers came to believe that Porter was "dead serious" and that he did in fact begin writing "Jewish tunes," which soon brought him wide popularity. In Rodgers's analysis, the melodies of "Night and Day," "Begin the Beguine," "Love for Sale," "My Heart Belongs to Daddy," and "I Love Paris" were "Jewish": "These minor-key melodies are unmistakably eastern Mediterranean."[26]

Contrary to Rodgers's judgment, there are in fact few explicit references to Jewish culture in Porter's repertoire. The most overt handling of Jewish subject matter may be found in "Hot-House Rose" (1927), commissioned by Fanny Brice. The song was inspired by the Brice vehicle "Second Hand Rose" by Grant Clarke and James Hanley, a song about a Jewish girl from the Lower East Side of Manhattan whose father trades in used wares ("Everyone knows that I'm just / Second hand Rose / From Second Avenue! . . . / Nu!"). Porter's song parodies Brice's early years, describing a poor girl who changes her name to one less recognizably Jewish: "My fam'ly name is Rosenbaum, / My other name is Rose." The narrator emulates the wealth and polish of other women but recognizes that she can never erase the indelible evidence of her class and ethnicity:

> I bought an ounce of nice perfume
> And now I smell just like a rose-in-bloom.
> But why take the trouble when ev'ryone knows
> That I'm only a hot-house rose.

Porter performed the song for Brice in the ballroom of the Ca' Rezzonico, and he recalled later that Brice found the friction between the song's description of poverty and the vast space, lined with frescos by Tiepolo, "wonderfully incongruous."[27] For reasons unknown, Brice never performed "Hot-House Rose." Perhaps she did not find an opportunity, though she frequently sang other Jewish novelty songs, including Irving Berlin's "Sadie Salome Go Home" (1909) and "Goodbye, Becky Cohen" (1910). Porter's song seems different in spirit from these earlier numbers, which celebrated Jewish assimilation even as they satirized it. Brice, born Fania Borach, changed her name and became a New York vaudeville darling, but in Porter's rendering, no pseudonym or amount of perfume could alter the fact that a New York native with a Jewish name was inevitably a "hot-house rose from God knows where, / The kind that grows without fresh air," and that everyone will always know who she really is—a perennial outsider as a Jew, the song implies. The pitfalls of assimilation and culture clash among Jewish immigrants, their children, and other ethnic groups were typical subjects in novelty songs, but Porter's sardonic take on assimilation as a transparent form of apery situates the song among the more cynical renditions of this theme.

Porter also referred to Jewish names in the song "I Am Gaston" (1938), in which the singer, remarking on his lack of a family name, states, "I'd gladly filch / The name of Zilch, / Or even sign / As Finkelstein." In "Midsummer Night" (1950), Porter writes, in a litany of the different "nights" that this night is not, "This is not Yom Kippur night, / This is not Jack the Ripper night." The Yiddish language made its way into "What a Ball" (1949), whose lyrics include the phrase "Oh, remember the waltz / So delightfully schmaltz." And the modern dialect of "Yinglish," the hybrid form of Yiddish and English that developed in the United States in the early twentieth century and could be heard in some Yiddish theater, radio, and cinema, is implied in "There Must Be Someone for Me" (1944). This list song, which invokes couplings of animals ("There's a boy mouse for ev'ry girl mouse") and features clever plays on words ("There's no boycott on any girl cot, / . . . There's a pa-poose for ev'ry ma-poose"), includes the lines "There's a boy chick for ev'ry girl chick," seemingly a pun on the word "boychik," a common American Yiddish diminutive for "boy." The cosmopolitan Jewish reference is heightened by the contrasting rural gentile subject of its rhyme, "There's a boy hick for ev'ry girl hick." Finally, Jewish music appears to be a likely model for the phrase "Da-da, da-da-da, da-da-da, dad!" in "My Heart Belongs to Daddy" (1938), whose repetitive turning musical pattern, set to vocables incorporating three augmented seconds, resembles techniques and scales associated with Hasidic *nigun*—a commonly wordless genre of religious music—and Yiddish song. Jack Gottlieb suggests that Porter's use of such elements in this song "can be construed . . . as a Jewish putdown," a pejorative mimicry of Jewish music in a song that plays on "the unsavory rich-Jew-with-mistress caricature."[28]

Given the overall paucity of explicit references to Jewish themes and music in Porter's oeuvre, the notion of Porter as a composer of "Jewish songs" seems far-fetched. Rodgers's opinion that Porter's use of the minor mode reflects the influence of the Jewish music of the eastern Mediterranean is also not persuasive: the minor mode seems insufficient to signify a particularly Jewish musical influence, given its ubiquity in art and popular music. Jeffrey Magee argues that it is not Porter's use of the minor alone but his "mixture of major and minor modality inflected by chromaticism" that qualifies his tunes as "Jewish."[29] He finds a precedent in Irving Berlin's Jewish novelty songs, which also juxtaposed major and minor and through which, Magee argues, this technique became popularly associated with American Jewish culture.[30] But the mixture of major and minor, common in so many musical genres and only loosely reflective of the Jewish music traditions heard in New York during that era, also seems insufficient to convey a "Jewish" inflection in the absence of Jewish subject matter in the songs' lyrics or in their theatrical contexts.[31] Perhaps Rodgers and later commentators have taken Porter's winking claim of writing "Jewish tunes" too literally, and Rodgers was in fact correct in initially believing Porter to be joking. Schwartz suggests that Porter's statement might in fact have been more hard-edged than light-hearted, reflecting the common stereotype about Jewish "domination" of American entertainment and a suspicion that he was unfairly shut off from success because he was not Jewish; indeed, Schwartz reads "undercurrents of anti-Semitism" in Porter's "'Jewish' formula."[32]

Whatever Porter's intention in making this comment, it is still informative to consider the possible impacts of American Jewish culture on Porter's work, in particular the ways in which both Jewish novelty songs and the popular Yiddish theater might have inspired his compositions and his conception of the Broadway musical, however indirectly. At the end of his discussion of Porter's "Jewishness" in his memoir, Rodgers muses, "It is surely one of the ironies of the musical theatre that despite the abundance of Jewish composers, the one who has written the most enduring 'Jewish' music should be an Episcopalian millionaire who was born on a farm in Peru, Indiana."[33] But the greater irony, if Rodgers's term is correct for characterizing the politics of identity in the early twentieth-century American popular song, was that the emergent genre of musical theater was so deeply influenced by the creative work of first- and second-generation Eastern European Jews. The effects of Yiddish theater, song, and sheet music on Broadway and Tin Pan Alley have remained underevaluated and are deserving of further study. This chapter is not an appropriate place to look into the matter in depth, but a brief discussion will help to provide a context for Porter's work and a sense of what Porter and his contemporaries might have meant when they claimed to detect Jewish inspiration in his songs.

The Yiddish theater, founded by the actor, writer, and director Abraham Goldfaden in Romania in 1876 and first performed in America by immigrant troupes as early as 1883, rapidly became the principal source of entertainment in New York for Eastern European Jewish immigrants. Yiddish theater was a thoroughly musical art form that featured songs, overtures, and orchestrated incidental music. Its richly hybrid scores frequently borrowed from disparate sources, including Yiddish folk song, Jewish liturgy, European operetta, American popular song, and modernist compositional techniques. This mixture led one reviewer in the Yiddish press to scoff, "Just imagine how it looks when, for example, a High Priest sings an aria of a Spanish gypsy or when a Jewish princess declares her love for a Jewish shepherd with a solo of a French prostitute [or when] . . . a Jewish servant dances a Spanish pirouette or a French Cancan, and that in the middle of the Temple in Jerusalem."[34] Although this writer evidently was unmoved by what he saw, the eclectic merging of genres and styles remained a common and often beloved characteristic of Yiddish theater among its broad audiences during the century's early decades. Yiddish theater's evocations of the Old Country, in both imported and newly composed "folk" songs, were often combined with representations of life in America in works such as Boris Thomashevsky's *The Jewish Yankee Doodle* and numerous plays about "green" immigrants such as *The Green Cousin*, *The Green Musician*, and *The Green Bride*.

Many audience members in the early years of Broadway were also frequent attendees of the Yiddish theater, and a number of Broadway's beloved performers got their start on Second Avenue stages.[35] The influence flowed in both directions: Yiddish plays appeared in translation on Broadway; English-language shows on Broadway formed the basis of works by leading Yiddish theater playwrights and composers; and plays by famous authors such as Ibsen and Shaw were produced on both stages, sometimes appearing in Yiddish translation in the first instance.[36] Yiddish theater is known to have held significant appeal for a number of Broadway's composers. E. Y. "Yip" Harburg, for example, attended Yiddish theater regularly as a youth; he recalled, "Everything in the Yiddish theater set me afire."[37] Joseph Rumshinsky, the prominent composer for the Yiddish theater, recalled in his autobiography that he once went to a dance hall where the pianist, a young man named George, surprised him by playing several of the numbers from his latest work, *Der tsebrokhene fidl* (The broken violin); the pianist told Rumshinsky that his parents regularly took him to Yiddish theater productions, and the family were avid fans. It was ten years later, at a new play he had written for the Yiddish theater and cinema actress Molly Picon, that Rumshinsky encountered this pianist again. George came with his brother Ira; they were the Gershwin brothers and had since achieved international acclaim.[38] The Gershwins attended Yiddish theater productions in Berlin and London as well, and George created piano rolls of the songs "Dos pintele yid" (The spark of Jewishness) and "Got un zayn mishpet iz gerekht" (God and his judgment are correct).[39] Rumshinsky also exhibited a cross-cultural influence in the opposite direction: he was known as the "Jewish Victor Herbert" and also incorporated techniques from Berlin's songs in his late Yiddish works.[40]

Jewish novelty songs in English by Berlin and others, like many Yiddish plays, also relied on humorous juxtapositions of ethnic cultural traditions and stereotypes, as exhibited in the titles of "Yonkle, the Cowboy Jew" (1907), "Yiddle on Your Fiddle Play Some Rag Time" (1909), "The Yiddish Rag" (1909), "Yiddisha Nightingale" (1910), "Yiddisher Irish Baby" (1915), "There's a Little Bit of Irish in Sadie Cohn" (1916), and "Yiddisher Jazz" (1921). Many of the most enduring works of Broadway and Tin Pan Alley similarly shared Yiddish theater's eclectic and often comic self-conscious thematic hybridity. The association of this shared sensibility with the processes of displacement and assimilation in modern Jewish culture was implied by a humorous interaction between Oscar Hammerstein II and Jerome Kern: when the two set out to create a theatrical adaptation of the biography of Marco Polo by Brian Oswald Donn-Byrne, Hammerstein remarked to Kern, "Here is a story laid in China about an Italian and told by an Irishman. What kind of music are you going to write?" to which Kern replied, "It'd be good Jewish music."[41]

Perhaps to Porter the word "Jewish," in the context of American popular music, meant nothing as simple as the use of minor scales or as reactionary as hostility to the Jewish presence in the entertainment business but was a more complex tendency toward the self-conscious assimilation of musical elements borrowed from disparate cultural contexts. In many of Porter's songs, including those listed by Rodgers as particularly "Jewish," it was a comparable sort of stylistic eclecticism that served as a metaphor for the reserves of romantic passion described by Porter's singers, for whom allusions to exotic sights and sounds alien to their daily life often express or awaken their innermost feelings.

Porter might never have seen the Yiddish theater, and it would be an exaggeration to argue that it had any direct inspiration on his work, but as he was an active composer in a genre in which so many of his contemporaries knew of or even worked in the Yiddish theater, it is likely that indirect but important instances of influence can be found. According to one anecdote, for example, when Bella Spewack pitched to him the idea of creating *Kiss Me, Kate*, she overcame his initial skepticism by arguing that the show was destined to make money because *The Taming of the Shrew* was "a Yiddish play at heart," representing codified gender roles and values about marriage resembling those depicted on Second Avenue.[42] The cross-cultural borrowing typical in early twentieth-century Jewish entertainment resembles Porter's own frequent references to the sounds of exotic, popular, and classical genres. Indeed, Porter's description of himself to the journalist Tex McCrary and actress Jinx Falkenburg pointed to an awareness of hybridity in his own life and music, his merging of the "lowbrow" and "highbrow," of Jewish humor and posh respectability, and of American entertainment and European art: "You might describe me as a cross between Eddie Cantor and the Duke of Windsor."[43]

At the same time, much of the music of the Jewish songwriters of Tin Pan Alley and Broadway was expressly *not* "Jewish" in its subject matter and musical materials: from Berlin's "Easter Parade" and "White Christmas" to Rodgers and Hammerstein's songs for *Carousel* and *Oklahoma!*, the music of popular Jewish composers frequently aimed to represent a secularized white Christian American culture. Adopting techniques from African American jazz and blues and portraying Americans on the stage allowed Berlin, Rodgers, and others to build careers in which they emphasized their participation in mainstream American culture rather than their membership in a marginalized minority group. As Stephen J. Whitfield observes, "In order not to write as a Jew, Berlin insisted that he wrote as a Caucasian (which entitled him to write in any dialect and on any theme)."[44] As a white, wealthy, Protestant midwesterner, Porter did not need to prove his assimilation, but as a homosexual man in the public eye, he understood what it was to be an outsider who adopted elements of conventional behavior to keep aspects of his private life from view. Chameleon-like, Porter created a heteronormative public persona by taking a wife and writing songs about heterosexual passion (though, as James Hepokoski's chapter in this volume shows, his songs occasionally included references to homosexual attraction as well). Thus Porter's joking comment about "writ[ing] Jewish songs" might ultimately be taken as a metaphor for his broader search to find his place not only among the Broadway musical greats but also in the American social mainstream.

The hybridity in many of Porter's works, as well as in their later interpretations, stems from their incorporation of the standard idioms of Tin Pan Alley with elements of its musical "others." Thus one hears the invocation of a gypsy guitar to express the passion in an American debutante's heart; a dance called a beguine that is played as a bossa nova or performed as a fusion of tap and flamenco; and a love song using minor harmonies that was reportedly based on the music of North Africa and was later interpreted as conveying a particularly "Jewish" sound. The aim of Porter's eclectic musical references was not ethnographic authenticity, but neither was it, in all cases at least, the perpetuation of ethnic stereotype. It was instead the expression of the mystery of what lurks within one's nature—of the indefinable thing called love and the passion that a character feels upon encountering his or her perfect match. In much of Porter's repertoire, it is with the evocation of eclectic musical techniques and genres, looking outward and evoking other styles through musical hybridity, that he creates his most introspective musical statements, turning back inwardly to examine the force and purity of the emotions that drive human feelings, relationships, and the quest for acceptance.

Notes

1. Porter often told multiple stories about what inspired his songs. This particular tale of origins appears in Ronald Schleifer, *Modernism and Popular Music* (Cambridge: Cambridge University Press, 2011), 130.

2. Stephen Citron, *Noel and Cole: The Sophisticates* (New York: Oxford University Press, 1993; reprint with new introduction, Milwaukee: Hal Leonard, 2005), 81. For further details on the production, see http://balanchine.org/balanchine/display_result.jsp?id=147&sid=&searchMethod=&current=&stagings=&refs=1&tvs=#refs, accessed 8 December 2012.

3. Gilbert Millstein, "Words anent Music by Cole Porter," *New York Times*, 20 February 1955, SM16, SM55, quote at SM55.

4. Charles Schwartz, *Cole Porter: A Biography* (New York: Da Capo Press, 1979), 56.

5. See Brendan Gill's introduction to Robert Kimball and Brendan Gill, eds., *Cole* (London: Michael Joseph, 1971), xii; and John Lahr, "King Cole: The Not So Merry Soul of Cole Porter," *New Yorker*, 12 and 19 July 2004, 102. Cole Porter mentions the inspiration of Gilbert and Sullivan in Millstein, "Words anent Music," SM55.

6. The text quote is from Robert Kimball, ed., *The Complete Lyrics of Cole Porter* (New York: Alfred A. Knopf, 1983), 86.

7. Ethan Mordden, "Rock and Cole," *New Yorker*, 28 October 1991, 96.

8. Matthew Shaftel, "From Inspiration to Archive: Cole Porter's 'Night and Day,'" *Journal of Music Theory* 43, no. 2 (1999): 323–24.

9. See Geoffrey Block, *Enchanted Evenings: The Broadway Musical from "Show Boat" to Sondheim and Lloyd Webber*, 2nd ed. (New York: Oxford University Press, 2009), 218–19;

and Joseph P. Swain, *The Broadway Musical: A Critical and Musical Survey* (New York: Oxford University Press, 1990), 138.

10. Shaftel, "From Inspiration to Archive," 324.

11. The self-consciousness of Porter's musical references can also make its way into the performance instructions. Allen Forte points out that in "What Is This Thing Called Love?" Porter added the words "In the manner of a 'blues'" ("The Secrets of Melody: Line and Design in the Songs of Cole Porter," *Musical Quarterly* 77, no. 4 [1993]: 617).

12. See Miriam Whaples, "Early Exoticism Revisited," in *The Exotic in Western Music*, ed. Jonathan Bellman (Boston: Northeastern University Press, 1998), 18–19.

13. On the perception of Heifetz as an exotic figure, see Joshua S. Walden, "'The Hora Staccato in Swing!': Jascha Heifetz's Musical Eclecticism and the Adaptation of Violin Miniatures," *Journal of the Society for American Music* 6, no. 4 (2012): 405–31.

14. See, for instance, "Gypsy Moon," Leo Camby and Ed Moebus, 1920; "Gypsy Moon," Winifred T. Barr, 1926; and "Gipsy Moon," Frank Eyton and Igor Borganoff, 1927.

15. Nicholas Saul, *Gypsies and Orientalism in German Literature and Anthropology of the Long Nineteenth Century* (London: Legenda, 2007), chap. 1.

16. Terry Castle, "Night and Day," *New Republic*, 21 December 1998, 43.

17. Citron, *Noel and Cole*, 136.

18. Monique Desroches, "Martinique," in *Garland Encyclopedia of World Music*, vol. 2: *South America, Mexico, Central America, and the Caribbean*, ed. Dale A. Olsen and Daniel E. Sheehy (New York: Garland, 1998), 915–17.

19. The published score of "Begin the Beguine" is almost the same as Porter's manuscript; other than the transposition to B-flat major from Porter's original C major, the few differences involve the incorporation of triplets in the piano in two measures and small changes in rhythmic notation. Folder 205, box 28, MSS 82, Cole Porter Collection, Irving S. Gilmore Music Library, Yale University.

20. The song's popularity provoked Porter to write a parody in 1944's "Dancin' to a Jungle Drum" (originally "Let's End the Beguine").

21. *Begin the Beguine* is also the title of a painting from 1946 by Max Beckmann depicting a claustrophobic, enigmatic, and exotic scene with dancers—one with a wooden leg—surrounded by other figures and objects, including a bound woman draped in sheer fabric, tropical birds, and a page of what might be sheet music to the song.

22. Tom Nolan, *Artie Shaw, King of the Clarinet: His Life and Times* (New York: W. W. Norton, 2010), 94.

23. Marty Paitch, "Begin the Beguine," folder 4, box 120, and folders 1–2, box 121, Ella Fitzgerald Collection, Music Division, Library of Congress, Washington, DC.

24. Richard Rodgers, *Musical Stages: An Autobiography* (New York: Random House, 1975; Cambridge, MA: Da Capo Press, 2002), 87.

25. Ibid., 88.

26. Ibid., 88. MGM executive producer Sam Katz similarly said that "Goodbye, Little Dream, Goodbye" was "beautiful—why, it's Jewish" (Schwartz, *Cole Porter*, 155).

27. Kimball, *Complete Lyrics*, 139.

28. Jack Gottlieb, *Funny, It Doesn't Sound Jewish: How Yiddish Songs and Synagogue Melodies Influenced Tin Pan Alley, Broadway, and Hollywood* (Albany: State University

of New York, with Library of Congress, 2004), 186–87. See also Schwartz, *Cole Porter*, 193, for further discussion of the song's mimicry of Jewish music.

29. Jeffrey Magee, "Irving Berlin's 'Blue Skies': Ethnic Affiliations and Musical Transformations," *Musical Quarterly* 84, no. 4 (2000): 540. See also Gottlieb, *Funny, It Doesn't Sound Jewish*, 189.

30. Magee, "Irving Berlin's 'Blue Skies,'" 541–48.

31. Stephen Citron also questions the association of Porter's major-minor juxtapositions with Yiddish song: "My ears tell me that some of this shifting from the major to minor mode more closely resembles the ambivalent French chansons popular around Pigalle than true Yiddish music" (*Noel and Cole*, 102).

32. Schwartz, *Cole Porter*, 117–18.

33. Rodgers, *Musical Stages*, 88.

34. Nina Warnke, "Yiddish Theater History, Its Composers and Operettas: A Narrative without Music," *Muzykalia* VII / *Judaica* 2 (2009): 5.

35. Stephen J. Whitfield, *In Search of American Jewish Culture* (Hanover, NH: Brandeis University Press, 1999), 61; and Nahma Sandrow, *Vagabond Stars: A World History of Yiddish Theater* (Syracuse, NY: Syracuse University Press, 1996), 154, 272.

36. See, for example, descriptions of Sholem Asch's *God of Vengeance* and Joseph Lateiner's adaptation of Broadway hits in Sandrow, *Vagabond Stars*, 183, 137. On Yiddish and Broadway productions of classic plays, see ibid., 259.

37. Howard Pollack, *George Gershwin: His Life and Work* (Berkeley: University of California Press, 2006), 43. See also Whitfield, *In Search of American Jewish Culture*, 63; and Harriet Hyman Alonso, *Yip Harburg: Legendary Lyricist and Human Rights Activist* (Middletown, CT: Wesleyan University Press, 2012), 7–9.

38. Joseph Rumshinsky, *Klangen fun mayn lebn* (New York: A. Y. Biderman, 1944), 497–500.

39. Pollack, *George Gershwin*, 44.

40. Ibid., 43.

41. Whitfield, *In Search of American Jewish Culture*, 61.

42. Schwartz, *Cole Porter*, 231.

43. William McBrien, *Cole Porter: A Biography* (New York: Alfred A. Knopf, 1998), 28.

44. Whitfield, *In Search of American Jewish Culture*, 99.

PART 3

Approaches to the Analysis and Criticism of Porter's Works

11

Licentious Harmony and Counterpoint in Porter's "Love for Sale"

MICHAEL BUCHLER

No one would mistake Cole Porter's "Love for Sale" for a love song. Yet this less-than-subtle song about the world's oldest profession, from the 1930 musical *The New Yorkers*, confronts the nature of love and, by extension, the love song genre. Because of its daring text, it not only was banned in Boston (honestly, what wasn't?) but was considered so risqué that at the time radio stations across America refused to play it.[1] Porter's musical setting of his infamous lyrics also deviated from the normative structures found in contemporaneous popular—and especially love—songs, and his structural departures were not simply motivated by relatively obvious concerns for text painting. This chapter attempts to unpack and understand these musical anomalies through close analyses of harmony, counterpoint, and text.

In the so-called golden age, love songs (and, indeed, most popular songs) tended to be relatively predicable numbers. With traditional foursquare phrase structure and resolutely functional harmonic syntax, the love song only rarely challenged our harmonic or formal expectations. Even Cole Porter—a sophisticate among sophisticates—seldom deviated from convention when portraying mutual affection.[2]

Example 1 reproduces the first sixteen bars of the refrain from Cole Porter's 1955 ballad "True Love." These four phrases follow an alternating pattern. In

EXAMPLE 1. "True Love" (from *High Society*), refrain, mm. 1–16. Words and music by Cole Porter. Copyright © 1955, 1956 Chappell & Co., Inc. Copyright renewed and assigned to John F. Wharton, Trustee of the Cole Porter Musical and Literary Property Trusts. Publication and Allied Rights Assigned to Chappell & Co., Inc. All Rights Reserved. Used by permission of Alfred Music.

the first and third phrases, the tonic is introduced and expanded through neighboring plagal motions and common-tone diminished seventh chords, followed in the even phrases by "true love, true love" set to a simple but firm dominant–tonic affirmation. It is charming, if a bit sappy, and still holds a deserved place in the wedding-reception canon.

In Porter's somewhat unconventional 1941 love song "I Hate You, Darling," the singer deceptively declares animosity for his or her true love. The opening sixteen bars are shown in example 2. While our protagonist is "hating" his darling, the accompanying harmonies are atypical, doing little to affirm the home key of E-flat major.[3] But everything settles down as we approach the initial section's end and the singer clarifies, "I hate you, darling . . . because I love you so." Porter set that affirmation with a strong dominant–tonic motion, quelling any of our notions that the singer might be harboring genuine animosity.

Mutual love did not typically inspire musical ingenuity during the golden age. Such happy matters of the heart befit virtuosity and repetition, but only

EXAMPLE 2. "I Hate You, Darling" (from *Let's Face It*), refrain, mm. 1–16. Words and music by Cole Porter.

seldom do they invoke harmonic originality.[4] But again, Cole Porter's "Love for Sale" is no love song. While the ostensible topic of the song and one of its most frequent lyrics is, in fact, "love," this song is more about the absence of love—not in the silly, playful manner of "I Hate You, Darling" but in a much more real and disturbing sense. One can, after all, sell sex but certainly not love. I believe this topic gave Porter license—perhaps even a mandate—to confront some of this genre's tonal, contrapuntal, and formal norms.

The Verse

Introductory verses are often omitted in music from this era, but in this song the verse forms something of a dramatic imperative. It comprises two exceptional ten-bar phrases. Phrases or subphrases that don't group into binary numbers of measures (two, four, eight, sixteen . . .) are atypical of this literature, but these phrases are also remarkable for the manner in which they establish the key. Contrapuntally, both phrases complete stepwise octave descents that meander through a variety of tonal regions. The overall linear motion seems goal directed; the moment-to-moment harmonic progression often does not.

Example 3 presents an analytical view of the verse, excluding the piano introduction. Almost throughout the first ten-bar phrase (mm. 5–14, shown in the top half of ex. 3), the melody and bass move in parallel sixths, each descending a complete octave. This stepwise pattern initially progresses by whole tone until measure 8 in the melody and measure 9 in the bass. Both parallel counterpoint and especially motion by whole tones effectively oppose any sense of tonal function or directionality, creating a musical fog that only lifts slightly at the "lonesome cop's" arrival in measure 10. The cop is the first character to enter this scene, and his presence is melodically uplifting. Structurally, however, the descending line presses onward. The "lonesome" G♭ arises from a voice exchange between the melody and bass; it signals an abandonment of the initial upper voice in the upper register.[5] As the beam in the first half of example 3 illustrates, that contrapuntal line continues in the accompaniment, where, in measure 10, the suspended E♭ descends to D♭, then to C in measure 11, and finally to B♭ in measure 13. To summarize: the initiating B♭4 in measure 5 descends an octave over the course of that first (unusual) ten-bar phrase, moving from outer to inner voice when the cop arrives.[6]

Meanwhile, the hopeful and unexpected leading tone (A4) sung in measure 11 is left unresolved in that register when the singer leaps down an augmented second just as her character "opens shop." That dominant in measure 11 is further undermined by the bass's stepwise descent in measure 12 (through a passing dominant $^4_2$), arriving at a weak first-inversion tonic at the cadence. The endpoints of this initial descent also highlight one of the song's central musical dichotomies: between major and minor tonic, or, more specifically, between D♮ and D♭, two notes that respectively signify hope and alienation throughout much of the song.

Contrapuntally, the second ten-bar phrase (mm. 15–24) resembles the first one, but the harmonies are now uniformly first-inversion dominant seventh

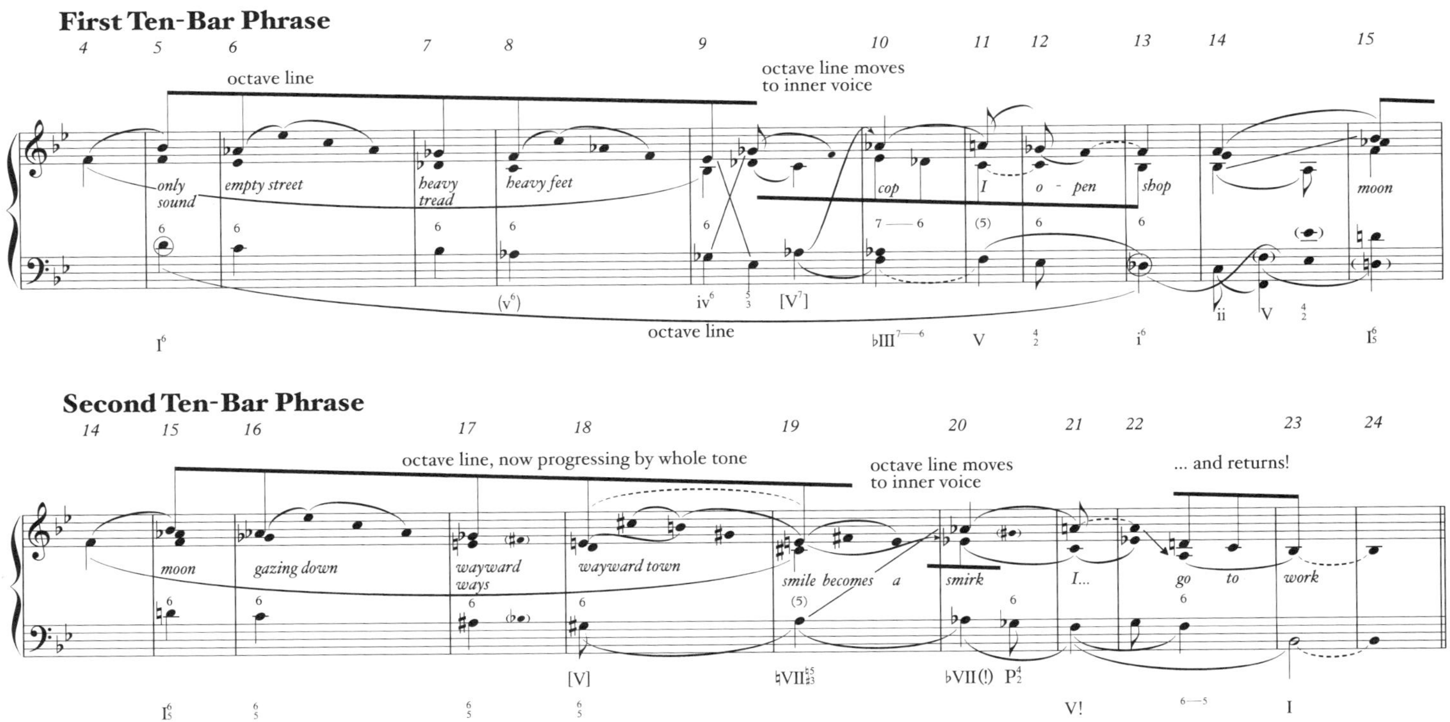

EXAMPLE 3. Voice-leading analysis of the introductory verse.

chords, not triads, and the octave descent progresses entirely by whole tone in the outer voices from measures 15–18. The tonally grounding half step from measures 7–8 is notably missing in measures 17–18, where the "wayward ways of this wayward town" initiate a wayward tonicization of A major, an especially cagey setting of the word "smile." The descending octave line briefly loses its momentum at this tonicization, but, as "smiles" turn to "smirks," any sense of A major as a local tonic is bluntly eradicated by Porter's surprisingly direct progressions to A-flat major and then F major triads. In very short order, Porter guides us from an extraordinary tonicization of the major leading-tone triad to a functional dominant in the home key. Only the smooth voice leading provides a measure of continuity throughout this passage. Indeed, were it not for the unfailingly parsimonious counterpoint, the melodic leading tone on which we circuitously arrive in measure 22 might not feel so badly abandoned as the vocal part leaps away yet again, this time diving a perfect fifth to complete the octave descent with a long-awaited perfect authentic cadence at "I go to work." Ella Fitzgerald, in her otherwise conservative *Cole Porter Songbook* recording (arranged and conducted by Buddy Bregman), took the liberty of resolving the leading tone in measure 22 properly.[7] It's a lovely rendition, but I am not sure that "lovely" is exactly what is called for here. To my ears, Porter's blatantly "improper" resolution acts as an important signifier in setting the words "I go to work" and preparing us—in a sense—for the well-known refrain.

Refrain

At least in terms of formal structure, the refrain is far more normative than the verse. It follows a standard AABA song form, with each section lasting sixteen measures, divided into four four-bar hypermeasures (not all are bona fide phrases).[8] The final A section concludes with an eight-bar coda-like cadential prolongation (mm. 89–96). Porter's adherence to standard formal design might well belie the highly idiosyncratic tonal and contrapuntal structure of this refrain.

The B-flat major foundation established in the introductory verse is immediately challenged at the beginning of the refrain. As I suggest on the sketch in example 4, the oscillating E-flat major and B-flat minor chords that occupy the first nine refrain bars (mm. 25–33) can reasonably be interpreted in at least two different tonal contexts. I hear this passage as tonic and minor dominant chords in E-flat major rather than as plagal motions in B-flat.[9] It is only with the words "slightly soiled" in measure 36 that I feel convinced we are genuinely

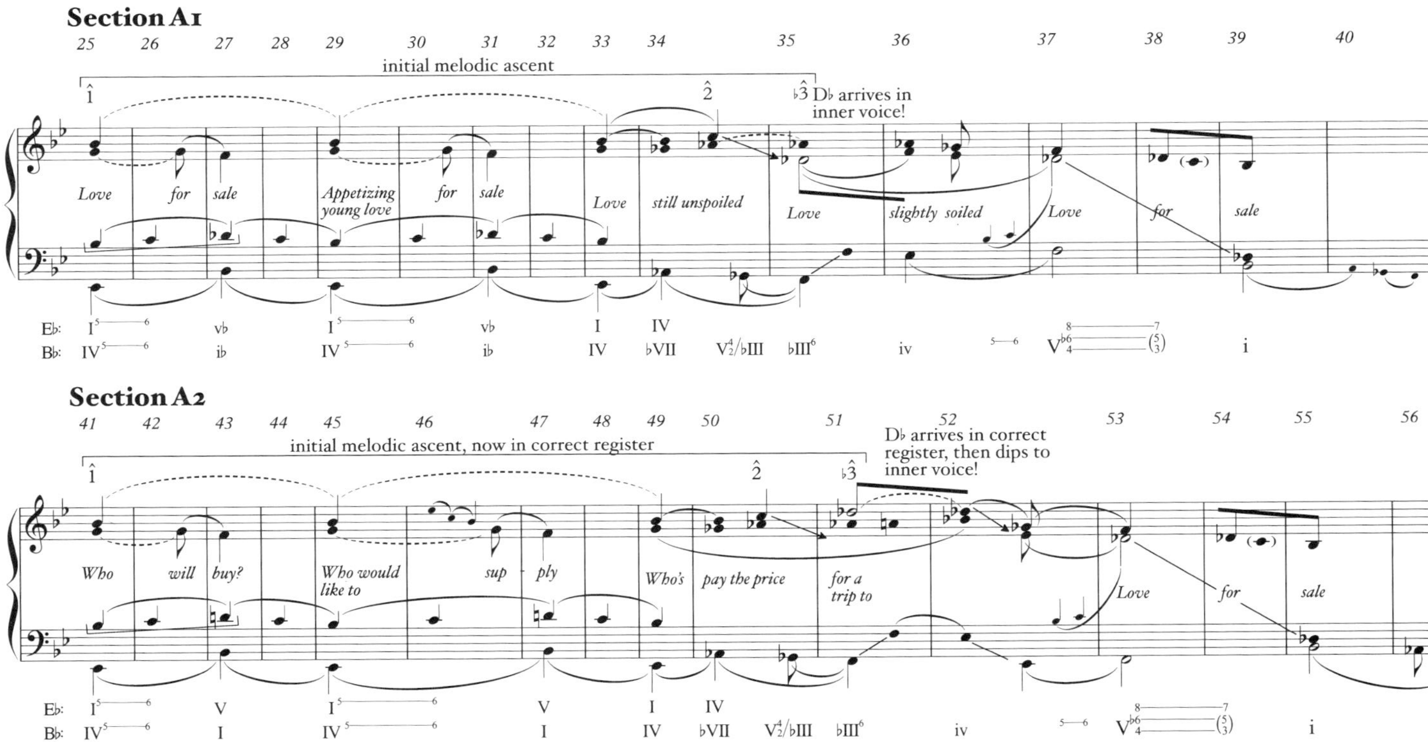

EXAMPLE 4. Voice-leading analysis of the refrain's A sections.

(continues on next page)

Section A3

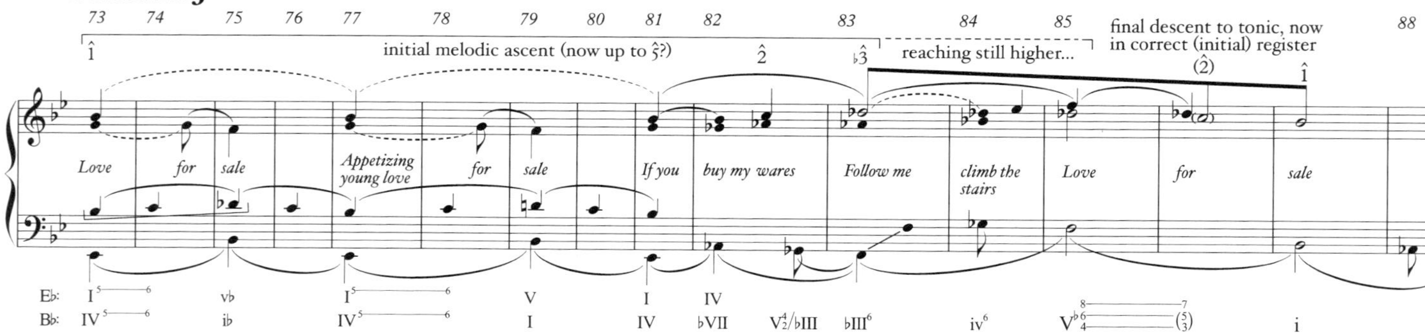

EXAMPLE 4. *(continued)*

in the key of B-flat. In an informal poll of students and colleagues, there was roughly an even mix of people who agreed with my auxiliary cadential reading (beginning off tonic) and those who heard it all in a modally mixed B-flat major.

This Chopinesque play of tonality that obscures the roles of tonic and subdominant commences all three A sections of the refrain. E-flat major plays a particularly prominent role at the beginning of the final A section (labeled A3), where it is tonicized by the climactic progression that ends the bridge (B section). This tonicization and its significance will receive considerably more attention a bit later in this chapter. Perhaps this bespeaks my own harmonic gullibility, or perhaps I am just overly willing to be swayed by tonicization, but I find myself convinced of E-flat major's viability each time we return to the tune's famous opening. I simply do not hear that section-initiating E-flat major chord as subdominant, even when I know that it must be by virtue of the cadence in B-flat that it both follows and eventually precedes.

Whether E-flat major is heard as tonic or subdominant, it seems to represent a certain hopeful optimism, whereas B-flat—especially B-flat minor—correlates with cold reality. E-flat major depicts "love" and even "appetizing young love"; B-flat minor sets the word "sale." B-flat (major) is our tonic, but perhaps the key of E-flat major is where we long to be. Porter's setting of "love" is hopeful, but in this song it simply is not real.

Cole Porter's counterpoint also reveals a great deal about the song's protagonist. As illustrated in examples 4 and 5, the refrain begins with a relatively static melody that operates in two distinct registers (see the opening eight bars, mm. 25–32). The upper line only begins to move in measure 33 at "love that's fresh and still unspoiled." B♭ ascends to C, and the accompanying harmonic motion suggests that the line should continue up to D♭. However, the ascending line is cut off at the next clause: "love that's only slightly soiled." The melodic A♭ that descends to G♭ at that point is not part of the same line of counterpoint; it originates as an inner voice and achieves melodic prominence.[10]

The line initiated by the B♭–C gesture in measures 33 and 34 does ascend, but only after being transferred into an inner voice. It reaches (the wrong) D♭ in measure 35 and continues to ascend to a neighboring E♭ in measure 36 before dropping back down to D♭ in measure 37. The textual connection involved with the subjugated upper voice seems almost too obvious. The ascending "love that's fresh and still unspoiled" is taken by the primary voice, while the descending "love that's only slightly soiled" is relegated to a contrapuntal inner voice. Analogously, "love" at the beginning of the refrain belongs to the primary voice, while "for sale" comes in an inner voice. The refrain's first legitimate dominant–tonic resolution underscores the section-ending lyric "love for sale" in measures 37–40. The melodic closure on a low B♭ marks the reunification of the vocal part with what had been the top contrapuntal voice. Though this utterance of the title lyric articulates a descending minor tonic triad, both the fifth and the third are supported by dominant harmony: a cadential six-four and its resolution.[11] As such, this authentic cadence is distinctly imperfect.

The second sixteen bars of the refrain, labeled section A2 on the sketches, follow essentially the same model as the first sixteen bars. The initial eight bars of A2 (text: "Who will buy? Who would like to sample my supply?") reflect little more than a surface-level elaboration of the refrain's opening: "Love for sale, appetizing young love for sale." But over the next eight bars, the melodic ascent from B♭ to C continues upward—in the same contrapuntal voice, that is—to D♭. The melodic goal here is the same as in the first sixteen-bar section, but where the character's line was initially derailed (text: "love that's only slightly soiled"), this time it clearly continues (text: "who's prepared to pay the price for a trip to paradise?"). However, just as soon as we arrive on D♭ in measure 52, that goal is undermined: at the word "paradise," the melody once again dips into the inner voice. Some measure of self-assurance has been gained, but the F in measure 53 that sets the word "love" still occupies the lower register, and "paradise," if ever gained at all, has pretty clearly been lost.

Only in the final refrain section (A3) does the melody ascend all the way to F5 ($\hat{5}$), the song's apex. This dramatic stepwise ascent to F5 is animated by the text "if you want to buy my wares, follow me and climb the stairs," reaching the high note on the following word, "Love." And while from a Schenkerian perspective it might seem that *this* note, not D♭, should serve as the song's true head tone (*Kopfton*), it simply appears too late. The arrival on F in measure 85 occurs at the structural dominant, and the song cannot at this point support a complete linear descent from $\hat{5}$. But by ascending to this height, Porter not only fulfills a long-standing melodic goal (suggested by the earlier E♭ neighbor tones) but also brings the singer to rest on B♭ in the initial (obligatory) register, creating a firmer sense of closure than in earlier cadences. The structural cadence in measure 87 really is the first contrapuntally *and* harmonically conclusive moment in the song. The three A-section ascents can be most easily compared in example 5, which provides an analytical summary.

In the song's final eight bars, which I rather equivocally deemed "coda-like," the title lyric is restated and melodically expanded. This passage is analytically

A1 (mm. 25–40)

A2 (mm. 41–56)

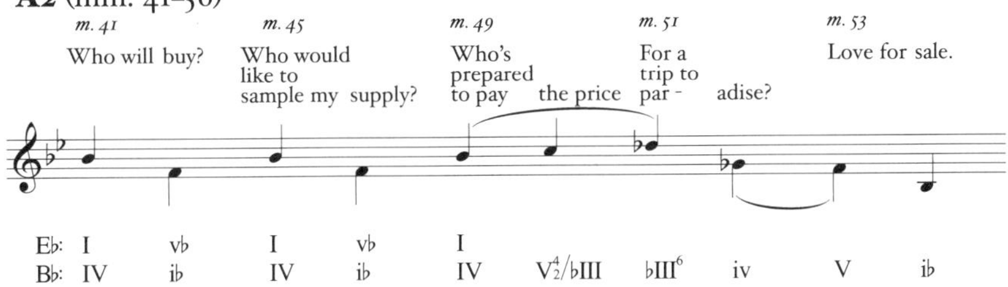

B [Bridge] (mm. 57–72) See Example 8

A3 (mm. 73–88)

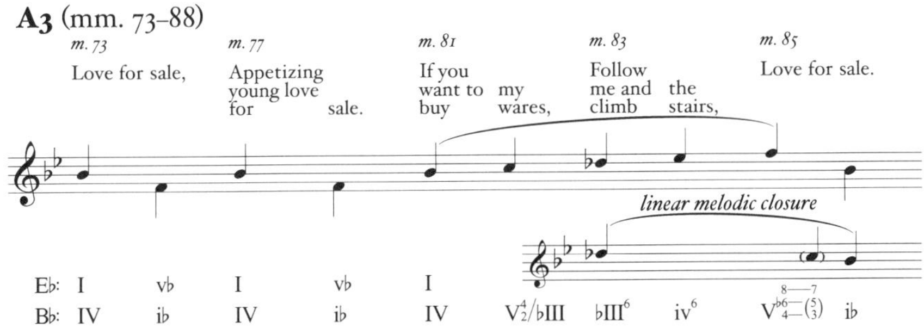

EXAMPLE 5. Analytical summary of the refrain's A sections (stem directions reflect distinct strands of voice leading).

sketched in example 6. Though the song has already attained structural closure by this point, Porter's harmonies here are worth at least brief comment. In particular, the word "sale" in measure 93, which should carry both melodic and harmonic resolution, instead conveys only the former. The harmonic denouement is extended with a chromatic motion to the minor subdominant (E-flat minor) in measure 94. This plagal ending—a mere surface interruption of the authentic cadence—reminds us of the plagal versus authentic ambiguities

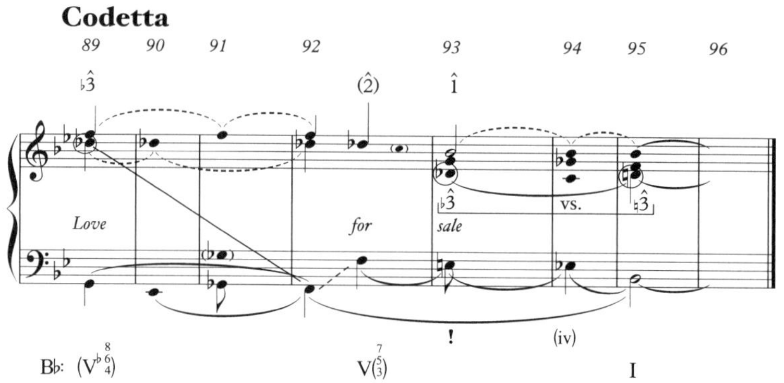

EXAMPLE 6. Voice-leading analysis of the codetta (mm. 89–96).

in the refrain's opening and definitively confirms the weaker role of E-flat, even while undermining the strong closure that we expect. If E-flat *major* represented love and hope, this E-flat *minor* gesture conveys something very different as the song concludes, finally, on B-flat major.

This conflict between major and minor tonic is subtly foreshadowed in the song's four-bar introduction, which initiates the dichotomy between D and D♭.[12] As the analytical sketch in example 7 shows, the introduction melodically outlines a B-flat *minor* triad, followed by a B-flat *major* triad, and yet Porter harmonically presents neither B-flat major nor minor in this passage. Instead, the initial tone is supported by a lowered submediant (♭VI), a harmony that plays a significant role in the song's B section (bridge).

There are several motivic connections between the bridge and the outer sections of the refrain, and linear analysis provides an effective means of elucidating them. A voice-leading sketch of the bridge appears in example 8. The

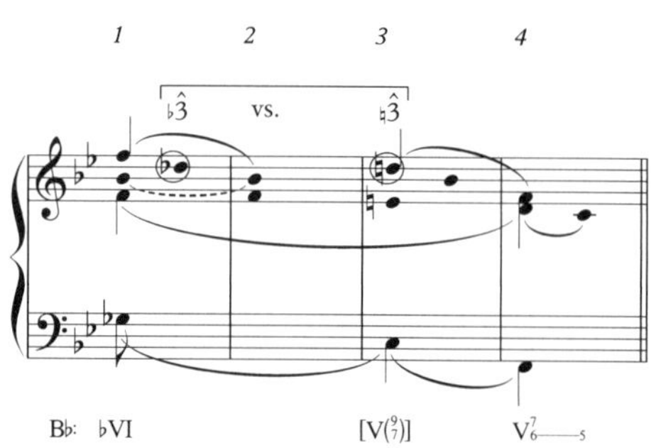

EXAMPLE 7. Voice-leading analysis of the piano introduction (mm 1.4).

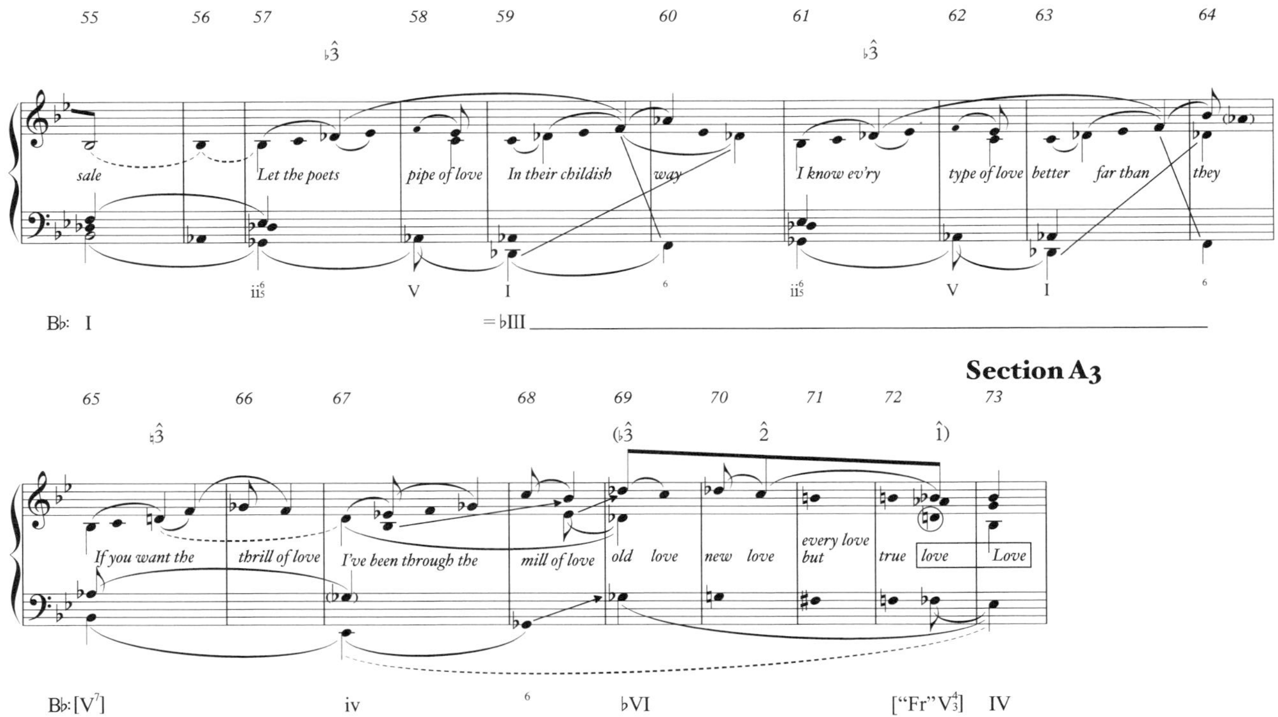

EXAMPLE 8. Voice-leading analysis of the bridge (B section).

play of D and D♭ becomes harmonically recontextualized in this section as those tones are stripped of their associations with the (major and minor) tonic triad. What I find most striking about this section, however, is the chromatic linear descent from D♭ to B♭, which, from a merely melodic or motivic standpoint, seems to mimic the way the song achieves melodic closure—except that this descent is built upon the shakiest of harmonic or contrapuntal pillars. The melodic D♭ (♭$\hat{3}$) is supported in Schubertian fashion by the expansion of the lowered mediant triad (♭III),[13] but in measures 70–72 the outer voices descend in parallel fourths, many of which are augmented. This musical passage underscores the climactic text "old love, new love, every love but true love," and the culminating words, "true love," are set with parallel tritones—quite a far cry from the sincere setting of "true love" in Porter's song of that title.

Porter creates a sort of enjambment as the bridge moves seamlessly into the last statement of the refrain tune at measure 73. He immediately reiterates the word "love" to create a seamless return to the head of the tune (text: "every love but true *love. Love* for sale"). Many singers have taken advantage of this by eliding the repeated word "Love."[14] Contrapuntally, the last tritone of "every love but true love" is harmonized as a dissonant dominant of E-flat (a so-called French V^4_3 of E-flat, or a second-inversion dominant seventh chord with a lowered fifth), providing a weak tonicized return to E-flat, which, as in the previous A sections, has only seemed to be our home (key). E-flat, in this sense, functions more as a hotel room than a residence. And love, by association, is both untrue and unreal.

Notes

1. In fact, it was not just his text that was socially problematic. According to William McBrien, the prostitute character in *The New Yorkers* was initially white. Porter switched to an African American prostitute to make the show more palatable to a white audience. William McBrien, *Cole Porter: A Biography* (New York: Alfred A. Knopf, 1998), 137.

2. Porter's status as a sophisticate has even been the subject of Stephen Citron's *Noel and Cole: The Sophisticates* (Oxford: Oxford University Press, 1993).

3. One particularly slippery (and beautiful) moment comes at the lyrics "all else above" in measures 11–12. At that location, a melodic B♭ is held as the bass descends from C to C♭, recalling the famous transition from verse to refrain in Porter's song "Night and Day" (at the lyrics "So a voice within me keeps repeating 'you, you, you.' Night and day, you are the one").

4. "Night and Day" (1932) stands apart as a notable exception in Porter's oeuvre. I do not mean to imply that Cole Porter's songs were formulaic; indeed, his works exhibit tremendous variety. Consider, for instance, love songs as diverse as "So in Love," "Do I Love You," "I Get a Kick Out of You," "I Love Paris," "Ev'ry Time We Say Goodbye," "I've

Got You Under My Skin," "Let's Do It (Let's Fall in Love)," "You're the Top," and "You'd Be So Nice to Come Home To." Any harmonic or contrapuntal anomalies, however, tend to be ironed out within sixteen bars, just as they were in "I Hate You, Darling."

5. I am invoking the contrapuntal sense of "voice," which moves by step and is distinct from a "melody," which can articulate several voices.

6. I'm using the octave-naming system of the Acoustical Society of America, where C4 = middle C.

7. *Ella Fitzgerald Sings the Cole Porter Songbook* (PolyGram Records MG V-4001-2, 1956, 1993).

8. See William Rothstein, *Phrase Rhythm in Tonal Music* (New York: Schirmer Books, 1989), 1–32.

9. Despite the tonally conclusive introductory verse, the refrain sounds to me like an auxiliary cadential structure.

10. Motivically, "love that's fresh and still unspoiled" and "love that's only slightly soiled" mirror each other, a clever association of musical and textual inversion.

11. In this literature, one frequently hears $\hat{3}$ substituting for $\hat{2}$ at the dominant (this might be called a "sub6" chord). However, this substitution is more complex: $\hat{2}$ is replaced by $\flat\hat{3}$ (rather than $\natural\hat{3}$), invoking the parallel minor mode.

12. As discussed elsewhere in the present volume, the introductions were typically composed after the remainder of the sheet music, often by Albert Sirmay, although sometimes by Porter himself. Regardless, they are thus able to "highlight important features of a song from the very outset" (Matthew Shaftel, "From Inspiration to Archive: Cole Porter's 'Night and Day,'" *Journal of Music Theory* 43, no. 2 [Fall 1999]: 325).

13. This expansion of ♭III is foreshadowed both in the first measure of the song's piano introduction and in the A sections of the refrain (e.g., "love that's only slightly soiled"). Like the instances of the lowered submediant in the A sections, here, too, the progression ultimately leads to a minor subdominant. What seems truly exceptional is that the bridge's subdominant never makes its way to a dominant but instead merges into the tonicized major subdominant chord that begins the A3 section.

14. A great example of this elision/enjambment can be heard in Libby Holman's 1931 version, one of the earliest recordings of this song. This recording was preserved by the Indiana Historical Society and rereleased in a three-disc set of Porter's songs from the thirties.

12

About Cole Porter's Songs

DON M. RANDEL

The first thing to establish is what about Cole Porter's songs this essay is not about. This entails addressing the nature of these songs, their genre, the modes of production at work in that genre, and the materials that these modes of production have left behind for the scholar. This entails setting aside a good many musicological habits.[1]

Before studying or performing a work, musicologists like to satisfy themselves that they have established a suitably reliable text of the work, or perhaps several such texts if the goal is to examine the compositional process over some period of time. Cole Porter's songs, however, do not lend themselves to such a pursuit, for complete autographs of both words and music are relatively rare, and the character of such autographs and of the first printed editions of this music were clearly shaped by the nature of the intended audiences and performances. For example, a song of this type was often first published in a form and for an audience that required it to be relatively easy to play on the piano. The songs' first public performances, on the other hand, were likely to be in orchestral arrangements made by Robert Russell Bennett or some other professional arranger for a Broadway show. Almost every performance thereafter is likely to have incorporated substantial modifications to harmonic progressions, as well as to tempo and rhythmic detail.

It is thus rather difficult to establish what features of any given song can be thought to be essential to its identity. This characterizes all of the repertory of popular song of the type that Porter composed. These songs retain their individual identity despite quite substantial transformations of their musical elements by different performers. What precisely are we talking about, then, when we talk about any Porter song? We will no doubt wish to get as close as we can to what Porter himself had in mind, but Porter himself almost certainly contemplated modifications by others to what he first produced in his own hand, even if he did not always like them. This greatly complicates anything we might like to produce in the way of voice-leading graphs (though some of the techniques of this type of analysis may indeed prove valuable), since apart from the melody itself, register is not in general specified at all as essential to the identity of a song, and there may be considerable variety even in the inversion in which a given harmony is presented. One will thus not be able to speak with much confidence about the importance of a pitch in the melody that is given root support in the bass.

Thus, this essay is not about analyzing the songs of Cole Porter as if they were by Robert Schumann, and it is certainly not about establishing a claim, based on techniques of analysis that we might agree are relevant to Schumann, that Porter's songs are equal in artistic merit to those of Schumann.[2] The claim of value is an entirely separate claim that must rest on independent value axioms, and it cannot be established by any analytical means absent such axioms.

Then there is the matter of the words. The musicological starting point is to assume that the words and the music might have something to do with one another. But the phrase "to do with" often brings along too much baggage. Through much of the history of Western art music, the words of vocal music have been thought necessarily to be "the mistress of the music" or some such formulation. The words are taken as the starting point, and the music is expected to "express" something about them and in that sense to derive from them in some degree. As I have suggested with respect to some repertories of Western art music, this view of the relationship between words and music in any given composition can easily lead into fantasy and distract from the ways in which music and poetry in general share certain features.

In the case of the songs of Cole Porter and the larger repertory to which they belong, the composition of the melody very often precedes the composition of the words, or "lyrics," as they are usually called, and this necessarily obviates the typical approach to the relationship between words and music in works of Western art music. It does not, however, preclude observations about what features words and music might share in any given song and how we might think about the words and the music in relation to one another. It makes the typical biographical question about what the composer may have had in mind in setting a particular text clearly irrelevant. That Porter was both the author of the lyrics and the composer of the song might seem to resurrect this question. Unfortunately, however, it will in general not be possible to know in any given case what went on in Porter's mind and the degree to which he may have conceived words and music each in terms of the other.

Robert Kimball, the leading authority on Porter's lyrics, writes as follows:

> To separate Porter's lyrics from his music is of course to provide only a partial impression of these songs, particularly because words and music were so intimately linked in his creative process. Usually he began with a title or an idea—an idea that could be musical or lyrical or both. He would then work from both the beginning and ending of a song, moving in both directions toward the middle. For the most part, he did not create music and lyrics separately, they came together. He worked largely at night, with a rhyming dictionary and other reference books, and he was a tireless reviser and polisher.[3]

The status of the words in this repertory has its own unusual character. Whereas the music of a song of this type may undergo considerable transformation while remaining clearly and legitimately identifiable, the words or lyrics are virtually never altered significantly by performers once the song has left the context of a show, if any, and established itself as a standard.[4] The words are either sung as originally produced or omitted altogether in a wide variety of instrumental arrangements. Performers of and listeners to the instrumental versions will know the song by a title consisting of the first few words of the lyrics but may not know much or any of the remainder of the lyrics. Certainly, no one minds their omission (as listeners to Schumann surely would), and the songs of this repertory are widely disseminated in lead sheets and fake books that omit the words. The words, too, may be disseminated in anthologies without the music, but principally as words to songs that the reader or performer would be expected to know and not as independent literary texts, though they might be admired as such in a few cases, like that of Porter.

Thus, this essay is also not about how Porter's songs "express" something about their lyrics, let alone about how Porter as both author and composer was uniquely able to give the ideal musical expression to his lyrics. Instead, it is about how the lyrics and the music of Cole Porter songs might be thought of in relation to one another in essentially musical and poetic structural terms. There may be moments at which something like word painting is clearly at work. The goal of my analysis, however, is more nearly to describe what the lyrics and the music sound like together rather than what they mean or express together. For this purpose it matters not whether lyrics or music came first or that they were created by the same man.

"Ev'ry Time We Say Goodbye," written in 1944 for *The Seven Lively Arts*, is a much-beloved example of Porter songs that became standards and continue to be performed and recorded in both vocal and purely instrumental versions. Figure 1 sets out the lyrics for the refrain in a way that hopes to clarify some of the relations between lyrics and music.[5] When the lyrics are printed separately,

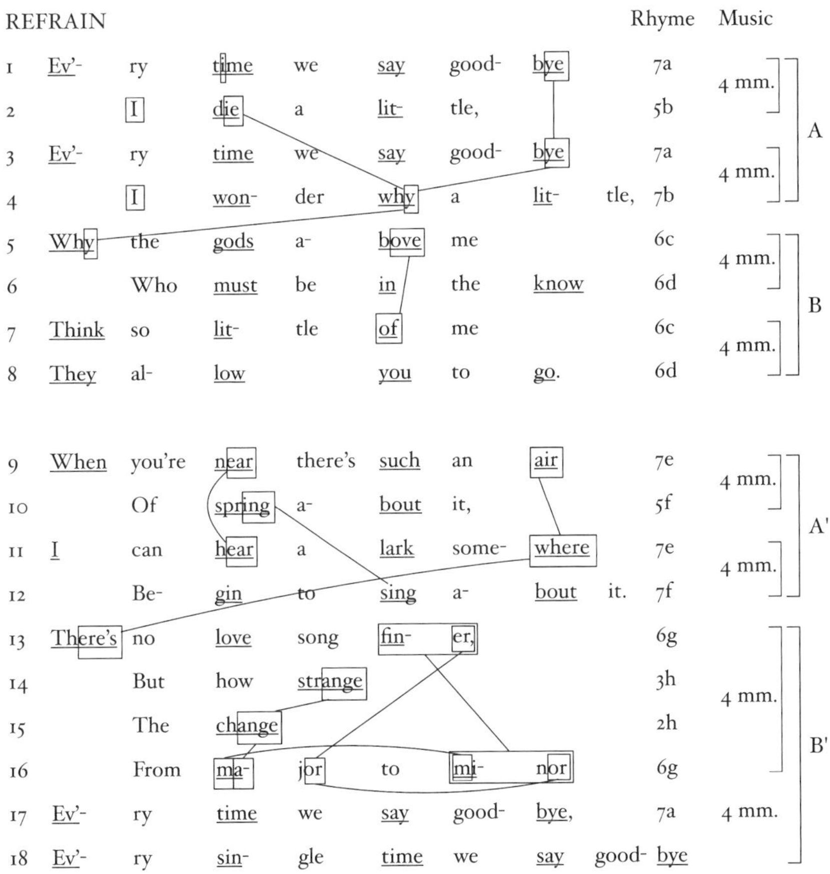

FIGURE 1. "Ev'ry Time We Say Goodbye" (from *Seven Lively Arts*), textual analysis. Words and music by Cole Porter. Copyright © 1944 Chappell & Co., Inc. Copyright renewed and assigned to John F. Wharton, Trustee of the Cole Porter Musical and Literary Property Trusts. Publication and Allied Rights Assigned to Chappell & Co., Inc. All Rights Reserved. Used by permission of Alfred Music.

none of the lines is indented. The indentation in figure 1 highlights the way in which the lyrics relate to the phrase lengths in the music. Like much poetry in English, this poetry is accentual, and I have underscored the accented syllables as if they were being recited without music. As we shall see, however, even the first steps in understanding the structure of the lyrics require reference to the music. In this respect, it really does seem to be the case that although it makes sense to read Heine independent of a setting by Schumann or anyone else, it proves difficult to understand Porter the poet independent of Porter the composer.

What strikes the eye and ear first is surely the density of sound created by end rhyme, internal rhyme, and additional instances of assonance and alliteration. In the first five lines, the long vowel *i* is everywhere, and it is of course the dominant sound in the single word around which the entirety of the lyrics revolves, "goodbye." In the first four lines, what might otherwise be the place for end rhyme simply repeats words. More important as rhyme is the internal rhyme between "die" and "why" in lines 2 and 4, which is based on the same long *i*. Syntactically, the first two lines might be thought to form a single line ending with "die," to which the descriptive "a little" is added almost parenthetically. Lines 3 and 4 then form a parallel pair, with the rhyming "why" followed by the descriptive "a little."

But the internal rhyme "why" occurs as the fourth syllable of line 4, whereas its rhyme in line 2 is the second syllable. Porter's music, nevertheless, places these two rhyming syllables in the analogous metrical positions, namely, on the first beat of the fourth measure of the four-measure phrase. Even though in line 4 there is an accented syllable (the first syllable of "wonder") that precedes the rhyming "why," Porter has set all of the first three syllables of line 4 as pickups to the downbeat of measure 8, which ends the four-measure phrase. See example 1, which, like the examples that follow, transcribes the original printed sheet music published by Chappell & Co. in 1944 in this particular case.

With these first four lines, the song begins to take on a shape that will be carried through in the remainder. The first line, the topic line we might call it, is recited in monotone on the third scale degree. And line 2 continues the slow-moving syllabic declamation of the first line, rising a semitone to A♭ for the rhyming syllable "die" set to a half note tied to an eighth starting on the downbeat. The musical setting of these two lines includes only three long notes, each two and one-half or three beats compared to surrounding quarters and eighths, and these set the syllables "time," (good-)"bye," and "die," which might be thought to condense what is elaborated in the remainder of the song.

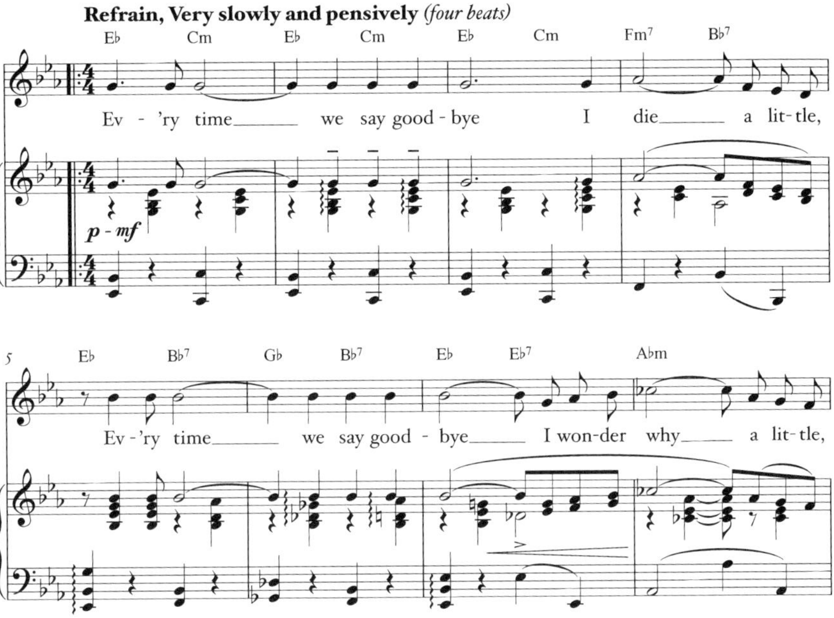

EXAMPLE 1. "Ev'ry Time We Say Goodbye," refrain, mm. 1–8.

Lines 3 and 4 are a rising sequence of lines 1 and 2, beginning now on the fifth scale degree. Line 3 repeats the words of line 1 and is identical rhythmically, but line 4 becomes more animated rhythmically with the additional syllables that lead to the rhyming "why." This syllable, like its counterpart in line 2, also rises a semitone above the "reciting tone" of the preceding line. But in this case, the semitone above is C♭, the flatted sixth scale degree in E-flat, thus introducing the parallel minor mode. The mixture of major and minor is crucial to the entire song in both text and music, and C♭ plays an important role throughout. The mixture is not restricted to the use of C♭, however. It begins in the bass line and accompanying harmony in measures 5 and 6, where there is a motion in the bass from E♭ to F to G♭, the lowered third degree of the parallel minor, which is harmonized with a G-flat major triad.

Thus, the first four-measure phrase, which sets the first two lines, is entirely diatonic, melodically unadorned, and rhythmically straightforward. The second four-measure phrase takes these materials and raises the tension of the whole. It rises to the fifth scale degree; it introduces the chromatic G♭ and C♭; it animates both melody and rhythm with the three pickup notes at the end of measure 7; and at the beginning of line 3 in measure 5 it introduces a syncopation (eighth rest, quarter note, eighth note) that will characterize the beginnings of lines until the very last, when the opening "Ev'ry time we say goodbye" is repeated for the final time, beginning directly on the downbeat as it had at the outset.

Lines 5 and 6, which are set with the third four-measure phrase, beginning in measure 9 (see ex. 2), increase the rising tension further. The melody begins by rising to the tonic, which is the highest pitch up until this point and will remain the highest pitch in the melody but for F in measure 25. The harmonic progression of the last two beats of measure 9 and the first two of measure 10 is the most chromatic progression in the song thus far. Here the bass descends stepwise through G♭, which recalls measure 6. The downbeat of measure 10 sounds the C♭ again that was so prominently heard in measure 8 and is here part of an implied chromatic inner voice moving from C through C♭ to B♭.[6] The chromaticism continues when D♭ is heard in the melody for the first time and becomes part of the dominant seventh chord on E♭ that tonicizes the A-flat major arrived at in measure 12. Looking ahead a bit, we can see that the melody here is part of a stepwise chromatic descent from the tonic E♭ of measure 9 to the fifth scale degree B♭ of measure 14. In addition to the intensification of the harmonic rhythm, the phrase rhythm of lines 5 and 6 accelerates slightly in that line 6 is a relative clause in relation to line 5 and thus introduces a slight separation of these two lines, implying the two

EXAMPLE 2. "Ev'ry Time We Say Goodbye," refrain, mm. 9–16.

two-measure subphrases that the pitch contours suggest rather than a more nearly continuous four-measure phrase, which has been the norm in setting pairs of lines.

As figure 1 makes clear, lines 9–12 have the same poetic structure as lines 1–4. Both the internal and the end rhymes follow the same pattern but with different words, and the word repetitions at the ends of lines 2 and 4 occur at the ends of lines 10 and 12 but with different words. Here conventions of musical form come into play. The refrains in much of this repertory consist of thirty-two measures in which phrases of eight measures (each consisting of two phrases of four measures) are combined in one of two ways as follows: AABA or ABAB' (or ABAC). In the former, which is perhaps the more common, the phrase designated A is stated three times with three different sets of words. The first two statements are most often a literal repetition and are notated only once, with a repetition sign and the second set of words written or printed directly under the first. The B section, called the bridge or the release, brings new words and some tonal contrast, often in the direction of the subdominant. The final A section incorporates a fourth set of words, and the music may or may not be altered slightly.

Although this AABA form is perhaps the more common of the two, it is relatively rare in Porter's songs. The refrain of "Anything Goes" is a literal example, though in the published sheet music, the repetition of A is written out. In the refrain of "I Love You," the second four measures of the A section are different each time. In the refrain of "From This Moment On," each section is sixteen measures long, the first two statements differ only slightly (the first statement ending on the dominant of the tonic G minor in preparation for the repetition, the second ending on the dominant of E-flat, which will be the key of the B section), and the final statement of A is more varied and extended. For present purposes I will not address the verses, which most often introduce the refrains, but these certainly require study as well.

"Ev'ry Time We Say Goodbye" is an example of the second scheme. In this scheme the music of A is repeated literally or very nearly literally, and the music of B is often varied somewhat at the end, especially when, as in this song, the first statement of B ends on a nontonic harmony, often the dominant, in preparation for the return to the tonic of the final statement of the A section. In both types there may be a coda of two or four measures, sometimes simply repeating or modifying very slightly the final line of the B section in both text and music. Porter's lyrics in this song clearly call for (or were written to fit) this standard form, as evidenced by the close structural similarity of lines 1–4 and 9–12. Equally clearly, the structure of the lines beginning with 13 calls for something quite different from lines 5–8, though lines 5 and 13 are structurally analogous.

In lines 13–16 we hear a density of sound created by rhyme and alliteration that is unprecedented and that in turn creates an accelerated phrase rhythm. This is plain to the eye if lines 14 and 15 are printed as separate lines, though one might think of them as forming a single line with internal rhyme and thus being part of a fourth group of four lines in the scheme of the text as a whole. In either case, it is hard to imagine that the music of what follows line 13 could be very much like the music of the lines that follow 5. And indeed it is not. Lines 13–16 are set musically to a single four-measure phrase, with the result that the syllabic rhythm is the fastest of any four-measure phrase in the song. A total of seventeen syllables occurs in this phrase, whereas the norm has been twelve syllables (four times) or fourteen (two times).

The acceleration of the syllabic rhythm and the increased density of sound in lines 14–16 have further musical parallels. Whereas in the analogous measures, 11 and 12, the dominant seventh of A-flat is given a whole measure, and the A-flat harmony itself is given another whole measure before the arrival in the melody at C♭ in measure 13, in measure 27 the dominant seventh lasts two beats and is followed on the third and fourth beats by A-flat major, and the C♭ (now in an inner voice) arrives on the downbeat of measure 28 (see ex. 3). This accelerated harmonic rhythm is accompanied in measure 27 by the only significantly disjunct melodic motion in the entire song. The leaps of fifths and fourths give increased prominence to the chromatic descent from D♭ to C first heard in the melody in measures 11–12. The harmony with C♭ heard in measure 13 marks the beginning of a phrase, but its analogue in measure 28 concludes a phrase as a result of the compression of the harmonic rhythm. This sets up the return to the tonic and to the first line of the lyrics in measure 29, forming the final four-measure phrase of the song.

Measure 28 and its C♭ require some further comment. The C♭ was first heard, perhaps somewhat surprisingly, as a very prominent pitch in the melody in measure 8, and it has been around ever since in regular alternation with C♮, both melodically and harmonically. If this song is about anything musically, it is about the mixture of major and minor. And of course it is in measure 28 that the lyrics speak explicitly of major and minor. The C♭ is actually heard on the word "major," but with F in the bass. The word "minor," however, sounds over a very prominent C♭ in the bass, and the appoggiatura on the third beat in the melody resolves to an A-flat minor chord in first inversion.[7]

EXAMPLE 3. "Ev'ry Time We Say Goodbye," refrain, mm. 25–31.

There is no doubt that this is word painting in every sense, and it is surely the case that Porter had this very much in mind. I am more interested, however, in the shape of the song that is created by the materials of both language and music independent of what is being "expressed." Porter works within a very conventional form with prescribed repetitions. But the song as a whole has a shape in which the materials of language and music—sound, pitch, rhythm, syntax—combine to produce a coordinated climax at the crux of the song, which also relates strongly to the song's semantic aspect.

How might we describe the shape of the song as a whole? The first eight lines of the lyrics describe the parting of the lovers in abstract, metaphorical, and one might say philosophical terms. At the parting, the speaker "dies" a little and wonders "why" life should be so constituted by the "gods." The repetition of line 1 in line 3 creates a slow-moving pace in that the first four lines are about one thing, about what happens on saying goodbye. This is strongly reinforced by the monotone recitation of lines 1 and 3. The second group of four lines, 5–8, takes up the question of "why" raised in line 4. Lines 5 and 7 also have the character of monotone recitation, though as we have seen the pitch level has risen from line 1 to line 3 to line 5.

The second group of eight (or nine) lines becomes more concrete and at the same time describes the positive situation from which the lovers do not wish to depart. Whereas lines 1–4 were about one thing because of the repetition of the first line, lines 9–12 consist of two pairs of lines with different subjects—first the air of spring and second the more concrete image of the lark and its song. Here one is bound to notice that "spring" in line 10 is sung to C♮ (though C♭ returns two syllables later in the same measure), whereas the corresponding syllable, "die" in line 2, introduced C♭ for the first time. This accelerated poetic motion leads to the high point of the song both poetically and musically in line 13. The monotone recitation of previous lines is here interrupted by the highest pitch of the song, F on "love" in measure 25, harmonized with C♮ (though here again, C♭ returns two beats later on the first beat of measure 26 with "fin[er]"). Then follows the metaphorical crux of the entire song, as described above, with its acceleration across all dimensions of both words and music. Thus, a conventional form with what might appear to be static repetitions nevertheless takes on a dramatic shape, reaching a moment of poetic and musical density before the concluding repetition of the first line, which restates the context for the whole.

"Ev'ry Time We Say Goodbye" is a particularly good example of Porter's art in relation to its tradition. But a good many others of his songs share features with this one. Especially characteristic is his treatment of the two most familiar forms for refrains, in which the opening phrase is repeated once (ABAB' or ABAC) or twice (AABA). In Porter's handling of these forms, the first four-measure phrase is likely to be repeated, but rarely is the whole of an eight- or sixteen-measure A section repeated literally. Similarly, when B is repeated, it is likely to be varied significantly, with the result that ABAB' and ABAC become difficult to distinguish from one another. This variation in the final section of the refrain, furthermore, often embodies a climactic effect in both words and music of the kind that "Ev'ry Time We Say Goodbye" incorporates, even if not as striking.

"You'd Be So Nice to Come Home To" can serve as a further example. Figure 2 shows once again a saturation of the first (here six) lines of the refrain with the sound of the long *i* and the repetition of the first words of the first line, "You'd be so nice," at the opening of the second. The "I" as a rhyming word at the end of line 5 is perhaps as well thought of as an internal rhyme in a line of eight syllables (labeled here as 5 and 6) and set with a four-measure phrase. In any case, lines 3, 4, and 5 are all shorter lines than the preceding and share a single rhyme. This sense of acceleration is captured in the succession of two-measure phrases to which they are set, all three of which are built on

REFRAIN

		Rhyme	Music	
1	You'd be so nice to come home to,	8 a	4 mm. a	A
2	You'd be so nice by the fire,	7 b	4 mm. b	
3	While the breeze on high	5 c	2 mm. c	B
4	Sang a lullaby,	5 c	2 mm. d	
5	You'd be all (E) that (E♭) I →	5 c	4 mm. e	
6	Could desire (verb).	3 b		
7	Under stars chilled by the winter,	8 d	4 mm. a	A'
8	Under an August moon burning above,	10 e	4 mm. b'	
9	You'd be so nice,	4 f	2 mm. f	C
10	You'd be paradise	5 f	2 mm. g	
11	To come home (E) to (E♭) and love (verb).	6 e	4 mm. h	

FIGURE 2. "You'd Be So Nice to Come Home To" (from *Something to Shout About*), textual analysis. Words and music by Cole Porter. Copyright © 1942 Chappell & Co., Inc. Copyright renewed and assigned to John F. Wharton, Trustee of the Cole Porter Musical and Literary Property Trusts. Publication and Allied Rights Assigned to Chappell & Co., Inc. All Rights Reserved. Used by permission of Alfred Music.

EXAMPLE 4. "You'd Be So Nice to Come Home To," refrain, mm. 8–16.

a three-pitch rhythmic-melodic element stated at successively higher pitch levels (mm. 8–14, F–D♯–E, D–B–C, E–C–E♭; see ex. 4). The final statement, in measures 13–14, reaches an E that is the highest pitch in the song and concludes with an E♭ heard here for the first time in the refrain.

How might we think of Porter's words in relation to this passage, which makes up the B section of the song? The clear sense of melodic, harmonic, and phrase-rhythmic climax of measures 13 and 14 rests on the E and E♭, which set the words "all" and "I," respectively. The subject of the preceding lines is the beloved who is being addressed, and these lines enumerate a series of concrete circumstances in which she or he would be "so nice." "All" on the climactic E sums up all of these circumstances and indeed all of what the singer could desire. E♭ introduces the singer specifically for the first time in the first-person pronoun, with "desire" being the only verb related to the singer. The verb "desire" ends the eight-measure B section on the tonicized dominant of A minor, which has been the key of the refrain up to this point. Desire, which by its nature demands an object, sounds on the dominant, which also demands an object or resolution and provides the structural turning point for the entire refrain.

The return to A minor follows immediately with the repetition of the A section. Here the words of lines 7 and 8 echo the structure of lines 1 and 2 in that line 8 begins with the same word that begins line 7, and the two lines return to an enumeration of further concrete circumstances. Comparing lines 1–4 with lines 7–10, however, we see an inversion in which lines 7 and 8 correspond to the concrete detail of lines 3 and 4 (and the end of line 2), and lines 9 and 10 return to the "You'd be" of lines 1 and 2. "You'd be" is the nugget (some critics might say the hypotext) of these lyrics, and Porter's inversion has placed them in a position to bring the form as a whole to its climactic conclusion.

Here again, as in lines 3–5, a succession of two-measure phrases built on a single three-pitch rhythmic and melodic element (mm. 24–32, E–F–A, A–B–D, C–D–E; see ex. 5) accelerates the phrase rhythm, and it is further intensified here by the repetition of "You'd be" at the beginnings of lines 9 and 10. Syntactically, line 9 is interrupted by line 10, as if the singer were at a loss to say just how nice "so nice" would be. Instead, the singer repeats "You'd be" in breathless fashion and instead of proceeding with the adjectival phrase "so nice" supplies the all-encompassing noun "paradise." Only then do we hear the continuation "To come home to" at the beginning of line 11. But this is at the beginning of line 11 rather than at the end, as in line 1. The end of line 11 is "and love," and here once again the singer appears, as at the end of the

EXAMPLE 5. "You'd Be So Nice to Come Home To," refrain, mm. 24–32.

B section in line 6. There the verb associated with the first-person singer is "desire." Here in line 11 it is "love," the ultimate inspiration of desire.

The melody of line 11 makes clear the parallel with lines 5 and 6 and intensifies their function. Line 9 first of all concludes in measure 26 on a chromatically prepared C major triad, which is where the song as a whole will conclude, and thus has an emphatic character as compared with the settings of "nice" in measures 2 and 6, where seventh chords require a continuation. Measure 27 continues the rising sequence with D as the principal pitch, as in the rising sequence of measure 11. The final step of the sequence brings the return of the highest pitch, E, as in measure 13, but E is then immediately followed stepwise by the E♭ heard in measure 14. The first occurrence of E♭ introduced the singer in the first person followed by the singer's desire. The final E♭ intrudes on the rhythmic space of the E and is suspended across the barline for four full beats, thus producing a large-scale suspension that is resolved with the singer's "and love" in C major. The downward direct chromatic motion of the melody in measures 29–30 and the chromaticism of the accompanying dissonance of the suspension produce the moment of greatest tension in the song. This tension is resolved with the resolution to C major at the end of a song that has dwelt largely in A minor, just as the lyrics, after describing possible circumstances in conditional grammatical constructions, concludes with the singer's declaring the single summarizing active verb (the "to" of the infinitive form being suppressed), "love."

"You'd Be So Nice to Come Home To" may call to mind "Easy to Love," since its complete first line is "You'd be so easy to love," and in this song too the conditional "You'd be" is a central device. And both songs end with the chromatic descent from the third scale degree through the flatted third scale degree to the second scale degree and then to the tonic. They have structural similarities as well that recur in other Porter songs.

Figure 3 shows how the conditional "You'd be" works in this case. Here it always incorporates "so," and all of the first four lines answer the question "You'd be so [what]?" The answers are all adverbial modifiers of a following infinitive: "easy to love," "easy to idolize," "sweet to waken with," and "nice to sit down to eggs and bacon with." The intensifying "so" occurs immediately after the "You'd be" that begins line 1 and is the first word in lines 2–4. Altogether "so" will occur in seven of the nine lines, being missing only in lines 7 and 8. Line 5 brings a shift from the second-person singular of "You'd be" to the first-person plural of "We'd be," which is also a conditional followed by "so." Following the pattern of lines 1 and 2, line 5 begins with "We'd be so," and line 6 begins with "so." In these two cases, paralleling the shift in person, there is a shift from the infinitive constructions of lines 1–4 to adjective phrases: "grand

REFRAIN

		Rhyme	Music	
1	You'd be so easy to love	7 a	4 mm.	A
2	So easy to idolize, all others above,	12 a	4 mm.	
3	So sweet to waken with,	7 c	4 mm.	B
4	So nice to sit down to eggs and bacon with.	11 c	4 mm.	
5	We'd be so grand at the game,	7 d	4 mm.	A
6	So carefree together that it does seem a shame →	12 d	4 mm.	
7	That you can't see	4 e	2 mm.	C
8	Your future with me,	5 e	2 mm.	
9	'Cause you'd be, oh, so easy to love.	9 a	4 mm.	

FIGURE 3. "You'd Be So Easy to Love," textual analysis. Used by permission of Alfred Music, PO Box 10003, Van Nuys CA 91410-0003.

at the game" and "carefree together." Unlike lines 2–4, however, each of which is syntactically complete, line 6 ends with an enjambment that requires the continuation in line 7, which in turn, ending with a verb, requires its object in line 8. Syntactically, then, lines 6–8 are much the most closely linked. Lines 7 and 8 are also the only lines in which, though the second-person singular returns as the subject, the subject is not part of a conditional expression. Instead, there is a straightforward declarative clause, "You can't see your future with me," formed by the two lines. All of this is captured as well in the sound of the words, in which the rhyming syllables "see" and "me" are closely linked by the short line lengths. Here again, as with the short lines in "You'd Be So Nice to Come Home To," one might be tempted to think of lines 7 and 8 forming only a single line with internal rhyme, given Porter's fondness for internal rhyme. In any case, these two lines, with their uniquely condensed syntax and sound, also reveal the condition around which the entirety of the lyrics revolve. Here we learn the condition that prevents the beloved from being "so . . ."

As in "You'd Be So Nice to Come Home To," the last line returns to the words of the first. And here, too, the "so" construction is intensified with the insertion not of a full phrase, as in the previous case, but of the rhyming "oh" just before the final "so."

The musical form of "Easy to Love" is the same thirty-two-bar ABAC, except that here the repetition of A is literal but for the final note (m. 24; see ex. 6). That note, however, is the highest in the song and is the note to which the final word of line 6, "shame," is sung. This is the word that drives forward into lines 7 and 8, the turning point in the lyrics. The analogous note in measure 8 at the end of the first statement of section A is a D harmonized with G major, the tonic. The E of measure 24, however, is harmonized with E major, which becomes the dominant seventh of A minor. Thus, just as the enjambment of lines 6 and 7 propels us into the climactic moment of the lyrics, the high E and its harmony demand a continuation into the following phrase.

As in "You'd Be So Nice to Come Home To," the arrival at the moment of accelerated rhyme in lines 7 and 8 is captured musically with a kind of motivic density not heard here before. Measures 24–27 consist of a series of four falling perfect fourths starting on E and descending stepwise to B. The overlapping pattern of falling fourth and rising third extends even into measure 28 and forms a phrase unlike any other for words unlike any others in the song.

The features that these two songs share in some detail point to somewhat broader similarities among Porter's songs, especially those that have entered the repertory as standards somewhat independent of the shows for which

EXAMPLE 6. Cole Porter, "You'd Be So Easy to Love," refrain, mm. 1–9 and 23–32. Used by permission of Alfred Music, PO Box 10003, Van Nuys CA 91410-0003.

they may have been originally composed. The verses are most likely to have a direct connection to the shows. For this reason they have tended to fall away as the songs entered the broader repertory, especially in purely instrumental performances. They remain, nevertheless, an important part of Porter's art. A few generalizations about the refrains, however, might include the following. Although they often draw on the two familiar forms (AABA and ABAC), they sometimes treat these forms rather flexibly. Repeated sections are most often not repeated literally. This has principally to do with the fact that these songs typically have a dramatic shape that moves to a climax in both lyrics and music in the latter part of the form. The form ABAC perhaps lends itself to the creation of this dramatic shape better than the form AABA. As stereotypical as the principal forms of this genre might appear to be, in Porter's songs, this movement toward and arrival at a climax are as clear in the lyrics as they are in the music. His ear was equally acute for the music of poetry and for the poetry of music. It might be best to say that for him the two were indistinguishable and that this makes irrelevant any attempt to place the two in some chronological order.

• • •

The three songs discussed here constitute less than 1 percent of Porter's output of songs, and as I have said, I have not even discussed the verses of those that have them or anything about their place in the musicals in which they first appeared. There is a great deal here that should attract sustained musicological attention and could expand the ways in which musicology often goes about its business. It is a repertory that is perched between written and oral traditions and that requires at a minimum a flexible notion of what constitutes the written and authentic text. It also poses questions about the ways in which music and poetry fit together and about how we might think about that relationship.

These three songs and others persuade me that Porter entirely confounds the notion of a song as a setting of a text and that his songs compel us to think of words and music in terms of one another and on an equal footing. This sharply subordinates any notion of the music "expressing" the meaning of the words and thus throws analysis back onto those features of music and words that are shared—things like rhythm, pitch, syntax, and sound in the sense that creates assonance and rhyme. In these terms, Porter's songs, while being cast often in some variation of a conventional form, have their own dramatic shapes and in sometimes quite intricate ways lead the listener along a purposeful progression from beginning to middle to end.

Notes

1. The essay by James Hepokoski elsewhere in this volume also takes up this matter from a slightly different angle.

2. Allen Forte is of course the great pioneer in the serious theoretical study of this song repertory, and his analyses are immensely illuminating. They do entail starting from an established text that is taken as authentic in detail. In the case of Porter, he has shown that such autographs as exist correspond very closely to the first editions of the printed sheet music and thus give one confidence that these sheet-music editions can be taken as representing something close to the composer's own version of the song. See his "Secrets of Melody: Line and Design in the Songs of Cole Porter," *Musical Quarterly* 77, no. 4 (1993): 607–47. I have followed his lead in this, though I rely rather less on specific details of these editions, and I believe that there is still much to learn about Porter's compositional process and the division of labor among Porter and others in the creation of his works. As for the goal of this analysis, there Forte concludes by writing, "Probably no analysis can reveal the inspirational moment, the key to the secrets, if you will, of a Cole Porter song. But I hope that the foregoing analytical discourse will at least provide an orientation to some of the major features of the songs and give further support—if any is needed—to the critical opinion that Porter's songs are of the highest artistic caliber." See also Forte's *The American Popular Ballad of the Golden Era 1924–1950* (Princeton, NJ: Princeton University Press, 1995); and *Listening to Classic American Popular Songs* (New Haven, CT: Yale University Press, 2001). The nature of the musical materials for the study of Porter's songs and the relationship of the types of materials to one another is also addressed in the essay in this volume by Matthew Shaftel.

3. Robert Kimball, ed., *Cole Porter: Selected Lyrics* (New York: Library of America, 2006), xvi. On this topic, see the essay in this volume by Rob Kapilow, who quotes Porter's own description of the process and who also takes up the question of the order in which words and music were composed. On the topic of words and music in this repertory more broadly, see Stephen Banfield, "Sondheim and the Art That Has No Name," in *Approaches to the American Musical*, ed. Robert Lawson-Peebles (Exeter: University of Exeter Press, 1996), 137–60.

4. Elsewhere in this volume, James Hepokoski gives an account of the long history of "Anything Goes," which was repeatedly revised as new versions of the show of the same title were created and as tastes changed with respect to what was and was not scandalous for certain audiences. That song and "You're the Top," furthermore, are of a type that invites the creation of a continuing series of verses exploiting the original conceit.

5. The complete song, like many, consists of a "verse," here of five lines, followed by the "refrain." In the case of this song, the verse is rarely performed, and lead sheets and fake books often omit it. Forte writes extensively about this song in all three publications cited in note 2. In *Listening to Classic American Popular Songs,* he provides a rich discussion of the sound of the lyrics themselves and the ways in which the music often captures this. My own account of the song will make similar observations

and in this sense merely supplements his analysis. Our emphases, however, will be somewhat different.

6. The omission of the C on beats 3 and 4 of measure 9 is surely just an artifact of the informal voice leading that often characterizes such piano accompaniments. Here it cannot be said to be a concession to the amateur pianist, however, since the first beat of measure 10 calls for a full four-pitch chord in the right hand of just the form that would have obtained with addition of the C at the end of the preceding measure. Many pianists would apply the C without thinking, especially if they were keeping an eye on the chord symbols above, and when this progression returns in measure 25, the C is in fact present. Furthermore, measures 9 through the first beat of measure 11 embody a conventional substitution for the ubiquitous I–vi–ii–V^7–I progression in which vi is replaced by a harmony built on the flatted third scale degree, often a minor seventh but sometimes a diminished seventh, as here. A pianist of the day would be likely to play tenths in the left hand (G–B♭, G♭–A♮, F–A♭), though the reader of popular sheet music could not be counted on to have large-enough hands. What is unusual here is the C♭, which would not be likely in the conventional progression of this type but which plays an important role throughout this song, being a part of the harmony on either ii or iv in the parallel minor.

7. The A-flat minor chord is variously treated as a chord in its own right (e.g., in mm. 8 and 12) or as part of a chord including F♮, which is sometimes clearly just an added sixth (e.g., the last chord of mm. 8 and 24), but sometimes, when F is in the bass (e.g., mm. 13 and 26), it is better thought of as having the function of a half-diminished seventh with F as the root and thus as ii^7 in the parallel minor that is followed by V^7 (e.g., m. 26). Sometimes F is in the bass, and A♭ is omitted (e.g., mm. 13 and 28). But tellingly, whoever supplied the chord symbols marked all of these possibilities as A-flat minor or A-flat minor sixth. Allen Forte ("Secrets of Melody," 639) describes the four-pitch chord as a Tristan chord, and in both *The American Popular Ballad* and *Listening to Classic American Popular Songs* he observes the presence of the Tristan chord in this and other songs, attributing to it a semantic value derived from Wagner. Forte also points to the prominence of the relative minor, C minor, at the beginning of this song, where the piano accompaniment of the first three measures in the sheet-music edition consists of an oscillation between E-flat major and C minor harmonies. This could be thought of as a part of the mixture of major and minor that is so important to the song and of the kind of word painting that it might represent. Certainly, everyone who composed or performed in this repertory knew very well that "major is happy" and "minor is sad." But the minor triad on the sixth scale degree is also part of the ubiquitous I–vi–ii–V–I progression and cannot always be thought to carry this particular semantic value, and this is the progression that underlies the first four-measure phrase of this song. Interestingly, very few performers of the song make use of this oscillation between I and vi, though the recording by the Benny Goodman Sextet that derives from their original performance of the song in *The Seven Lively Arts* does include it as well as other details of the accompaniment given in the sheet music that are certainly not a part of the song's later performance tradition.

13
You Never Know
Anatomy of a Flop

CLIFF EISEN

Of all Porter's shows, from *Paris* (1928) to *Silk Stockings* (1955), only *Around the World in Eighty Days* (1946) had a shorter run than *You Never Know*'s meager seventy-eight. And *Around the World*, which lasted only seventy-five performances, was not really a Porter show: it was an Orson Welles "extravaganza" financed, produced, directed by, and starring him. When it failed, Porter's minimal contribution, a handful of songs and some instrumental music, was collateral damage. Lewis Nichols, who reviewed *Around the World* for the *New York Times*, wrote that "it is questionable whether the Cole Porter manner is the ideal one for a frantic evening."[1] However, with *You Never Know*, the musical produced by the Shubert Organization that ran at the Winter Garden Theatre from 21 September to 26 November 1938, the blame is often laid at the composer's feet—as if a musical lives and dies primarily by the success or failure of its songs.

The *New Yorker* reported that Clifton Webb (as the valet Gaston) danced "stylishly" and Libby Holman (as the high-society Mme Baltin) could still make the reviewer's "hair stand up when she digs her feet in and lets go." But the reviewer added that "Cole Porter's music and lyrics only occasionally suggest that intricate and fascinating gift."[2] And Brooks Atkinson, writing for the *New York Times*, dismissed most of the score with the off-hand remark, "There is one of his patter serenades, 'Alpha to Omega,' that is gay and clever, and some of the rest of them may, as Mark Twain said of classical music, be better than they sounded."[3] Atkinson also described the show as a kind of "rummage sale"—not necessarily with respect to the music (or at least Porter's music, since in the end several songs by other composers were interpolated in the show) but certainly with respect to the plot, the vaudeville and revue routines, the dancing girls, and some lavish spectacle.[4] Most, if not all, of this "rummage" had been introduced into the show by its producer, John Shubert, who at the time was striking out on his own in an attempt to rival the legacy of the recently deceased Florenz Ziegfeld. Shubert stage-managed this failure by manipulating and deceiving his writers—probably including Porter, who appears to have given up on the show by the summer of 1938—and by unilaterally insisting on the inclusion of gratuitous material that was unsuited to the original, small-scale, intimate character of the show.

You Never Know was based in the first instance on Siegfried Geyer's *Kleine Komödie* (also known as *Bei Kerzenlicht*), a three-act play produced in Vienna in 1927 that was subsequently adapted for the English-language stage (as *Candle Light*) by P. G. Wodehouse and ran for 128 performances at the Empire Theatre in New York between September 1929 and January 1930. Starring Gertrude Lawrence and Leslie Howard, it was described by Brooks Atkinson as "sardonic[ally] elegan[t]."[5] In 1933 the play was also produced as a film (*By Candlelight*), starring Paul Lukas and Elissa Landis and directed by James Whale. Like both Geyer's *Kleine Komödie* and *Candle Light*, the film was a modest success, noted chiefly for its lightweight, unpretentious, and sometimes obvious humor: "With its philandering prince and a butler who also has an eye for feminine beauty, a countess who welcomes flattery from the opposite sex, and a very artful and comely girl, 'By Candlelight,' the present film at the Roxy, affords a pleasantly amusing diversion. It is shallow and somewhat obvious in spots, but its little intrigue is set forth with admirable cunning by James Whale and others."[6]

That "little intrigue"—the basis for all iterations of the *Kleine Komödie* irrespective of minor changes and differences—was a fairly standard, partly deliberate, and partly accidental confusion-of-identity love quadrangle: Mme Baltin's maid, Maria, impersonates her mistress during an assignation with Baron de Romer's valet, Gaston, whom she believes to be the Baron. When the Baron discovers them, he pretends to be the valet in order to help Gaston. Mme Baltin, however, is horrified and exposes the couple, although in the end—predictably—the play comes to a happy conclusion, and the four leads dine by candlelight. Incidental characters in the show include the Baron's friend Ida Courtney and Mme Baltin's husband, Henri, the "dry goods king of France."

It was this plot that was the basis for the immediate antecedent of *You Never Know,* a musical version titled *Bei Kerzenlicht* of Geyer's play, with a book by Karl Farkas and music by Robert Katscher.[7] It premiered at the Deutsches Volkstheater in Vienna on 30 April 1937.

> In his comedy "Le jeu de l'amour et du hazard" (1730), the French dramatist Pierre Carlet de Chamblain de Marivaux, the originator of the *Konversationslustspiel*, invented an immortal plotline. It might be called the "quadrille of the quid pro quo": the master plays the servant, the servant plays the master, the maid pretends to be the lady and the lady the maid. Two hundred years later, the humorous and deft Viennese authors Hans Adler, Paul Frank, and Siegfried Geyer turned this story into a charming *Lustspiel*, the "Kleine Komödie," which has conquered the theatrical world. . . . Robert Katscher decorates this story with a charming musical score. The original authors have modestly retreated into the background, and Robert Katscher alone is given as the author of the comedy "Bei Kerzenlicht," which premiered yesterday at the Deutschen Volkstheater. He abstains from describing it as a *Lustpiel*, *Komödie* or operetta: instead he gives it the subtitle, "Twelve Songs for a little Comedy." . . . Everything is managed with exceptional skill and humor, and Katscher's graceful music contributes to the audience's great enjoyment. This music is elegant and spirited, not only in the main numbers . . . but also in the amusing parlando scenes. It is, in a manner of speaking, French in conception but feels Viennese.[8]

The Shuberts apparently kept a close eye on Continental theater—or perhaps just on Katscher, whose *The Wonder Bar* they had produced at the Nora Bayes Theatre in New York in 1931, though without much success either as a play or musically.[9] And within days of *Bei Kerzenlicht*'s Viennese premiere, they concluded an agreement with Katscher and his publishers, Georg Marton Verlag and Ludwig Doblinger, for the rights to *Bei Kerzenlicht* "as produced at the Deutsche Volkstheater."[10]

Porter's involvement with *You Never Know*—indirect at first—probably began in the summer of 1937 while he was in Paris; on 13 September he wrote to Albert Sirmay, the music director at Chappell & Co. who edited (or even produced) piano-vocal scores of many of his songs, "requesting he keep himself free to work on the Clifton Webb show after September 27."[11] And on 17 September the *New York Times* reported that "the [Shubert] management would like to bring Adele Astaire (Lady Cavendish) back to the stage in [*Greek to You*], and that Cole Porter would write the score for it. In fact, negotiations with Mr. Porter have already begun and will be continued on his impending arrival here."[12] *Greek to You*, the Shuberts' original idea for a Clifton Webb / Cole Porter vehicle, was never produced. But even by the date of the *New York Times* report, the decision may already have been taken to prioritize *You Never Know* instead. On board the SS *Normandie* during his return trip to New York, Porter sketched out lyrics for "At Long Last Love" on ship's stationery (fig. 1).[13] According to Eells, by the time of Porter's riding accident on 24 October, he had already

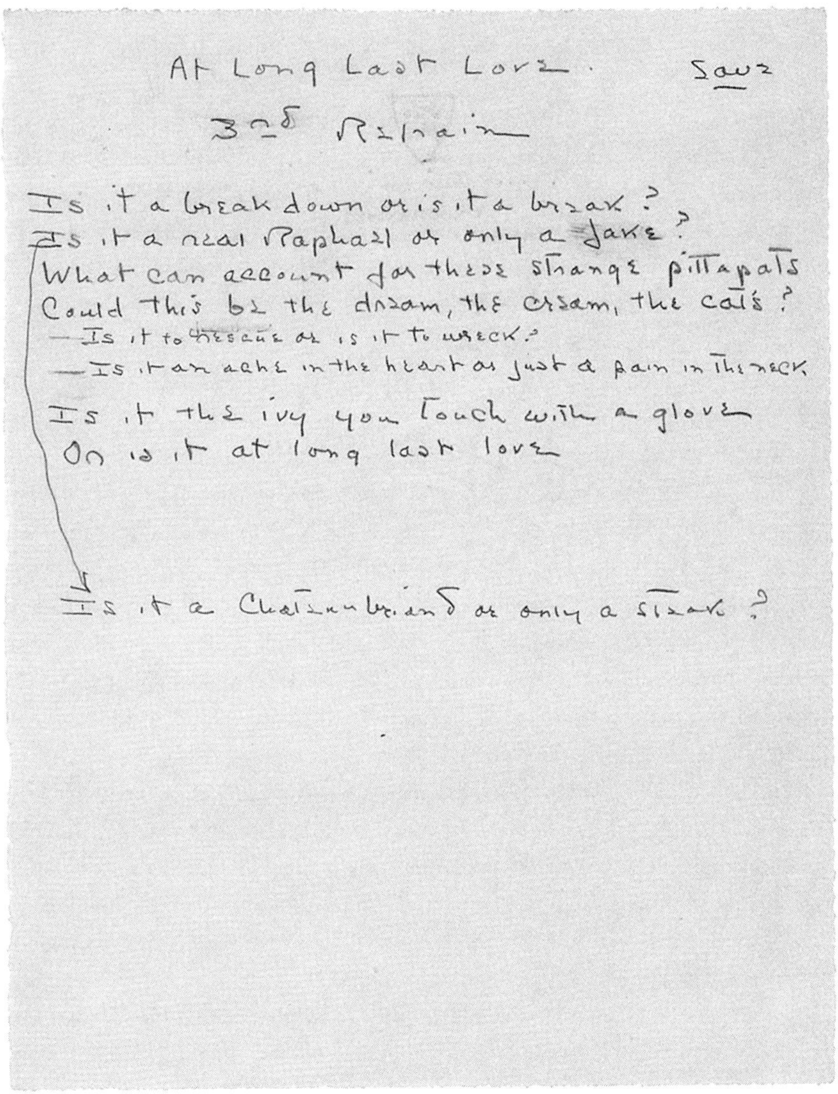

FIGURE 1. Undated autograph sketch for "At Long Last Love." (The present location of this sketch is unknown; it was auctioned by RRauction.com on 18 June 2014.)

written, in addition to "At Long Last Love," "From Alpha to Omega" and "You Never Know."[14] The earliest surviving script, by Rowland Leigh, is also dated October 1937.[15]

Porter's riding accident and the two major surgeries he underwent between the date of the accident and 8 December put a temporary halt to all his composing activities. But he was also encouraged by his doctors to go back to work as a kind of therapy, and on 31 December he signed a contract with the Shubert Organization for the writing of *You Never Know*, promising to deliver the songs within a month.[16]

In the meantime, the Shuberts, now fully committed to the show, began the search for a cast. Clifton Webb, who played Gaston, had long been assured the lead in a new Shubert musical—whether *Greek to You* or *You Never Know*—but casting for the rest of the show proved problematic. Libby Holman, whose name first surfaced in December as a possible Mme Baltin, did not sign until 3 February 1938 (and then only reluctantly, as she had more or less given up on Broadway after her appearance in the Howard Dietz–Arthur Schwartz show *Revenge with Music*, which ran for 158 performances between November 1934 and April 1935).[17]

In early January it was reported that Marlene Dietrich was being sounded out for the lead role previously taken by Gertrude Lawrence (as the maid Maria). Other names mentioned at the time included June Knight, Jane Pickens, Tallulah Bankhead, and Joan Crawford.[18] But it was Lupe Velez, who had revived her flagging career earlier that year with her performance as a maid (also named Maria) in the film *High Flyers*, who finally took the part.[19] Velez came to *You Never Know* with a reputation as a troublemaker, and during the tryouts, tensions ran high between her and Holman.[20] According to several reports, Velez was offended when Holman was offered additional songs in the show, just about the time that the director, Rowland Leigh, wrote to John Shubert: "Confidentially, I believe we are going to lose Libby next season. Velez has been making some pretty serious threats of what she is going to do to Holman some time, even being indiscreet enough to mention them to Libby's chauffeur. I only hope that this bitterness will cool off during the summer."[21] If anything, however, matters got worse, and the disputed songs remained central to Velez's disgruntlement. The *Milwaukee Journal* for 30 August 1938 reported: "A temperamental clash between Lupe Velez and Libby Holman has left the new Broadway play, 'You Never Know,' rehearsing without a director Tuesday. The director, Rowland Leigh, walked out Saturday and announced that he would not return until the girls composed their differences. The fireworks started when Miss Holman, who had announced that all she wanted was a small part and perhaps one little song, was assigned two new Cole Porter numbers. Miss Velez did not, to put it mildly, quite like the idea."[22] Whatever the tensions between Holman and Velez, their disagreements seem neither to have affected their performances nor to have been obvious to audiences. Press reports fairly consistently praise Velez as perhaps the most effective cast member. The *Los Angeles Examiner* for 8 March 1938, reporting on the Boston tryout, carried the headline "Show Stopped by Lupe Velez."[23] The *Los Angeles Times* for 8 April, reporting on the Philadelphia tryout, noted that "Lupe Velez Wins Ovation in Cole Porter Musical."

What was becoming apparent, though, was a growing tension between the director, Rowland Leigh, and John Shubert. When the tryouts reached Pittsburgh, Shubert sent George Abbott (according to Shubert, at Cole Porter's request, but see below) to see the show and suggest improvements.[24] Leigh had no advance warning of Abbott's visit, and he wrote angrily to Shubert on 30 April:

> Dear John:
>
> This, I'm afraid, will be a rather disagreeable letter. However, as I am being foolish enough to give way, it will be worth your while to read it to the end.
>
> On receipt of your telegram I was, frankly, very angry, especially as I had just read in the local paper that George Abbott had been sent to Pittsburg [*sic*] to try and save "You Never Know."[25] Also, being able to read, I had managed to see the cute little article in the weekly Variety saying that John Shubert had sent writers to Pittsburg. Now, John, I am not pretending that if a show is not right outside writers should not be called in, especially when the original writer is forced to be in Hollywood. Nor would I enlarge upon the arrant discourtesy of doing things without one word to the original author. But I will set down for the benefit of the show precisely how things have come to be in a mess.
>
> The original book of "By Candle-Light" was a light comedy at moments bordering on farce. The original idea your father had (this was long before you became presentor of the show) was to make a small intimate musical such as he had seen in Vienna (where, by the way, it flopped badly).[26] As I remember, in the early days when you first became interested, you also held this very sensible view. The book of the show was written by myself in that light. Cole wrote the music in that spirit, and in three and one half weeks, under the greatest physical difficulties, I put the show on, also in that spirit. . . .
>
> The last performance in New Haven was the best performance that "You Never Know" has yet had. Since this time a determined effort has been made

> to broaden the show, to vulgarize it, to enlarge it, to make it drearily old-fashioned, and to remove from it every possible hint of taste and distinction. From innumerable members of the audience I have had letters protesting that the show which they have seen two or three times has disintegrated beyond belief. This is due to several causes:
>
> 1. Putting in the show girls from "Between The Devil." They can neither act, sing nor look like ladies.[27]
> 2. Putting in a dainty little troop of dancing boys whose very name, "The Debonairs," show what the wretched audience has to expect. And if you tell me that they stop the show with their old routine from "Between The Devil" I can only answer that applause and showmanship do not go hand in hand, especially when you follow six dancing girls with six singing boys.
> 3. A series of old burlesque jokes shoved into the show regardless of character, not to mention good taste.
> 4. The fact that Lupe has not only been allowed but encouraged to run riot.
>
> Lupe is a brilliant, vital person with almost unlimited talent. She is very similar in her capabilities to Gertie Lawrence, but apparently what has occurred to no one is the fact that Gertie wrecked the original "By Candle-Light" through doing what Lupe is now allowed to do. Lupe was my original choice as you know and I do not go back on it for one moment, because as long as she was under my control she was magnificent. She and Clifton and Rex were marvelously balanced because though she had the vitality and they had the subtlety they had a common meeting point. Remove that meeting point and your only alternative is to put nice red noses on Clifton and Rex and play the whole thing as a vulgar romp. Unfortunately, "By Candle-Light" cannot be made into a big successful, flashy, vulgar musical. You have to play it (undoubtedly with improvements) as it was originally intended and produced, or not at all. There has obviously been no one in charge of the show. Everybody has been allowed to do as they please and any additions that have been made have perfectly obviously been in the wrong direction. Therefore, can you blame me, John, when I get annoyed at reading in the newspapers adverse criticism directed against myself for things that have been done without my knowledge, let alone my approval . . . ?
>
> As I telegraphed you, I spoke to Cole for a long time at my expense. Cole is, I think I may say, one hundred per cent in agreement with me that the show has disintegrated completely since my departure.[28]

Shubert reassured Leigh in a letter of 23 May that "Abbott's work to date has been cutting out perhaps 25 minutes of dialogue and the including of five lines in Mme Baltin's boudoir where Lupe is discovered on the telephone talking to Clifton, and then the Baltins enter and play their scene as you originally wrote it. Instead of I'll Knock 'Em Down, Toby Wing and Kemper now do Rhyme Or Reason." But apparently oblivious to Leigh's more serious concerns, he added: "Abbott has another suggestion. He feels that right after Clifton goes out to order the dinner at Fyot's we will have a straight scene with Libby and some gigolos (The Debonairs) and have Clifton and Libby do a song together. This is terribly important. I quite agree with Abbott that Holman and Webb made their name by working in different shows together. It is just the germ of an idea in his head and he feels that the audience demands those two personalities to do something together."[29] Not only was Leigh not mollified, but further changes to the script—almost all of them contrary to the spirit in which the show was conceived (not to mention Shubert's willful disregard of Leigh's artistic investment in the quality of the book as he saw it, as well as his rudeness)—seem to have exacerbated matters to the extent that Leigh wrote again to Shubert, on 19 September:

> I am informed that last night after I was denied the author's right of presence in the theatre during rehearsal (my grounds for this statement are based on your words shouted at me in front of some fifty members of the company—"I don't give a damn what you like—get the hell out of here"), a new scene was written and put into rehearsal. This was done against my knowledge and consent. . . .
>
> You will kindly delete this new scene or have Mr. Abbott write it and submit it to me. You will also be good enough to delete the scene written, I believe, by yourself or Mr. Gilbert, in which Mr. Kemper and Miss Wing appear in bathing suits, and in which Miss Wing has been instructed to make an objectionable gesture patting Mr. Kemper's stomach and posterior. You will note in my letter of yesterday, I objected to this whole sequence. This particular portion, however, is visually vulgar and highly detrimental to the name of any writer who has been advertised as sole author and director of a play.
>
> Kindly also delete the words: "I have given you the best years of my wife"—on the grounds that it is not and has not been an original joke in the last ten years—and I am making myself liable to a suit for plagiarism by including it in the book of a play advertised as written by myself.[30]

From the very start of his complaints, beginning with his letter of 30 April, Leigh apparently put his finger on what seems to have been the chief problem with *You Never Know*—John Shubert's attempt to turn an intimate show into a spectacular. The extent to which Porter may have been involved with or sanctioned these changes is uncertain. On the one hand, Shubert intimated it was Porter's idea to send George Abbott to Pittsburgh to see the show and make changes to it. But at the same time, Shubert also claimed that Porter agreed with Leigh—and Leigh said as much himself, in his letter of 30 April—that at least some of Abbott's changes, in particular the scene with the gigolos and the Debonairs mentioned in his letter of 23 May, were detrimental to the play.[31] In this respect, Shubert appears to have deceived, if not outright lied to, Leigh, since the Debonairs not only figured prominently in the show when it was produced in New York, in act 1, scene 3 ("Ladies' Room" at the Club Bali), act 1, scene 6 ("Don't Let It Get You Down"), and act 2, scene 2 ("Gendarme"), but Shubert also arranged, at a very late stage, for a duet with Holman and Webb ("No," composed by Dana Suesse).

In the end, not even George Abbott was happy with the changes, pulling rank on John Shubert by writing to his father, J. J. Shubert, on 26 September: "I am very sorry that you were not on hand when it was arranged that I go to work on YOU NEVER KNOW, for it seems a little unjust that you should be hooked with my version, and then decide to do an entirely different kind of show, and put it in the Winter Garden."[32] Even after Abbott's revisions and the production of a more or less final script for Clifton Webb on 22 August, significant changes continued to be made to the text.[33] Scenes were added and deleted, including bar and swimming pool scenes, as well as chorus girls.[34] Songs were cut, rearranged, or newly imported by composers other than Porter and Katscher (see the appendix).

As for Porter, it may be that he was not consulted as much as Shubert claimed, that he simply acquiesced, or that he even more or less washed his hands of the show altogether. There is virtually no evidence of Porter's engagement with *You Never Know* after the spring and summer of 1937. In part this may have been a legacy of his horse-riding accident, which prevented him from attending rehearsals or out-of-town performances, which he was contractually allowed to miss.[35] And in part it may have been that, contrary to his usual working habits, Porter in 1938 produced two musicals more or less simultaneously, *You Never Know* and *Leave It to Me*, the show that opened at the Imperial Theatre on 9 November 1938 and that catapulted Mary Martin to fame with her rendition of "My Heart Belongs to Daddy." During September and October, Porter apparently spent most of his time working on *Leave It to Me*. He is unlikely to have been party to the additional changes made then that infuriated both Leigh and Abbott. Certainly, several of Porter's original songs for *You Never Know* were dropped either before or during the spring tryouts, including "By Candlelight" and "I'm Going In for Love." Both hew to the show's original intimate conception. "By Candlelight," composed as early as January 1938, is a charming piano-accompaniment-only number intended for private performance in the Baron's drawing room.[36] During the course of the song, the lights are intended to be turned off, and Gaston appears with a lit candelabra—all part of the Baron's gentle attempts at seduction (fig. 2). "I'm Going In for Love," written for the character of Mme Baltin in March 1938 but apparently never used (or certainly dropped before the Philadelphia tryouts

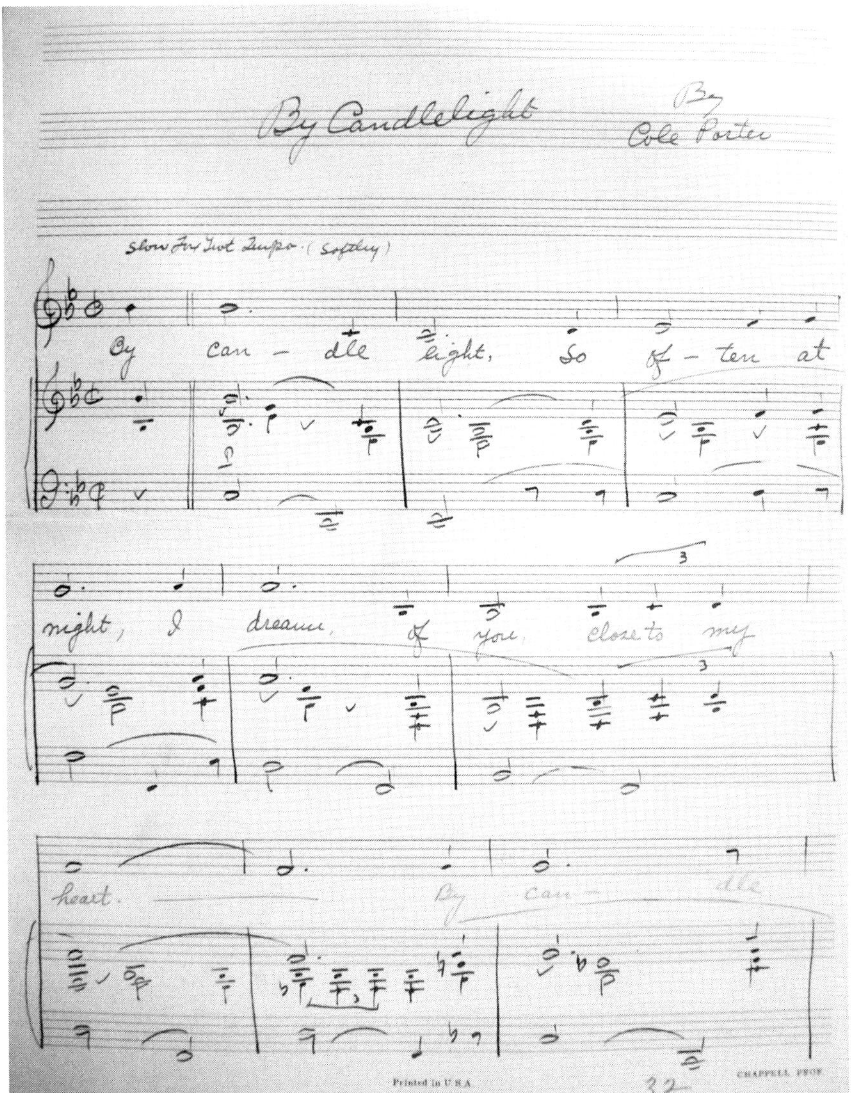

FIGURE 2. Copyist's piano-vocal score of "By Candlelight." Folder 214, box 30, MSS 82, Cole Porter Collection, Irving S. Gilmore Music Library, Yale University.

at the end of that month), is more exuberant but nevertheless small-scale.[37] Tellingly, perhaps, the tempo indication reads "with graceful Viennese swing" (see fig. 3). Yet both songs were dropped, as were "Just One Step Ahead of Love" and "I'm Yours," among others.

If anything, then, *You Never Know* fell victim to John Shubert's meddling in and mismanagement of the show, as well as his disingenuousness in playing Porter against Leigh, Leigh against Abbott, and all three of them against his own intentions to expand the show beyond what any of the principals, and eventually the critics, thought it could bear. This meddling was itself a result of internal strife within the Shubert Organization. John Shubert had previously been allied with his uncle Lee Shubert, one of the three brothers—Sam S. Shubert, Lee, and J. J. (Jacob J.) Shubert—who had founded the theatrical empire in the late nineteenth century. In 1937 J.J. co-opted John, his son, in an attempt not only to take control of the organization but also to crush the theatrical competition through the sheer size and elaborateness of his productions and through the sheer size of his theaters, among them the Winter Garden Theatre, the venue the Shuberts settled on for *You Never Know*.[38] Of the numerous theaters owned or operated by the Shuberts, the Winter Garden was the second largest, with a seating capacity of 1,526; only the Majestic held more, at 1,645.[39] And during the Shuberts' tenure, the Winter Garden had been home chiefly to large-scale revues and variety shows, including the *Ziegfeld*

FIGURE 3. Copyist's piano-vocal score of "I'm Going for Love." Folder 213, box 30, MSS 82, Cole Porter Collection, Irving S. Gilmore Music Library, Yale University.

Follies for 1934 and 1936. Given the theater's size and traditions and the audience's expectations, John Shubert's decision to stage *You Never Know* at the Winter Garden militated against the success of what was at heart an intimate period farce. It also militated against the show's financial success because it imposed prohibitive costs on the production, even though the cast, directors, writers, and composers had to agree to pay cuts or a reduction in royalties to keep the show afloat.[40]

• • •

Without perhaps much knowledge of the convoluted history of *You Never Know* or of the specifics of Porter's, Leigh's, Abbott's, and John Shubert's dealings and double-dealings during the writing and revising of the show, the anonymous reviewer in *Theatre Arts Monthly* nevertheless identified its chief problems: "As an intimate revue it might have passed, but it dies under the weight of musical comedy routine and the size of the theatre."[41] Porter was not to blame for these problems, but he was either unable or unwilling to do anything about them. And at least some of the songs, notably songs cut from the final New York production, have become part of the Porter canon, including "From Alpha to Omega," "You Never Know," and "At Long Last Love."

Appendix: Comparison of Nonmusical Sources for *You Never Know*

28 March 1938: Philadelphia script (SOA, scripts box 610)	**1 May 1938: Chicago (*Playbill*)**	**22 August 1938: Clifton Webb's script (breaks off after act 2, scene 2; SOA, scripts box 610)**	**21 September 1938: New York (*Playbill*)**
Act 1, scene 1	**Act 1, scene 1**	**Act 1, scene 1**	**Act 1, scene 1**
	Prologue		I Am Gaston
The Café Society Set (chorus)	The Café Society Set		Au Revoir Cher Baron
Eyes Shine More Divinely by Candlelight (Baron)	Eyes Shine More Divinely by Candlelight reprise: By Candlelight	Eyes Shine More Divinely by Candlelight	By Candlelight (music by Robert Katscher)
Maria (Gaston)	Maria	Maria	Maria Reprise: Maria
From Alpha to Omega (Maria, Gaston)	From Alpha to Omega		
reprise: By Candlelight			
Act 1, scene 2	**Act 1, scene 2**	**Act 1, scene 2**	**Act 1, scene 2**
You Never Know (Mme Baltin)	You Never Know	You Never Know	You Never Know

28 March 1938: Philadelphia script (SOA, scripts box 610)	1 May 1938: Chicago (*Playbill*)	22 August 1938: Clifton Webb's script (breaks off after act 2, scene 2; SOA, scripts box 610)	21 September 1938: New York (*Playbill*)
			Act 1, scene 3
Hat Check Scene: Yes, Yes, Yes (Ida)	Yes, Yes, Yes	Ladies Room (show girls and Miss Crawford)	Ladies Room (with The Debonairs)
	Dance		
Reprise: From Alpha to Omega	Reprise: From Alpha to Omega		
Baltin's Song (The One I Adore, I'll Black His Eye) (Mme Baltin, chorus)			
Act 1, scene 3	**Act 1, scene 3**	**Act 1, scene 3**	**Act 1, scene 4**
repeat of Maria (Gaston)	Baltin's Song (I'll Black His Eye)	What's The Name of That Tune (Gaston, Mme Baltin)	What Is That Tune?
	Act 1, scene 4	**Act 1, scene 4**	
	Reprise: From Alpha to Omega		
What Shall I Do? (Maria, chorus)	What Shall I Do?	No Rhyme or Reason (Ida, Baltin)	For No Rhyme or Reason
	Finale		
		Act 1, scene 5	**Act 1, scene 5**
		From Alpha to Omega	From Alpha to Omega
		Reprise: By Candlelight	Reprise: By Candlelight
			Act 1, scene 6
			Don't Let it Get You Down*
			Act 1, scene 7
		What Shall I Do?	What Shall I Do?
Act 2, scene 1	**Act 2, scene 1**	**Act 2, scene 1**	**Act 2, scene 1**
For No Rhyme or Reason (Ida, Debonairs)	No Rhyme or Reason		Let's Put It to Music (by Edwin Gilbert and Alex Fogarty)
At Long Last Love (Gaston)	At Long Last Love	At Long Last Love	At Long Last Love
	Act 2, scene 2	**Act 2, scene 2**	**Act 2, scene 2**
Platform scene: Gendarme (lyrics by Rowland Leigh, music by Robert Katscher)**	Platform scene		Platform scene: Take Yourself a Trip (by Edwin Gilbert and Alex Fogarty)
			Yes, Yes, Yes (by Edwin Gilbert and Alex Fogarty)
			Gendarme

28 March 1938: Philadelphia script (SOA, scripts box 610)	**1 May 1938: Chicago (*Playbill*)**	**22 August 1938: Clifton Webb's script (breaks off after act 2, scene 2; SOA, scripts box 610)**	**21 September 1938: New York (*Playbill*)**
Act 2, scene 2	**Act 2, scene 3**		**Act 2, scene 3**
Just One Step Ahead of Love (Mme Baltin)	One Step Ahead of Love		No (by Dana Suesse)
	Act 2, scene 4		
	Waiter's reprise: You Never Know		
Act 2, scene 3			
Good Evening Princess (Gaston, Maria)	Good Evening Princess	Good Evening Princess	Good Evening Princess
Finale: Who Are You (lyrics by Rowland Leigh with notation: "In Place of 'YOURS' in last scene of play, with no verse"; last page with another version of verse)			

* Written for the film *Break the News*, first released in Sweden on 30 April 1938 but not used. See http://www.imdb.com/title/tt0029944/releaseinfo?ref_=tt_ov_inf+.

** The text of this otherwise unpublished song runs:

> Don't we look superb in our uniforms?
> Don't you think our smiles seraphic
> Considering our jobs
> Controlling Paris traffic.
> Maybe it's because of our uniforms
> All the women here adore us
> They swarm around in droves.
> And serenade in chorus.
> REFRAIN: Oh Gendarme—Mon Cheri
> I wish you would come off your beat
> Won't you consent to make merry
> With me "toute suite"
> Gendarme: My beau gosse
> Forget your deduction of crime
> I promise to show you with no loss
> The hell of a time
> Stop arresting Apaches—
> Let those taxis collide.
> We should care what the crash is
> When we're not inside.
> Oh Gendarme—my fond arm
> Won't give you a moment of calm
> Till you are my own Gendarme.

(SOA, April 1938 Philadelphia script)

Notes

1. Lewis Nichols, "'Around the World': Note on the Good and Bad in the New Musical and on Mr. Welles, Showman," *New York Times*, 9 June 1946.

2. Wolcott Gibbs, "Words and Sad Music," *New Yorker*, 1 October 1938, 30.

3. Brooks Atkinson, "Clifton Webb, Lupe Velez and Libby Holman Appearing in a Cole Porter Musical," *New York Times*, 22 September 1938. Later critics have dismissed the score as well. For example, Stephen Citron wrote: "The score is third-rate Porter. . . . [T]he missing element here—and throughout the show—was Cole's apparent loss of melodic invention" (*Noel and Cole: The Sophisticates* [New York: Oxford University Press, 1993; reprint with new introduction, Milwaukee: Hal Leonard, 2005], 163). Some, however, such as Ethan Mordden, praised many of the songs, including numbers that were dropped from the show during the tryouts but subsequently revived (*Sing for Your Supper: The Broadway Musical in the 1930s* [New York: Palgrave Macmillan, 1995], 249–51).

4. Atkinson, "Clifton Webb."

5. Siegfried Geyer (1883–1945) was a Jewish Austrian author, playwright, and dramaturge who fled Vienna following the Anschluss, was interned in Hungary during the war, and was shot dead on the Hungarian-Slovakian border in late 1944 or early 1945. The *Kleine Komödie* was perhaps his best-known and most successful work. For Brooks Atkinson's review, see "Bringing the Season Up to Date," *New York Times*, 13 October 1929.

6. Mordaunt Hall, review of *By Candlelight*, *New York Times*, 6 January 1934. Also see http://www.imdb.com/title/tt0023860/.

7. Karl Farkas (1893—1971) was an Austrian actor and cabaret performer who, like Geyer, fled Austria in 1938. Traveling by way of Paris to New York, he returned to Vienna in 1946 and reestablished his career there. Several recordings of his work are available on Presier Records, including *Unvergessener Karl Farkas* (released 1987, recorded 1960, 1961, and 1965); Karl Farkas and Ernst Waldbrunn, *Doppelconferencen* (released 1990, recorded 1960 and 1964); and *Altmeister des Humors: Fritz Grünbaum, Karl Farkas, Franz Engel* (released 1990, recorded 1908, 1930, 1931, 1932, 1934, and 1937). Robert Katscher (1894—1942) was an Austrian composer. His *Lustspiel* titled *Die Wunder-Bar* premiered in Vienna in 1930 and was given on Broadway in 1931 as *The Wonder Bar,* with Al Jolson as the male lead. Jolson also played the male lead in the 1934 film. See http://ibdb.com/production.php?id=11341 and http://www.imdb.com/title/tt0026007/?ref_=nm_flmg_wr_2. Katscher immigrated to the United States in 1938 (see *New York Times*, 26 June 1938).

8. *Neues Wiener Journal*, 1 May 1937, 27. All translations are my own.

> Der französische Dramatiker Pierre Carlet de Chamblain de Marivaux, der als der Schöpfer des Konversationslustspiels gilt, hat in seiner Komödie "Le jeu de l'amour et du hazard" (1730) eine unsterbliche Situation geschaffen. Man könnte sie die Quadrille der Quidproquos nennen: Der Herr spielt den Diener, der Diener spielt den Herrn, die Zose gibt sich für die Gnädige aus und die Gnädige für die Zose. Zwei Jahrhunderte später machten drei witzige und gewandte Wiener Autoren, Hans Adler, Paul Frank und Siegfried Geyer, aus disem Stoff ein überaus reizendes

> Lustpiel, die "kleine Komödie," die alle Theater der Welt eroberte. . . . Robert Katscher gab diesem Gewand weichen musikalischen Schmuck. Die Originalautoren sind bescheiden in den Hintergrund getreten, und Robert Katscher zeichnet allein als Autor der Komödie "Bei Kerzenlicht," die gestern im Deutschen Volksteather Ihre Uraufführung erlebt. Er verzichtet auf die Bezeichnung Lustspiel, Komödie oder Operette, sondern gibt als Untertitel nur an: "Zwölf Chansons um eine kleine Komödie. . . ." Das alles ist mit ausserordentlicher Geschicklichkeit und mit allerbester Laune gemacht, und Katschers graziöse Musik trägt das ihrigen zum großen Vergnügen der Zuschauer bei. Diese Musik ist elegant und schmissig sowohl in den Hauptnummern . . . wie auch in den sehr lustigen Parlando-Szenen. Sie ist sozuzagen französisch gedacht und wienerische empfunden.

The *Wiener Zeitung*, 1 May 1937, described the work as "an enchanting, thoroughly entertaining instance of refined theater" (eine entzückenden, restlos amüsante Gabe kultivierten Theaters).

9. An Al Jolson vehicle, *The Wonder Bar* had a limited run of seventy-six performances. According to the *New York Times*, 18 March 1931, "The story of the piece is hackneyed enough; although the cast is long the talent is thin. . . . The songs are undistinguished."

10. For the Shuberts' 3 May agreement with Georg Marton Verlag on behalf of Robert Katscher and their 5 May agreement with Doblinger, see folder 7, box 85, Show Series, Shubert Organization Archive, New York (hereafter SOA). In fact, the wording of the agreement precluded a production—like Porter's *You Never Know*—that was chiefly the work of another composer. On 7 December, shortly after a draft contract with Porter had been drawn up, the Shuberts' lawyer, Adolph Kaufman, wrote a memo that highlighted the problem: "I want to call your attention to several basic matters, which should receive your careful judgment before you conclude any contract with Cole Porter. . . . The proposed agreement with Cole Porter, is to do a complete score. You understand that under his form of agreement you would not be entitled to interpolate into the score written by Porter, not even parts of the original score by Katcher [*sic*]. Furthermore, Cole Porter's name would have to be announced as the composer. You therefore immediately have a conflict, irrespective of anything else." This document and records of later negotiations to resolve the problem with Katscher, Marton, and Doblinger are in folder 7, box 85, Show Series, SOA.

11. George Eells, *The Life That Late He Led: A Biography of Cole Porter* (New York: G. P. Putnam's Sons, 1967), 162.

12. *New York Times*, 17 September 1937.

13. Both Eells, *The Life That Late He Led*, 162, and William McBrien, *Cole Porter: A Biography* (New York: Alfred A. Knopf, 1998), 209, state that Porter traveled on the *Estonia*, which left Le Havre on 4 October. As both a report in the *New York Times* for 1 October and the sketch sheet for "At Long Last Love" show, however, Porter traveled on the SS *Normandie*, which arrived on 30 September. "At Long Last Love" was, as McBrien points out (211), copyrighted early in October, although it apparently lacked a verse, which perhaps gives some credence to the well-known story of Porter working on the song while trapped under his fallen horse on 24 October.

14. Eells, *The Life That Late He Led*, 165.

15. Scripts, box 610, SOA. Porter nevertheless continued to work on *Greek to You*, possibly even into 1938. Drafts of three numbers for the show, "Greek to You," "Wild Wedding Bells," and an opening for act 2, scene 1, survive in folder 213, box 30, MSS 82, Cole Porter Collection, Irving S. Gilmore Music Library, Yale University.

16. For Porter's contract, see folder 7, box 85, Show Series, SOA.

17. Holman as Mme Baltin is mentioned in the *New York Times*, 21 December 1937. Her contract with Shubert is in folder 7, box 85, Show Series 7.

18. *New York Times*, 7 January 1938 and 12 January 1938. See also "Cole Porter Musical Is Coming Here," *Pittsburgh Press*, 5 February 1938. June Knight had recently appeared as Karen O'Kane in the Shubert production of Porter's *Jubilee*, Jane Pickens had been featured in the *Ziegfeld Follies of 1936* with Fanny Brice and Gypsy Rose Lee, Tallulah Bankhead had starred with Conway Tearle as Cleopatra in *Antony and Cleopatra*, and Joan Crawford had appeared in the Shuberts' *The Passing Show of 1924*.

19. A draft of her contract, dated 1 February 1938, is in folder 7, box 85, Show Series, SOA.

20. For numerous incidents that strengthened Velez's troublemaking reputation, see Michelle Vogel, *Lupe Velez: The Life and Career of Hollywood's "Mexican Spitfire"* (Jefferson, NC: McFarland, 2012).

21. It remains unclear exactly what additional songs were offered to Holman and when. "You Never Know" was added during the initial tryouts; "I'm Yours," which is known in two versions, was revised in March 1938 but later dropped; "Just One Step Ahead of Love" was written in late March, revised for the Philadelphia tryout, but dropped before the show reached New York; and "I'll Black His Eye" was composed in February 1938 but dropped during the tryouts. See Robert Kimball, *The Complete Lyrics of Cole Porter* (New York: Da Capo Press, 1992), 225–35. According to Citron, there had been tension between Holman and Velez right from the start, and during the New Haven tryouts in early March, "[Holman and Velez] engaged in a tussle between curtain calls that ended with Lupe blacking one of Libby's eyes" (*Noel and Cole*, 164). Rowland Leigh to John Shubert, 23 May 1938, folder 5, box 10, Solo Series, SOA.

22. *Milwaukee Journal*, 13 May 1938, based on an AP press report from New York.

23. Vogel, *Lupe Velez*, 291.

24. Tryouts for *You Never Know* began on 3 March 1938 at the Shubert Theatre in New Haven and continued on 7 March at the Shubert Theatre in Boston; 21 March at the National Theatre in Washington, DC; 28 March at the Forrest Theatre in Philadelphia; 18 April at the Nixon Theatre in Pittsburgh; 24 April at the Cass Theatre in Detroit; 1 May at the Grand Opera House in Chicago; 22 May at the Shrine Auditorium in Des Moines; 23 May at English's Theatre in Indianapolis; 27 May at the Hartman Theatre in Columbus; and 29 May at the Erlanger Theatre in Buffalo. After a summer off and further revisions, the show also played at the Bushnell Theatre in Hartford beginning 16 September. See John Shubert to Rowland Leigh, 28 April 1938: "Dear Rowley Cole Porter had George Abbott see You Never Know in Pittsburg Abbott is now willing to revise book and partially restage Needless to say Abbotts prestige great asset for New York opening" (folder 5, box 10, Solo Series, SOA).

25. Although the Pittsburgh notice has not been traced, it was probably similar or nearly identical to a report published in the *New York Times* a few days earlier (26 April): "George Abbott went to Pittsburgh to see last Saturday's two performances [of *You Never Know*]—this as a favor to his friend, Cole Porter, composer of the show, to whom he reported his opinion yesterday."

26. *Bei Kerzenlicht* was not a flop, as Leigh claims; see the review in the *Neues Wiener Journal* cited above. Leigh does appear to be correct, however, in claiming that the original idea was for an intimate musical; see the *New York Times* for 12 January 1938: "The musical version of 'By Candlelight' is expected to start practicing early next month. . . . Rowland Leigh, the adaptor, will direct, and the cast will boast seven principal players and no chorus."

27. *Between the Devil* was a comedy with music by Arthur Schwartz and a book and lyrics by Howard Dietz that the Shuberts had produced at their Imperial Theatre between 22 December 1937 and 12 March 1938. Like *You Never Know*, it had a limited and unsuccessful run of only ninety-three performances.

28. Copy in the folder Correspondence 1938, Cole Porter Literary and Musical Trust.

29. Folder 5, box 10, Solo Series, SOA.

30. Ibid.

31. See John Shubert to Leigh, 1 June 1938: "Dear Rowley: Saw Porter the other day, and he evidently had a long talk with Abbott on the 'phone. I would not worry too much about the gigolo idea and those damn Debonairs" (ibid.).

32. Folder 7, box 85, Show Series, SOA.

33. The final script for Webb is in scripts, box 610, SOA.

34. See Eells, *The Life That Late He Led*, 176–77.

35. See Porter's 31 December 1937 contract with the Shuberts and in particular the following clause: "It is explicitly understood that in view of the partial physical disability of the Composer, of which the Manager is completely informed, the Composer shall not be required to be present at each and every rehearsal. It is the Composer's intention, however, to exercise every effort to be present whenever it is essential and definitely necessary" (folder 7, box 85, Show Series, SOA). What is more, Porter spent much of the spring recuperating in Havana.

36. See Kimball, *The Complete Lyrics*, 235, where the copyright date January 1938 is noted.

37. See ibid., 233, for the March 1938 date. It seems likely that the song was never tried in the show. The Philadelphia script has in its place the similar song "Just One Step Ahead of Love." See the appendix.

38. For a description of those productions, see Foster Hirsch, *The Boys from Syracuse: The Shuberts' Theatrical Empire* (New York: Cooper Square Press, 2000), esp. chap. 6, "All in the Family," 163–87. The Winter Garden was originally built in 1896 as the American Horse Exchange but then leased as a theater by the Shuberts in 1911 and renovated and enlarged in 1922. See *The Cambridge Guide to American Theatre*, ed. Don B. Willmeth and Tice L. Miller (Cambridge: Cambridge University Press, 1993), 408.

39. Other theaters owned or operated by the Shuberts whose seating capacities are known included the Ambassador (built in 1921, seating capacity 1,088), the Belasco

(1907, 1,016), the Broadhurst (1917, 1,156), the Cort (1912, 1,082), the Ethel Barrymore (1928, 1,058), the Imperial (1923, 1,443), the Longacre (1913, 1,091), the Lyceum (1903, 922), and the Shubert (1913, 1,460). Among other theaters operating on Broadway, only the Marquis (1919, 1,611), the Palace (1913, 1,740), and the St. James (1927, 1,620) had seating capacities comparable to or greater than the Winter Garden and the Majestic. See http://www.newyorktheatreguide.com/broadwayTheatres/.

40. For example, a list of furs supplied to Select Theatres for use in the production by the high-end furrier I. J. Fox included a Russian ermine wrap at $1,500, a silver fox jacket at $700, a pair of silver foxes at $500, a pair of blue foxes at $300, a pair of cross foxes at $250, five skin sets of stone martens at $400, two blue-dyed white fox muffs at $75 each, two white fox muffs at $100 each, one Persian muff at $150, one black Caracul muff at $200, and one Kolinsky muff at $250 (excluding insurance). Invoices also survive for the hiring or purchase of trunks, suitcases, and hat boxes from Oppenheimer & Sherman and for pianos from Mathubeck Pianos. Shubert attempted to offset at least some of these costs by selling product placements in the show to Guerlain perfume, Schieffelin cognac, and Canada Dry ginger ale. All of the relevant documents are in folder 7, box 85, Show Series, SOA. For the cast's pay cuts and royalty agreements, see ibid.

41. See Nichols, "'Around the World.'"

14

A Consideration of Drama, Lyrics, and Musical Structure in a Porter Film

Broadway Melody of 1940

MATTHEW SHAFTEL

Although King Shaw (George Murphy) has only received the call to audition for the new Cole Porter musical due to a case of mistaken identity—he is mistaken for Johnny Brett (Fred Astaire)—he sings with emotion and dances with aplomb. From the way Shaw is looking at his costar-to-be, Clare Bennett (Eleanor Powell), it is clear that he is after more than a part in the show. Indeed, the sultry tune and poignant harmonies that accompany the title phrase of the song, "Between you and me, / You're something spectacular," reveal the depth of his feelings. And yet, something unresolved in the music—unexpected musical events, some of which literally fall "between" the words "you" and "me"—suggest that Shaw's love is unrequited. As the movie audience will discover, Shaw's engagement with the bottle drives Bennett into Brett's arms, as Brett ultimately takes his rightful place as the leading man in the musical production, as well as in the movie itself.

With its spiffy dance numbers and moments of slapstick humor, the final installment to the four-film *Broadway Melody* movie series, *Broadway Melody of 1940*, is easy to dismiss as entertaining but cliché. However, the musical score provided by Cole Porter, along with top-drawer performances by Fred Astaire,

George Murphy, Eleanor Powell, and three operatic voices (Douglas McPhail, Carmen D'Antonio, and Lois Hodnott), add a sophistication that elevates the film far beyond the previous installments of the series. The film, like its three predecessors, follows the long dramatic tradition of *mise en abyme*, embedding a plot focused on the making of a Broadway musical within the context of a musical film. The technique provides plentiful opportunities for deliberate on-screen (diegetic) music making and dancing, and Porter's songs offer hidden glimpses into the characters' psyches, their relationships, and their overarching objectives.[1] Not only does the film include the first film reprise of Porter's 1935 signature ballad, "Begin the Beguine," but it also includes three lesser-known gems newly composed for the film: "Between You and Me," "I Concentrate on You," and "I've Got My Eyes on You."[2] The three ballads written expressly for the film present a particularly Porterian musical portrait, offering an opportunity to explore intricate aspects of musical design and lyrical interface in a context that is a bit less familiar to most Porter fans. In addition, an examination of the songs' filmic context and multiple musical arrangements reveals a deeper connection to the film's narrative than their conventional song and dance routines might suggest.

The movie opens with Brett (Astaire) and Shaw (Murphy) working at a dance club, where they are paid to dance with the ladies. Shaw has shown up late for work, having overindulged in liquor and female company (very scandalous in the 1940 context). The two then sing and dance the only comic number in the movie, "Please Don't Monkey with Broadway," for the gathered crowd at the club:

> So move Grant's Tomb to Union Square
> And put Brooklyn anywhere,
> But please, please, I beg on my knees,
> Don't monkey with old Broadway.

The lyrics are distinctly Porterian, as noted by their droll engagement with American landmarks (Grant's Tomb in Union Square), biting commentary on contemporary events, alliterative juxtaposition (Brooklyn vs. Broadway), and internal rhymes (please, knees).[3] Play with poetic meter is not uncommon in the movie/Broadway music of the time, but here the threefold change in metric patterns surely reflects Porter's rhythmically intricate hand, moving in direct succession from a regular alternation of weak and strong syllables in "So *move* Grant's *Tomb* to Union *Square*," to a syncopated strong–weak pattern in

"*And* put *Brook*lyn *anywhere*," followed by a completely irregular distribution of strong syllables in "But *please, please*, I *beg* on my *knees*."

Brett is so convincing in his song-and-dance routine that he catches the eye of an agent, who asks him to audition for the new musical he is producing. In a relatively expected plot twist worthy of Mozart, the partners briefly switch names to avoid a creditor who is after Shaw, the result of which is the case of mistaken identity mentioned at the opening of this chapter: Shaw gets the invitation instead of the intended recipient, Brett. In a brief episode, we learn the important detail that Brett has long been watching Clare Bennett from afar while she performs in a different Broadway show. This yields to the scene in which Shaw, now also completely taken with Bennett, takes his audition, singing "Between You and Me" to Bennett and then dancing with her as the song evolves through three stylistically distinct musical arrangements: first, a high-style ballet, then a high-style waltz, and lastly a vaudeville-type tap dance.

Not only does the song's intricate musical design allow for the flexibility of multiple arrangements, but it also reveals much about the rather one-way relationship between Shaw and Bennett. And later in the movie, it also becomes a two-step dance background to a comic scene between the agent and a young woman who, like Bennett toward Shaw, does not return the affections of her wooer.

The song's title hints at the intimacy of a shared secret, but the only thing that is shared in the lines of the first half of the refrain is a one-sided list of compliments: "You're something spectacular," "You're a prize," and so forth (see table 1 for the complete text). The second half of the refrain reveals that "you," in this case, Bennett, is not *yet* "mine," that is, that Bennett and Shaw are *not* courting, although he certainly wishes to make a "love" relationship into a "formality." Several elements in the structure of both the lyrics and the music point to a rather dim future for this relationship, which, despite a few nights out on the town, turns out not to have the "oomph" that Shaw desires.

Porter's lyrics often exhibit a distinctive paradoxical quality. In subject, they often juxtapose the most mundane, and often cliché, with clever references to contemporary issues and/or society. Here, for instance, "You're something spectacular" and "You're a prize" are followed by the clear reference to the war developing in Europe: "Your heart I'll bombard to get." The line "And chuck the formality" places the "vernacular" term of "chuck," with its short,

	Rhyme	Noteworthy sonic qualities	Syllables, accents, and metric patterns	No. of feet and immediately repeated syllabic patterns
Between you and me,	a	*oo* vs. *ee*	5 (3) ˘ ¯ ¯ ˘ ¯	2 (¯ ¯)
You're something spectacular,	b	*s* alliteration	7 (2) ˘ ¯ ˘ ˘ ¯ ˘ ˘	2 (˘ ˘; ˘ ˘)
Between you and me,	a		5 (3) ˘ ¯ ¯ ˘ ¯	2 (¯ ¯)
You're a prize,	c	"you're" "I"	3 (2) ¯ ˘ ¯	1
Between you and me,	a		5 (3) ˘ ¯ ¯ ˘ ¯	2 (¯ ¯)
To use the vernacular	b	"To" "use"	7 (2) ˘ ¯ ˘ ˘ ¯ ˘ ˘	2 (˘ ˘; ˘ ˘)
You've got what they call	d	"you've"	5 (3) ˘ ¯ ¯ ˘ ¯	2 (¯ ¯)
"Oomph" in your eyes.	c	"Oomph" "your"	4 (2) ¯ ˘ ˘ ¯	1 (˘ ˘)
Till I make you mine,	e	"I"	5 (3) ˘ ¯ ¯ ˘ ¯	2 (¯ ¯)
Your heart I'll bombard to get,	f		7 (2) ˘ ¯ ˘ ˘ ¯ ˘ ˘	2 (˘ ˘; ˘ ˘)
No matter how hard to get	f	"heart" "hard"	7 (2) ˘ ¯ ˘ ˘ ¯ ˘ ˘ !	2 (˘ ˘; ˘ ˘)!
It may be.	a	"get" "It"	3 (1) ˘ ˘ ¯ !	1 (˘ ˘)
So why not combine	e	"combine" "mine"	5 (3) ˘ ¯ ¯ ˘ ¯	2 (¯ ¯)
And chuck the formality	a	*ch* and *ck* vs. *f*	7 (2) ˘ ¯ ˘ ˘ ¯ ˘ ˘	2 (˘ ˘; ˘ ˘)
Between love and	g (a)	"love" distinct!	4 (2) ˘ ¯ ¯ ˘	2 (¯ ¯)
Between you and me.	a		5 (3) ˘ ¯ ¯ ˘ ¯	2 (¯ ¯)!

TABLE 1. Poetic structure of "Between You and Me" (from *Broadway Melody of 1940*). Words and music by Cole Porter.

rhythmic consonance, in direct contrast to "formality," a term whose meaning is supported by its soft, fricative consonant and unusual metric structure (a secundus paeon, ˘ ¯ ˘ ˘, like "vernacular").

In a similar vein, as displayed in table 1, the poetic structure provides a large-scale regularity to contain and contrast with the high degree of surface spontaneity in rhyme, alliteration, vowel manipulation, and metric adjustment. "Between You and Me" breaks evenly into two eight-line halves, each of which divides neatly into two quatrains, and on the whole, the metric structure is fairly consistent quatrain to quatrain. However, near the end of the poem, Porter disrupts the pattern at two telling points: the first, "No matter how hard to get," suggests that Shaw and Bennett may not be a sure thing, and the second, the lines "Between love and / Between you and me," hints that there may be some undesirable distance between the three essential elements of this song: "you," "me," and "love."

In addition to the end rhymes of the lines, which present their own game with the listener by following no predictable pattern, the song's internal play with sounds gives the lyric cohesiveness. As summarized in table 1, the first half makes repeated use of the long vowel sound of *oo* ("oomph"), particularly in the context of the words "you," "you've," "you're," and "your." Shaw leaves little doubt as to the target of his love! This long *u*-vowel is contrasted with *ee* and *i* (as in "me" and "mine"), and interestingly, the *u*-vowel largely disappears from the second half of the song. When it returns as the final line of the song, the doubt expressed in the *ee*- and *i*-voweled statements ("hard to get / It may be," "So why not combine," and "Till I make you mine") forces a reinterpretation of the title phrase: "Between you and me lies something impassable."

Before turning an ear toward the song's inner workings, I will briefly consider the hot-button issue of urtext, outlining what and whose music this analysis will address. As Lawrence Zbikowski demonstrates in his thoughtful exploration of the skeletal schematic "identity" of "Bye, Bye, Blackbird" through its many different stylistic and musical reinterpretations, essentializing the features of any particular song is potentially a complex endeavor.[4] Even in its most publicly available form, the sheet music that was sold by the ream to the amateur music-making public (along with the ubiquitous ukulele arrangements) included a great degree of filigree in the piano parts that was attributed to Albert Sirmay (1880–1967), who, after completing a degree at the Academy of Music in Budapest, worked as the music editor for Harms and, later, Chappell & Co. Sirmay (né Szirmai) edited and arranged the works of many of the Broadway composers of the era, including Kern, Rodgers, Gershwin, and, of course, Porter. As stated by William McBrien, "He was a superb editor . . . who excelled at preserving the composer's intention."[5] As has already been made evident in the present volume, Porter was a well-trained musician, having undertaken university study and (in all likelihood) conservatory training in Paris. He was entirely capable of composing all aspects of his songs, and, as can be seen in the few extant Porter sketches, he would lay out all the critical details of both harmony and melody before turning the songs over to Sirmay.[6] A draft of Porter's 1944 song, "I'm Afraid I Love You," that almost exactly matches the sheet music can be found in the substantial Yale archive, and it shows a careful sketching of melody, harmony, and bass (but no lyrics) and a number code to show where the bass pattern should be repeated. Above one particular moment of pianistic filler, Porter has written, "the Sirmay touch," probably to tease Sirmay, who would eventually have completed the final version for publication. On the second page of the draft over another florid moment Porter has written "another Sirmay, to hell with him."

Sirmay did much of the orchestration and arrangement for the Broadway and film versions of Porter's tunes, and the arrangements in *Broadway Melody of 1940* are lush, varied, and extensive, particularly for the danced portions of the songs. Yet, the sung portions of the songs in Porter's films and musicals generally match the basic harmonic and melodic outlines of the sheet music. A conductor's score used for the opening night of *Kiss Me, Kate*, also found in the Yale archive, for instance, consists of a piano-vocal reduction of the musical. Outside of its incidental music and reprises, this conductor's score matches the sheet music to a stunning degree, suggesting a musical proximity that may be closer than some critics might claim. The analyses below recall specific elements of the score as heard in the movie itself (no doubt, a "fixed" urtext), but the harmonic and melodic details are replicated in the sheet music, except where noted.

A complete linear melodic/contrapuntal sketch of the refrain can be found in example 3. The thirty-two measures of the refrain divide neatly into two similar halves (AA'), each of which can itself be subdivided into eight-bar phrases (ab a'c), replicating the hierarchical structure of the text. A half-cadential arrival on the dominant in measure 16 allows the song to be heard as a single parallel period (with important variation in the consequent).[7] Thus, the parallel phrase structure mirrors the dependent relationship between the two halves of the text: the hopeful desire of the first half contextualized by the harsh realities of the second.

The five-syllable lines at the beginning of each quatrain allow each eight-measure phrase to open with similar musical material: typically an eighth-note-delayed entrance of the voice, followed by three repeated quarter notes, and then a step (or small skip) up to a long note on the downbeat of the following measure (see ex. 1, with melody and a summary of harmonic function abstracted from the sheet music). The repeated between-you-and-me rhythm/contour figure accommodates the many bacchius-type feet (˘ ¯ ¯) in the lyrics and puts the fullest possible weight on the long note at the end, emphasizing the words "me," "mine," "com-*bine*." When Murphy (playing Shaw) sings Porter's rhythm, he foreshortens the third note ("you") and anticipates "me" by almost an eighth note. This rhythmic liberty puts further emphasis on "me" while reducing the emphasis on "you," an ironic reflection of Shaw's overt self-centeredness.

The between-you-and-me figure can also be heard at the halfway points of phrases 1 and 2, and, in fact, various manifestations of this between-you-and-me (b-y-a-m) figure account for nearly half the measures in the entire

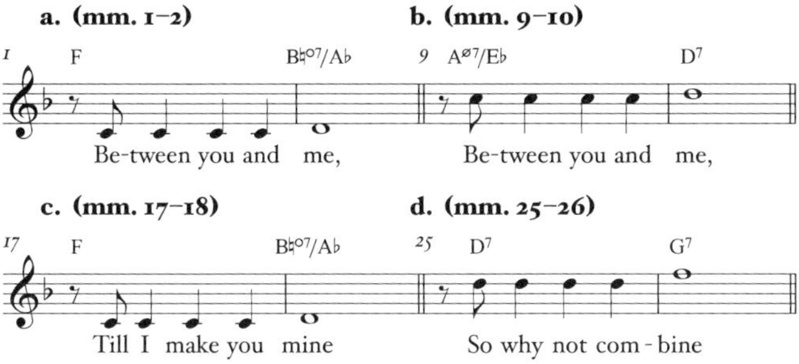

EXAMPLE 1. "Between You and Me," opening of each eight-measure phrase. The chord symbols above the staves are summaries of the actual harmonies found in the film and sheet music.

EXAMPLE 2. Additional occurrences of the between-you-and-me figure.

refrain. Like the repetitious use of vowel sounds cited above, this unifies the melodic material and betrays the extent to which Shaw is obsessed with Bennett (and, perhaps, given the emphasis on the word "me," with himself).[8] And yet, just as the surface unity of Porter's lyrics gives way to foreground variation, there is a great degree of variety between the b-y-a-m figures. The b-y-a-m figure that opens each half of the song (1a and 1c) are identical except for the text, evoking the antecedent-consequent relationship described earlier: both make use of the structural 5–6 neighbor motion from C4 to D4 (see the graph in ex. 3), and both include a move from the F-major tonic to a poignant nonfunctional $B^{\circ}{}^{4}_{2}$ that resolves linearly to a G minor triad (ii).[9] Thus, although the close neighbor motion in the melody has the potential to suggest a closeness between "you" and "me," the highly dissonant setting of "me" suggests otherwise.

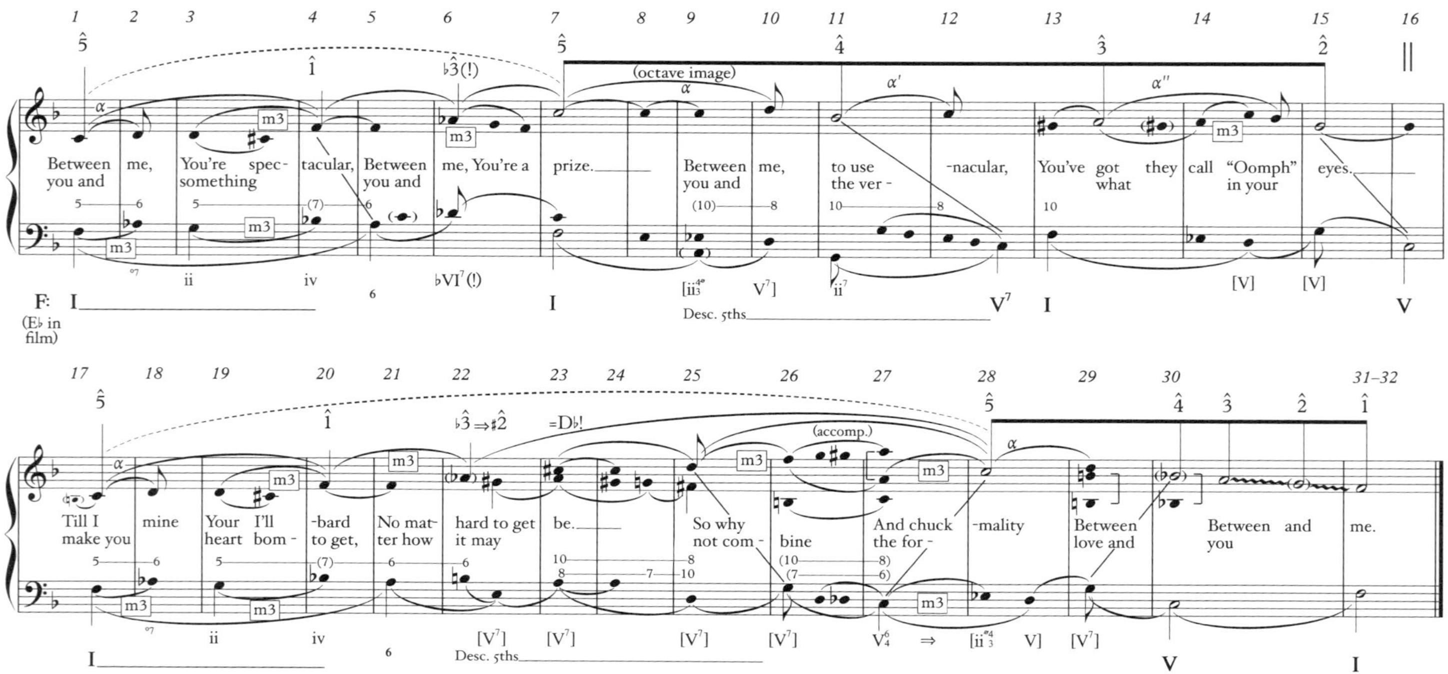

EXAMPLE 3. "Between You and Me," linear graph of entire refrain.

The minor third in the bass from F to A♭ that accompanies measures 1–2 (and 17–18) also bodes ill for the future of the Shaw-Bennett relationship. Indeed, the minor third is immediately sequenced in measures 3–4 and 19–20 as G–B♭ (the minor iv over B♭ is also a bad sign), part of a third ascent in the bass—F–G–A—expanding tonic: I–I^6. The next iteration of the b-y-a-m figure (mm. 5–6; ex. 2a) transfers the F–A♭ minor third from the bass to the melody, evoking lowered scale degree $\hat{3}$ as a "blue note." This A♭ blue note on "me" is set with a D♭^{7} harmony (♭VI^7) that arises out of neighbor motion from the fifth of the tonic harmony and resolves back to C with the return of the primary tone in measure 7. This D♭^{7} chord takes the place of a missing dominant and is a sign of the gulf that lies between Shaw and Bennett—D♭ is the pitch that literally falls in-between C and D (i.e., between "you" and "me").

The second phrase opens with a new recontextualization of the b-y-a-m figure, again with foreshadowing poignancy. Here, the octave image of the opening C–D neighbor again accompanies the title phrase, but now the first bar is set with that most poignant of Porter harmonies, the famed half-diminished seventh (which is none other than the Tristan chord; ex. 1b). This initiates a descending-fifth sequence (mm. 9–13; A–D–G–C–F root motion), which supports the descent of the fundamental line from $\hat{5}$ to $\hat{4}$ to $\hat{3}$ with a series of incomplete neighbors that recall the opening motive: C5–D5; B♭4–C5; A4–B♭4 (again, this is graphed in ex. 3). The A4 of the final b-y-a-m figure (mm. 13–14; ex. 2b) is decorated by a G♯4 lower neighbor, providing variety and, more importantly, emphasizing the sonic/poetic relationship between "you've" and "you," literally giving rise to the line "*Oomph* in your eyes."[10]

The final three occurrences of the b-y-a-m figure strike three final blows to Shaw's hopes for a union. First, however, I'd like to consider the *missing* b-y-a-m figure that should have occurred in measure 21 (see ex. 4), the parallel spot to measure 5 (ex. 2a). Porter replaces the expected title figure with a

EXAMPLE 4. The surprising replacement for the missing b-y-a-m figure!

repetition of measures 19–20 a minor third higher, using the surprise to set the only immediately successive end rhyme in the lyric: “Your heart I’ll bombard to get / No matter how hard to get / It may be.” But rather than the expected “blue note” of A♭ (♭$\hat{3}$), as in measure 5, Porter spells this as G♯, which launches the song temporarily to the distant key area of A major (III). Shaw thus misses the C5 primary tone altogether and instead lands in measure 23 on C♯5, right in the middle of the ever-widening gulf between Bennett’s “you” (C) and Shaw’s “me” (D). But rather than correcting this misstep by recapturing a proper C5 primary tone, Shaw’s C♯ resolves upward to D5 at the start of the fourth and final phrase. (Indeed, C5 as a fully supported primary tone never does return in its native register.)

In measure 25, C♯5 resolves up to D5, which itself is an upper neighbor to the C5 in measure 28, recalling the opening motive in retrograde. This entire excursion from the first half of the refrain takes the form of a circle-of-fifths motion from measures 22 to 27. Measure 25 includes another minor-third manifestation of the b-y-a-m figure, arriving on the song’s F5 apex, which suggests a certain desperation to the question “So why not combine?” F5 is supported by a G dominant seventh harmony, but the question that the dissonant seventh raises sees no resolution in this register. Instead, the melody returns to earth to “chuck the formality” in the previous register and with yet another minor third, from A4 to C5 (see ex. 5). Although a C dominant-seventh harmony in measure 27 would have continued the descending fifths and, as shown in my recomposition in example 5b, would have supported B♭$\hat{4}$ allowing a “stepwise closure of the fundamental line (parallel to m. 11), Porter opts for a suspended dominant in measure 27 with an A4 in the melody and another motivic minor-third motion from A4 to C5 (see ex. 5a). Measures 27–28 may

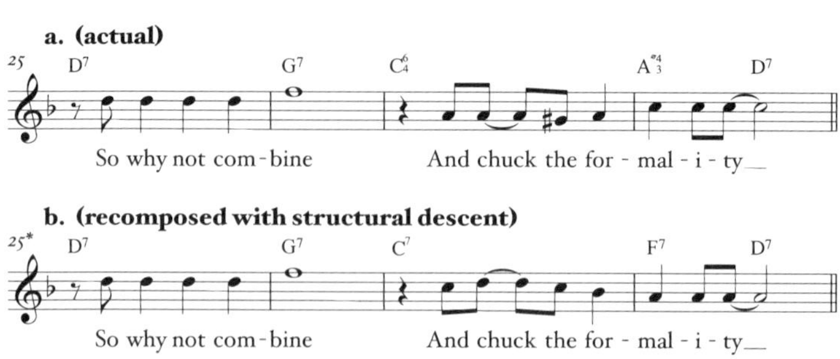

EXAMPLE 5. “Between You and Me,” mm. 25–28, actual (a) and recomposed with structural descent (b).

be best interpreted as an elision between the dominant and a V^4_2 of IV, which, in the absence of a structural descent here, supports (albeit quite weakly) the return of the C5 primary tone.

The graph in example 3 shows a descent that is somewhat "regularized" and compressed into the penultimate measure of the song (the B♭ occurs in the alto voice), but it is the very *lack* of the connection between "combine," the primary tone, and the remainder of the song that bodes so ill for Shaw. When Porter ends the song with a twofold repetition of the b-y-a-m figure, he again references the C–D neighbor, moving from C5 on "formality" to D5 on "between love," with Shaw finally stating what he *wishes* were between him and Bennett: "love." However, the final motion to tonic (ex. 2d) is by major third, again thwarting a true linear closure.[11]

As if Shaw's inability to close the deal from a linear perspective were not enough, what occurs in the dance that follows is a gradual metric and rhythmic deformation of the song to a point where it is hardly recognizable as the poignant love song where Shaw had begun. Here is a summary of the order of events:

1. Shaw sings the version discussed above in a slow, sultry fashion.
2. The b-y-a-m figure is slowed down to nearly half tempo as an introduction to a high-style pas de deux, accompanied by a heavy dose of syrupy *Empfindsamkeit* (sensibility) in the violins.
3. There is a transformation to a fully orchestrated Straussian waltz, complete with violin flourishes (see ex. 6).
4. There is a frilly big-band arrangement of a vaudeville-style tap-dance waltz.

The high-style dance at least has the potential to suggest intimacy, but when it gives way to the courtly waltz and, eventually, to the vaudeville-style tap

EXAMPLE 6. "Between You and Me," waltz arrangement. Words are supplied only to aid in the mapping of the two versions. The waltz version is only danced, *not* sung.

dance, there is nothing left of Shaw's love croon. Indeed, there is little for Shaw to do in the movie but return to the bottle, which is exactly what he does.

Whereas the poetic and musical structures seem to conspire against a love between Bennett and Shaw in every detail, a different pairing deserves a much more optimistic assessment. During a break in one of the dress rehearsals for the show, Brett, who has been secretly coaching Shaw in his dancing (remember, Brett was the one who was *supposed* to have been called for the audition), wanders onto the empty stage and finds a piece of Cole Porter (!) sheet music on the rehearsal piano. On the cover is a picture of Claire Bennett, which causes Brett to swoon. He cannot resist opening the music, and he plays and sings (and, ultimately, dances) the clever little song "I've Got My Eyes on You."

With its references to "spying" from afar and its quintessentially Porterian ending twist, this is the perfect anthem for Brett, who has been secretly admiring Bennett, but whenever she is close, he is too nervous to speak with her (as evidenced by a running gag where he runs into a statue every time she's nearby). The text of the refrain is relatively simple and employs many of the same techniques that were discussed above. Unfortunately, the verses of both "Between You and Me" and "I've Got My Eyes on You" were cut from the film. Whereas the Broadway musicals of the time would almost invariably include the verse, the enormous cost of film and the limitations of a feature-length movie generally led producers to cut the verses in the movie musicals of the same time period. This is particularly tragic in the case of "I've Got My Eyes on You," since its extended verse is unusually intricate and musically linked to the refrain. I've included the text in table 2 and, later, will briefly mention some of its musical features, since Porter intended the verse to be included in the film.

The refrain presents a humorous juxtaposition with the verse, virtually insuring a sense of paranoia in the person to whom this song is directed! The verse's opening denial—"I don't want you to feel when you step out for a meal"—is undercut by the list of ways and places that the singer could be spying on the target. Thus it is hardly surprising when the refrain reveals the truth. The immediate end rhymes of the verse take on an obsessive quality, particularly when they culminate in the alliterative explosion of "date down in the dale / There's a Dictaphone." The foreshortening of the lines "There's a Dictaphone / Under ev'ry stone" enhances the sense of climax here, allowing the "bloodhound" reference to seem truly hyperbolic.

The refrain does not result in the same degree of hyperbole and obsessiveness, which, in the film, allows Brett to seem more charming than creepy. Yet the multiple rhymes with "eyes" (the keyword in the song), particularly the surprising "spies," and the numerous alliterations (see table 2) do retain the repetitive quality of the verse. This quality is also supported by the fact that the meter of this refrain is far more regular than that of "Between You and Me." The most notable break from the fairly regular iambs is the word "I've," the accent of which pairs it with "you." Whereas the initial quatrain alternates end rhymes, the second half of the refrain begins to resemble the verse in its

	Rhyme	**Noteworthy sonic qualities**	**Syllables**	**Number of feet**
Verse				
I don't want you to feel	a		6 (3)	
When you go out for a meal	a		7 (3)	
With my rivals in town	b		6 (2/3)	
That I mean to track you down,	b		7 (3)	
Or that when you sail	c		5 (3)	
For a date down in the dale	c	*d* alliteration	7 (3)	
There's a Dictaphone	d	More *d*	5 (3)	
Under ev'ry stone	d		5 (3)	
And a bloodhound on your trail	c		7 (3)	
However—				
Refrain				
I've got my eyes on you,	e	"I've" "eyes"	6 (4) ¯ ¯ ˘ ¯ ˘ ¯	3 largely iambic
So best beware where you roam,	f	*b* alliteration "where" "ware"	7 (4) ˘ ¯ ˘ ¯ ¯ ˘ ¯	3 except "I've"
I've got my eyes on you,	e		6 (4) ¯ ¯ ˘ ¯ ˘ ¯	3
So don't stray too far from home.	f	*s* alliteration; *f* + *r* alliteration	7 (4) ˘ ¯ ˘ ¯ ¯ ˘ ¯	3
Incidentally,				
I've set my spies on you,	e	*s* alliteration "spies"/"eyes"	6 (4) ¯ ¯ ˘ ¯ ˘ ¯	3
I'm checking on all you do	e	"you"/"do"	7 (4) ˘ ¯ ˘ ˘ ¯ ˘ ¯	3
From A to Zee.	g		4 (2) ˘ ¯ ˘ ¯	2
So, darling, just be wise	h	"wise"/"eyes"/"spies"	5 (2) ˘ ¯ ˘ ¯ ˘ ¯	2
Keep your eyes	h		3 (2) ¯ ˘ ¯	1
On me.	e		2 (2) ¯ ¯	1 (2)

TABLE 2. Poetic structure of "I've Got My Eyes on You" (from *Broadway Melody of 1940*). Words and music by Cole Porter.

immediately repeated end rhymes and its foreshortening of the lines from five to first three and then to two syllables. The song's playful ending twist, "Keep your eyes / On me," throws a humorous light on what could otherwise be misinterpreted.

From the very beginning of the film, the act of gazing and admiring while hiding or without direct mutual engagement is central to the plot. The agent who accidentally brings Shaw in for an audition secretly watches Shaw and Brett's opening dance number together. Brett secretly watches Bennett's first dance number, and then secretly watches the rehearsals in order to help Shaw with his dancing. In the scene where this song is sung, not only does Brett dance not with Bennett but rather with her cover photo on the sheet music, but Bennett herself is "spying" on Brett, observing the entire scene, "incidentally" acting out the very twist at the end of the song. Later, when Bennett finally convinces Brett to take her out for lunch, one hears "I've Got My Eyes on You" playing in the background as a German shadow artist makes portraits of the couple. Here, the protagonists gaze intently at each other's shadow, but not at each other directly. Finally, when Brett must take over for Shaw in the first scene of the show because Shaw is too drunk to go onstage, Brett and Bennett are both wearing masks. They dance to the similarly obsessive "I Concentrate on You," which resolves much of the unfinished business of the earlier two ballads, but they do so while looking at each other from behind masks. This special interaction between the dramatic elements of the film and the songs is noteworthy.[12]

The refrain of "I've Got My Eyes on You" bears some structural resemblance to "Between You and Me," although less so than "I Concentrate on You," which will be discussed shortly. Most noteworthy is the motivic use of a nonharmonic structural neighbor. In the earlier song, this was the whole-step motion from $\hat{5}$ to $\hat{6}$ (C4–D4) in the b-y-a-m figure; here, however, the neighbor tone is elongated to a whole note plus a dotted half from tonic to supertonic (also a whole step): E♭4–F4 (see ex. 7). The sheet music for this song includes a four-measure tonic pedal, which makes the F4 neighbor tone and its lingering stepwise descent to $\hat{5}$ (B♭3 in m. 4) quite dissonant. Particularly noteworthy

EXAMPLE 7. "I've Got My Eyes on You," refrain, mm. 1–5.

is the strong metrical placement of dissonant pitches on "eyes" ($\hat{7}$) and "you" ($\hat{6}$), the latter of which lasts a full three beats. The effect of these dissonances is quite unsettling, and it may be worth noting that the two pitches are C4 and D4, the exact pitches of the b-y-a-m neighbor figure. All three ballads written for the movie were written within a month of each other, suggesting that, although "Between You and Me" ended up being transposed down a whole step to accommodate George Murphy's baritone range, specific pitch references among them, at least in Porter's own conception of these songs, are a distinct possibility.[13]

Whereas the sheet music's obdurate pedal emphasizes an almost eerie obsessiveness, more closely aligning with Shaw's one-sided emotions for Bennett, the version that Brett plays and sings at the piano in the film de-emphasizes the pedal and sets the dissonant tones with nonfunctional parallel harmonies in the middle voices. While the harmonic context does ease the dissonant landscape, it even more closely recalls the fully diminished seventh setting of the upper neighbor in "Between You and Me." In the film, however, "I've Got My Eyes on You" is clearly meant to be more playful, particularly when Brett breaks into a ragtime version of the tune at the piano, interrupted by brief tap-dance breaks that involve kicking and slapping the instrument. In fact, during the dancing we see Bennett peaking behind the curtain (doing her own spying) and smiling with delight. Although Brett is not yet aware of it, the emotion suggested here is a shared one!

The warning of the second line ("So best beware . . .") clarifies the true point of the song and causes the melody and harmony to come into firm agreement, arpeggiating from the B♭3 octave image of the primary tone up to its actual registral home on B♭4 ($\hat{5}$). This arpeggiation recalls the opening arpeggiated ascent from low $\hat{5}$ to upper $\hat{5}$ in "Between You and Me" (and points to a similar event in "I Concentrate on You"). The arpeggiation here stays in major, at least temporarily, while in both of the other songs in the film the arpeggiation borrows from the parallel minor. Porter does work in the parallel minor, however, emphasizing the homophonic "beware where you roam" with a skip to a ♭$\hat{7}$ blue note on D♭5. Note that D♭ was the pitch that fell between "you" and "me" in the previous song and its setting—a fully diminished seventh chord (vii$^{\circ 7}$ of ii)—also poignantly recalls the earlier song. (Perhaps it is Brett who stands between Shaw and Bennett?) As shown in the graph of the refrain found in example 8, the D♭5 immediately returns by step to the dominant primary tone, and the piano paints the word "roam" with a bassline flourish and a voice exchange with the alto voice. In the sheet music this is a chromatic descent

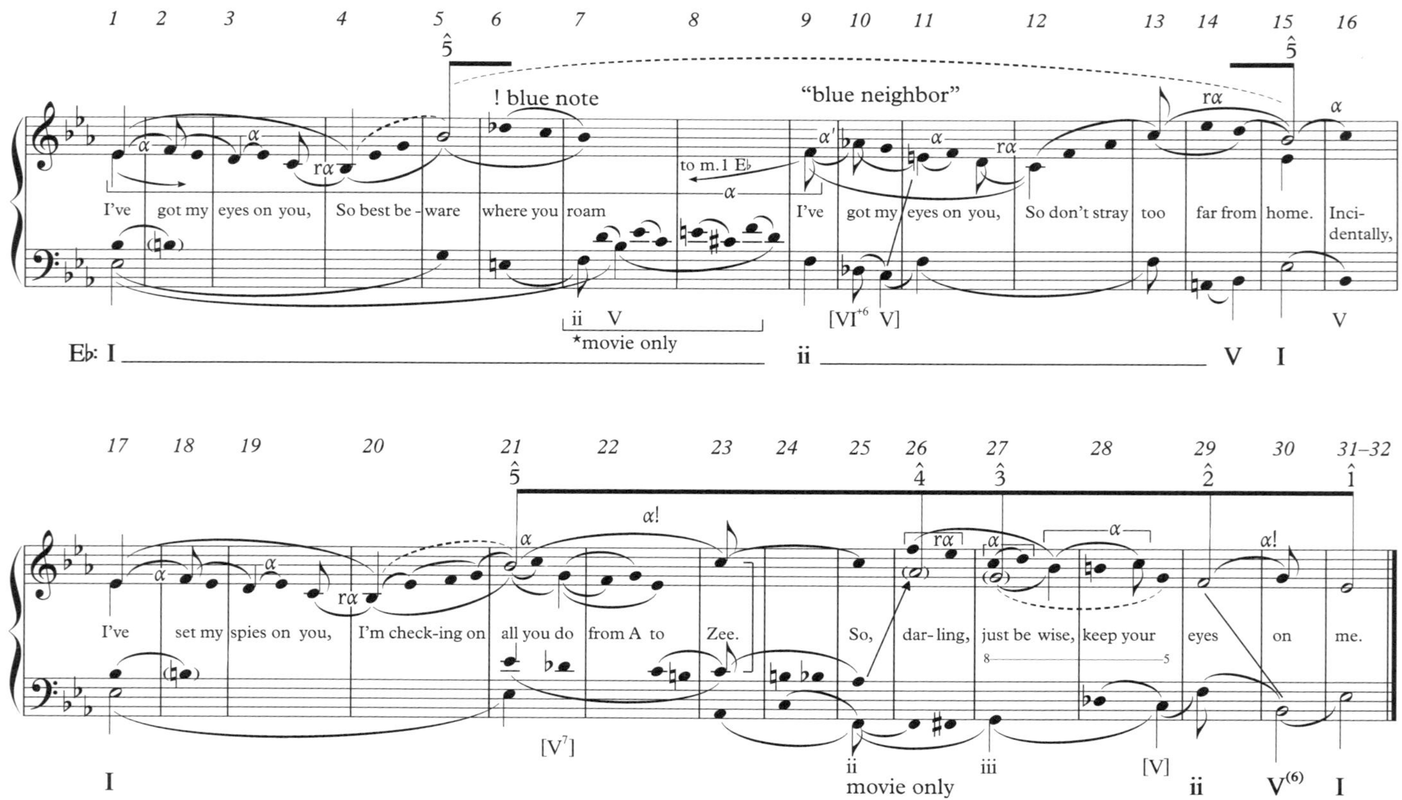

EXAMPLE 8. "I've Got My Eyes on You," linear graph of entire refrain.

from F to D, but Brett is turning the page of the music in the film, so he plays a simple expansion of the dominant through one-handed thirds: D–B♭, E♭–C, E♮–C♯, F–D.

Although the structural layout of the lyrics contrasts to that of the earlier song, the musical form is quite similar, with each of its two dependent halves, AA', lasting sixteen measures. The larger sections break into eight-measure phrases, of which the second and fourth are contrasting: aa' a"b. Although the sheet music thwarts a cadential dominant–tonic arrival in measure 15 by inverting the E♭ tonic, in the film Brett plays a root-position tonic, providing a greater degree of finality despite the fact that he is still singing the scale-degree $\hat{5}$ primary tone. The dominant implication of measure 16's quip, "incidentally," seems to fall outside of the phrase as a linking gesture, and Brett appropriately delivers the line as an aside.

Porter makes another pitch-specific reference to "Between You and Me" in the second eight-measure phrase when he transposes the title phrase to F minor and makes a small adjustment to the E♭–F neighbor, such that the whole step becomes a minor third from F4 to A♭4, still functionally an incomplete neighbor tone, but one calling upon the neighboring "blue" note rather than the neighboring diatonic tone—a "blue neighbor" (see ex. 9). The F–A♭ minor third here recalls the second iteration of the b-y-a-m figure, setting the A♭ with the same D♭7 whose function was rather mysterious in the previous song. Here is another reference to the parallel objectives of Brett and Shaw, but the D♭7 in "I've Got My Eyes on You" functions in the more expected German fashion, slipping down by semitone to the dominant.

Moving from the title figure in E♭ to its transposition to F minor creates a large-scale motivic parallelism, wherein the opening E♭ moves in the background to the F neighbor in measure 9, followed by the stepwise descent down to B♭. This is summarized in example 10, which shows measures 1–2, then omits nonrelevant pitches from measures 9–15, showing the large-scale arrival on B♭ that parallels the opening motive. That both the foreground and background structures include the spying motive is a reflection of the action's pervasiveness in the film itself.

EXAMPLE 9. "I've Got My Eyes on You," opening of a' (mm. 9–11).

EXAMPLE 10. "I've Got My Eyes on You," motivic parallelism in first sixteen measures.

Two additional features of the song also support the consistency of the spying eye. First, unlike either of the other two ballads written for (and included in) the movie, only the second half of the refrain includes a complete descent from the primary tone, with the first half prolonging B♭ $\hat{5}$ through a double neighbor (A♭4 in m. 10 and C5 in m. 13), which is supported by the F minor excursion discussed above. This use of the neighbor figure (now a neighbor to B♭ rather than E♭) and the constancy of B♭ suggest that Brett's watchful eye will not wander far. Second, while the second half of the refrain does include a descent to the tonic, it incorporates a number of similar neighbor figures. The largest of these, in measures 21–22, is motivated by the addition of the minor seventh to the tonic harmony after the repetition of the titular motive. The harmonic impetus of this V^7 of IV drives the harmony to a long expansion of the predominant, a relatively rare event in Porter's songs. This motion to an A♭ harmony *should* recall the initial neighbor tone of the verse (G–A♭–G), the A♭ of which sets "you" with a syncopated half note, but this reference is lost in the film with the omission of the verse. I've included example 11a to demonstrate the musical connection between verse and refrain and have also included an

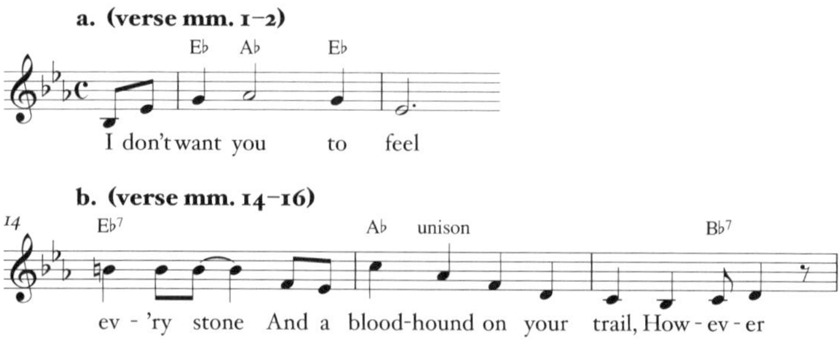

EXAMPLE 11. "I've Got My Eyes on You," verse mm. 1–2 (a) and mm. 14–16 (b).

example of the A♭ harmony from the end of the verse, which gives way to a piano-voice unison delivery of "bloodhound on your tail"—text painting of the cleverest sort (see ex. 11b to envision the "bloodhound" coming into unison with the target).

In the refrain, the arrival on the A♭ subdominant supports a large-scale upper neighbor C5 (see m. 23; ex. 8), setting the culmination of the line "I'm checking on all you do / From A to Zee." The expansion of the predominant leads to the apex of the refrain (which, incidentally, matches the apex of the verse) on F5 in measure 26, which, as the octave image of the F4 in measure 9, recalls the F minor iteration of the title motive. This resemblance is supported by a direct rhythmic and contour recall of the opening motive, which is enhanced by a similar descent to B♭, and the use of the pitches F–E♭–C–D and B♭. Even the reordering of the C5 and D5 so that D acts as an escape tone, rather than a firm member of a stepwise descent, recalls the initial motive (see ex. 12).

By emphasizing the endearment, "darling," on the apex, Porter shifts the tone of the song, clarifying that this really *has* been a declaration of love. Thus, the final lines of the text, with their veiled request that Bennett return Brett's love, can descend from the primary tone B♭ to the tonic. The descent, however, is itself veiled, beginning in the bass of measures 27 and 28 (the bass notes are identified on the right side of the chord-symbol slashes in ex. 12b; cf. ex. 8) and not revealing itself in the upper voice until the whole note F in measure 29 on the word "eyes." It is fitting that the descent doesn't become evident until the shift from "my eyes" to "your eyes." Porter even treats "your eyes on me" to a recall of the opening motive, albeit with a reversal of the F4 and E♭4. The film's shift in camera perspective at this point adds renewed emphasis, as

EXAMPLE 12. "I've Got My Eyes on You," titular motive (a) as transformed in mm. 25–27 (b).

it moves away from Bennett's eyes to accommodate Brett's fanciful ragtime tap at the piano. As a viewer, we too are directed to "keep our eyes" on Brett, and, given the virtuosity of the performance, we can do nothing else!

A varied reprise of "I've Got My Eyes on You" with different lyrics was originally planned for the film.[14] It borrows much of the text of the verse and then replaces the title phrase with "I'm so in love with you," beginning and ending with the same line. That this bald declaration is quite contrasting with the highly veiled nature of the initial lyrics may be the reason it was cut from the film. Instead, Brett's shyness around Bennett seems much better suited to the declaration of love in "I Concentrate on You."

When Shaw shows up drunk for the opening night of the show, Brett has no choice but to replace him onstage, dancing with Bennett to the song "I Concentrate on You," which is masterfully sung in an operatic style by the baritone Douglas McPhail. A ten-minute dance arrangement of "Begin the Beguine," complete with exoticist visions of scantily clad persons in tropical garb, follows, but this song was imported directly from the musical *Jubilee* (1935), where it was the hit song, and was included purely as a marketing ploy.[15] Thus, the drama of the film truly culminates in the revelation of "I Concentrate on You," after which the shared love of Brett and Bennett is a foregone conclusion.

In many ways, "I Concentrate on You" acts as a direct response to the earlier ballads, particularly "Between You and Me." In this way, the first and final ballads of the film (those that were actually written for the film, at least) function as "pendants," a group of individual artworks that can only be understood when viewed together. Pendants were initially found in the visual arts and were particularly popular among the paired portraits of the Renaissance and Baroque eras. Pendant arias are also common in Baroque opera, where the pairing of arias across a work provides multiple perspectives on a single event or character.[16] A full-fledged linear approach to "I Concentrate on You" is found in Allen Forte's insightful article on Cole Porter, which was the first substantive musical consideration of the composer's music.[17] I have reproduced his linear reduction in example 13 for ease of comparison, but my focus here is on the substantial intersections between the first and final ballads that were written for the film: "I Concentrate on You" and "Between You and Me," two songs that, despite some important differences, contain a number of striking similarities.

As in "Between You and Me" (and as echoed in "I've Got My Eyes on You") the ballad opens with an octave projection of the scale-degree $\hat{5}$ primary tone (B♭4, as in "I've Got My Eyes on You"). The motion through the octave evokes the parallel minor, using the minor $\hat{3}$, as in the opening ballad of the musical.

EXAMPLE 13. Linear analysis of "I Concentrate on You," from Allen Forte, "Secrets of Melody: Line and Design in the Songs of Cole Porter," *Musical Quarterly* 77, no. 4 (Winter 1993): 607–47.

There it seemed to reflect a troubling distance between Shaw and Bennett, whereas here it sets the generally troubling mood that is found in the lyric's description of stormy winter skies: "whenever skies look grey." Other similarities between the two songs' openings include the opening ascending fourth, with its distinctive $\hat{5}$–$\hat{6}$–$\hat{1}$ approach to tonic, and its use of embedded structural neighbor tones, C4–D4, which is a pitch-specific reference to the b-y-a-m figure. These neighbor tones also recall "I've Got My Eyes on You" (also a pitch-specific reference). Thus the C–D neighbor motion of the b-y-a-m figure underlies the entire film, wherein the primary plot point is the relationship between "you" and "me," as well as the very definition of who "me" might turn out to be.

All three ballads that Porter wrote for the film adopt similar formal strategies: four eight-bar phrases that make up a larger AA' form, but where the fourth eight-bar phrase contains a surprising excursion. Unlike "Between You and Me" and the sheet-music version of "I've Got My Eyes on You," Porter ends each half of this ballad with an authentic cadential arrival, allowing a complete fifth descent in each half. This links closely to the resolution in the text: whenever things are bad, "I concentrate on you." That both descents use the lowered $\hat{3}$ blue note from the parallel minor recalls important blue notes from the other two ballads and reinforces the E-flat *major* home tonic arrival on the word "you." It is the message that "you" provide the refuge from all that is negative that is the answer to the question marks in the earlier ballads. Here there is nothing standing "between" Brett and Bennett; the clouds of Shaw's drunkenness and the darkness of the previous identity confusion are cleared by Brett's newfound relationship with Bennett.

Like "Between You and Me," the apex of the final ballad seems disconnected to what occurs around it. A somewhat ironic arrival on a dissonant E♭ (it is the home tonic, after all) over a D♭ dominant seems nearly as far removed from the primary tone as the F5 home tonic dissonant apex in "Between You and Me." The surprising shift in the second half of the refrain leads to the key of ♭III (G-flat major), not so far from the surprising move to III in the same location of "Between You and Me." As Forte points out, the tonicization of G-flat major lends a musical weight to the tone that had originally been introduced as a blue note in measure 5.[18] This potential was also available in "Between You and Me," but, as mentioned above, the brief move to an unprepared A major there illustrated "how hard to get" she will be. Nonetheless, G♭ as a key area, and, in particular, the D♭ dominant seventh that supports the apex in measure 25 and later resolves by semitone to a bass C in measure 28 demonstrate a connection with both earlier ballads. D♭7 sets the A♭ of the F minor iteration of the titular theme in "I've Got My Eyes on You," and Porter uses a surprisingly uncontextualized D♭7 to set the blue note A♭ in measure 6 of "Between You and Me." Now the setting of A♭ with D♭7 seems to have found its native context, and in "I Concentrate on you," it ultimately leads to a D♭5–C5–B♭4 descent back to the primary tone (mm. 26–28), recalling the same descent in "I've Got My Eyes on You" ("where you roam"), but now set in major. The prevalence of blue notes in the previous two songs and their problematic descents to tonic can now be resolved in a complete and unveiled stepwise descent to the E-flat major tonic: "Whenever the blues becomes my only song / I concentrate on you."

The heavily orchestrated version of this song in the film and Brett and Bennett's ballet-inspired dance never deteriorate into the waltz or fanciful tap of the earlier ballads. With no rhythm section and an operatic baritone accompanied by Wagnerian "ahhs" from a soprano-laden choir, this song is meant to have a serious impact. It is only in the gratuitous and bombastic, but terribly entertaining, "Begin the Beguine" number that the lightheartedness returns. When Shaw, Brett, and Bennett dance a short final number while a women's chorus sings a reprise of "I've Got My Eyes on You," the audience no longer has a doubt as to who "me" and "you" might be, and a Hollywood ending is assured.

Through a close examination of the lyrics and musical structure of the three ballads that Porter wrote in the fall of 1939 for the movie musical *Broadway Melody of 1940*, this chapter has underscored Porter's attention to detail not only in his intricate texts and musical designs but also in his consideration of plot, story, and dramatic impulse. Even in the filmic medium, where Porter had a great deal less control over the final product than in his more native Broadway context, his work reveals an interconnectedness that allows for a deeper understanding of the film. Although the film's plot hardly represents high drama, the musical questions set up by the opening two ballads, "Between You and Me" and "I've Got My Eyes on You," are answered in a beautiful and quite serious manner by "I Concentrate on You," a Porter masterwork of the highest order.

Notes

1. *Kiss Me, Kate* is also centered on the *mise en abyme* paradigm of a show-within-a-show.

2. In addition to the bombastic arrangement of "Begin the Beguine," the movie also includes the hilariously funny number "Please Don't Monkey with Broadway" and a single non-Porter dance number, "All Ashore" (by Roger Edens), but the pres-

ent discussion will focus primarily on the three ballads that Porter wrote specifically for the film.

3. In his pleas to leave Broadway alone, Porter may have been referencing efforts to clean up Broadway in the 1930s and 1940s, as the streetcar lines were eventually removed and a shift away from its well-documented debauchery seemed to be warranted.

4. See chapter 5 of Lawrence Zbikowski's *Conceptualizing Music: Cognitive Structure, Theory, and Analysis* (New York: Oxford University Press, 2002). Hepokoski's chapter in the present volume lays out a very nuanced discussion of the many problems inherent in establishing a stable text for analysis in this repertoire. The layers of complexity he unfolds may well apply to any text in any repertoire; indeed, the understanding of any work is highly dependent on the delivery and reception, as well as the circumstances thereof.

5. See William McBrien, *Cole Porter: A Biography* (New York: Alfred A. Knopf, 1998; reprinted in 2000); and Howard Pollack, *George Gershwin: His Life and Work* (Berkeley: University of California Press, 2007), 192.

6. I have explored this ground at length in my article "From Inspiration to Archive: Cole Porter's 'Night and Day,'" *Journal of Music Theory* 43, no. 2 (Fall 1999): 315–47.

7. The thirty-two-bar parallel-period form was particularly common in the popular songs from about 1910 to 1930 and can be seen in such early Porter songs as "An Old-Fashioned Garden" (1919).

8. This sort of obsessive infatuation is found in a number of Porter songs, including, most famously, "I've Got You Under My Skin."

9. Octaves will be designated such that C4 represents middle C and all pitches within the octave immediately above middle C will be indicated with a "4." The C above middle C is designated C5, while the C below middle C is designated as C3.

10. In the film, Shaw actually oscillates between the A4 and the G♯4, giving even greater emphasis to the reversal of the neighbor. When he begins the consequent phrase in measure 16, he approaches the C4 by another unwritten chromatic lower neighbor: B♮.

11. Note, though, that in performance Murphy glissandos from A4 to F4, sliding through the normative G4 scale degree $\hat{2}$.

12. It would be presumptuous to assume that these connections were all drawn by Porter, since, of course, the movie director, Norman Taurog, may well have decided to develop this idea in the visual medium. Nonetheless, there is a surprising interconnectedness here that is worth exploring.

13. Even if there had been no transposition for the film, the audibility of specific pitch connections is doubtful. They are mentioned here, however, as evidence of a surprisingly unified conception of the three ballads that Porter wrote for this film.

14. Robert Kimball shows the lyrics of the revised refrain as follows:

> I'm so in love with you
> I can't tell sunshine from rain.
> I'm so in love with you
> I don't know pleasure from pain.

Confidentially,
Whenever you appear
And tell me you're riding high,
Why am I Blue? You know the answer, dear,
I'm so in love with you.

See *The Complete Lyrics of Cole Porter* (New York: Knopf, 1983; reprint, New York: Da Capo Press, 1992), 254.

15. An extended engagement with this awe-inspiring rendition of "Begin the Beguine" can be found in Joshua Walden's essay in the present volume. Walden situates this and other exoticist fantasies in Porter's work as a whole.

16. I am ever grateful to Jonathan Easey (in a personal correspondence) and Gregory Decker for sharing their work on pendants. Gregory Decker, "Pastorals, Passepieds, and Pendants: Interpreting Characterization through Aria Pairs in Handel's *Rodelinda*," *Music Theory Online* 19, no. 4 (2013). A cursory discussion can also be found in his dissertation, "The Language of Baroque Opera: Topic, Structure, and Characterization in Handel's Italian-Language Operas" (Ph.D. diss., Florida State University, 2011).

17. Allen Forte, "Secrets of Melody: Line and Design in the Songs of Cole Porter," *Musical Quarterly* 77, no. 4 (Winter 1993): 607–47.

18. Forte, "Secrets of Melody," 634.

15

Kiss Me, Kate

LYNN LAITMAN SIEBERT

No examination of Cole Porter's contributions would be complete without an assessment of his acknowledged masterpiece, *Kiss Me, Kate*. Written in 1948, it holds a unique place in Porter's career and represents the fullest flowering of his mature talent. Porter's enormous successes in the thirties were followed by setbacks in the early forties. World War II changed the theater and its audiences as it changed the world. Plagued by extreme physical pain from his damaged legs and by the frequent professional disappointments that sapped his self-esteem, dampened his spirit, and undermined his reputation, Porter described his feelings after the failure of his 1948 film score, *The Pirate*: "I felt I was out of work: that no one wanted me. 'Spread the word that I'm set to do another show,' I told my agent. He shook his head. 'Right now no one wants you, Cole,' he said. 'They think you're old fashioned.'"[1] Richard G. Hubler wrote:

> But his kingdom of gaiety was beginning to dissolve around him. He had ruled the musical world of the late twenties and thirties so long—where a Porter song was the indubitable hallmark of distinction and sophistication—that he could hardly believe in the new era. The lyrical ingenuity, the amusing *risqué*, the freshness and abandon of his works had been amazing then. Now they had to give way to a new style of musical comedy. In 1943 *Oklahoma!* of Rodgers and Hammerstein hit the boards. It was a smash from the start. Porter knew it. "The librettos are much better and the sources are much closer to the book than they used to be," he said. "They are, let us say, more musicianly." It was

undoubtedly the success of *Oklahoma!* which inspired him toward his *Kiss Me, Kate* five years later.[2]

It was in 1948, amid rumors he was "written out," that Porter composed *Kiss Me, Kate*, meeting the challenge of the "new style musical comedy" and simultaneously surpassing his past triumphs while establishing a new standard for the genre. The score's subtle refinement, depth of expression, and inventiveness, as well as the total integration of music, lyrics, and libretto, distinguish *Kiss Me, Kate* as Porter's masterwork. The genesis of the work was documented in a BBC program produced in 1970 titled *The Making of "Kiss Me, Kate."* Interviews with Porter and others revealed that Arnold Saint Subber, coproducer of *Kate*, conceived the play-within-a-play format based on *The Taming of the Shrew* after watching actors Alfred Lunt and Lynn Fontanne bicker offstage during their production of the Shakespeare classic.[3] Saint Subber approached Bella Spewack to write the script, and she suggested Porter compose the score. After several discussions with Saint Subber concerning the overall plan of the book, Porter wrote "Another Openin', Another Show," "I've Come to Wive It Wealthily in Padua," and "Where Is the Life That Late I Led?" Bella Spewack, who coauthored the book with her husband, Sam, worked closely with Porter, constantly encouraging him to forget his pain through his work. She often suggested song titles from Shakespeare's own lines and from her own contributions to the script, knowing that Porter usually built his songs around a striking textual phrase. A masterful adaptation of Shakespeare's *The Taming of the Shrew,* incorporating a parallel, contemporary love story, Bella and Sam Spewack's script was the only one in Porter's long career to match his talents, and the resulting blend is magical.

The story portrays Fred Graham, director and leading man of a second-rate acting company, and his relationship with Lilli Vanessi, his ex-wife and leading lady, in their upcoming performance of Shakespeare's *The Taming of the Shrew*. Although divorced and dating others, Lilli and Fred are still in love with one another, and their arguments, jealousies, and eventual reconciliation form the basis for the plot. The secondary romantic characters are Lois Lane and Bill Calhoun, whose plans to marry are frustrated by his compulsive gambling and her questionable fidelity. Both relationships are ingeniously paralleled in *The Taming of the Shrew*, interweaving contemporary and Shakespearean worlds through the play-within-a-play framework. Fred/Petruchio tames Lilli/Kate, thus allowing Lois/Bianca to marry Bill/Lucentio. Porter's music and lyrics consistently reflect and support *Kate*'s interweaving of two worlds: twentieth-century America and sixteenth-century Padua.

Kiss Me, Kate opened on Broadway at the New Century Theatre on 30 December 1948, with a run of 1,077 domestic performances and subsequent international performances. Produced by Arnold Saint Subber and Lemuel Ayres and choreographed by Hanya Holm, *Kate* starred Alfred Drake (Fred Graham / Petruchio), Patricia Morison (Lilli Vanessi / Kate), Lisa Kirk (Lois Lane / Bianca), and Harold Lang (Bill Calhoun / Lucentio). The music was orchestrated by Robert Russell Bennett.

Structurally, the first act of *Kate* is considerably longer than the second. The numbers included on the New York program are listed below:

ACT 1
"Another Openin', Another Show"
"Why Can't You Behave?"
"Wunderbar"
"So in Love"
"We Open in Venice"
"Dance" (end Padua Street scene)
"Tom, Dick or Harry"
"Rose Dance"
"I've Come to Wive It Wealthily in Padua"
"I Hate Men"
"Were Thine That Special Face"
"I Sing of Love"
First Act Finale, "Kiss Me, Kate"
"Tarantella"

ACT 2
"Too Darn Hot"
"Where Is the Life That Late I Led?"
"Always True to You in My Fashion"
"Bianca"
"Brush Up Your Shakespeare"
"I Am Ashamed That Women Are So Simple"
Second Act Finale, "Kiss Me, Kate"

Although not indicated on the program, an overture and an entr'acte were included in the actual production. It is not known if several instrumental numbers such as "Bianca's Theme (incidental music)," "Grand Finale," "Padua Street Scene. We Open in Venice," "Pavane (Why Can't You Behave?)," and "Petruchio's Theme" were also included, since they are neither listed on the program nor standard features of the score (as are the overture, entr'acte, etc.). Additional numbers written for *Kate* but unused in the actual production are "If Ever Married I'm," "I'm Afraid, Sweetheart, I Love You," "It Was Great Fun the First Time," "We Shall Never Be Younger," "What Does Your Servant Dream About?," and "A Woman's Career."

Since a fuller exploration of this show's complexities is beyond the scope of this chapter, the more detailed discussion below focuses on a limited selection of numbers that illustrate Porter's mature compositional skills, mastery of multiple musical styles, and incisive musical characterization. These numbers also contributed to the novel shape of the full score.

From Act 1

"Another Openin', Another Show"

"Another Openin', Another Show" is a rousing show business anthem rivaling Irving Berlin's landmark "There's No Business Like Show Business" from *Annie Get Your Gun* (1946). Sung by Fred Graham's acting troupe, it differs from Berlin's approach by omitting a verse and instead opens directly with a seventy-two-measure standard refrain: AAB (sixteen measures each), followed by A^1 (a twenty-four-measure cadential extension). With seasoned mastery, Porter forcefully propels the number via his melodic and rhythmic organization, using ascending melodic sequences to build tension in both the A and B material. The first two A sections "climax" on E♭5 in their final phrases, while the B section, providing contrast with its repeated notes, pushes farther upward to F5 (mm. 44–48). As expected, the melodic climax of the song occurs in the final A section (mm. 48–72), which organically expands the closing figure, ascending to the melodic highpoint, G5, on the final note. This sustained, highly cohesive thematic growth, which drives the melody over an unusually large range (an octave and a sixth from B♭3 to G5) and imbues the piece with a sense of inevitability, is one of the hallmarks of Porter's mature compositional style (ex. 1).

Porter's deft use of rhythm is evidenced in the two related rhythmic patterns that characterize the A and B material and utilize syncopations and beat anticipations to help generate momentum (ex. 2). The most striking rhythms, however, occur at the end of each section, where accent displacements imply triple meter, dramatically thrusting the music forward not only at the close of the "release" (mm. 45–48) but also at the close of each A statement. Through this skillful use of accent displacement at the conclusion of all four sections

EXAMPLE 1. "Another Openin', Another Show" (from *Kiss Me, Kate*), mm. 1–72.

of the song (rather than just one), Porter uses rhythm to further articulate the overall structure and amplify the propulsive drive of the song.

Rather than emulating the unique, groundbreaking model of Rodgers and Hammerstein's *Oklahoma!* opening, Porter's "Another Openin', Another Show" instead conforms to the more typical "big production number" model. However, regardless of the model employed, the concinnity of melodic, rhythmic, and harmonic elements in this opening is masterful, combining a structural and musical clarity with a sense of irresistible drive, both of which admirably fulfill the dramatic purpose of any successful opening number: to capture audience attention and generate excitement and anticipation for the show to follow.

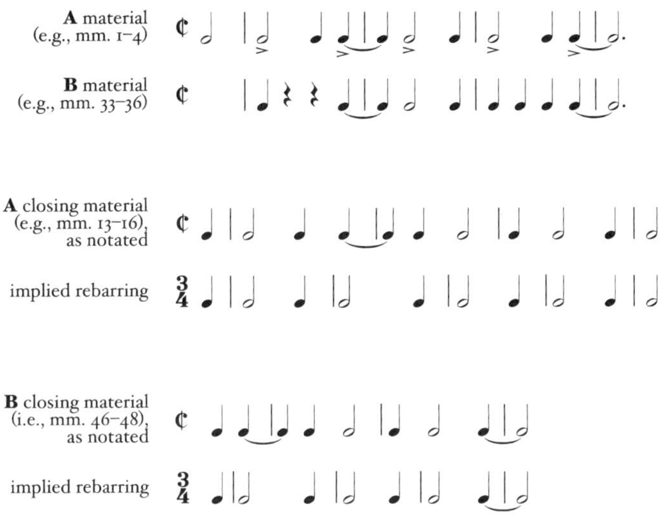

EXAMPLE 2. Rhythmic figures of "Another Openin', Another Show."

"Why Can't You Behave?"

What makes the score of *Kate* so unique is Porter's creation of a musical mirror of the play-within-a-play, reflecting the romances within Shakespearean Padua and the contemporary world. Here, with his skillful integration of music and script, Porter employs a blues idiom within his "popular" style to effectively create a twentieth-century portrait of the romance between secondary characters Lois and Bill. What better way to portray Lois's dismay at Bill's continued gambling (and resulting postponement of their wedding) than to employ harmonies replete with altered chords, chromaticism, parallelism, cross-relations, and blues coloration? The bass establishes the harmonic focus, outlining the root and/or fifth of the chord, while the upper parts chromatically enrich the bass harmonies (ex. 3). Chromatic parallelism in the penultimate phrase of each of the three subsections (mm. 12–16, 28–32, 44–48) enhances the underlying functional harmonies.

Chromaticism also pervades the melody, whose disjunct, unusual motion relies on chromatically descending lines. Lois's disappointment could not be more effectively conveyed than here, with Porter's daring leaps down a minor seventh and up a diminished seventh in the opening phrase (see ex. 3; mm. 5–6, uppermost line; also see ex. 4); these leaps embellish the G–G♭–F–E♭ descent. Similarly, the use of chromatically descending lines (C5–B♭4–A4–A♭4–G4), coupled with a mix of leaps and stepwise motion in the penultimate phrases

EXAMPLE 3. "Why Can't You Behave?" (from *Kiss Me, Kate*), mm. 5–16. Copyright © 1949 Cole Porter. Copyright renewed and assigned to John F. Wharton, Trustee of the Cole Porter Musical and Literary Property Trusts. Publication and Allied Rights Assigned to Chappell & Co., Inc. All Rights Reserved. Used by permission of Alfred Music.

of each of the three subsections, enhances the character's sense of sorrow as she pleads, "After all the things you told me / And the promises that you gave" or "Won't you turn that new leaf over . . . ?" (see ex. 3; mm. 13–16 uppermost line).[4] Such passages illustrate how Porter's deliberate choice of thematic material brilliantly captures the essence of the character and situation.

His mature mastery is also evident in his strikingly original organization of this song. Structurally inventive, the fifty-two-measure song omits any verse and varies the internal thematic disposition of the refrain, with four measures for the introduction and sixteen measures each for A, A, and A[1]. One of the few Porter songs to lack a contrasting B section, "Why Can't You Behave?" is nevertheless thematically varied. Each sixteen-measure A section is subdivided into four equal phrases (a microcosm of the AABA refrain form), providing internal contrast and rounded form within the A material. The sustained, "bluesy" opening phrase, sequentially repeated in the second phrase, also closes each A section. This musical "framing," often setting the title lyrics, is used as an organizational technique in other *Kate* songs as well ("I've Come to Wive It Wealthily in Padua," "Too Darn Hot," and "Always True to You in My Fashion"). The third phrase of each A section (a "microrelease") is subdivided into two smaller phrases, which, along with shorter rhythmic values and repeated notes, provide thematic and phrasing contrast to the surrounding material (ex. 4).

The A^1 material provides additional variety with its elaboration of the opening phrases (ex. 5). Porter manages to simultaneously build into his song internal linkages, which reinforce cohesion while preserving a sense of contrast and variety. "Why Can't You Behave?" also exemplifies Porter's thorough integration of music and script. Through his use of blues, Porter simultaneously captures Lois's emotional dismay at Bill's continued gambling and further reinforces the "vernacular," twentieth-century setting of the scene, so distinct from Shakespeare's Padua.

"So in Love"

What better way to convey the central dramatic message of the show, that although the two leading characters, Fred and Lilli, are divorced, they still love one another deeply? Porter's exquisite dramatic love ballad fulfills that purpose, using the music to encapsulate the intense emotional bond between the two main characters. One of the most beautifully crafted songs in this entire show, "So in Love" is first sung by Lilli and later reprised by Fred, and it embodies Porter's most refined compositional skills. As one might expect,

EXAMPLE 4. "Why Can't You Behave?," mm. 5–20.

EXAMPLE 5. "Why Can't You Behave?," mm. 37–40.

Porter utilizes an unusual structure, building this eighty-nine-measure song in the following distinctive fashion: introduction (twelve measures, including the refrain theme, eight measures, and the transition, four measures), A (sixteen measures), A[1] (sixteen measures), B (eight measures), B[1] (eight measures), and A[2] (twenty-nine measures). This format, however, merely supplies the framework within which Porter expands his opening germinal idea (a repeated note followed by an ascending step), constantly (and masterfully) building the range, length, and intensity of line to heighten the meaning and power of the text. In the A section, the opening idea expands intervallically, ascending from C4 to D♭5 before "falling off" to a G4 at the cadence in measures 27–28 (see ex. 6). The A[1] section repeats the procedure, pushing higher still, reaching E♭5 in

EXAMPLE 6. "So in Love" (from *Kiss Me, Kate*), mm. 13–81. Copyright © 1949 Cole Porter. Copyright renewed and assigned to John F. Wharton, Trustee of the Cole Porter Musical and Literary Property Trusts. Publication and Allied Rights Assigned to Chappell & Co., Inc. All Rights Reserved. Used by permission of Alfred Music.

the corresponding location and descending to A4 at the cadence in measures 43–44. The upward drive continues in the release, whose two phrases ascend first to E♭5 (mm. 46–47) and then to F♭5 (m. 54). The song builds in intensity, growing from the initial germinal idea, with each subsequent A phrase spanning a melodic arc that reaches slightly higher (via ever larger leaps) than its predecessor, inexorably anticipating the ultimate climactic moment in the final A² section. At this point, the urgent passion of the text ("So taunt me and hurt me, / Deceive me, desert me") climaxes on the dramatic words "I'm yours 'til I die," set to the final version of that arc melody, with the largest vocal leap (a fifth, from B4 to F5) reaching the melodic high point (F5) in measure 70 before releasing tension through the gradually descending setting of the repeated title phrase ("so in love . . . so in love") in an expanded closing section (mm. 72–89).[5] The supportive accompaniment delineates thematic areas with changes in figuration and strategic modulations.

In the release (BB¹), the shift to A♭ is reinforced by a tonic pedal (on A♭) that ceases only with the return to F minor (in mm. 56–60; ex. 7). Changes in accompanimental figuration in the A² section, such as the scalar, quarter-note triplets in the bass (mm. 66, 68) and the striking, disjunct bass line (mm.

EXAMPLE 7. "So in Love," mm. 45–60.

EXAMPLE 8. "So in Love," mm. 65–72.

69–70), accentuate the mounting intensity and the climax of the melodic line (ex. 8). As Alec Wilder states, this song is "carefully, astutely, suavely conceived; it builds, never loses intensity, indeed, is a marvel of craftsmanship."[6] Related to earlier Porter songs such as "Mysteriously," "I'm Yours," and "It Was Written in the Stars," "So in Love" far surpasses them in depth and power of expression because of its tight, highly organic construction and exquisite integration of melody, rhythm, harmony, and text. The other songs are not as tightly cohesive in their construction, nor do they convey the same quality of drama and inexorability as does "So in Love." Here, Porter is remarkably economical, utterly focused, at the height of his compositional skill, creating an emotional intensity rarely seen outside of the great lied tradition.

"I Hate Men"

Selected specifically to illustrate how Porter's shift in musical style is his means of reflecting the play-within-a-play structure, the brief and concise number "I Hate Men" at once transports the audience to sixteenth-century Padua and demonstrates Porter's skill at characterization through music. It conveys Kate's stubborn, shrewish personality through its pointed lyrics and its declamatory style. Only twenty-four measures long (repeated three times for three stanzas), "I Hate Men" adopts the following unconventional form: introduction (two measures, includes "motto"), A (four measures), B (eight measures), B[1] (eight measures), postlude (two measures). As in Petruchio's earlier song, "I've Come to Wive It Wealthily in Padua," the music is primarily a vehicle for the lyrics. Accordingly, Porter employs a motto, which sets the title phrase,

EXAMPLE 9. "I Hate Men" (from *Kiss Me, Kate*), motto. Copyright © 1949 Cole Porter. Copyright renewed and assigned to John F. Wharton, Trustee of the Cole Porter Musical and Literary Property Trusts. Publication and Allied Rights Assigned to Chappell & Co., Inc. All Rights Reserved. Used by permission of Alfred Music.

capturing Kate's personality. With three increasingly elaborate recurrences (ex. 9a, b, and c), evoking a sense of variations on a theme, this motto unifies the otherwise loose structure; delineates the beginning, middle, and end of the song; and, similar to the motto in "I've Come to Wive It Wealthily in Padua," follows a textual "punch line" ("He may have hair upon his chest but, sister, so has Lassie").[7] Through these three stanzas, Kate details her cynicism about men and, as in "I've Come to Wive It Wealthily in Padua," the remainder of "I Hate Men" incorporates patter style to project the humorously antagonistic lyrics. Consistent with the Shakespearean setting, "I Hate Men" avoids the musical characteristics of Porter's popular, "contemporary, vernacular" style (chromaticism, syncopation, etc.) in favor of even rhythms, diatonic harmonies, and Baroque-influenced Alberti bass figuration, ornamentation, and sequential development (ex. 9).

From Act 2

"Where Is the Life That Late I Led?"

A key number of act 2 that anchors the characterization of the male lead in the play-within-a-play, this substantial number further heightens appreciation of Porter's musical versatility and skill. Following the jazz-inspired, quintessentially contemporary act 2 opener, "Too Darn Hot," "Where Is the Life That Late I Led?" abruptly returns the audience from the twentieth to the sixteenth century as Shakespeare's character, Petruchio, bemoans his newly married status. In this song, Porter masterfully demonstrates his skill at characterization through music, mining musical resources from his extensive classical training and his broad travels throughout Europe to convey the forceful, virile character of Petruchio. Porter establishes the sixteenth-century Paduan setting through the use of "classical" musical style, complete with an operatic, triadic, arching vocal line. In fact, the introduction and part of the opening vocal line are identical with the corresponding passages in the first act song "I Sing of Love," which is sung by Bianca, another sixteenth-century Shakespearean character, as part of the play-within-a-play format. However, the similarity ends there, and, perhaps sensing the limitations of the earlier song, Porter continues this song in a different and extremely effective manner.

Conforming to both the verse-refrain format and the internal arrangement of verse = AA^1 and refrain = BB^1CB^2, this substantial 122-measure song nevertheless includes several internal variations, as indicated in table 1.

Consistent with the character and setting, "Where Is the Life That Late I Led?" employs a classical rather than popular musical idiom, but, in contrast to the other "classical" *Kate* songs, "Where Is the Life That Late I Led?" uses the classical idiom to underscore the humorous lyrics.[8] The dramatic recitative style of the transition gravely mocks Petruchio as he bewails his loss of freedom as a newly married man (ex. 10).

Petruchio recalls his carefree bachelor days in a rollicking $\frac{6}{8}$ refrain that resembles the Italian song "Funiculi-Funicula" (ex. 11).[9] The most humorous section, the patter, is quite unusual, avoiding the more common, rapid-fire, repeated-note patter style (reminiscent of Gilbert and Sullivan) seen earlier in Porter's music and, instead, parodying the style of an Italian boat song. It is also no accident that Porter, through his operatic vocal scoring and the actual text for the patter section, evokes a comparison of Petruchio with the Don Juan / Don Giovanni characters of operatic tradition. One cannot help referencing Leporello's famous "list" of the Don's amorous conquests in Mozart's *Don Giovanni* when Petruchio catalogs his own past loves. That Porter had an intimate knowledge of Italy is evident in his numerous textual references to Italian landmarks and his inimitable internal rhymes such as "Lisa," who gave a "new meaning to the leaning tower of Pisa," or "Lina" with "Still peddling your pizza in the streets o' Taormina?"[10] Porter further underscores the

Introduction	**Verse**			**Refrain**				**Patter**		**Refrain**				
	A	A^1	transition	B	B^1	C	B^2	D	D^1	B	B^1	C	B^2	cadential extension
10 mm.	8 mm.	8 mm.	8 mm.	8 mm.	8 mm.	8 mm.	8 mm.	8 mm.	8 mm.	8 mm.	8 mm.	8 mm.	8 mm.	8 mm.
10 mm.	24 mm.			32 mm.				16 mm.		40 mm.				

TABLE 1. Internal variations in "Where Is the Life That Late I Led?"

EXAMPLE 10. "Where Is the Life That Late I Led?" (from *Kiss Me, Kate*), mm. 27–34.

EXAMPLE 11. "Where Is the Life That Late I Led?," mm. 35–42.

humor and exaggerates the comic impact of the lyrics with overexpressive harmonies, fluctuations between major and minor, recurrent "sigh" motifs, frequent rubato and tempo changes, and the general performance marking "slowly, with over-emphasized expression" (ex. 12). A final amusing touch is provided by the operatic vocal cadenza, which adds "drama" to the final cadence (ex. 13).

EXAMPLE 12. "Where Is the Life That Late I Led?," mm. 66–81.

(*continues on next page*)

EXAMPLE 12. *(continued)*

EXAMPLE 13. "Where Is the Life That Late I Led?," mm. 110–14.

Conclusion

The 1940s were a difficult time for Porter. He contended with continuous pain from his shattered legs, professional setbacks, and a keen awareness that musical theater tastes were shifting with the impacts of World War II and the new emphasis on more substantive libretti and more universal themes than those available to Porter during his earlier years. Porter had to reimagine his approach to musical theater after four decades in the field. Yet, with the deft hand of a master, he totally integrated the Spewacks' first-rate, complex libretto's play-within-a-play format, seamlessly transitioning from dialogue into song and meticulously crafting music and lyrics to reflect every nuance of style, timeframe, and character. At the height of his powers, Porter demonstrates his ability to write music in a dizzying variety of genres, reflecting the duality of the script (two centuries, four hundred years apart), each number capturing its own moment of drama and characterization with far more economy of means and power than words alone could achieve. Textually, Porter effortlessly alternates between Shakespeare's elegant phrases and colloquial English and utilizes his classical musical training, employing organic thematic development, a rich harmonic language, and techniques such as ostinato, secondary dominants, rubato, modulations, modal ambiguity, and deceptive cadences, among others, to lend his music its internal logic, sense of cohesion, and inevitability. Clearly, Porter still draws on previous features of his style such as humorous patter sections, internal rhymes, a highly literate vocabulary, and the use of verse/refrain forms, as well as many varieties of musical styles. Yet in this score, he transcends his earlier work—perhaps in response to having such a fine libretto, perhaps due to the maturation of his skills and spirit or to his recognition that post–World War II audiences wanted "more." In *Kate* his work exhibits a new cohesiveness throughout the score, more nuanced characterizations, and a sophisticated, seamless sense of structural integrity. The emotional depth and timeless quality of the *Kiss Me, Kate* score set it apart as a personal triumph for Porter and a true marvel of musical theater.

Notes

1. Richard Hubler, *The Cole Porter Story, as Told to Richard G. Hubler* (Cleveland: World Publishing Company, 1965), 50.

2. Ibid., 90.

3. British Broadcasting Corporation, *The Making of "Kiss Me, Kate,"* 23 December 1970. A tape of this program is housed at the Cole Porter Musical and Literary Property Trusts. It includes interviews with Porter, Saint Subber, Bella and Sam Spewack, Alfred Drake, Robert Russell Bennett, and Brooks Atkinson, as well as excerpts from the original Broadway cast album.

4. Robert Kimball, *The Complete Lyrics of Cole Porter* (New York: Knopf, 1983; reprint, New York: Da Capo Press, 1992), 387.

5. Ibid., 388.

6. Alec Wilder, *American Popular Song: The Great Innovators, 1900–1950* (New York: Oxford University Press, 1972), 250.

7. Kimball, *The Complete Lyrics*, 390.

8. Ibid., 393–94.

9. I am grateful to the late H. Wiley Hitchcock for having called this similarity to my attention.

10. Kimball, *The Complete Lyrics*, 393.

PART 4

Materials for the Study of Cole Porter's Music

16

Cole Porter's Papers

MARK EDEN HOROWITZ

Until you've experienced it firsthand, it's hard to appreciate the wonders of working with someone's personal papers, particularly someone you admire. I was fortunate to be the archivist for the Cole Porter Collection in the Music Division of the Library of Congress, and what follows are some of the things that touched and fascinated me from that collection.[1]

First, some history. There are two Cole Porter Collections. There's something of a mystery about how the collection got divided, but, after some recent investigation, the truth seems clearer. In his will, Porter left his papers to Yale, his alma mater. So at some point after Porter died on 15 October 1964, his executors sent his existing papers to Yale. But in April 1962 Porter was sent a letter by Harold Spivacke, chief of the Music Division of the Library of Congress. It read in part: "Dear Mr. Porter: We have been organizing a campaign to strengthen our collection of holograph manuscripts of works of the American musical theater. As you may have heard, we already have almost all the extant manuscripts of Victor Herbert, George Gershwin, Sigmund Romberg, Richard Rodgers, Oscar Hammerstein and others. We would be highly honored if we could add the manuscripts of Cole Porter to that list." Within six months, the first of four shipments of Porter's papers arrived at the Library. That shipment included manuscripts for one of Porter's first shows, *See America First*, and one of his last, *Kiss Me, Kate*. The final shipment arrived in September 1964, a month and a half before he died. That shipment included manuscripts for *Silk Stockings*, *High Society*, and *Les Girls*.

There are differing opinions, but here's what I think happened. In 1927, when Yale fired Monty Woolley as director of undergraduate dramatics, Porter was furious at the institution's ill treatment of his close friend. Thus began an estrangement that lasted several decades. Apparently, things changed in 1960, when Yale awarded Porter an honorary doctorate. To accommodate Porter's difficulty in traveling, the university did the unprecedented and presented the award off-campus in Porter's Waldorf Towers' apartment. By all accounts, Porter was extraordinarily moved by this gesture, and, presumably, it was shortly thereafter that he placed the bequest in his will (we don't know the date, as the details of Porter's will are closely held by the estate). My guess is that when Porter was approached by the Library two years later, he had forgotten about the bequest (though it is odd that his attorney wouldn't have picked up on it). Perhaps he meant to change his will to leave the remainder of his papers to the Library. Perhaps if he'd remembered his bequest he wouldn't have given the Library what he did. Though the collection at Yale is significantly larger than the collection at the Library, much of what's at the Library is, as they say, *cherce*.

The Library's Porter collection is oddly divided. Its most important contents are from very early in Porter's career, and then—with a few odd bits and pieces between—it jumps to Porter's last four Broadway musicals: *Kiss Me, Kate*, *Out of This World*, *Can-Can*, and *Silk Stockings*, plus a bit of *High Society* and *Les Girls*. Without question, the most fascinating and important materials are Porter's lyric sketches for those four final Broadway shows. But before we get to them . . .

The Student

There are about thirty pages of musical exercises in Porter's hand—two- and four-part harmonizations, exercises in voice leading, a fugue, and so on. Some of them may be from his studies at Harvard starting in the fall of 1914 or from his private studies with Pietro Yon shortly thereafter, and some may come from his studies at the Schola Cantorum in Paris in 1920—particularly those with notes in French. I'm told that some of his exercises would have likely met with disapproval—flirting with the odd blue note, or daring a parallel fifth.

It's good to know that Porter studied such things, but what I find most interesting are his doodles. Was Porter bored in class? Did he take breaks to clear his mind while working out homework exercises? Whatever it was, many pages have margins that are decorated with drawings. Mostly drawings of people. Mostly women. Women in hats—cloches and the like. There's an air of the flapper about many of them. There are a couple of men whom one might describe as louche. There's also a suggestion of what might be an Apache dancer here and there. Who imagined this side of Porter? And there's one page where he writes his name at the top with the initials bold and stylized. A bit of ego? One almost hopes that most of this is from the earlier period, as he was nearly thirty years old when he was at the Schola Cantorum. Whatever the truth, they humanize Porter.

Early Years

The largest group of music manuscripts we have in Porter's hand are for his first professional show, *See America First* (1916). There are over thirty songs and numbers represented—surely many more than the show could have included (a typical musical includes twelve to fifteen numbers). In some cases there are two versions of a song, including of the title number. Porter's "fair copies" are clear and neat. In addition, there are some forty leaves of sketches, one of the richest examples I know of Porter's early compositional process.

While the lyrics for all the songs are reproduced in Robert Kimball's *Complete Lyrics of Cole Porter*, most of the music remains unrecorded and largely forgotten. Porter himself made clear his admiration for Gilbert and Sullivan. But while the influence of W. S. Gilbert's lyrics is clear, I see less influence from Sullivan, particularly among the sketches.

In fact, to my ear, Porter has not yet found his musical voice, though there are hints. Much of the music sounds fairly generic of its time, but then there are sudden moments of more daring bits—an unusual leap here, a more daring harmony there. It's a bit like early Jerome Kern (also before I think he found his mature voice), but with more flirtations with ragtime, jazz, and blues.

Music Manuscripts

One unexplained mystery is the lack of music manuscripts in Porter's hand. Other than the previously mentioned early works, there are very few in the Library's collections. The Yale Collection has more, but even there they are few and far between and in some instances include only photocopies of manuscripts (at least according to the finding aid). What happened to them? The fact that they are described as photocopies makes one wonder all the more, as it suggests the manuscripts existed at least into the 1960s (the photocopier was introduced in 1959). Aside from that mystery, it seems likely that he gave his manuscripts to a copyist, arranger, and/or publisher to prepare their versions and simply didn't ask for or want the manuscripts back. There would have been no need, however, to turn lyric sketches over to anyone. I've also been told that he wasn't as much of a saver as one might hope and expect.

Speaking of copyists, editors, and publishers, it's important to bring up Albert "Doc" Sirmay. Sirmay seems largely forgotten and unappreciated, but Porter clearly respected him, and one might legitimately call him a collaborator with Porter. A composer in his own right, Sirmay became music director of the Chappell music publishing company and worked closely with their roster of composers, including Kern, Gershwin, and especially Porter. Many of the published piano-vocal scores of standards of the mid-1920s to the mid-1960s owe their elegance, clarity, and playability to Sirmay. He could convert a lead sheet to a richly accompanied song; he could wed melodies to accompaniment figures to make the totality of a song playable on the piano; he was a master of chord voicings. Many of the Porter music manuscripts in both the Library and Yale collections are in Sirmay's clear and flowing hand.

The Times, the World

There are unexpected items that suggest all manner of things about the times and the world Porter inhabited and some clues to how he thought. For example, Porter's audition notes for *Out of This World* are typed, three-hole punched, and bound with string. On the cover there's a note: "Under 'N'—*Negroes* for part of HATTIE in *Kiss Me, Kate*." Next to the name of auditioner Doretta Morrow is written: "Mezzo but can high G. Blonde, beautiful face. Understudy for Helen or ensemble." The next year Morrow originated the role of Tuptim in *The King and I*. My favorite audition note is next to Mel Torme's name: "5 ft. 7 1/2—small voice / stylist / moves well."[2]

For opening night of *Out of This World* there's a carbon of a letter and list from Porter's secretary to Mr. Phillips at Goldfarb's Flower Shop: "Mr. Porter would like you to send flowers to the persons whose names are listed on the enclosed sheet. . . . These are all to be long-stemmed RED ROSES—2 dozen to each person except Charlotte Greenwood, who is to get 4 dozen. I know that you will take care of this order in your usual excellent fashion. . . . Please enclose Mr. Porter's card with each order. . . . I shall shortly send you a Christmas order also." The six women listed, in addition to Charlotte Greenwood, include Priscilla Gillette, Hanya Holm (choreographer), and Agnes De Mille (director).

Of course, there are also the various lists for who gets opening night tickets, where they should sit, and who gets invited to the party. These lists are peopled with names like Elsa Maxwell, Countess di Zoppola, and Jack Warner.

Among Porter's clippings is one dated 16 July 1953. *Can-Can* has opened, and he's in Hollywood to look in on the film being made of *Kiss Me, Kate*. The clipping includes the following: "I just get burned at the critics. Every time I write songs for a show, they say 'the music is not up to Mr. Porter's standard.' One time my wife and I got so peeved that we decided to find out what my 'standard' was. She keeps vast books of clippings and we went back to my first Broadway show, which I did with a friend of mine from Harvard. The critics then said, 'these boys should leave New York and never come back!'" I shared this quote with a major musical theater songwriter of today; his response, "It makes me feel less lonely."

Research and Collaboration

This leads us to another quote from the same clipping: "[Porter] admitted that shows are harder to compose these days and he good-naturedly blames that on Rodgers and Hammerstein. 'It was easier to turn out tunes in the old days,' he sighed. 'But then Rodgers and Hammerstein began writing great shows in which the songs were related to the plot. Now you can't just write a song and throw it into the show in any spot.'"

The following is speculation, but speculate I shall. Although expectations for musicals had changed because of the Rodgers and Hammerstein revolution, I think it's fair to say that all of Porter's late shows are still musical comedies. The songs may relate more directly to the plot, but the songs are mostly still entertainments—respites—rather than dramatically necessary and dense with subtext. Seduction excepted. But one possible effect is that with *Can-Can* and *Silk Stockings*, Porter's papers for the first time (I've seen) also include research materials. Songs are no longer just informed by Porter's worldview—admittedly, educated and worldly—but now include appropriate details from specific sources. As for Hammerstein being the model of this evolution, his own papers for *Carousel* are full of research on the flora and fauna of New England, the role of women, how cotton mills worked, phrases and pronunciation common to Maine, history, and even recipes for clam bakes.

In the case of Porter, *Can-Can* is particularly rich in research materials. There are typed and detailed précis on over a dozen topics, the longest at nineteen pages. Subjects include Jane Avril (with extracts from her memoirs); Senator Beranger; the jury system in France; the first national congress against pornography; society manners in 1900; random notes on the law; and occupations for women 1890–95. It's fascinating stuff. There are some markings by Porter, but there's no indication of who compiled this material. It's also clear that Porter actually used at least some of it while he wrote his lyrics. Somehow one can't imagine that Porter would have had similar research prepared on ocean liner operations, gangster behavior, or evangelical practices when writing *Anything Goes* (though, to be fair, I suspect he had to have done some research in order to have included all the body parts cataloged in "The Physician" from 1933's *Nymph Errant*).

Though I feel guilty taking the space here, I think it's instructive to have an example. The following excerpt not only gives a wonderful sense but, for those who know *Can-Can*, is fascinatingly revealing of the show's source:

> Senator Berenger brought up the question of indecent balls in the Senate. This came up as a result of two highly successful dances in Montmartre, the Quat's Arts and Fin de Siecle. Henri Guillaume, one of the organizers, a painter whose morality by [*sic*] beyond doubt, was dragged into court, together with a group of girls who starred in the balls. The theme of the first ball was the Cortege of Cleopatra; the impersonator of the Egyptian queen was a girl known as Sarah Brown (Marie Rayer was her real name); beside her, there was Emma Denne, Yvonne (Clarisse Roger), and Manon (Josephine Lavol), the latter the most beautiful model in Paris. The charge against them was disorderly conduct. One of the accusation's chief witnesses was La Goulue. She gave a moving account of her innocent attire, her shocked surprise at the shameless horde of women who invaded the planks of her stage. She explained that she lifted her skirts slightly and that too only so as to keep in tune with [the] milieu where, that night, her chastity suffered martyrdom. The suit was brought by Mr. Berenger, the miscreants were found guilty but sentence was suspended because, the attorney remarked; "Their records are clean and also in the circumstances, they surrendered to the general tendency of the world of painters and artists where they worked as models."

But the change in the creation of musicals that is arguably more important than research is the level of collaboration among the creators. It's been said of *Oklahoma!* that it's not only the integration of the score and script that was revolutionary but that the choreography looked like the costumes, looked like the set, sounded like the orchestrations, and so on. Porter doesn't seem to have quite been able to change his approach as dramatically as the times began calling for. It's particularly disappointing given at least one thrilling possibility. There's the *potential* for a song from *Can-Can* that's brilliantly suggested and described in a letter to Porter from the show's librettist, Abe Burrows, dated 8 July 1952:

> In regard TO THINK THAT THIS COULD HAPPEN TO ME, I am not quite sure of the situation that will surround it, but I am fairly certain that there will be a situation that such a song would fit.
>
> Our hero is going to fall in love with the girl and he is going to be astounded by this fact. I should think it would be a good idea if the lyrics would contain, in addition to the hero's happiness, something about the fact that he is surprised by all this. This is a fellow who never thought he would fall in love with a woman, never thought he was capable of emotions like that. He was sure that his only interest was the law.
>
> Incidentally, I have developed a little sidelight on this fellow's character I would like to tell you about: I think the key is the fact that he is a judge at the age of, let's say, 37, certainly no more than 40. A man who becomes a judge at this age must have really worked hard. He is a sort of legal Wunderkind, and he must have had time for very little else besides the law in his life. Women would have been a distraction; normal emotions would have been a bother. Consequently, there is a whole segment missing from our hero's life, and, therefore, he has some very unFrench lack of interest in all the amenities and delights of life.
>
> Consequently, when love hits this man, his reactions will be slightly atomic. He'll be frightened, happy, chilled, warmed, ecstatic, puzzled, upset, shocked and delighted. This sounds like the love reaction of a schoolboy, but it's my theory that our hero's emotional growth stopped temporarily the day he entered school.
>
> Anyway, you can see from all this that TO THINK THAT THIS COULD HAPPEN TO ME is actually what our hero would say. However, I do think you are right in not wanting to rush into doing the lyrics until you know a little more about the situation.
>
> As to whether he sings it to the girl or alone, I couldn't say anything about that either as yet. Of course, that would affect the song very much. If she is present, I guess he wouldn't expose his thrilled bewilderment as much as if he were alone.

If ever a letter should have inspired a spectacular song, this is that letter. Unfortunately, the song—or, rather, *songs*—that Porter wrote is among the most pedestrian of his career. There are two unused and incomplete versions of a song—"To Think That This Could Happen to Me" and "Am I in Love?"—and then a complete song that ended up in the show, "I Am in Love." While the song Porter wrote for the spot would have been perfectly acceptable in the

1930s, the character who sings it comes across as generic, the song doesn't really go anywhere, and there are no details specific to the time, the place, or the situation. Here's a portion:

> I am dejected,
> I am depressed,
> Yet resurrected
> And sailing the crest.
> Why this elation,
> Mixed with deflation?
> What explanation?
> I am in love!

It deteriorates from there.

In his next show, *Silk Stockings* (1955), there is evidence of a collaboration with a librettist that did have a more direct influence on a final song, but here both the input and the result are of lesser, though funnier, import. Among the show's librettists was the legendary George S. Kaufman. There are two letters from Kaufman in which he gives very specific suggestions for—well, here's how he puts it: "Here is the revised scene leading to the song for the three boys. And here are at least some subjects for the Siberia song." I won't quote the entire letters, but here are some of the lines he provides:

> There is great skating all year round. You can cut figure eights and your throat.
> You get rid of your in-laws.
> Take along plenty of anti-freeze.
> You never burn your tongue on the soup, because it's always cold.
> Where all day the sun shines bright. And I'm also told that it shines all night.
> Anything about sighing for Siberia?
> You get free salt with your beer.
> You never run out of ice at your cocktail parties.

It's hard to believe he was one of the great humorists of the twentieth century. But he did indeed inspire Porter, who used and improved several of Kaufman's suggestions: "When it's cocktail time 'twill be so nice / Just to know you'll not have to phone for ice" and "Where they say all day the sun shines bright, / And they also say that it shines all night." Notice how he gets the inner rhyme of "day" and "say." And "Since the big salt mines will be so near, / We can all have salt to put in our beer." Which clarifies where the salt comes from. He also takes advantage of the "sighing for Siberia" but in a way that isn't clear in just reading the lyric. Porter's sketches also reveal that he tried to craft some other of Kaufman's notions into lyrics but gave up. He tried desperately to make something of the "anti-freeze." Manipulating the options somewhat, the best version might be: "We can motor far with perfect ease / If the boss is not anti anti-freeze."

The research for *Silk Stockings* is of a far less serious nature than that for *Can-Can*, primarily relating to perfume. All to inform a song called "The Perfume of Love," which was incomplete and unused. But if anyone wants to complete such a song, the material is all here waiting. There's the pamphlet, *McCall's Perfume Guide*. (Did you know that "perfume is the fourth dimension of your personality. It gives you a lift when you wear it, brings pleasure to those you meet. It gives you a deep sense of self-confidence in your own womanliness.") And there's a four-page handwritten letter to Porter from a Gladys H. Givin of Bullock's, Westwood Village, Los Angeles. She lists over eighty perfumes and helpfully indicates which ones have matching colognes and toilet waters. Their names are mostly French and leave one rather breathless. I particularly like the sequence: Narcisse Noir, Arpège, Prétexte, Scandal, Rumeur, and My Sin . . . and was a tad shocked by Russian Leather.

Lyric Writing

While there's been some discussion of it above, the most fascinating materials in the collections are Porter's lyric sketches and how much they reveal of his process. I've examined the sketches of lyricists such as Irving Berlin, Ira Gershwin, Oscar Hammerstein, and Stephen Sondheim. All of them have things in common. They all make lists, be they rhymes, synonyms, or nouns appropriate for a given song. They all consider alternate words in a given line—verbs and adjectives that might have slightly different colors or number of syllables or that just might be more appropriate in a given line. In "My Favorite Things," Hammerstein considers "snowflakes that stay/sit/rest on my nose or eyelashes."

But there are also differences. Of all I've seen, Porter is probably the neatest, the most organized, the most consistent. His handwriting is always regular. He maintains layers of indentations as appropriate. He neatly crosses out lines or words he's abandoned. I've tried to come up with an analogy to a profession that most closely equates, considering cabinetmaker, gem cutter, mosaicist (if that's even a word), and I finally settled on stonemason—with Porter's stones being lines, couplets, and quatrains. He identifies a spot and selects a stone, puts it in place, tries another, then another. He chips at one here and there to make it fit perfectly. And it's not only the size and shape but also the color and texture that must be right. And the balance of stones over the whole wall.

While "stonemason" suggests Porter's effort and craft, it doesn't fit the grace and elegance. And, less flattering, the prissiness.

For more complicated songs, there may be a dozen to three dozen pages of lyric sketches written in pencil in a neat but odd hand. (His *f*'s tend to be simple vertical lines; his *e*'s are like *m*'s turned on their sides.) Occasional couplets or quatrains that are written on smallish note pages of hotel stationery may be intermingled with his typical lined paper. His lists, often of rhymes, are wonderful, but one of my favorites is the following sequence of what he calls "synonisms" (great word) that fill a page. It's for the song "I Hate Men" from *Kiss Me, Kate* (I've tried to replicate his indentations as closely as possible):

I HATE MEN
(Synonisms of *hate*)

I dislike	flinch
disrelish	fly or flee from
object to	scamper
do not care for	abominate
have an aversion to	
no taste for	
no stomach for	
shun	
eschew	
recoil from	
cannot bear	enrage
abide	irritate
endure	vex
shrug my shoulders	irk
shudder at	tire
loathe	annoy
abominate	they nauseate me
detest	repel
abhor	sicken
shun	disgust
oppose	revolt
elude	offend
dodge	
recoil	

But it's the crafting of individual lines that becomes so extraordinary. You can see the thought processes—how one idea leads to another. How once he has a notion he'll try several different ways to express it, including changing the order of words; or once he has a line, rewriting it so it includes an inner rhyme. One of my favorite examples is this page—one of many pages—for just one section of "Always True to You in My Fashion" from *Kiss Me, Kate*. Again, this is an approximation; some words and phrases are written above those that are crossed out; some lines are inserted with arrows; *x*'s seem to indicate favorite lines (I'm told the Clifton Webb / diapers apposition at the end is a reference to the film *Sitting Pretty*, where he played an acid-tongued eccentric who's forced to become a babysitter):

FASHION

xI'm so crazy , I confess
xFor a brand new evening dress
That I guess I'd acquiesce ____ to
And I could be very good to Mainbocher
xI'd undress, ~~well~~ much more ~~or~~ than less for "
I confess I might undress " "
But I'm say yes to " "
Though my agent says I could
Play in pictures and be good,
A producer says I could
Be a star in Hollywood
~~I'd be~~ When you're good in Hollywood ~~just~~ crime doesn't pay
So I'm If I'm good " " then crime does pay

xI've a sexy beau called "Tex"
And he only talks of sex
And he's happiest when he necks
So I let him think that sex
Isn't his checks + not his sex are/is here to stay
And he tells me dear that sex is here to stay
And his sex controls his checks
And I've always said that sex is here to
And I know, my dear that " " "
xAnd he gives me pretty checks
xSo I always tell him sex is here to stay
I should love like ev'rey deb,
To be starred with Clifton Webb
~~But with Clifton diapers shiftin/liftin' I wont play~~
~~But when Clifton richest fifty " "~~
~~with dypers on the ebb~~

It's also worth remembering that Porter is one of those extraordinary musical theater songwriters who is both a composer and a lyricist. Often described as a rare combination, it strikes me as surprisingly common: George M. Cohan, Irving Berlin, Noël Coward, Frank Loesser, Stephen Sondheim, Harold Rome, Jerry Herman, and others. Of that list, Porter and Sondheim are the most trained and sophisticated composers. As a result, their lyric sketches share another attribute: many of the lyrics include musical indications, usually vertical lines between words that suggest where the measures might come, indications of which syllables might be accented, and rhythmic values above words. Perhaps surprising to some, this suggests that when the lyric comes first, it initially inspires a rhythm, with the melody to come later, though both Porter and Sondheim are musically best known for their exquisite tunes with dense and surprising harmonies. (This early focus on rhythm seems fairly typical; there are also examples of Richard Rodgers being supplied lyrics by Oscar Hammerstein, and Rodgers marks some of them with rhythmic possibilities in exactly the same way, and Jerry Herman has discussed that he conceives his songs while walking to get a visceral sense of their tempo and meter.)

Conclusion

There is no conclusion, as Porter's manuscripts and papers are a near-inexhaustible source for research and fascination. One can get lost in the craft, the detail, the life, and the history. No, not lost, seduced and fascinated by. And one thing always leads to another. What surprises me more than anything is how few people take advantage of papers like Porter's that were saved and donated and are now available for study. Take this chapter as a challenge and an invitation.

Notes

1. The seed for this chapter came from a segment of an article by the author titled "The Craft of Making Art," *Studies in Musical Theatre* 7, no. 2.

2. This is reminiscent of the purported report from Fred Astaire's RKO screen test: "Can't sing. Can't act. Balding. Can dance a little."

17

Secondary Materials and the Study of Cole Porter

GREGORY J. DECKER

This chapter comprises an annotated list of secondary sources whose major focus is either Cole Porter and his music or subjects closely related to his life and works. The bibliography will be of use to researchers who study Porter, his music, and the historical and cultural milieu in which he worked; it will also be of interest to those wishing to grasp the state of the field, as it serves as a general overview of the available research. I have organized the sources into six categories: biography; critical interpretation; musical construction; studies of particular songs, shows, or lyrics; contextual sources; and encyclopedic sources. Several sources that do not fall easily into any of these groupings have been listed separately.

Readers will likely not be surprised to see that the majority of the sources surveyed (about 75 percent) were written in 1990 or later, since the past twenty-five years have seen a great increase in scholarly interest in popular music. This time period has also seen the rise of the "new musicology," which is no longer new and which has provided space for contextualized critical studies such as those found in sections 2 and 5 of this bibliography. The majority of monographs and other books about Porter specifically are primarily biographical, presenting narratives of his career and sometimes his personal life. The significant exception in this regard is the work of Allen Forte, who analyzes music structure in Porter's songs and its intersection with textual readings (see section 3). It seems clear that there is much room for sustained academic inquiry into the music of Cole Porter and American popular song more generally.

The bibliography below includes 101 annotated entries, almost all of which are available at libraries across the United States. (There are only two exceptions to this—see Smith 1984, section 4; and Cooney 1980, section 7.) About two-thirds of the sources are books or dissertations, while articles and separate book chapters constitute the last third. Of course, there are many sources that could fall into several of the above-named categories; in these cases, I have tried to place the source according to the spirit of its main focus. Not included in this bibliography are resources written in a language other than English, published music by Cole Porter, anthologies that include his music, and items deemed too broad or derivative to be of use to most readers; otherwise, it is a comprehensive account of relevant sources as of May 2013.

Section 1: Biography

Many of the materials included in this chapter contain at least a cursory sketch of Porter's life and work. The sources in this section, however, are focused primarily on chronicling his personal and professional life. Three major biographies about Porter were published in the 1960s, not long after his death in 1964 (Eells 1967; Ewen 1965; and Hubler 1965); all three are understandably dated, though at least two of these authors knew Porter personally, and their respective narratives are based on those personal relationships. Charles Schwartz's 1977 biography is more detailed than the first three and is the first major source to deal directly with the influence of Porter's homosexuality on his relationships and his career. The most recent biography and the most carefully researched is William McBrien's, published in 1998. Other sources in this list are either less robust (often based on one or more of the major sources), or they deal with the lives of other artists in addition to Porter.

Citron, Stephen. *Noel and Cole: The Sophisticates*. New York: Oxford University Press, 1993. Reprint with new introduction, Milwaukee: Hal Leonard, 2005.

Chronological biographies of Noël Coward and Cole Porter meant to highlight these figures as two major artistic voices of the same generation; information in the biographies is primarily professional but is sometimes contextualized with personal information. The author offers his opinions and commentary, especially with regard to particular works.

Eells, George. *The Life That Late He Led: A Biography of Cole Porter*. New York: G. P. Putnam's Sons, 1967.

This biography is chronological and provides an account of Porter's professional life written by a personal friend; some notes regarding the reception of his works are included, as well as a list of stage works and songs.

Ewen, David. *The Cole Porter Story*. New York: Holt, Rinehart & Winston, 1965.

Very similar to Eells (1967) in the type of information included. An appendix provides a list of original stage and film productions of his shows, casts, songs; a list of his "greatest songs"; and a small discography.

Grafton, David. *Red, Hot and Rich! An Oral History of Cole Porter*. New York: Stein & Day, 1987.

A chronological biography enlivened by the number of quotes from Porter, people he knew and worked with, and contemporaneous critics. The reader should note, though, that Grafton discusses Porter's homosexuality in a condescending light, calling it a "perversion."

Howard, Jean. *Travels with Cole Porter*. New York: Harry N. Abrams, 1991.

Visually oriented book chronicling the friendship between Porter and Howard and her experiences traveling with Porter.

Hubler, Richard. *The Cole Porter Story, as Told to Richard G. Hubler*. Cleveland: World Publishing Company, 1965.

Mostly a chronicle of Porter's career but with some information regarding his early life. The author was a friend of Porter's, and the chapters stem from interviews with the composer. The narrative mixes third- and first-person perspectives (as if told by Porter himself).

Lahr, John. "King Cole: The Not So Merry Soul of Cole Porter." *New Yorker*, 12–19 July 2004, 100–104.

A review of the film *De-Lovely* (which recounts Porter's life and relationship with his wife) that includes contextualizing information, especially about the hardship Porter endured after his riding accident and how his life and homosexuality influenced his writing style.

McBrien, William. *Cole Porter: A Biography*. New York: Alfred A. Knopf, 1998.

The most complete and well-researched biography available. The author intertwines Porter's personal and professional life chronologically and cites sources, interviews, and correspondences. Porter's sexual orientation is dealt with openly and respectfully.

Schwartz, Charles. *Cole Porter*. New York: Dial Press, 1977.

A more open, mature chronological biography than those that were published prior to 1977. This book marks the first biography to incorporate Porter's homosexuality as an important aspect of his life and work. It was considered the standard biography until McBrien (1998).

Section 2: Interpretation and Critical Approaches

The resources in this section all link structural, textual, or dramatic devices in Cole Porter's works to biographical or broader cultural interpretation. Examinations along these same lines but with both a broader historical component and an inquiry into works by composers or artists other than Porter can be found in section 5. A number of the following essays take Porter's sexuality into account and therefore engage with queer theory in analyzing his works. Others employ feminist criticism or investigate the ways in which Porter depicted social class and interactions among different classes. Several sources produce more general semiotic readings through examinations of musical structure and drama. Note that Berry (1999) and Buchler (2008) do not analyze Porter's music specifically, but both authors mention that their analytical approaches may be applicable to his output.

Bergeron, Katherine. "Uncovering Cole." *Repercussions* 4, no. 2 (1995): 10–29.

A historical framing and critical review of the 1990 album *Red Hot + Blue* and how musical style and visual cues recontextualize Porter's songs.

Berry, David Carson. "Dynamic Introductions: The Affective Role of Melodic Ascent and Other Linear Devices in Selected Song Verses of Irving Berlin." *Intégral* 13 (1999): 1–62.

Mentions that Porter's music can be profitably analyzed using Schenkerian analysis and the methodology delineated by the author for songs written by Irving Berlin.

Block, Geoffrey. *Enchanted Evenings: The Broadway Musical from "Show Boat" to Sondheim and Lloyd Webber.* 2nd ed. 1997. Reprint, New York: Oxford University Press, 2009.

Author compiles history and critical reception for a number of musicals by various composers; for each show, he also discusses the content with respect to theatrical and cultural contexts more broadly and examines some of the music analytically, offering brief hermeneutic interpretations. He states in the introduction that he wishes to address with specific examples broader elements and shifts in the Broadway show, especially the "song-and-dance vs. integrated" issue and the perceived tension between selling tickets and "artistic integrity" (asserting that all combinations have value). The two Porter shows are *Anything Goes* and *Kiss Me, Kate*.

Buchler, Michael. "Modulation as a Dramatic Agent in Frank Loesser's Broadway Songs." *Music Theory Spectrum* 30, no. 1 (2008): 35–60.

Buchler mentions Porter as a fellow songwriter and lyricist, and he states that a particular nonfunctional sequence in Loesser's "My Time of Day" from *Guys and Dolls* is also found in Porter's "Love for Sale." The analytical concepts he details may be useful for those studying Porter's music.

Clum, John M. *Something for the Boys: Musical Theater and Gay Culture*. New York: St. Martin's Press, 1999.

Monograph regarding the intersections between American/British musical theater and gay culture, particularly gay male culture between the end of World War I and the 1970s. Each chapter is an essay that explores different aspects of this relationship. Porter and shows are mentioned throughout the book, but pages 69–75 specifically focus on queer interpretation of his lyrics.

Fearnow, Mark. "Let's Do It: The Layered Life of Cole Porter." In *Staging Desire: Queer Readings of American Theater History*, edited by Kim Marra and Robert A. Schanke. Ann Arbor: University of Michigan Press, 2002.

Author discusses Porter's "dual life" as public heterosexual and private homosexual and how these "layers" relate to double readings of his song lyrics (e.g., "baby, I'm the bottom, you're the top!").

Ford, Andrew. "Eminem and Cole Porter." In *Undue Noise: Words about Music*. Sydney, Australia: ABC Books, 2002.

A brief comparison of the lyric-writing prowess of contemporary rapper Eminem and Porter, in which the author concludes that the words of both have "a brilliant artifice" in their virtuoso rhyming.

Greher, Gena R. "Night & Day: Cole Porter, Hip Hop, Their Shared Sensibilities and Their Teachable Moments." *College Music Symposium* 49–50 (2009–10): 158–63.

Author briefly considers how music educators might compare the creative wordplay and inclusion of high- and low-style elements in Porter's songs to those in hip hop today.

Knapp, Raymond. "'How Great Thy Charm, Thy Sway How Excellent!': Tracing Gilbert and Sullivan's Legacy in the American Musical." In *The Cambridge Companion to Gilbert and Sullivan*, edited by David Eden and Meinhard Saremba. Cambridge: Cambridge University Press, 2009.

Briefly explores the musical, poetic, and dramatic legacy of Gilbert and Sullivan shows in twentieth-century American musicals, including text setting and "images of Englishness" in Porter's *Anything Goes*. The author specifically mentions *H.M.S. Pinafore* in this context.

Lawson-Peebles, Robert. "Brush Up Your Shakespeare: The Case of *Kiss Me, Kate*." In *Approaches to the American Musical*, edited by Robert Lawson-Peebles. Exeter: University of Exeter Press, 1996.

Essay explores a number of contrasts that create meaning with respect to Shakespeare's plays in the film version of *Kiss Me, Kate*, including high society vs. low society, Shakespearean texts vs. American vernacular, and onstage action vs. real-life action. Another essay in the collection ("Sondheim and the Art That Has No Name" by Stephen Banfield) briefly analyzes meter, rhyme, and the use of punctuated silence in Porter's "You're the Top."

Mordden, Ethan. "A Critic at Large: Rock and Cole." *New Yorker*, 28 October 1991, 91–113.

Article commemorating Porter's centennial year. It includes a chronology of his professional life but also commentary on Porter's music, lyrics, and style. The author demonstrates that Porter's lyrics are subversive to the dominant patriarchal system and contain double entendres regarding sex and homosexuality; his music, Mordden asserts, uses rhythm and melody to embody sex and sex appeal. The final section of the article centers on the *Red Hot + Blue* album, contending that this work brings together America's two disparate pop music traditions (rock and Broadway).

Morella, Joe, and George Mazzei. *Genius and Lust: The Creativity and Sexuality of Cole Porter and Noel Coward*. New York: Carroll & Graf Publishers, 1995.

Explores Porter's and Coward's lives and work in terms of their homosexuality, especially text, characters, and dramatic situations.

Pessen, Edward. "The Great Songwriters of Tin Pan Alley's Golden Age: A Social, Occupational, and Aesthetic Inquiry." *American Music* 3, no. 2 (1985): 180–97.

Explores the influences of social class, education, nationality, identity, and location (i.e., New York) on the work of Tin Pan Alley composers from the 1920s to the 1940s.

Schleifer, Ronald. "What Is This Thing Called Love? Cole Porter and the Rhythms of Desire." *Criticism* 41, no. 1 (Winter 1999): 7–23. Reprinted in *Modernism and Popular Music*, by Ronald Schleifer. Cambridge: Cambridge University Press, 2011.

An examination of Porter's lyrics, use of rhyme, and syncopation (textual and musical) in select pieces within the context of modernism in the first half of the twentieth century. The author posits that these effects create a sense of "moving around," or "homelessness in his music."

Severn, John R. "A (White) Woman's (Ironic) Places in *Kiss Me, Kate* and Post-war America." *Studies in Musical Theatre* 6, no. 2 (2012): 173–86.

Demonstrates that contrasts between the "offstage" and "onstage" storylines in Porter's show reveal divergent strategies for "negotiating [women's places] in post-war America" (174). The analysis focuses mostly on plot and lyrics but extends to music in a few instances.

Stout, Janis P. *Coming Out of War: Poetry, Grieving, and the Culture of the World Wars*. Tuscaloosa: University of Alabama Press, 2005.

Book explores poetry and song in the period from World War I through World War II from a variety of angles; author briefly discusses Porter's "Ev'ry Time We Say Goodbye" and "When I Had a Uniform On."

Swain, Joseph P. *The Broadway Musical: A Critical and Musical Survey*. 2nd ed. 1990. Reprint, Lanham, MD: Scarecrow Press, 2002.

Author states that his purpose in the book is to "survey the achievements of [musical theater's] music as a dramatic element," and each chapter is an analysis of a different show. There are numerous mentions of Porter's work, but one chapter is devoted entirely to *Kiss Me, Kate*. The analyses examine text, drama, and music.

Ullestad, Neal. "Diverse Rock Rebellions Subvert Mass Media Hegemony." In *Rockin' the Boat: Mass Music and Mass Movements*, edited by Reebee Garofalo. Boston: South End, 1992.

Author cites and discusses the album *Red Hot + Blue* (1990) to benefit AIDS research as part of a string of subversive acts, shows, and songs featuring pop/rock artists at the time. The author asserts that the juxtaposition of older recordings and videos with new ones creates a political statement that Porter's songs did not originally contain.

Section 3: Composition and Musical Construction

Surprisingly little has been written that has a specific focus on Porter's method of composition and musical construction. The majority of sources make only passing reference to this area of inquiry and examine instead his life, lyrics, and cultural contributions. Allen Forte has been the sole major contributor to the study of musical structure in Porter's songs, with several other authors offering case studies or methodologies for analysis that could apply to Porter's music.

Choi, Jaehee. "They Do That Voodoo So Well: A Critical Examination of Selected Songs of the Founders of the American Standard Songbook." Ph.D. diss., University of Southern California, 2007.

An investigation of the musical construction and text of songs by Jerome Kern, Irving Berlin, George Gershwin, and Cole Porter. The analyses describe each song's construction in terms of motive, counterpoint, and text; hermeneutic readings of text-music relationships are offered. Examined songs by Porter include "What Is This Thing Called Love," "Night and Day," "Just One of Those Things," "Begin the Beguine," "I've Got You Under My Skin," "Easy to Love," "You'd Be So Nice to Come Home To," "Ev'ry Time We Say Goodbye," and "So in Love."

Ferencz, George J. *The Broadway Sound: The Autobiography and Selected Essays of Robert Russell Bennett*. Eastman Studies in Music, No. 12. Rochester, NY: University of Rochester Press, 1999.

In the autobiographical portion of this book, Bennett, who was a Broadway and Hollywood orchestrator and composer, spends a few pages talking about his experience working with Porter and his observations about Porter's compositional process.

Forte, Allen. *The American Popular Ballad of the Golden Era, 1924–1950*. Princeton, NJ: Princeton University Press, 1995.

Construction of songs is explored, including lyrics, harmony, melody, rhythm, motive, and voice leading. Preliminary chapters provide basic analytical information, and subsequent chapters take up analyses of ballads by a number of composers who worked within the titular time period. The included Porter songs are "After You, Who," "Easy to Love," "Ev'rything I Love," "You'd Be So Nice to Come Home To," "Ev'ry Time We Say Goodbye," and "So in Love."

———. *Listening to Classic American Popular Songs*. New Haven, CT: Yale University Press, 2001.

Forte explores a number of songs from the 1920s to the 1940s, including three by Porter ("What Is This Thing Called Love," "I've Got You Under My Skin," and "Ev'ry Time We Say Goodbye"). Elements of construction, including lyrics, form, harmony, melody, rhythm, and range, are explored for each song, situating them within the context of the time period. These structural attributes are incorporated into brief analyses that suggest how music and lyrics interact.

———. "Secrets of Melody: Line and Design in the Songs of Cole Porter." *Musical Quarterly* 77, no. 4 (1993): 607–47.

Forte says that he seeks to remedy the situation in which Porter's (and other "light") music has had no discussion in the analytical and musicological literature (although it should be noted that this is less true more recently). Principal aspects of Porter's surface melodic construction, motivic design, harmonic characteristics, modulatory progressions, form, and long-range line are detailed.

Gilbert, Steven E. "Reflections on a Few Good Tunes: Linear Progressions and Intervallic Patterns in Popular Song and Jazz." In *Music Theory in Concept and Practice*, edited by David W. Beach, James M. Baker, and Jonathan W. Bernard. Rochester, NY: University of Rochester Press, 1997.

Covers how linear progressions and linear intervallic patterns (LIPs) often work in the music of Broadway composers like Porter, Gershwin, Berlin, and others. The author discusses how songs that are controlled by the same LIP for much of the music allow for variation that jazz players need; this construction is the reason that many of these songs and their underlying structures found their way into jazz composition and performance. Cole Porter tunes are not analyzed, but the author mentions that they operate similarly.

Johns, Donald. "Funnel Tonality in American Popular Music, ca. 1900–70." *American Music* 11, no. 4 (Winter, 1993): 458–72.

Author describes funnel tonality as a "term for pieces that begin away from the tonic, out of the key, or in an otherwise unstable tonal state. It is a dynamic process in which the composer seeks to achieve a tonality, to reach an ultimate arrival point that is appropriate, that sounds right, but is not always obvious from the beginning" (460). Two of Porter's songs are noted with respect to this construction, "Love for Sale" and "You'd Be So Nice to Come Home To."

Larson, Steve. "Swing and Motive in Three Performances by Oscar Peterson." *Journal of Music Theory* 43, no. 2 (1999): 283–314.

Author discusses different ways a piece can "swing" and how swing changes in three different performances of Porter's "Night and Day" by Oscar Peterson.

Luttrell, Matthew David. "An American Songwriter in Paris: Cole Porter's Ballet *Within the Quota* with Comparison to Darius Milhaud's *La Création du monde*." D.M.A. document, Arizona State University, 2010.

Author examines the influences, style, instrumentation, harmonic materials, thematic materials, and reception in Porter's ballet *Within the Quota*. Porter's work is compared to Milhaud's *La création du monde*, since the author posits that Porter's "serious music" in the ballet falls in line stylistically with compositions by Les Six and Stravinsky.

Siebert, Lynn Laitman. "Cole Porter: An Analysis of Five Musical Comedies and a Thematic Catalogue of the Complete Works." Ph.D. diss., City University of New York, 1974.

Offers brief analyses of songs from five shows the author believes to be representative of several periods in Porter's output; analyses focus on melody, harmony, motive, form, and style, with comparisons to other Porter songs. The five shows analyzed are *The Pot of Gold* (1912), *Fifty Million Frenchmen* (1929), *Du Barry Was a Lady* (1939), *Kiss Me, Kate* (1948), and *Out of This World* (1950). There is also a thematic catalog for all known songs by Porter organized chronologically and by show (where applicable). Musical and textual incipits are given for both verse and refrain. Publication information and primary source references are given where appropriate. Sketches, fragments, reprises, incidental music, and arrangements of Porter's music are not included.

Section 4: Sources Specific to Songs and Lyrics

The following sources deal either with Porter's lyrics and their interpretation or with one or more specific songs or shows from his output. A number of sources are simply collections of Porter's lyrics, Robert Kimball's volume ([1983] 1992) being the most comprehensive. Remaining materials on the lyrics are more probing, attempting to define Porter's writing style and suggest interpretation (e.g., Hischak 1991). Other sources listed below investigate one or several specific songs: analyzing numerous jazz arrangements of one song is common (e.g., Strunk 1999), while other authors, such as Shaftel (1999) and Buchler (2008), investigate structure and hermeneutic interpretation in a particular piece of music. Finally, several sources in this list delineate production information for individual shows, in one case (Krasker and Kimball 1988) detailing the extent and location of original materials. Buckalew (1995) is the most comprehensive source in this vein, providing specific information on changes to and reception of *Anything Goes* from its premiere in 1934 through the 1987 Broadway revival.

Alper, Garth. "'What Is This Thing Called Love?' as Conceptualized by Nine Jazz Pianists." *Jazz Perspectives* 5, no. 2 (2011): 115–34.

The titular song is used as a case study for how jazz piano style has changed over time.

Baker, Russell, ed. *The Norton Book of Light Verse*. New York: W. W. Norton, 1986.

Lyrics of "You're the Top," "Always True to You in My Fashion," and "Brush Up Your Shakespeare" are printed without commentary.

Buchler, Michael. "Every Love but True Love: Unstable Relationships in Cole Porter's 'Love for Sale.'" In *PopMusicology: Perspektiven der Popmusikwissenschaft*, edited by Christian Bielefeldt and Rolf Grossman. Luneberg, Germany: Transcript Verlag, 2008.

An earlier version of Buchler's contribution to the present volume.

Buckalew, Flora Christina. "Cole Porter's *Anything Goes*: Its Making and Remaking." Ph.D. diss., Pennsylvania State University, 1995.

Offers a detailed look at the creation of the show within the dramatic and cultural contexts of the time and goes on to examine how its reincarnations onstage and in film have differed from and coincided with the original. Reception of each version is also surveyed.

Burns, Lori. "Genre, Gender, and Convention Revisited: k. d. lang's Cover of Cole Porter's 'So in Love.'" *Repercussions* 7–8 (Spring–Fall 1999): 299–325.

Examines the melodic and harmonic structure of the song, its musical narrative, its dramatic context in the original show and movie *Kiss Me, Kate*, and k. d. lang's 1991 cover. The author explores how lang reinterprets the song with a feminist narrative both musically and visually.

Friedwald, Will. *Stardust Melodies: A Biography of Twelve of America's Most Popular Songs*. New York: Pantheon, 2002.

Porter's chapter profiles his song "Night and Day," with some information on the structure of the song itself and the cultural context surrounding its composition, but the author mostly details its performance history.

Furia, Philip. *The Poets of Tin Pan Alley: A History of America's Great Lyricists*. New York: Oxford University Press, 1990.

Each chapter is devoted to an American song lyricist. Porter's lyrics are explored within the context of contemporary lyricists, Tin Pan Alley lyrics more generally, and Porter's life and homosexuality. The author characterizes Porter's lyrics as sometimes witty and modern, sometimes overly sentimental.

Gopnik, Adam, ed. *Americans in Paris: A Literary Anthology*. New York: Library of America, 2004.

A collection of writings by Americans visiting or living in Paris from Benjamin Franklin to Dorothea Tanning; Cole Porter's song "You Don't Know Paree" from *Fifty Million Frenchmen* (1929) is included as an example of how Porter's lyrics and his persona helped to create a vision of Paris as "the paradise of pleasure," as Gopnik puts it. The song itself is an interesting choice because it actually promotes the idea that the pleasurable side of Parisian society and culture is a facade for a harsher reality.

Gottlieb, Robert, and Robert Kimball. *Reading Lyrics*. New York: Pantheon Books, 2000.

A collection of song lyrics from a number of different composers. Includes a short biography of Porter and lyrics for thirty-seven of his most famous songs.

Gross, John, ed. *The Oxford Book of Comic Verse*. New York: Oxford University Press, 1994.

Contains the lyrics to "I'm a Gigolo" and "Brush Up Your Shakespeare" without commentary.

Harmon, William, ed. *The Oxford Book of American Light Verse*. New York: Oxford University Press, 1979.

Six of Porter's song lyrics are printed without commentary: "Anything Goes," "Let's Do It," "My Heart Belongs to Daddy," "You're the Top," "Well, Did You Evah," and "Brush Up Your Shakespeare."

Hischak, Thomas S. *Word Crazy: Broadway Lyricists from Cohan to Sondheim*. New York: Praeger, 1991.

The discussion of Porter's lyrics includes some biographical information and describes his lyrics as witty, full of innuendo, topical, and tinged with upper-class detachment. The author offers his own critical commentary on "Night and Day" and "I Get a Kick Out of You."

Johnson, John. "Cole Porter, 1944–1948: 'Don't Fence Me In.'" In *Musical Theatre in America: Papers and Proceedings of the Conference on the Musical Theatre in America*, edited by Glenn M. Loney. Contributions in Drama and Theatre Studies, No. 8. Westport, CT: Greenwood Press, 1984.

A reception and critical history of the shows *Mexican Hayride* (1944), *Seven Lively Arts* (1944), and *Around the World in Eighty Days* (1946). The connection between the shows' critical failures and their overbearing producers (Michael Todd, Billy Rose, and Orson Welles, respectively) is examined.

Kimball, Robert, ed. *Cole Porter: Selected Lyrics*. New York: Library of America, 2006.

Lyrics from a number of songs, including popular and less well known ones, are reprinted. The author offers an introduction with commentary and contextualization. Note that each song's corresponding show is not listed.

———. *The Complete Lyrics Of Cole Porter*. New York: Knopf, 1983. Reprint, New York: Da Capo Press, 1992.

Lyrics for all extant songs from 1909 (college songs) through 1958 (*Aladdin*), organized chronologically by show. The foreword by John Updike is reprinted in Updike and Christopher Carduff, *Higher Gossip: Essays and Criticism* (New York: Alfred A. Knopf, 2011) and in Updike, "Top of the Pops," *Institute for Studies in American Music* 20, no. 2 (May 1991): 1–2, 15.

Kimball, Robert, and Brendan Gill. *Cole*. New York: Holt, Rinehart & Winston, 1971. First reprint, New York: Dell, 1992. Second reprint, Woodstock, NY: Overlook Press, 2000.

A visually oriented book with a short biographical essay. There are reproductions of photos, letters, and newspaper articles, as well as a chronology of shows and songs with some lyrics.

Kimball, Robert, and Richard M. Sudhalter. *You're Sensational: Cole Porter in the 20's, 40's & 50's*. Indianapolis: Indiana Historical Society, 1999.

Follows the same concept as Kimball and Sudhalter (1992).

———. *You're the Top: Cole Porter in the 1930's*. Indianapolis: Indiana Historical Society, 1992.

This book is the companion to a set of recordings and includes background information about the shows Porter wrote in the 1930s, the songs and the performances on the recordings, and the performers featured. There are also photographs of Porter, his wife, and the performers. Note that not all recordings are from the 1930s. The recordings were drawn from the Yale Collection of Historical Sound Recordings.

Kornick, Rebecca Hodell. *Recent American Opera: A Production Guide*. New York: Columbia University Press, 1991.

Lists Porter's *Kiss Me, Kate* with brief descriptions of the plot, roles, and production requirements, including orchestration.

Krasker, Tommy, and Robert Kimball. *Catalog of the American Musical: Musicals of Irving Berlin, George & Ira Gershwin, Cole Porter, Richard Rodgers & Lorenz Hart*. Washington, DC: National Institute for Opera and Musical Theater, 1988.

A catalog of the completeness and location of original piano-vocal scores, lyrics, libretti, and orchestral scores and parts for the book musicals of the composers in the title. There is also information about how to acquire or rent materials for performance, some performance requirements, numbers that exist in different versions or were cut from the production, and differences between different productions of the same show (e.g., Broadway vs. London). The information is likely somewhat out of date.

Mast, Gerald. *Can't Help Singin': The American Musical on Stage and Screen.* Woodstock, NY: Overlook Press, 1987.

The chapter on Porter's music focuses mainly on his lyrics and interprets them through the lens of his life and contemporaneous culture.

Morgan, David. "Superimposition in the Improvisations of Herbie Hancock." *Annual Review of Jazz Studies* 11 (2000): 69–90.

Author describes "superimposition" as "the technique by which an improviser plays a melody implying a chord, chord progression, or tonal center other than that being stated by the rhythm section" (69). He analyzes Herbie Hancock's versions of several numbers, including Porter's "All of You" from 1955.

Shaftel, Matthew. "From Inspiration to Archive: Cole Porter's 'Night and Day.'" *Journal of Music Theory* 43, no. 2 (Fall 1999): 315–47.

Details the composition of "Night and Day," including the circumstances surrounding its composition and its popularity after its premiere. The bulk of the article details the song's musical construction, and Shaftel demonstrates its musical and textual sophistication.

Smith, Carole June. "Cole Porter's Ironic Vision: A Study of the Lyrics, 1909–1958." Ph.D. diss., University of California, Berkeley, 1984.

The author has made this dissertation unavailable for viewing or downloading from the ProQuest UMI database; according to *WorldCat*, the only library that holds this item is the University of California, Berkeley, and it will not or cannot lend it to other libraries. Still, for those wishing to carry out a serious study of Porter's lyrics, it may be worth pursuing the source further.

Strunk, Steven. "Chick Corea's 1984 Performance of 'Night and Day.'" *Journal of Music Theory* 43, no. 2 (Fall 1999): 257–81.

Details how Chick Corea alters the form and harmony of "Night and Day" from Porter's original version and how motivic cells are manipulated throughout his version of the song.

Weremchuk, George. "A Comparative Analysis of Improvised Solos Based on the Popular Songs 'Body and Soul,' 'Night and Day,' and 'Out of Nowhere' as Performed by Selected Jazz Tenor Saxophonists Representing Different Styles." D.M.A. document, University of Miami, 1998.

Seeks to examine how a single composition has been treated differently in melody, harmony, and rhythm by a number of different jazz soloists. In chapter 3, the author analyzes Porter's "Night and Day" as played by Zoot Sims, Joe Henderson, and Jerry Bergonzi; transcriptions of each of these three arrangements are offered as appendixes.

Wilder, Alec. *American Popular Song: The Great Innovators, 1900–1950*. New York: Oxford University Press, 1972.

In a chapter about Porter's music, the author discusses the lyrics, interpretation, and basic compositional devices. Songs include "Let's Do It (Let's Fall in Love)," "You Do Something to Me," "I'm a Gigolo," "What Is This Thing Called Love?," "Love for Sale," "Night and Day," "I've Got You on My Mind," "It's Bad for Me," "All Through the Night," "Anything Goes," "I Get a Kick Out of You," "You're the Top," "Just One of Those Things," "Why Shouldn't I?," "Ev'ry Day a Holiday," "I've Got You Under My Skin," "Get Out of Town," "I Concentrate on You," "Ev'rything I Love," "Ev'ry Time We Say Goodbye," and "Another Openin', Another Show."

Section 5: Historical, Cultural, and Artistic Contexts

The sources in this section all deal not just with Porter and his music but also with artists who knew or worked with him, contemporaneous musical theater composers, the changing structure of Broadway shows from 1920 to 1960, and the historical and cultural forces shaping artistic output during Porter's most active professional years. Items surveyed here range from critical commentaries to attempts at structural, dramatic, and musical generalizations about musical theater during Porter's time. Many sources discuss or mention the commonly held notion that the hallmark of Porter's writing was a witty mixture of low-style tropes and sexual innuendo with the high style of American society and European culture.

Block, Geoffrey. "The Broadway Canon from *Show Boat* to *West Side Story* and the European Operatic Ideal." *Journal of Musicology* 11, no. 4 (1993): 525–44.

Explores which shows written between *Showboat* (1927) and *West Side Story* (1957) have become part of a Broadway canon and why; also considered are the ways in which these shows' structures are similar to the operatic canon and how they affected the Broadway genre. Cole Porter's contribution, according to the author, is *Kiss Me, Kate*.

———. "The Melody (and the Words) Linger On: American Musical Comedies of the 1920s and 1930s." In *The Cambridge Companion to the Musical*, edited by William A. Everett and Paul R. Laird. Cambridge: Cambridge University Press, 2002.

Details cultural contexts for shows, plots, and lyrics during the 1920s and 1930s, including those of Porter.

Ewen, David. *Composers for the American Musical Theatre*. New York: Dodd, Mead, 1968.

A history of musical theater in the United States organized by prominent composers, beginning with Victor Herbert and ending with Leonard Bernstein. Porter's chapter is a chronology of shows and songs along with some information about reception and the author's criticism.

———. *Great Men of American Popular Song*. Englewood Cliffs, NJ: Prentice Hall, 1972.

Each chapter gives a brief account of composers whom the author deems to be representative of American popular songs from the time of William Billings through the 1960s. The section on Porter is a condensed version of Ewen 1965 (see section 1) with some commentary on Porter's musical style and lyrics.

Garber, Michael G. "Reflexive Songs in the American Musical, 1898 to 1947." Ph.D. diss., City University of New York, 2006.

An investigation and hermeneutic interpretation of songs that are explicitly, figuratively, or tangentially about music, singing, dancing, or other activities that take place in musicals. Porter's music is mentioned but not dealt with specifically; still, these types of songs are ubiquitous in musical theater, and this source may be of interest to those studying Porter's music.

Greenspan, Charlotte, and Geoffrey Block. *Pick Yourself Up: Dorothy Fields and the American Musical*. New York: Oxford University Press, 2010.

Professional and personal biography of Dorothy Fields, who wrote the book (along with her brother Herbert) for three of Porter's musicals; includes information about the time she spent working with Porter.

Guest, Ann Hutchinson. "The Golden Age of the Broadway Musical: A Personal Reminiscence." *Dance Chronicle: Studies in Dance and the Related Arts* 16, no. 3 (1993): 323–71.

Dance researcher Guest recalls her personal experiences as a Broadway dancer in six shows in the 1940s and 1950s, including *Kiss Me, Kate*.

Gussow, Mel. "A Writer at His Wit's End? He Winds Up in the Library." *New York Times*, 19 April 2001, E1, E3.

Author attests to the usefulness of the Abe Burrows Collection at the New York Public Library, which contains letters between Burrows and Cole Porter.

Hemming, Roy. *The Melody Lingers On: The Great Songwriters and Their Movie Musicals*. New York: Newmarket Press, 1986. Reprint, New York: Newmarket Press, 1999.

The chapter on Porter contains synopses of his movie-musicals, including information about the productions and how they may have differed from the Broadway production on which they were based.

Hornby, Richard. "The Decline of the American Musical Comedy." *Hudson Review* 41, no. 1 (Spring 1988): 182–88.

The author criticizes Broadway shows of the 1970s and 1980s as being dull and pseudointellectual and holds up the success of the revival of Porter's *Anything Goes* in 1987 as evidence that the golden age of the American musical is behind us.

Hyland, William G. *The Song Is Ended: Songwriters and American Music, 1900–1950*. New York: Oxford University Press, 1995.

A chronological history of Broadway shows and the professional lives of the composers who wrote them. Porter's chapter covers the beginning of his career; his shows and professional life after *Anything Goes* are grouped together with those of other composers in two subsequent chapters.

Knapp, Raymond, Mitchell Morris, and Stacy Wolf. *The Oxford Handbook of the American Musical*. New York: Oxford University Press, 2011.

Consists of a number of essays that deal with different aspects of musical theater, including its history, appearance in different media, performance, reception, and critical approaches to meaning and drama. Porter and his music make several appearances throughout these essays, specifically in regard to his music and "camp," his musical style and Tin Pan Alley, and sexual themes and references.

Kreizenbeck, Alan. "1931–1940." *The Passing Show: Newsletter of the Shubert Archive* 3, no. 2 (1979): 8.

Lists the musicals that were produced by the Shubert Organization in the 1930s (including Porter's *You Never Know* [1938]) and advertises that the Shubert Archive holds scripts, lyrics, production photos, and some autograph music for the productions during that period.

Lindberg, Ulf. "Popular Modernism? The 'Urban' Style of Interwar Tin Pan Alley." *Popular Music* 22, no. 3 (2003): 283–98.

Examines the connections between Tin Pan Alley music of the interwar period, culture, modernization, and modernism. The author suggests that these connections play out for Porter in the use of "self-reflexive irony" and witty wordplay that subtly hint that the singer is always aware of an audience or a third party; he posits that this detachment is part of what we mean when we describe Porter's music and lyrics as "sophisticated."

Mordden, Ethan. *Beautiful Mornin': The Broadway Musical of the 1940s*. New York: Oxford University Press, 1999.

Author writes a critical history of musicals in the 1940s, contending that two things changed the nature of shows during this period: the production of cast albums and the rise of the integrated show. He writes about Porter's shows in the early 1940s (*Something for the Boys* and *Panama Hattie*) briefly, especially their connection to Ethel Merman; *Kiss Me, Kate* gets a longer treatment, in which the author criticizes the show's construction but not its music.

———. *Coming Up Roses: The Broadway Musical in the 1950s*. New York: Oxford University Press, 1998.

Contains a brief discussion of the makings of Porter's *Silk Stockings*.

———. *Sing for Your Supper: The Broadway Musical in the 1930s*. New York: Palgrave Macmillan, 2005.

In the same vein as Mordden (1999). Author mentions Porter's sexuality and has a brief discussion about how this may have affected his work, especially in his writing—both musical and textual—for women's voices.

Nolan, Frederick. "Cole Porter." In *American Song Lyricists, 1920–1960*, edited by Philip Furia. Detroit: Gale, 2002.

A brief personal and professional biography that includes a list of famous songs from shows and films and a small discography. The book contains sections with similar information on a number of other lyricists such as Dorothy Fields, Ira Gershwin, and Lorenz Hart.

Patinkin, Sheldon. *"No Legs, No Jokes, No Chance": A History of the American Musical Theater*. Evanston, IL: Northwestern University Press, 2008.

Plot summaries of representative shows with some commentary by the author; also provides some recommendations of recordings for each show.

Pells, Richard H. *Modernist America: Art, Music, Movies, and the Globalization of American Culture*. New Haven, CT: Yale University Press, 2011.

The book explores how modernist ideas were expressed in American culture in the twentieth century and how American culture became global culture. Porter's music and shows are discussed several times in the book: in connection with the exportation of American culture around the globe in the period between the wars; the importance of lyrics over vocal quality in the first half of the twentieth century; the emphasis on story over hit songs in the 1940s; and Porter's music as a blend of high and low culture.

Plotkins, Marilyn Jane. "Irving Berlin, George Gershwin, Cole Porter and the Spectacular Revue: The Theatrical Context of Revue Songs from 1910 to 1937." Ph.D. diss., Tufts University, 1982.

Details historical, textual, and musical contexts for three revues by each composer over three different decades. Musical analyses usually detail how lyrics and phrases are set musically.

Rimler, Walter. *Not Fade Away: A Comparison of Jazz Age with Rock Era Pop Song Composers*. Ann Arbor, MI: Pierian Press, 1984.

Includes a basic professional biography of Porter.

Sheed, Wilfrid. *The House That George Built: With a Little Help from Irving, Cole, and a Crew of About Fifty*. New York: Random House, 2007.

The chapter on Porter includes a brief biography and the author's critical take on his work.

Sheed, Wilfrid, and Edward Sorel. "The Songwriters in Hollywood." *American Heritage* 44, no. 6 (1993): 82–94.

An account of how American songwriters were aided and hindered by Hollywood musicals beginning in the 1920s. Porter is mentioned along with the Gershwins as being sought out because of their "brand" and expected to write numerous "hits" for just one movie.

Silverberg, Carol E. "If It's Good Enough for Shakespeare: The Bard and the American Musical." Ph.D. diss., State University of New York at Binghamton, 2009.

Author examines five musicals based on plays by William Shakespeare, including *Kiss Me, Kate* (1948). In each chapter, the creation of the show, its critical and popular reception, and the show's content are discussed with a focus on how changes to the source material reflect contemporaneous cultural and social contexts.

Stempel, Larry. *Showtime: A History of the Broadway Musical Theater*. New York: W. W. Norton, 2010.

Includes basic bibliographic and professional information on Porter with commentary on how his lyrics fused high and low culture and were often reactions to contemporaneous events. Specific examples are given.

Tibbetts, John C. "The New Tin Pan Alley: 1940s Hollywood Looks at American Popular Songwriters." In *Perspectives on American Music 1900–1950*, edited by Michael Saffle. New York: General Music Publishing, 2000.

Chapter examines the "biopics" made in the 1940s about Tin Pan Alley composers like George M. Cohan and Cole Porter (in *Night and Day*). The section on *Night and Day* discusses the willful lack of factuality in the movie and how it was meant to substantiate Porter's public persona.

Zinsser, William. *Easy to Remember: The Great American Songwriters and Their Songs*. Jaffrey, NH: David R. Godine Publisher, 2000.

A brief personal and professional biography mixed with commentary on Porter's witty and urbane lyrics that helped to define and comment on high culture in America.

Section 6: Encyclopedic Sources

A number of resources that contain information about Porter and his music are encyclopedic in nature. These works contain chronologies of Porter's professional life, including shows for which he composed music, songs within those shows, and sometimes information about the original productions.

Of those works included, only Bordman and Norton ([1978] 2010) offers a larger narrative—these authors chronicle composers, music, authors, and texts that were instrumental in the development of the American musical. The remaining sources in this list will be most helpful for those seeking general or preliminary information.

Bordman, Gerald, and Richard Norton. *American Musical Theatre: A Chronicle*. 4th ed. 1978. Reprint, New York: Oxford University Press, 2010.

A history of musical theater as we understand the term today, starting with the eighteenth-century ballad opera but focusing from 1866 onward. Details the music and shows that were instrumental in the development of the American musical—information regarding famous songs, first casts, runs, plots, and critical reception is offered for each show. Note that the text is organized by show, not composer.

Bordman, Gerald Martin, and Thomas S. Hischak. *The Oxford Companion to American Theatre*. 3rd ed. Reprint, New York: Oxford University Press, 2004.

Offers a very brief description of Porter's career, including some famous songs and singers with whom he worked.

Ewen, David. *American Songwriters: An H. W. Wilson Biographical Dictionary*. New York: H. W. Wilson, 1987.

An encyclopedia of songwriters ranging from Stephen Foster to Fats Domino. Porter's entry is 8.5 pages long, with chronological biographical and professional information.

Studwell, William E. "From Hammerstein to Hammerstein: The American Musical, 1927–1943: An Essay and Bibliography." *Music Reference Services Quarterly* 3, no. 2 (1994): 17–28.

A list of major shows and songs by Jerome Kern, Irving Berlin, George and Ira Gershwin, Cole Porter, and Rodgers and Hart.

Suskin, Steven. *Show Tunes: The Songs, Shows, and Careers of Broadway's Major Composers*. New York: Oxford University Press, 2000.

Porter's entry gives a professional biography and a list of shows, including premiere date, place, number of performances, cast and production personnel, notable revivals, and published songs from each show.

Section 7: Other

The following do not easily fall into the categories outlined above. Still, they may be of interest to those researchers wishing to study Porter and his music, so they are included here separately.

Cooney, Mary Ellen. "A Director's Approach to Cole Porter's *Anything Goes* in Community Theatre: A Production Thesis." M.A.T. thesis, University of Louisville, 1980.

This source is unavailable through the ProQuest UMI database; according to *WorldCat*, only the University of Louisville and the Chicago Public Library hold this item, and it seems that they will not or cannot lend it to other libraries. Still, interested researchers may wish to pursue the source further.

Hass, Richard W., and Robert W. Weisberg. "Career Development in Two Seminal American Songwriters: A Test of the Equal Odds Rule." *Creativity Research Journal* 21, nos. 2–3 (2009): 183–90.

Authors use the song output and recording history of Cole Porter and Irving Berlin as case studies to help determine whether the quality of creative output by an artist is determined by the proportion of major works to minor works in his or her output or by expertise, which would theoretically increase across an artist's career. They suggest that their results tend to support the "expertise" theory. See also Richard W. Hass, "Development of Creative Expertise in Music: A Quantitative Analysis of the Songs of Cole Porter and Irving Berlin" (Ph.D. diss., Temple University, 2008).

Miesel, Victor. "Begin the Beguine by Max Beckmann." *Bulletin: Museums of Art and Archaeology* 6 (1983): 1–29.

An examination of Max Beckmann's painting by the same name as Porter's song. The author considers the affinity between the two works. Also available on the journal's archival website at http://quod.lib.umich.edu/b/bulletin.

Ramczyk, Suzanne Mary. "A Performance Demands Analysis of Six Major Female Roles of the American Musical Theatre." Ph.D. diss., University of Oregon, 1986.

Author considers voice-type, vocal endurance, vocal range, vocal style, acting ability, and dancing ability for a number of female roles, including Reno Sweeney in *Anything Goes*. She bases her analysis on the script and score for the 1962 revival but also examines Ethel Merman's influence on the creation of the role.

Section 8: Discography

Although a number of the entries in this bibliography contain small or partial discographies as appendixes or endnotes, there is only one comprehensive guide to the recording of Porter's music. Rimler's discography is an impressive list, organized by song (not show) and then by artist and album title. It includes indexes of compositions, recording artists, album titles, and show titles, which allow flexibility in a search. The source is somewhat dated, since it is twenty years old, but it is exhaustive in its scope until 1995.

Rimler, Walter. *A Cole Porter Discography*. San Francisco: N. Charles Sylvan, 1995.

Selected Bibliography

GREGORY J. DECKER

Archived Primary-Source Materials

Library of Congress Cole Porter Collection, ML31.P67, Music Division, Library of Congress, Washington, DC: music manuscripts, lyric sheets, correspondence, playbills, and other miscellaneous sources, totaling about 2,700 items and spanning the years 1912 to 1957, although the majority of the sources date from 1948 to 1957 (see http://hdl.loc.gov/loc.music/eadmus.mu009008)

Yale University Cole Porter Collection, MSS 82, Irving S. Gilmore Music Library, Yale University, New Haven, CT: manuscripts, correspondence, photographs, and other miscellaneous items spanning the years 1901 to 1992 (the collection is considerably larger than the one at the Library of Congress; see http://hdl.handle.net/10079/fa/music.mss.0082)

Secondary Sources

Advertisement for *Seven Lively Arts*. *New York Daily News*, 21 November 1944.

Albert, Allan, and Bobby Short. *You're the Top: The Cole Porter Story*. Produced by Kirk D'Amico. 56 min. New York: WinStar Home Entertainment, 1998. DVD.

Alper, Garth. "'What Is This Thing Called Love?' as Conceptualized by Nine Jazz Pianists." *Jazz Perspectives* 5, no. 2 (2011): 115–34.

Altman, Rick. *The American Film Musical*. Bloomington: Indiana University Press, 1987.

Alonso, Harriet Hyman. *Yip Harburg: Legendary Lyricist and Human Rights Activist*. Middletown, CT: Wesleyan University Press, 2012.

American Society of Composers, Authors and Publishers. *30 Years of Motion Picture Music: The Big Hollywood Hit Tune since 1928*. New York: ASCAP, 1958.

———. *The ASCAP Biographical Dictionary of Composers, Authors and Publishers*. 3rd ed. Compiled and edited by Lynn Farnol Group. New York: ASCAP, 1966.

Baker, Russell, ed. *The Norton Book of Light Verse*. New York: W. W. Norton, 1986.

Barron, James. "Cole Porter's Lost Show Unearthed." *New York Times*, 23 June 2014, C1, C6.

Barron, Mark. "New York Notes: Hammerstein Will Make 'Carmen' Over into 'Carmen Jones.'" *Los Angeles Times*, 30 August 1942.

Barry, Edward. "50,000 Attend Park Program of Porter Airs." *Chicago Daily Tribune*, 21 August 1951, 21.

Baskerville, David. *Jazz Influence on Art Music to Mid-Century*. Berkeley: University of California Press, 1975.

———. "Jazz Influences on Art Music to Mid-Century." Ph.D. diss., University of California, Los Angeles, 1965.

Beasley, Maurine H. *Eleanor Roosevelt and the Media: A Public Quest for Self-Fulfillment*. Urbana: University of Illinois Press, 1987.

Beebe, Lucius. "Stage Asides: Billy Rose Fears Public Will Think Him Artistic." *Herald Tribune*, 3 December 1944.

Beiswanger, George. "Carmen Jones: The Team behind the Show." *Theatre Arts* 27, no. 3 (March 1944): 155–62.

Bergeron, Katherine. "Uncovering Cole." *Repercussions* 4, no. 2 (1995): 10–29.

Berry, David Carson. "Dynamic Introductions: The Affective Role of Melodic Ascent and Other Linear Devices in Selected Song Verses of Irving Berlin." *Intégral* 13 (1999): 1–62.

Block, Geoffrey. "The Broadway Canon from *Show Boat* to *West Side Story* and the European Operatic Ideal." *Journal of Musicology* 11, no. 4 (1993): 525–44.

———. *Enchanted Evenings: The Broadway Musical from "Show Boat" to Sondheim and Lloyd Webber*. 2nd ed. 1997. Reprint, New York: Oxford University Press, 2009.

———. "The Melody (and the Words) Linger On: American Musical Comedies of the 1920s and 1930s." In *The Cambridge Companion to the Musical*, edited by William A. Everett and Paul R. Laird. Cambridge: Cambridge University Press, 2002.

Bordman, Gerald. *American Musical Revue: From the "Passing Show" to "Sugar Babies."* New York: Oxford University Press, 1985.

Bordman, Gerald, and Richard Norton. *American Musical Theatre: A Chronicle*. 4th ed. 1978. Reprint, New York: Oxford University Press, 2010.

Bordman, Gerald Martin, and Thomas S. Hischak. *The Oxford Companion to American Theatre*. 3rd ed. 1984. Reprint, New York: Oxford University Press, 2004.

Bourdieu, Pierre. *The Field of Cultural Production*. New York: Columbia University Press, 1993.

———. *Outline of a Theory of Practice*. Translated by Richard Nice. Cambridge, MA: Harvard University Press, 1984.

Bourne, Steven. *Elisabeth Welch: Soft Lights and Sweet Music*. Metuchen, NJ: Scarecrow Press, 2005.

Bowen, José. "Finding the Music in Musicology: Performance History and Musical Works." In *Rethinking Music*, edited by Nicholas Cook and Mark Everist. New York: Oxford University Press, 1999.

Brecht, Bertolt, and John Willet. *Brecht on Theatre: The Development of an Aesthetic.* New York: Hill and Wang, 1966.

Breese, Charlotte. *Hutch.* London: Bloomsbury, 1999.

Bricktop and James Haskins. *Bricktop.* New York: Atheneum, 1983.

British Broadcasting Corporation. *The Making of "Kiss Me, Kate."* 23 December 1970. Videotape. Available at the Cole Porter Musical and Literary Property Trusts.

Buchler, Michael. "Every Love but True Love: Unstable Relationships in Cole Porter's 'Love for Sale.'" In *PopMusicology: Perspektiven der Popmusikwissenschaft*, edited by Christian Bielefeldt and Rolf Grossman. Luneberg, Germany: Transcript Verlag, 2008.

———. "Modulation as a Dramatic Agent in Frank Loesser's Broadway Songs." *Music Theory Spectrum* 30, no. 1 (2008): 35–60.

Buckalew, Flora Christina. "Cole Porter's *Anything Goes*: Its Making and Remaking." Ph.D. diss., Pennsylvania State University, 1995.

Burns, Lori. "Genre, Gender, and Convention Revisited: k. d. lang's Cover of Cole Porter's 'So in Love.'" *Repercussions* 7–8 (Spring–Fall 1999): 299–325.

Castle, Terry. "Night and Day." *New Republic*, 21 December 1998, 39–43.

Chapman, John. "N.Y. Stage Suffers Acute Real Estate Shortage." *Chicago Daily Tribune*, 3 October 1943.

———. "'Seven Lively Arts' Crowds Laugh at Gags and Not Critic." *Daily News*, 3 March 1945.

Chauncey, George. *Gay New York: Gender, Urban Culture, and the Making of the Gay Male World, 1890–1940.* New York: Basic Books, 1994.

Chicago Daily Tribune. "All-Negro Cast Will Present New 'Carmen.'" 6 September 1942.

———. Stage Notes. 13 July 1944.

Choi, Jaehee. "They Do That Voodoo So Well: A Critical Examination of Selected Songs of the Founders of the American Standard Songbook." Ph.D. diss., University of Southern California, 2007.

Citron, Stephen. *Noel and Cole: The Sophisticates.* New York: Oxford University Press, 1993. Reprint with new introduction, Milwaukee: Hal Leonard, 2005.

Clum, John M. *Something for the Boys: Musical Theater and Gay Culture.* New York: St. Martin's Press, 1999.

Cocteau, Jean. *Cock and Harlequin: Notes Concerning Music.* Translated by Rollo H. Myers. London: Egoist Press, 1921.

Coleman, Robert. "The Theatre: Rose's $24 Show Is Well Worth It." *Daily Mirror*, 8 December 1944.

Cooke, Charles. The Talk of the Town: "Op." *New Yorker*, 2 January 1937, 12.

Cooke, Richard P. "The Theatre: Lively Lillie." *Wall Street Journal*, 9 December 1944.

Cooney, Mary Ellen. "A Director's Approach to Cole Porter's *Anything Goes* in Community Theatre: A Production Thesis." M.A.T. thesis, University of Louisville, 1980.

Coward, Noël. *The Noël Coward Songbook.* London: Michael Joseph, 1953.

Crichton, Kyle. "Carmen Jones." *Collier's*, 15 January 1944, 60.

Cunningham, Paul. *40 Years of Show Tunes: The Big Broadway Hits from 1917–1957.* New York: ASCAP, 1958.

Dash, Irene G. *Shakespeare and the American Musical*. Bloomington: Indiana University Press, 2010.

Dash, Thomas R. "The Week in the Theatre: Seven Lively Arts." *Retailing Home Furnishings*, 18 December 1944.

Davis, Lee. *Bolton and Wodehouse and Kern: The Men Who Made Musical Comedy*. New York: James H. Heineman, 1993.

Day, Barry. *The Complete Lyrics of P. G. Wodehouse*. Lanham, MD: Scarecrow Press, 2004.

———, ed. *The Letters of Noël Coward*. New York: Alfred A. Knopf, 2007.

Decker, Gregory. "The Language of Baroque Opera: Topic, Structure, and Characterization in Handel's Italian-Language Operas." Ph.D. diss., Florida State University, 2011.

de Mille, Agnes. *Speak to Me, Dance with Me*. Boston: Little, Brown, 1973.

Denby, Edwin. "'Scene De Ballet' at Billy Rose's." *Herald Tribune*, 24 December 1944.

Desroches, Monique. "Martinique." In *Garland Encyclopedia of World Music*. Vol. 2, *South America, Mexico, Central America, and the Caribbean*, edited by Dale A. Olsen and Daniel E. Sheehy. New York: Garland Publishing, 1998.

Dolin, Anton. *Autobiography*. London: Oldbourne Book Company, 1960.

Du Bois, William. "Erstwhile Mahout Captures Sixth Avenue." *New York Times*, 10 December 1944.

Eells, George. *The Life That Late He Led: A Biography of Cole Porter*. New York: G. P. Putnam's Sons, 1967. Reprinted in 1972.

Ewen, David. *American Songwriters: An H. W. Wilson Biographical Dictionary*. New York: H. W. Wilson, 1987.

———. *The Cole Porter Story*. New York: Holt, Rinehart & Winston, 1965.

———. *Composers for the American Musical Theatre*. New York: Dodd, Mead, 1968.

———. *Great Men of American Popular Song*. Englewood Cliffs, NJ: Prentice Hall, 1972.

Fauser, Annegret. "Dixie Carmen: War, Race, and Identity in Oscar Hammerstein's *Carmen Jones* (1943)." *Journal of the Society for American Music* 4, no. 2 (May 2010): 127–74.

Fearnow, Mark. "Let's Do It: The Layered Life of Cole Porter." In *Staging Desire: Queer Readings of American Theater History*, edited by Kim Marra and Robert A. Schanke. Ann Arbor: University of Michigan Press, 2002.

Feinstein, Michael, and Ian Jackman. *The Gershwins and Me: A Personal History in Twelve Songs*. New York: Simon and Schuster, 2012.

Ferencz, George J. *The Broadway Sound: The Autobiography and Selected Essays of Robert Russell Bennett*. Eastman Studies in Music, No. 12. Rochester, NY: University of Rochester Press, 1999.

Fitzgerald, Ella. *Ella Fitzgerald Sings the Cole Porter Songbook*. 1956. PolyGram Records MG V-4001-2, 1993.

Flanner, Janet. *Paris Was Yesterday: 1925–1939*. New York: Viking Press, 1972. Reprint, London: Virago, 2003.

Ford, Andrew. "Eminem and Cole Porter." In *Undue Noise: Words about Music*. Sydney, Australia: ABC Books, 2002.

Forte, Allen. *The American Popular Ballad of the Golden Era, 1924–1950*. Princeton, NJ: Princeton University Press, 1995.

———. *Listening to Classic American Popular Songs*. New Haven, CT: Yale University Press, 2001.

———. "Secrets of Melody: Line and Design in the Songs of Cole Porter." *Musical Quarterly* 77, no. 4 (1993): 607–47.

Franklin, Rachel. "American Jazz in the Works of Jean Wiéner, Maurice Ravel, and Darius Milhaud." DMA document, Peabody Conservatory, 1995.

Friedwald, Will. *Stardust Melodies: A Biography of Twelve of America's Most Popular Songs*. New York: Pantheon, 2002.

Friends of the Library. *Cole Porter: The Life That Late He Led*. Los Angeles: University of Southern California, 1967.

Furia, Philip. *The Poets of Tin Pan Alley: A History of America's Great Lyricists*. New York: Oxford University Press, 1990.

Garber, Michael G. "Reflexive Songs in the American Musical, 1898 to 1947." Ph.D. diss., City University of New York, 2006.

Garland, Robert. "'Seven Lively Arts' at Ziegfeld Theater." *Journal American*, 8 December 1944.

Gaver, Jack. "New York." *San Francisco Chronicle*, 10 September 1944.

Gibbs, Wolcott. "The Theatre." *New Yorker*, 16 December 1944.

Gilbert, Steven E. "Reflections on a Few Good Tunes: Linear Progressions and Intervallic Patterns in Popular Song and Jazz." In *Music Theory in Concept and Practice*, edited by David W. Beach, James M. Baker, and Jonathan W. Bernard. Rochester, NY: University of Rochester Press, 1997.

Gill, Brendan. *A New York Life: Of Friends and Others*. New York: Poseidon Press, 1990.

———. "Profiles: Wouldn't It Be Fun?" *New Yorker*, 18 September 1971, 48–66.

Goldberg, Albert. "Porter Tunes Provide Entertaining Evening." *Los Angeles Times*, 4 August 1952, B8.

Gopnik, Adam, ed. *Americans in Paris: A Literary Anthology*. New York: Library of America, 2004.

Gottlieb, Robert, and Robert Kimball. *Reading Lyrics*. New York: Pantheon Books, 2000.

Graf, Herbert. *Opera for the People*. Minneapolis: University of Minnesota Press, 1951.

Grafton, David. *Red, Hot and Rich! An Oral History of Cole Porter*. New York: Stein & Day, 1987.

Grant County and Who's Who [1831–1909]. Marion, IN: Special Company, [1909].

Greenspan, Charlotte, and Geoffrey Block. *Pick Yourself Up: Dorothy Fields and the American Musical*. New York: Oxford University Press, 2010.

Greher, Gena R. "Night & Day: Cole Porter, Hip Hop, Their Shared Sensibilities and Their Teachable Moments." *College Music Symposium* 49–50 (2009–10): 158–63.

Grieve, Victoria. *The Federal Art Project and the Creation of Middlebrow Culture*. Urbana: University of Illinois Press, 2009.

Gross, John, ed. *The Oxford Book of Comic Verse*. New York: Oxford University Press, 1994.

Guest, Ann Hutchinson. "The Golden Age of the Broadway Musical: A Personal Reminiscence." *Dance Chronicle: Studies in Dance and the Related Arts* 16, no. 3 (1993): 323–71.

Gussow, Mel. "A Writer at His Wit's End? He Winds Up in the Library." *New York Times*, 19 April 2001, E1, E3.

Hammerstein, Oscar, II. *Carmen Jones*. New York: A. A. Knopf, 1945.

Harmon, William, ed. *The Oxford Book of American Light Verse*. New York: Oxford University Press, 1979.

Harriman, Margaret Case. *Take Them Up Tenderly: A Collection of Profiles*. New York: Alfred A. Knopf, 1944.

Hart, Moss. *Act One: An Autobiography*. New York: Random House, 1959.

———. Foreword to *The Cole Porter Songbook*. New York: Simon and Schuster, 1959.

Haskins, James. *Mabel Mercer: A Life*. New York: Atheneum, 1987. Reprint, New York: Welcome Rain, 2000.

Hass, Richard W., and Robert W. Weisberg. "Career Development in Two Seminal American Songwriters: A Test of the Equal Odds Rule." *Creativity Research Journal* 21, nos. 2–3 (2009): 183–90.

Hawley, Douglas. "Billy Rose as Modern Ziggy." *Dallas Times-Herald*, 8 December 1944.

Hemming, Roy. *The Melody Lingers On: The Great Songwriters and Their Movie Musicals*. New York: Newmarket Press, 1986. Reprint, New York: Newmarket Press, 1999.

Hemingway, Ernest. *A Moveable Feast*. New York: Charles Scribner's Sons, 1964. Multiple reprints. Reprint cited, London: Arrow Books, 1996.

Heritage, Donald. "Seven Lively Arts? Billy Rose Is Eighth." *Philadelphia Record*, 12 November 1944.

Hischak, Thomas S. *Word Crazy: Broadway Lyricists from Cohan to Sondheim*. New York: Praeger, 1991.

Hitchcock, H. Wiley. *Music in the United States: A Historical Introduction*. 2nd ed. Prentice Hall History of Music Series, edited by H. Wiley Hitchcock. Englewood Cliffs: Prentice Hall, 1974.

Hoffman, Irving. "Tales of Hoffman." *Daily Reporter*, 5 September 1944.

Holden, Stephen. "Recalling the Life of the Party: 'Tribute to Bobby Short' at Lincoln Center." *New York Times*, 16 May 2013.

Hornby, Richard. "The Decline of the American Musical Comedy." *Hudson Review* 41, no. 1 (Spring 1988): 182–88.

Horst, George Hoyningen-Huene, and Valentine Lawford. *Salute to the Thirties*. New York: Viking Press, 1971.

Howard, Jean. *Travels with Cole Porter*. New York: Harry N. Abrams, 1991.

Hubler, Richard. *The Cole Porter Story, as Told to Richard G. Hubler*. Cleveland: World Publishing Company, 1965.

Hyland, William G. *The Song Is Ended: Songwriters and American Music, 1900–1950*. New York: Oxford University Press, 1995.

Johns, Donald. "Funnel Tonality in American Popular Music, ca. 1900–70." *American Music* 11, no. 4 (Winter 1993): 458–72.

Johnson, John. "Cole Porter, 1944–1948: 'Don't Fence Me In.'" In *Musical Theatre in America: Papers and Proceedings of the Conference on the Musical Theatre in America*, edited by Glenn M. Loney. Contributions in Drama and Theatre Studies, No. 8. Westport, CT: Greenwood Press, 1984.

Kahan, Sylvia. *Music's Modern Muse: A Life of Winnaretta Singer, Princesse de Polignac*. Rochester, NY: University of Rochester Press, 2003.

Kammen, Michael. *American Culture, American Tastes: Social Change and the 20th Century*. New York: Alfred A. Knopf, 1999.

Kapilow, Robert. *All You Have to Do Is Listen: Music from the Inside Out*. Hoboken: John Wiley and Sons, 2008.

———. *What Makes It Great? Short Masterpieces, Great Composers*. Hoboken: John Wiley and Sons, 2011.

Kimball, Robert. "The Cole Porter Collection at Yale." *Yale University Library Gazette* 44, no. 1 (July 1969): 8–15.

———, ed. *Cole Porter: Selected Lyrics*. New York: Library of America, 2006.

———. *The Complete Lyrics of Cole Porter*. New York: Knopf, 1983. Reprint, New York: Da Capo Press, 1992.

———. Foreword to *Cole Porter 100th Anniversary*. Piano/Vocal Selections. Secaucus, NJ: Warner Bros. Publications, 1991.

———. Introduction to *Music and Lyrics by Cole Porter: A Treasury of Cole Porter*. New York: Chappell, 1972.

———. Liner notes to Cole Porter, *Overtures & Ballet Music*. 1989. EMI 7 54300 2, 1991, compact disc.

———. Liner notes to *Cole Porter's Out of This World*. DRG 94764, 1995, compact disc.

———. Liner notes to *Unmined Cole: Unpublished Gems of Cole Porter*. Centaur CRC 2387, 1998, compact disc.

———. *The Unpublished Cole Porter*. New York: Simon and Schuster, 1975.

Kimball, Robert, and Alfred Simon. *The Gershwins*. New York: Bonanza Books, 1973.

Kimball, Robert, and Brendan Gill. *Cole*. New York: Holt, Rinehart & Winston, 1971. First reprint, New York: Dell, 1992. Second reprint, Woodstock, NY: Overlook Press, 2000.

Kimball, Robert, and Richard M. Sudhalter. *You're Sensational: Cole Porter in the '20s, '40s & '50s*. Indianapolis: Indiana Historical Society, 1999.

———. *You're the Top: Cole Porter in the 1930's*. Indianapolis: Indiana Historical Society, 1992.

Knapp, Raymond. *The American Musical and the Formation of National Identity*. Princeton, NJ: Princeton University Press, 2005.

———. "'How Great Thy Charm, Thy Sway How Excellent!': Tracing Gilbert and Sullivan's Legacy in the American Musical." In *The Cambridge Companion to Gilbert and Sullivan*, edited by David Eden and Meinhard Saremba. Cambridge: Cambridge University Press, 2009.

Knapp, Raymond, Mitchell Morris, and Stacy Wolf, eds. *The Oxford Handbook of the American Musical*. New York: Oxford University Press, 2011.

Kochno, Boris. *Diaghilev and the Ballets Russes*. New York: Harper & Row, 1970.

Kornick, Rebecca Hodell. *Recent American Opera: A Production Guide*. New York: Columbia University Press, 1991.

Krasker, Tommy, and Robert Kimball. *Catalog of the American Musical: Musicals of Irving Berlin, George & Ira Gershwin, Cole Porter, Richard Rodgers & Lorenz Hart*. Washington, DC: National Institute for Opera and Musical Theater, 1988.

Kreizenbeck, Alan. "1931–1940." *The Passing Show: Newsletter of the Shubert Archive* 3, no. 2 (1979): 8.

Lahr, John. "King Cole: The Not So Merry Soul of Cole Porter." *New Yorker*, 12–19 July 2004, 100–104.

———. *Notes on a Cowardly Lion: The Biography of Bert Lahr*. New York: Alfred A. Knopf, 1969.

Larson, Steve. "Swing and Motive in Three Performances by Oscar Peterson." *Journal of Music Theory* 43, no. 2 (1999): 283–314.

Lawford, Valentine. *Horst: His Work and His World*. Harmondsworth: Viking, 1984.

Lawson-Peebles, Robert. "Brush Up Your Shakespeare: The Case of *Kiss Me, Kate*." In *Approaches to the American Musical*, edited by Robert Lawson-Peebles. Exeter: University of Exeter Press, 1996.

Levine, Lawrence. *Highbrow/Lowbrow: The Emergence of Cultural Hierarchy in America*. Cambridge, MA: Harvard University Press, 1988.

Lindberg, Ulf. "Popular Modernism? The 'Urban' Style of Interwar Tin Pan Alley." *Popular Music* 22, no. 3 (2003): 283–98.

Luttrell, Matthew David. "An American Songwriter in Paris: Cole Porter's Ballet *Within the Quota* with Comparison to Darius Milhaud's *La Création du monde*." D.M.A. document, Arizona State University, 2010.

Lynes, Russell. "Highbrow, Lowbrow, Middlebrow." *Harper's Magazine*, February 1949, 19–28.

Lyons, Leonard. "Times Square Tattle." *Washington Post*, 11 January 1944.

Macdonald, Dwight. *Against the American Grain*. New York: Random House, 1962.

Maloney, Russell. The Talk of the Town: "Ziegfeld Restored." *New Yorker*, 29 July 1944, 14.

———. The Talk of the Town. *New Yorker*, 16 November 1935, 14.

Martin, Linton. "'Seven Arts,' Rose Revue, Super-Show." *Philadelphia Inquirer*, 26 November 1944.

———. "'Seven Lively Arts' Opens at Forrest." *Philadelphia Inquirer*, 25 November 1944.

Mast, Gerald. *Can't Help Singin': The American Musical on Stage and Screen*. Woodstock, NY: Overlook Press, 1987.

Matthews, Jessie, and Miles Kreuger. *Opening Night*. Tapes made for the radio program on 21–22 February 1960, Institute of the American Musical.

Maxwell, Elsa. "Elsa Maxwell's Party Line: 7 Come 11 Lively Arts." *New York Post*, 14 December 1944.

———. *R.S.V.P.: Elsa Maxwell's Own Story*. New York: Little, Brown, 1954.

McBrien, William. *Cole Porter: A Biography*. New York: Alfred A. Knopf, 1998. Reprinted in 2000.

McGinley, Phyllis. "Elegy with a Pewter Lining." *New Yorker*, 19 August 1939, 19.

McGlinn, John. "The Original 'Anything Goes'—a Classic Restored." Program booklet for *Anything Goes*. EMI 7 49848 2, 1989, compact disc.

McMillin, Scott. *The Musical as Drama*. Princeton, NJ: Princeton University Press, 2006.

Merman, Ethel, and George Eells. *Merman: An Autobiography*. New York: Simon and Schuster, 1978.
Middleton, Richard. *Studying Popular Music*. Philadelphia: Open University Press, 1990.
Miesel, Victor. "Begin the Beguine by Max Beckmann." *Bulletin: Museums of Art and Archaeology* 6 (1983): 1–29.
Milhaud, Darius. *Études*. Paris: Éditions Claude Aveline, 1927.
———. *Ma vie heureuse*. Paris: Belfond, 1973.
———. *Notes without Music: An Autobiography*. Translated by Donald Evans. New York: Alfred A. Knopf, 1953. Reprint, New York: Da Capo Press, 1970.
Millstein, Gilbert. "Words anent Music by Cole Porter." *New York Times*, 20 February 1955.
Mingus, Charlie. *Ah Um*. Columbia CL1370, 1959.
M.L. "Alicia Markova, Anton Dolin Partners of Long Standing." *Christian Science Monitor*, 20 September 1945.
Mordden, Ethan. *Beautiful Mornin': The Broadway Musical of the 1940s*. New York: Oxford University Press, 1999.
———. *Broadway Babies: The People Who Made the American Musical*. New York: Oxford University Press, 1983.
———. *Coming Up Roses: The Broadway Musical in the 1950s*. New York: Oxford University Press, 1998.
———. "A Critic at Large: Rock and Cole." *New Yorker*, 28 October 1991, 91–113.
———. *The Guest List: How Manhattan Defined American Sophistication from the Algonquin Round Table to Truman Capote's Ball*. New York: St. Martin's Press, 2010.
———. *Make Believe: The Broadway Musical in the 1920s*. New York: Oxford University Press, 1997.
———. *Sing for Your Supper: The Broadway Musical in the 1930s*. New York: Palgrave Macmillan, 2005.
Morehouse, Ward. "'Seven Lively Arts' Big and Beautiful—and It Has Beatrice Lillie." *New York Sun*, 8 December 1944.
Morella, Joe, and George Mazzei. *Genius and Lust: The Creativity and Sexuality of Cole Porter and Noel Coward*. New York: Carroll & Graf Publishers, 1995.
Morgan, David. "Superimposition in the Improvisations of Herbie Hancock." *Annual Review of Jazz Studies* 11 (2000): 69–90.
Nelson, Stephen Clarke. "Only a Paper Moon: The Theatre of Billy Rose." Ph.D. diss., New York University, 1985.
Newsweek. "Billy Rose Is Now a Different Rose but Same Gay Lillie Guilds His 'Arts.'" 18 December 1944.
———. Theater: "Carmen Gone Broadway." 13 December 1943, 91.
New Yorker. The Talk of the Town: "Hippodrome." 11 September 1926, 17.
New York Times. "Dr. Albert Sirmay, Composer, Editor." Obituary. 17 January 1967, 35.
———. "Yale's Musical Clubs Had Fine Western Trip." 5 January 1913: X8.
Nichols, Lewis. "About 'Carmen Jones.'" *New York Times*, 12 December 1943.
———. "Happy Old Year." *New York Times*, 26 December 1943.

———. "The Play." *New York Times*, 8 December 1944.
———. "Ring Out Wild Bells." *New York Times*, 17 December 1944.
Nolan, Frederick. "Cole Porter." In *American Song Lyricists, 1920–1960*, edited by Philip Furia. Detroit: Gale, 2002.
Nolan, Tom. *Artie Shaw, King of the Clarinet: His Life and Times*. New York: W. W. Norton, 2010.
Orledge, Robert. *Charles Koechlin (1867–1950): His Life and Works*. Chur, Switzerland: Harwood, 1989.
———. "Cole Porter's Ballet 'Within the Quota.'" *Yale University Library Gazette* 50, no. 1 (July 1975): 19–29.
Orodenker, Maurice. "Seven Lively Arts." *Billboard*, 2 December 1944.
Parsons, Schuyler Livingston. *Untold Friendships*. Boston: Houghton Mifflin, 1955.
Patinkin, Sheldon. *"No Legs, No Jokes, No Chance": A History of the American Musical Theater*. Evanston, IL: Northwestern University Press, 2008.
Peck, Seymour. "The King of Clarinetists." *P.M.*, 6 December 1944.
Pells, Richard H. *Modernist America: Art, Music, Movies, and the Globalization of American Culture*. New Haven, CT: Yale University Press, 2011.
Perloff, Nancy Lynn. *Art and the Everyday: Popular Entertainment and the Circle of Erik Satie*. New York: Oxford University Press, 1991.
Pessen, Edward. "The Great Songwriters of Tin Pan Alley's Golden Age: A Social, Occupational, and Aesthetic Inquiry." *American Music* 3, no. 2 (1985): 180–97.
Philip, Robert. *Early Recordings and Musical Style: Changing Tastes in Instrumental Performance, 1900–1950*. Cambridge: Cambridge University Press, 2004.
———. "The Twentieth Century: 1900–1940." In *Performance Practice after 1600*, edited by Howard Mayer Brown and Stanley Sadie. New York: Macmillan, 1989.
Plotkins, Marilyn Jane. "Irving Berlin, George Gershwin, Cole Porter and the Spectacular Revue: The Theatrical Context of Revue Songs from 1910 to 1937." Ph.D. diss., Tufts University, 1982.
Pollack, Howard. *George Gershwin: His Life and Work*. Berkeley: University of California Press, 2007.
Pope, Virginia. "Design—a Lively Art." *New York Times*, 3 December 1944.
Porter, Cole. *Adios, Argentina*. Private recordings. Cole Porter Musical and Literary Property Trusts, Paul, Weiss, Rifkind, Wharton & Garrison LLP, New York.
———. "Another Openin', Another Show." New York: Buxton Hill Music Corporation, 1949. Sole selling agent, T. B. Harms.
———. *Anything Goes [2011 Revival Cast Recording]*. Ghostlight 8-4452, 2011, compact disc.
———. "'Anything Goes' from *Anything Goes*." Victor 24825-A, [1930s], 78 rpm recording.
———. *Anything Goes: London 1989 Cast Recording*. First Night / Traditions Alive recording, B000024XEM, 1989, compact disc.
———. *Anything Goes: A Musical Comedy*. Musical score. New York: Harms, 1936.
———. *Anything Goes: The New Broadway Cast Recording*. RCA Victor 7769-2-RC, 1987, compact disc.

———. *Classic Cole*. Jan De Gaetani, mezzo-soprano, and Leo Smit, piano. Columbia M 34533, 1977, LP. Reissued Sony Music A34533, 1992, compact disc.

———. *Cole Porter Song Album*. New York: Harms, 1935.

———. *Cole Sings Porter: Rare and Unreleased Songs from "Can-Can" and "Jubilee."* Koch International Classics 3-7171-2H1, 1994, compact disc.

———. "I Hate Men." New York: Buxton Hill Music Corporation, 1948. Sole selling agent, T. B. Harms.

———. *Kiss Me, Kate* vocal score. New York: T. B. Harms, 1948.

———. *Let's Misbehave!: A Cole Porter Collection, 1927–1940*. Naxos 8-120533, 2001, compact disc.

———. "So in Love." New York: Buxton Hill Music Corporation, 1948. Sole selling agent, T. B. Harms.

———. "Where Is the Life That Late I Led?" New York: Buxton Hill Music Corporation, 1949. Sole selling agent, T. B. Harms.

———. "Why Can't You Behave?" New York: Buxton Hill Music Corporation, 1948. Sole selling agent, T. B. Harms.

———. *You're the Top: A Testimonial*. Viper's Nest, UN-CD-180, 1995.

Ramczyk, Suzanne Mary. "A Performance Demands Analysis of Six Major Female Roles of the American Musical Theatre." Ph.D. diss., University of Oregon, 1986.

Rascoe, Burton. "Theater: 'The Seven Lively Arts'—New Era in Magnificence." *World Telegram*, 8 December 1944.

Rialto Gossip. "Theatre Guild Makes Plans for Its Season Here and on the Road." *New York Times*, 9 August 1942.

Richard, Stanley, ed. *Ten Great Musicals of the American Theatre*. Radnor, PA: Chilton Book Company, 1973.

Rimler, Walter. *A Cole Porter Discography*. San Francisco: N. Charles Sylvan, 1995.

———. *Not Fade Away: A Comparison of Jazz Age with Rock Era Pop Song Composers*. Ann Arbor, MI: Pierian Press, 1984.

Rodgers, Richard. *Musical Stages: An Autobiography*. New York: Random House, 1975. Reprint, Cambridge, MA: Da Capo Press, 2002.

Rothstein, William. "On Implied Tones." *Music Analysis* 10 (1991): 289–328.

———. *Phrase Rhythm in Tonal Music*. New York: Schirmer Books, 1989.

Rubin, Joan Shelley. *The Making of Middlebrow Culture*. Chapel Hill: University of North Carolina Press, 1992.

Rumshinsky, Joseph. *Klangen fun mayn lebn*. New York: A. Y. Biderman, 1944.

Rust, Brian. *The Complete Entertainment Discography*. New Rochelle, NY: Arlington House, 1973.

Salsini, Paul. *Cole Porter: Twentieth Century Composer of Popular Songs*. Charlotteville, NY: SamHar Press, 1972.

Samuels, Ernest. *Bernard Berenson: The Making of a Connoisseur*. Cambridge, MA: Belknap Press, 1979.

———. *Bernard Berenson: The Making of a Legend*. Cambridge, MA: Belknap Press, 1987.

Sandrow, Nahma. *Vagabond Stars: A World History of Yiddish Theater*. New York: Harper & Row, 1977. Reprint, Syracuse, NY: Syracuse University Press, 1996.

Saul, Nicholas. *Gypsies and Orientalism in German Literature and Anthropology of the Long Nineteenth Century*. London: Legenda, 2007.

Savran, David. *Highbrow/Lowdown: Theater, Jazz, and the Making of the New Middle Class*. Ann Arbor: University of Michigan Press, 2009.

Schenker, Heinrich. *Free Composition*. Edited and translated by Ernst Oster. New York: Longman, 1979.

Schiff, David. "One Swell Party." *Atlantic Monthly*, July 2004. http://www.theatlantic.com/past/docs/issues/2004/07/schiff.htm.

Schleifer, Ronald. *Modernism and Popular Music*. Cambridge: Cambridge University Press, 2011.

———. "What Is This Thing Called Love? Cole Porter and the Rhythms of Desire." *Criticism* 41, no. 1 (Winter 1999): 7–23. Reprinted in *Modernism and Popular Music*, by Ronald Schleifer. Cambridge: Cambridge University Press, 2011.

Schloss, Edwin H. "Billy Rose's 'Seven Lively Arts' Has Premiere." *Philadelphia Record*, 25 November 1944.

Schoenberg, Arnold. "Why No Great American Music?" In *Style and Idea*, edited by Leonard Stein. New York: St. Martin's Press, 1989.

Schuller, Gunther. *Early Jazz: Its Roots and Musical Development*. New York: Oxford University Press, 1968.

Schwartz, Charles. *Cole Porter: A Biography*. New York: Dial Press, 1977. Reprint, New York: Da Capo Press, 1979.

Seldes, Gilbert. *The Seven Lively Arts*. 1924. Reprint, Mineola: Dover, 2001.

Sensenderfer, R. E. P. "Billy Rose in Bloom in New Revue." *Evening Bulletin*, 25 November 1944.

"'Seven Lively Arts' Is Launched by Billy Rose with Champagne." *New York Herald-Tribune*, 8 December 1944, *Seven Lively Arts* Scrapbook, reel 2, MSS 82, Irving S. Gilmore Music Library of Yale University.

Severn, John R. "A (White) Woman's (Ironic) Places in *Kiss Me, Kate* and Post-war America." *Studies in Musical Theatre* 6, no. 2 (2012): 173–86.

Shaftel, Matthew. "From Inspiration to Archive: Cole Porter's 'Night and Day.'" *Journal of Music Theory* 43, no. 2 (Autumn 1999): 315–47.

Shakespeare, William. *The Complete Works of William Shakespeare: With the Temple Notes*. Cleveland: World Syndicate Publishing, 1935.

Shattuck, Roger. *The Banquet Years: The Origins of the Avant Garde in France, 1885 to World War I*. New York: Random House, 1968.

Sheed, Wilfrid. *The House That George Built: With a Little Help from Irving, Cole, and a Crew of About Fifty*. New York: Random House, 2007.

Sheed, Wilfrid, and Edward Sorel. "The Songwriters in Hollywood." *American Heritage* 44, no. 6 (1993): 82–94.

Siebert, Lynn Laitman. "Cole Porter: An Analysis of Five Musical Comedies and a Thematic Catalogue of the Complete Works." Ph.D. diss., City University of New York, 1974.

Silverberg, Carol E. "If It's Good Enough for Shakespeare: The Bard and the American Musical." Ph.D. diss., State University of New York at Binghamton, 2009.

Simon, Henry. "Don't Be Serious." *P.M.*, 17 December 1944.

Simon, Robert A. "Musical Events." *New Yorker*, 22 November 1941, 74–75.

Smit, Leo. "The Classic Cole Porter." *Saturday Review*, 25 December 1971, 48–49.

Smith, Carole June. "Cole Porter's Ironic Vision: A Study of the Lyrics, 1909–1958." Ph.D. diss., University of California, Berkeley, 1984.

Smith, Cecil. *Musical Comedy in America*. New York: Theatre Arts Books, 1950.

Smith, Jane S. *Elsie de Wolfe: A Life in the High Style*. New York: Atheneum, 1982.

Spewack, Bella, and Samuel Spewack. "The Complete Text of *Kiss Me, Kate*." *Theatre Arts* 39, no. 1 (January 1955): 33–57.

———. "*Kiss Me, Kate*: A Musical Play [libretto]." Typescript. New York: Hart Stenographic Bureau, 1948.

Spewack, Samuel, and Bella Spewack. *Kiss Me, Kate* [libretto]. New York: T. B. Harms, 1949.

Spiegel, Irving. "Negro Cast Will Sing Carmen." *New York Times*, 23 August 1942.

Staggs, Sam. *Inventing Elsa Maxwell: How an Irrepressible Nobody Conquered High Society, Hollywood, the Press, and the World*. New York: St. Martin's Press, 2012.

Stempel, Larry. *Showtime: A History of the Broadway Musical Theater*. New York: W. W. Norton, 2010.

Stout, Janis P. *Coming Out of War: Poetry, Grieving, and the Culture of the World Wars*. Tuscaloosa: University of Alabama Press, 2005.

Strunk, Steven. "Chick Corea's 1984 Performance of 'Night and Day.'" *Journal of Music Theory* 43, no. 2 (Fall 1999): 257–81.

Studwell, William E. "From Hammerstein to Hammerstein: The American Musical, 1927–1943: An Essay and Bibliography." *Music Reference Services Quarterly* 3, no. 2 (1994): 17–28.

Sullivan, Arthur Seymour, and William Schwenck Gilbert. *A Treasury of Gilbert and Sullivan*. Edited by Deems Taylor, arrangements by Albert Sirmay. New York: Simon and Schuster, 1941.

Suskin, Steven. *Show Tunes: The Songs, Shows, and Careers of Broadway's Major Composers*. 4th ed. New York: Oxford University Press, 2010.

Swain, Joseph P. *The Broadway Musical: A Critical and Musical Survey*. 2nd ed. 1990. Reprint, Lanham, MD: Scarecrow Press, 2002.

Thomson, Andrew. *Vincent d'Indy and His World*. Oxford: Clarendon Press, 1997.

Tibbetts, John C. "The New Tin Pan Alley: 1940s Hollywood Looks at American Popular Songwriters." In *Perspectives on American Music 1900–1950*, edited by Michael Saffle. New York: General Music Publishing, 2000.

Time. "'Carmen Jones': An All-Negro Cast Makes Oscar Hammerstein II's Modernization of Bizet's Opera Memorable Theater." 13 December 1943, 111.

Tomkins, Calvin. *Living Well Is the Best Revenge*. 1962. Reprint, New York: New American Library, 1998.

Ullestad, Neal. "Diverse Rock Rebellions Subvert Mass Media Hegemony." In *Rockin' the Boat: Mass Music and Mass Movements*, edited by Reebee Garofalo. Boston: South End, 1992.

Vaill, Amanda. *Everybody Was So Young: Gerald and Sara Murphy: A Lost Generation Love Story*. Boston: Houghton Mifflin, 1998. Reprint, London: Warner Books, 1999.

Van den Brande, Wilifried, Simon Van den Brande, and Lou Demeyere. *Looking for Cole*. Directed by Simon Van den Brande. Canvas Television (Vlaamse Radio- en Televisieomroep), October 2014.

Vreeland, Diana. *D.V.* New York: Alfred A. Knopf, 1984.

Walden, Joshua S. "'The Hora Staccato in Swing!': Jascha Heifetz's Musical Eclecticism and the Adaptation of Violin Miniatures." *Journal of the Society for American Music* 6, no. 4 (2012): 405–31.

Walser, Robert. "Highbrow, Lowbrow, Voodoo Aesthetics." In *Microphone Fiends: Youth Music and Youth Culture*, edited by Andrew Ross and Tricia Rose. New York: Routledge, 1994.

Warnke, Nina. "Immigrant Popular Culture as Contested Sphere: Yiddish Music Halls, the Yiddish Press, and the Processes of Americanization, 1900–1910." *Theatre Journal* 48, no. 3 (October 1996): 321–35.

———. "Yiddish Theater History, Its Composers and Operettas: A Narrative without Music." *Muzykalia* VII / *Judaica* 2 (2009): 1–11.

Waters, Ethel. *His Eye Is on the Sparrow*. Garden City, NY: Doubleday, 1951.

Watkins, Glenn. *Pyramids at the Louvre: Music, Culture, and Collage from Stravinsky to the Postmodernists*. Cambridge, MA: Belknap Press of Harvard University Press, 1994.

Webb, Clifton, and David L. Smith. *Sitting Pretty: The Life and Times of Clifton Webb*. Jackson: University Press of Mississippi, 2011.

Weremchuk, George. "A Comparative Analysis of Improvised Solos Based on the Popular Songs 'Body and Soul,' 'Night and Day,' and 'Out of Nowhere' as Performed by Selected Jazz Tenor Saxophonists Representing Different Styles." D.M.A. document, University of Miami, 1998.

Whaples, Miriam. "Early Exoticism Revisited." In *The Exotic in Western Music*, edited by Jonathan Bellman. Boston: Northeastern University Press, 1998.

Whitfield, Stephen J. *In Search of American Jewish Culture*. Hanover, NH: Brandeis University Press, 1999.

Wiéner, Jean. *Allegro Appassionato*. Paris: Belfond, 1978.

Wilder, Alec. *American Popular Song: The Great Innovators, 1900–1950*. New York: Oxford University Press, 1972.

Woolf, S. J. "Beatrice Lillie's Recipe for Laughter." *New York Times*, 26 November 1944.

Wright, Les, ed. *The Bear Book: Readings in the History and Evolution of a Gay Male Subculture*. New York: Haworth, 1997.

Yang, Sandra Sedman. "The Composer and Dance Collaboration in the Twentieth Century: Darius Milhaud's Ballets, 1918–1958." Ph.D. diss., University of California, Los Angeles, 1997.

Ybarra, T. R. "'Jazz 'er Up!': Broadway's Conquest of Europe." *New York Times Book Review*, 18 December 1921, 3, 17.

Zinsser, William. *Easy to Remember: The Great American Songwriters and Their Songs*. Jaffrey, NH: David R. Godine Publisher, 2000.

Zolotow, Sam. "News of the Stage." *New York Times*, 19 June 1944.

———. "Opening Tonight of 'Carmen Jones.'" *New York Times*, 2 December 1943.

About the Contributors

The Editors

DON MICHAEL RANDEL attended Princeton University, where he earned A.B. (1962), M.F.A. (1964), and Ph.D. (1967) degrees in music. His scholarly interests include medieval liturgical chant, especially in Spain, medieval Arabic music theory, secular polyphony in France and Spain in the fifteenth and sixteenth centuries, Latin American popular music, and the songs of Robert Schumann and Cole Porter. He is the editor of *The Harvard Dictionary of Music*, *The Harvard Biographical Dictionary of Music*, and *The Harvard Concise Dictionary of Music and Musicians* and has served as editor in chief of the *Journal of the American Musicological Society*. After two years on the faculty of Syracuse University, he joined the faculty of the Department of Music of Cornell University, where he remained for thirty-two years. During that time he held a series of administrative posts, including department chair, vice-provost, dean of the College of Arts and Sciences, and provost. In 2000 he became president of the University of Chicago, serving there until 2006, when he became president of the Andrew W. Mellon Foundation, from which he retired in 2013. He is a member of the board of the Carnegie Corporation of New York, Carnegie Hall, the Lyric Opera of Chicago, and CNA Financial, and he is chairman of the board of the American Academy of Arts and Sciences. He has also served on the boards of the Chicago Symphony Orchestra, the Argonne National Laboratory, and Rockefeller University.

MATTHEW R. SHAFTEL, Dean of Westminster College of the Arts at Rider University, previously distinguished professor of music theory at Florida State University, received Ph.D. and M.Phil. degrees from Yale University. He holds a B.A. degree in music and education, also from Yale University. He has won three major teaching prizes and was a quarterfinalist for the Grammy Music Educator Award. Previously president of Music Theory Southeast, he recently completed four years as editor of *MTO*, a journal of the Society for Music Theory, and was an editor for *College Musical Symposium*. His numerous publications and presentations reflect an interest in opera as well as in texted music from 1845 to 1945, including articles on Schubert, Schoenberg, Webern, Stephen Foster, and Cole Porter. His book-length publications include a critical edition of Anton Webern's early music, a textbook published by Hayden McNeil, and an aural skills textbook published by Oxford University Press in 2013. Finally, he also has a great deal of practical experience as a performer of these songs. He has given solo recitals throughout the United States and parts of Europe and spent six years as the director of the Asolo Song Festival and Institute for Song Interpretation, which took place in northern Italy.

SUSAN FORSCHER WEISS is professor and past chair of musicology at the Peabody Institute and holds a joint appointment in the Department of German and Romance Languages, Krieger School of Arts and Sciences, at Johns Hopkins University. She received her B.A. degree from Goucher College, an M.A. degree from Smith College, and a Ph.D. from the University of Maryland. In the fall of 2014 she held the Robert Lehman Visiting Professorship at the Harvard Center for Italian Renaissance Studies at Villa i Tatti, where, among other things, she examined the correspondence between Bernard Berenson and the Porters. Her numerous publications and presentations in leading journals and books focus on her interest in Renaissance music, musical instruments, and ways of learning. Since 1994 she has taught at both the Peabody and Homewood campuses of Johns Hopkins University. Currently she is working on the subject of images and memory in music, on marginalia in printed musical texts, and on the prosopography of Renaissance musicians. She is the recipient of numerous awards, including grants from the NEH, Harvard University, and the Folger Shakespeare Library, as well as several from Johns Hopkins University for innovations in teaching and from the Johns Hopkins School of Medicine for programs in music cognition.

The Authors

WILLIAM BOLCOM won the Pulitzer Prize for composition in 1988 and has won four Grammy Awards. He taught composition at the University of Michigan from 1973 to 2008. In the fall of 1994 the University of Michigan named him the Ross Lee Finney Distinguished University Professor of Composition. His published work includes *Reminiscing with Sissle and Blake*, with Robert Kimball (New York, 1973).

MICHAEL BUCHLER is associate professor at the Florida State University College of Music. He recently completed a term as vice president of the Society for Music Theory and has previously served as an elected member at large and as chair of SMT's Program Committee. He works principally on American music, and his range of scholarship includes Tin Pan Alley, musical theater, Hollywood music, and atonal theory and analysis. His articles appear in many journals, including *Music Theory Spectrum, Journal of Music Theory,* and *Music Theory Online,* and he has given numerous conference presentations and guest lectures. At Florida State University, he has won both undergraduate and graduate teaching awards, and he currently serves as faculty director of the Music Living-Learning Community.

ERIC DAVIS is a musician and researcher who specializes in early American popular music. He is coeditor of *The Complete Lyrics of Johnny Mercer,* published in 2009 by Alfred A. Knopf. His composition *Thanksgiving for Heroes* for soprano, baritone, mixed chorus, and dancers was performed by the San Francisco Bach Choir on a program featuring several of his works. In 2004, he received a grant from the California State Library to preserve and catalog 2,000 historical recordings of theatre music from shows that opened on Broadway between 1844 and 1939. He is the associate director of the Institute of the American Musical in Los Angeles and cofounder of Theatre Comique, a performance ensemble dedicated to the repertoire of early American musical theatre. He received his B.A. from Indiana University and is a Ph.D. candidate in musicology at the University of Southern California. His dissertation concentrates on the art of orchestration for Broadway musicals before 1920. He is currently a lecturer in music history at the Colburn School Conservatory of Music.

GREGORY J. DECKER is assistant professor of music theory at Bowling Green State University (Ohio). He is the winner of the National Opera Association's Outstanding Dissertation Award for 2012, and his publications can be found in *Music Theory Online, The Opera Journal,* and *Intégral.* He has given numerous papers at regional, national, and international meetings on topics ranging from sixteenth-century vocal polyphony to Handel's opera seria to Broadway. He is currently coediting a volume of essays for Oxford University Press titled *Singing in Signs: New Semiotic Explorations of Opera.*

CLIFF EISEN is professor of music history at King's College London. He has published widely on Mozart and other late eighteenth-century topics and is a member of the steering committee of the Akademie für Mozartforschung, Salzburg. His current projects include a new edition of the Mozart family letters and a study of Cole Porter's musicals, among others.

JAMES HEPOKOSKI is a professor of music and chair of the Department of Music at Yale University. Specializing primarily in broad aspects of musical form and hermeneutics in European art music, 1750–1950, he is the author of numerous articles and seven books, including (with Warren Darcy) *Elements of Sonata Theory: Norms, Types, and Deformations in the Late-Eighteenth-Century Sonata* (New York: Oxford University Press, 2006), a study that was awarded the Wallace Berry Prize (best book) from the Society for Music Theory in 2008.

MARK EDEN HOROWITZ is a senior music specialist in the Music Division of the Library of Congress, where he has been the archivist or coarchivist of collections that include Leonard Bernstein, Oscar Hammerstein II, Cole Porter, Richard Rodgers, and many others. His book *Sondheim on Music,* which won the ASCAP Deems Taylor Special Recognition Award and the ARSC Award for Best Research in Recorded Popular Music, was reissued in a second edition in 2010. He has taught courses in the history of musical theater at Georgetown University and Catholic University. Contributing editor to the *Sondheim Review* for ten years, he also wrote the ten-article series Biography of a Song.

ROBERT KAPILOW is a composer, conductor, author, and commentator. Kapilow received degrees from Yale and Eastman and was on the faculty at Yale for six years. He is best known for his *What Makes It Great?®* presentations (now for over fifteen seasons in New York and Boston), his family compositions and Family Musik® events, his "Citypieces," and residencies with institutions as diverse as the National Gallery of Canada and Stanford University. Kapilow's popularity and appeal are reflected in notable invitations and achievements: he appeared on NBC's *Today Show* in conversation with Katie Couric; he presented a special *What Makes It Great?®* event for broadcast on PBS's *Live from Lincoln Center*; and he has written two highly popular books published by

Wiley / Lincoln Center: *All You Have to Do Is Listen,* which won the PSP Prose Award for Best Book in Music and the Performing Arts, and *What Makes It Great?* (2011), the first book of its kind to be especially designed for the iPad with embedded musical examples.

ROBERT KIMBALL is the artistic advisor for the Cole Porter Musical and Literary Property Trusts. The foremost expert on the lyrics of Cole Porter, he has authored more than seven books on the lyrics of the great songwriters from 1930 to 1950. Kimball received B.A. and J.D. degrees from Yale University. He was the principal advisor to the Cole Porter archives at Yale Unviersity.

SIMON MORRISON is a professor of music at Princeton University. His publications include *The Love and Wars of Lina Prokofiev* (2014), *The People's Artist: Prokofiev's Soviet Years* (2009), *Russian Opera and the Symbolist Movement* (2002), essays on ballets by Debussy and Ravel, and contributions to such large-circulation publications as the *London Review of Books*, the *New York Times*, and the *New York Review of Books.*

MITCHELL MORRIS, associate professor at UCLA, received his Ph.D. from the University of California, Berkeley. He specializes in music at the fin de siècle, Russian and Soviet music, twentieth-century American music, opera, rock and soul, and gay/lesbian studies. He has published essays on gay men and opera, disco and progressive rock, musical ethics, and contemporary music in journals such as *repercussions* and *American Music,* as well as in collections such as *Beyond Structural Hearing?*, *Musicology and Difference*, *En travesti*, and *Audible Traces*. He is currently preparing a book titled *The Persistence of Sentiment: Essays on Pop Music in the 70s* and is at work on a project entitled *Echo of Wilderness: Music, Nature, and Nation in the United States, 1880–1945*. He is the coeditor (with Raymond Knapp and Stacy Wolf) of *The Oxford Handbook of the American Musical.*

JAMES O'LEARY is Frederick R. Selch Assistant Professor of Musicology at Oberlin. He received his Ph.D. from Yale University. His publications include "*Oklahoma*'s 'Lousy Publicity' and the Politics of Formal Integration in the American Musical Theater," *Journal of Musicology* 31, no. 1 (Winter 2014): 139–182; Yolanda Kondonassis, *Ravel: Intimate Masterpieces* (Oberlin Music, 2013), liner notes; "From Left to *Gauche* and 'In Between': the Politics of Voice in Duke Ellington's *Beggar's Holiday* (1946)," in *Sillages critiques* (Paris: Les Presses Universitaires Paris Sorbonne), forthcoming online; and "A Guide to *The Enchanted Island*," Metropolitan Opera Educator Guides, December 2011.

LYNN LAITMAN SIEBERT, a Juilliard-trained violinist, graduated with a B.A. magna cum laude from Vassar College, studied with Nadia Boulanger at Fontainebleau, France, and holds an M.A. in musicology (Rutgers) and a Ph.D. in music/musicology (CUNY). For three decades Dr. Siebert has taught music theory and history (including world music and history of jazz) at Baruch College, Drew University, and College of St. Elizabeth, and she continues to perform as a solo and chamber violinist. She is the author of a two-volume study on the music of Cole Porter, "Cole Porter: An Analysis of Five Musical Comedies and a Thematic Catalogue of the Complete Works" (Ph.D. diss., Graduate Center of CUNY, 1975) and the lead essay in *Eternal Woman*, a 2012 monograph on the art of Lyanne Malamed. She is also a biographee in the *International Who's Who in Music* and thirteen similar references. Currently, she is the director of Arts Participation & Communications at Morris Arts.

WILFRIED VAN DEN BRANDE is a performer/scholar and the founder of ColePorterAnthology.com. He is a highly successful Belgian baritone, and his five-CD set of over eighty Porter songs was released in 2010. He has since embarked on a complete recording of the extant Porter works, with over three hundred already recorded. He received his Ph.D. from the Royal Conservatory and Free University of Brussels, and his dissertation was titled "Cole Porter's Legacy." His documentary *Looking for Cole* is distributed by EuroArts.com.

JOSHUA S. WALDEN is on the faculty of musicology at the Peabody Institute of Johns Hopkins University. Before joining Peabody he held an Andrew W. Mellon postdoctoral appointment at Johns Hopkins and a junior research fellowship at the University of Oxford. His book *Sounding Authentic: The Rural Miniature and Musical Modernism* (Oxford University Press, AMS Studies in Music Series, 2014) won the Association for Recorded Sound Collections Award for Excellence in Historical Research on Classical Music: Discography. He is the editor of *The Cambridge Companion to Jewish Music* (2015) and *Representation in Western Music* (Cambridge University Press, 2013; paperback 2015). His articles appear in the *Journal of the American Musicological Society, Journal of the Society for American Music, Musical Quarterly,* and elsewhere. He won the ASCAP Deems Taylor/Virgil Thomson award for his article on Yiddish theater in the *Journal of the Royal Musical Association.*

Index

Music in American Life

Only a Miner: Studies in Recorded Coal-Mining Songs *Archie Green*
Great Day Coming: Folk Music and the American Left *R. Serge Denisoff*
John Philip Sousa: A Descriptive Catalog of His Works *Paul E. Bierley*
The Hell-Bound Train: A Cowboy Songbook *Glenn Ohrlin*
Oh, Didn't He Ramble: The Life Story of Lee Collins, as Told to Mary Collins *Edited by Frank J. Gillis and John W. Miner*
American Labor Songs of the Nineteenth Century *Philip S. Foner*
Stars of Country Music: Uncle Dave Macon to Johnny Rodriguez *Edited by Bill C. Malone and Judith McCulloh*
Git Along, Little Dogies: Songs and Songmakers of the American West *John I. White*
A Texas-Mexican *Cancionero*: Folksongs of the Lower Border *Américo Paredes*
San Antonio Rose: The Life and Music of Bob Wills *Charles R. Townsend*
Early Downhome Blues: A Musical and Cultural Analysis *Jeff Todd Titon*
An Ives Celebration: Papers and Panels of the Charles Ives Centennial Festival-Conference *Edited by H. Wiley Hitchcock and Vivian Perlis*
Sinful Tunes and Spirituals: Black Folk Music to the Civil War *Dena J. Epstein*
Joe Scott, the Woodsman-Songmaker *Edward D. Ives*
Jimmie Rodgers: The Life and Times of America's Blue Yodeler *Nolan Porterfield*
Early American Music Engraving and Printing: A History of Music Publishing in America from 1787 to 1825, with Commentary on Earlier and Later Practices *Richard J. Wolfe*
Sing a Sad Song: The Life of Hank Williams *Roger M. Williams*
Long Steel Rail: The Railroad in American Folksong *Norm Cohen*
Resources of American Music History: A Directory of Source Materials from Colonial Times to World War II *D. W. Krummel, Jean Geil, Doris J. Dyen, and Deane L. Root*
Tenement Songs: The Popular Music of the Jewish Immigrants *Mark Slobin*
Ozark Folksongs *Vance Randolph; edited and abridged by Norm Cohen*
Oscar Sonneck and American Music *Edited by William Lichtenwanger*
Bluegrass Breakdown: The Making of the Old Southern Sound *Robert Cantwell*
Bluegrass: A History *Neil V. Rosenberg*
Music at the White House: A History of the American Spirit *Elise K. Kirk*
Red River Blues: The Blues Tradition in the Southeast *Bruce Bastin*
Good Friends and Bad Enemies: Robert Winslow Gordon and the Study of American Folksong *Debora Kodish*
Fiddlin' Georgia Crazy: Fiddlin' John Carson, His Real World, and the World of His Songs *Gene Wiggins*
America's Music: From the Pilgrims to the Present (rev. 3d ed.) *Gilbert Chase*
Secular Music in Colonial Annapolis: The Tuesday Club, 1745–56 *John Barry Talley*
Bibliographical Handbook of American Music *D. W. Krummel*
Goin' to Kansas City *Nathan W. Pearson, Jr.*
"Susanna," "Jeanie," and "The Old Folks at Home": The Songs of Stephen C. Foster from His Time to Ours (2d ed.) *William W. Austin*
Songprints: The Musical Experience of Five Shoshone Women *Judith Vander*
"Happy in the Service of the Lord": Afro-American Gospel Quartets in Memphis *Kip Lornell*

Paul Hindemith in the United States *Luther Noss*
"My Song Is My Weapon": People's Songs, American Communism, and the Politics of Culture, 1930–50 *Robbie Lieberman*
Chosen Voices: The Story of the American Cantorate *Mark Slobin*
Theodore Thomas: America's Conductor and Builder of Orchestras, 1835–1905 *Ezra Schabas*
"The Whorehouse Bells Were Ringing" and Other Songs Cowboys Sing *Collected and Edited by Guy Logsdon*
Crazeology: The Autobiography of a Chicago Jazzman *Bud Freeman, as told to Robert Wolf*
Discoursing Sweet Music: Brass Bands and Community Life in Turn-of-the-Century Pennsylvania *Kenneth Kreitner*
Mormonism and Music: A History *Michael Hicks*
Voices of the Jazz Age: Profiles of Eight Vintage Jazzmen *Chip Deffaa*
Pickin' on Peachtree: A History of Country Music in Atlanta, Georgia *Wayne W. Daniel*
Bitter Music: Collected Journals, Essays, Introductions, and Librettos *Harry Partch; edited by Thomas McGeary*
Ethnic Music on Records: A Discography of Ethnic Recordings Produced in the United States, 1893 to 1942 *Richard K. Spottswood*
Downhome Blues Lyrics: An Anthology from the Post–World War II Era *Jeff Todd Titon*
Ellington: The Early Years *Mark Tucker*
Chicago Soul *Robert Pruter*
That Half-Barbaric Twang: The Banjo in American Popular Culture *Karen Linn*
Hot Man: The Life of Art Hodes *Art Hodes and Chadwick Hansen*
The Erotic Muse: American Bawdy Songs (2d ed.) *Ed Cray*
Barrio Rhythm: Mexican American Music in Los Angeles *Steven Loza*
The Creation of Jazz: Music, Race, and Culture in Urban America *Burton W. Peretti*
Charles Martin Loeffler: A Life Apart in Music *Ellen Knight*
Club Date Musicians: Playing the New York Party Circuit *Bruce A. MacLeod*
Opera on the Road: Traveling Opera Troupes in the United States, 1825–60 *Katherine K. Preston*
The Stonemans: An Appalachian Family and the Music That Shaped Their Lives *Ivan M. Tribe*
Transforming Tradition: Folk Music Revivals Examined *Edited by Neil V. Rosenberg*
The Crooked Stovepipe: Athapaskan Fiddle Music and Square Dancing in Northeast Alaska and Northwest Canada *Craig Mishler*
Traveling the High Way Home: Ralph Stanley and the World of Traditional Bluegrass Music *John Wright*
Carl Ruggles: Composer, Painter, and Storyteller *Marilyn Ziffrin*
Never without a Song: The Years and Songs of Jennie Devlin, 1865–1952 *Katharine D. Newman*
The Hank Snow Story *Hank Snow, with Jack Ownbey and Bob Burris*
Milton Brown and the Founding of Western Swing *Cary Ginell, with special assistance from Roy Lee Brown*

Santiago de Murcia's "Códice Saldívar No. 4": A Treasury of Secular Guitar Music from Baroque Mexico *Craig H. Russell*
The Sound of the Dove: Singing in Appalachian Primitive Baptist Churches *Beverly Bush Patterson*
Heartland Excursions: Ethnomusicological Reflections on Schools of Music *Bruno Nettl*
Doowop: The Chicago Scene *Robert Pruter*
Blue Rhythms: Six Lives in Rhythm and Blues *Chip Deffaa*
Shoshone Ghost Dance Religion: Poetry Songs and Great Basin Context *Judith Vander*
Go Cat Go! Rockabilly Music and Its Makers *Craig Morrison*
'Twas Only an Irishman's Dream: The Image of Ireland and the Irish in American Popular Song Lyrics, 1800–1920 *William H. A. Williams*
Democracy at the Opera: Music, Theater, and Culture in New York City, 1815–60 *Karen Ahlquist*
Fred Waring and the Pennsylvanians *Virginia Waring*
Woody, Cisco, and Me: Seamen Three in the Merchant Marine *Jim Longhi*
Behind the Burnt Cork Mask: Early Blackface Minstrelsy and Antebellum American Popular Culture *William J. Mahar*
Going to Cincinnati: A History of the Blues in the Queen City *Steven C. Tracy*
Pistol Packin' Mama: Aunt Molly Jackson and the Politics of Folksong *Shelly Romalis*
Sixties Rock: Garage, Psychedelic, and Other Satisfactions *Michael Hicks*
The Late Great Johnny Ace and the Transition from R&B to Rock 'n' Roll *James M. Salem*
Tito Puente and the Making of Latin Music *Steven Loza*
Juilliard: A History *Andrea Olmstead*
Understanding Charles Seeger, Pioneer in American Musicology *Edited by Bell Yung and Helen Rees*
Mountains of Music: West Virginia Traditional Music from *Goldenseal* *Edited by John Lilly*
Alice Tully: An Intimate Portrait *Albert Fuller*
A Blues Life *Henry Townsend, as told to Bill Greensmith*
Long Steel Rail: The Railroad in American Folksong (2d ed.) *Norm Cohen*
The Golden Age of Gospel *Text by Horace Clarence Boyer; photography by Lloyd Yearwood*
Aaron Copland: The Life and Work of an Uncommon Man *Howard Pollack*
Louis Moreau Gottschalk *S. Frederick Starr*
Race, Rock, and Elvis *Michael T. Bertrand*
Theremin: Ether Music and Espionage *Albert Glinsky*
Poetry and Violence: The Ballad Tradition of Mexico's Costa Chica *John H. McDowell*
The Bill Monroe Reader *Edited by Tom Ewing*
Music in Lubavitcher Life *Ellen Koskoff*
Zarzuela: Spanish Operetta, American Stage *Janet L. Sturman*
Bluegrass Odyssey: A Documentary in Pictures and Words, 1966–86 *Carl Fleischhauer and Neil V. Rosenberg*
That Old-Time Rock & Roll: A Chronicle of an Era, 1954–63 *Richard Aquila*

Labor's Troubadour *Joe Glazer*
American Opera *Elise K. Kirk*
Don't Get above Your Raisin': Country Music and the Southern Working Class *Bill C. Malone*
John Alden Carpenter: A Chicago Composer *Howard Pollack*
Heartbeat of the People: Music and Dance of the Northern Pow-wow *Tara Browner*
My Lord, What a Morning: An Autobiography *Marian Anderson*
Marian Anderson: A Singer's Journey *Allan Keiler*
Charles Ives Remembered: An Oral History *Vivian Perlis*
Henry Cowell, Bohemian *Michael Hicks*
Rap Music and Street Consciousness *Cheryl L. Keyes*
Louis Prima *Garry Boulard*
Marian McPartland's Jazz World: All in Good Time *Marian McPartland*
Robert Johnson: Lost and Found *Barry Lee Pearson and Bill McCulloch*
Bound for America: Three British Composers *Nicholas Temperley*
Lost Sounds: Blacks and the Birth of the Recording Industry, 1890–1919 *Tim Brooks*
Burn, Baby! BURN! The Autobiography of Magnificent Montague *Magnificent Montague with Bob Baker*
Way Up North in Dixie: A Black Family's Claim to the Confederate Anthem *Howard L. Sacks and Judith Rose Sacks*
The Bluegrass Reader *Edited by Thomas Goldsmith*
Colin McPhee: Composer in Two Worlds *Carol J. Oja*
Robert Johnson, Mythmaking, and Contemporary American Culture *Patricia R. Schroeder*
Composing a World: Lou Harrison, Musical Wayfarer *Leta E. Miller and Fredric Lieberman*
Fritz Reiner, Maestro and Martinet *Kenneth Morgan*
That Toddlin' Town: Chicago's White Dance Bands and Orchestras, 1900–1950 *Charles A. Sengstock Jr.*
Dewey and Elvis: The Life and Times of a Rock 'n' Roll Deejay *Louis Cantor*
Come Hither to Go Yonder: Playing Bluegrass with Bill Monroe *Bob Black*
Chicago Blues: Portraits and Stories *David Whiteis*
The Incredible Band of John Philip Sousa *Paul E. Bierley*
"Maximum Clarity" and Other Writings on Music *Ben Johnston, edited by Bob Gilmore*
Staging Tradition: John Lair and Sarah Gertrude Knott *Michael Ann Williams*
Homegrown Music: Discovering Bluegrass *Stephanie P. Ledgin*
Tales of a Theatrical Guru *Danny Newman*
The Music of Bill Monroe *Neil V. Rosenberg and Charles K. Wolfe*
Pressing On: The Roni Stoneman Story *Roni Stoneman, as told to Ellen Wright*
Together Let Us Sweetly Live *Jonathan C. David, with photographs by Richard Holloway*
Live Fast, Love Hard: The Faron Young Story *Diane Diekman*
Air Castle of the South: WSM Radio and the Making of Music City *Craig P. Havighurst*
Traveling Home: Sacred Harp Singing and American Pluralism *Kiri Miller*
Where Did Our Love Go? The Rise and Fall of the Motown Sound *Nelson George*
Lonesome Cowgirls and Honky-Tonk Angels: The Women of Barn Dance Radio *Kristine M. McCusker*

California Polyphony: Ethnic Voices, Musical Crossroads *Mina Yang*
The Never-Ending Revival: Rounder Records and the Folk Alliance *Michael F. Scully*
Sing It Pretty: A Memoir *Bess Lomax Hawes*
Working Girl Blues: The Life and Music of Hazel Dickens *Hazel Dickens and Bill C. Malone*
Charles Ives Reconsidered *Gayle Sherwood Magee*
The Hayloft Gang: The Story of the National Barn Dance *Edited by Chad Berry*
Country Music Humorists and Comedians *Loyal Jones*
Record Makers and Breakers: Voices of the Independent Rock 'n' Roll Pioneers *John Broven*
Music of the First Nations: Tradition and Innovation in Native North America *Edited by Tara Browner*
Cafe Society: The Wrong Place for the Right People *Barney Josephson, with Terry Trilling-Josephson*
George Gershwin: An Intimate Portrait *Walter Rimler*
Life Flows On in Endless Song: Folk Songs and American History *Robert V. Wells*
I Feel a Song Coming On: The Life of Jimmy McHugh *Alyn Shipton*
King of the Queen City: The Story of King Records *Jon Hartley Fox*
Long Lost Blues: Popular Blues in America, 1850–1920 *Peter C. Muir*
Hard Luck Blues: Roots Music Photographs from the Great Depression *Rich Remsberg*
Restless Giant: The Life and Times of Jean Aberbach and Hill and Range Songs *Bar Biszick-Lockwood*
Champagne Charlie and Pretty Jemima: Variety Theater in the Nineteenth Century *Gillian M. Rodger*
Sacred Steel: Inside an African American Steel Guitar Tradition *Robert L. Stone*
Gone to the Country: The New Lost City Ramblers and the Folk Music Revival *Ray Allen*
The Makers of the Sacred Harp *David Warren Steel with Richard H. Hulan*
Woody Guthrie, American Radical *Will Kaufman*
George Szell: A Life of Music *Michael Charry*
Bean Blossom: The Brown County Jamboree and Bill Monroe's Bluegrass Festivals *Thomas A. Adler*
Crowe on the Banjo: The Music Life of J. D. Crowe *Marty Godbey*
Twentieth Century Drifter: The Life of Marty Robbins *Diane Diekman*
Henry Mancini: Reinventing Film Music *John Caps*
The Beautiful Music All Around Us: Field Recordings and the American Experience *Stephen Wade*
Then Sings My Soul: The Culture of Southern Gospel Music *Douglas Harrison*
The Accordion in the Americas: Klezmer, Polka, Tango, Zydeco, and More! *Edited by Helena Simonett*
Bluegrass Bluesman: A Memoir *Josh Graves, edited by Fred Bartenstein*
One Woman in a Hundred: Edna Phillips and the Philadelphia Orchestra *Mary Sue Welsh*
The Great Orchestrator: Arthur Judson and American Arts Management *James M. Doering*

Charles Ives in the Mirror: American Histories of an Iconic Composer *David C. Paul*
Southern Soul-Blues *David Whiteis*
Sweet Air: Modernism, Regionalism, and American Popular Song *Edward P. Comentale*
Pretty Good for a Girl: Women in Bluegrass *Murphy Hicks Henry*
Sweet Dreams: The World of Patsy Cline *Warren R. Hofstra*
William Sidney Mount and the Creolization of American Culture *Christopher J. Smith*
Bird: The Life and Music of Charlie Parker *Chuck Haddix*
Making the March King: John Philip Sousa's Washington Years, 1854–1893 *Patrick Warfield*
In It for the Long Run *Jim Rooney*
Pioneers of the Blues Revival *Steve Cushing*
Roots of the Revival: American and British Folk Music in the 1950s *Ronald D. Cohen and Rachel Clare Donaldson*
Blues All Day Long: The Jimmy Rogers Story *Wayne Everett Goins*
Yankee Twang: Country and Western Music in New England *Clifford R. Murphy*
The Music of the Stanley Brothers *Gary B. Reid*
Hawaiian Music in Motion: Mariners, Missionaries, and Minstrels *James Revell Carr*
Sounds of the New Deal: The Federal Music Project in the West *Peter Gough*
The Mormon Tabernacle Choir: A Biography *Michael Hicks*
The Man That Got Away: The Life and Songs of Harold Arlen *Walter Rimler*
A City Called Heaven: Chicago and the Birth of Gospel Music *Robert M. Marovich*
Blues Unlimited: Essential Interviews from the Original Blues Magazine *Edited by Bill Greensmith, Mike Rowe, and Mark Camarigg*
Hoedowns, Reels, and Frolics: Roots and Branches of Southern Appalachian Dance *Phil Jamison*
Fannie Bloomfield-Zeisler: The Life and Times of a Piano Virtuoso *Beth Abelson Macleod*
Cybersonic Arts: Adventures in American New Music *Gordon Mumma, edited with commentary by Michelle Fillion*
The Magic of Beverly Sills *Nancy Guy*
Waiting for Buddy Guy *Alan Harper*
Harry T. Burleigh: From the Spiritual to the Harlem Renaissance *Jean E. Snyder*
Music in the Age of Anxiety: American Music in the Fifties *James Wierzbicki*
Jazzing: New York City's Unseen Scene *Thomas H. Greenland*
A Cole Porter Companion *Edited by Don M. Randel, Matthew Shaftel, and Susan Forscher Weiss*

The University of Illinois Press
is a founding member of the
Association of American University Presses.

Composed in 10.25/14 Adobe Chaparral Pro
with Myriad Pro display
by Kirsten Dennison
at the University of Illinois Press
Manufactured by Sheridan Books, Inc.

University of Illinois Press
1325 South Oak Street
Champaign, IL 61820-6903
www.press.uillinois.edu